ORIGINAL WORK **FUNA**

MANGA **Hibiki Kokonoe**

CHARACTER DESIGN **Sukima**

SCHOOL SPIRIT!

7

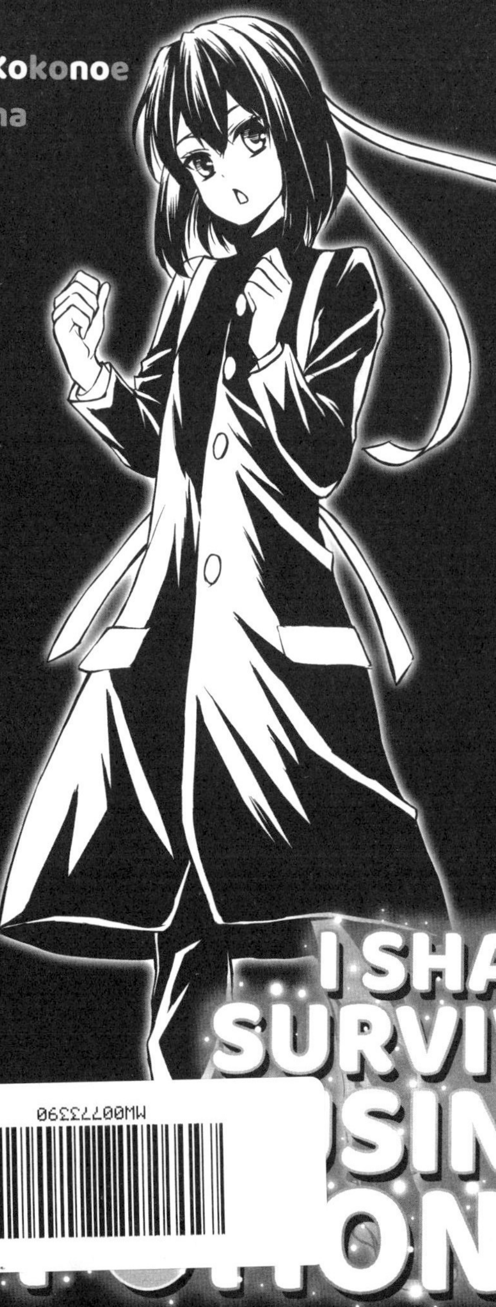

I SHALL SURVIVE SING ONS!

TABLE OF CONTENTS

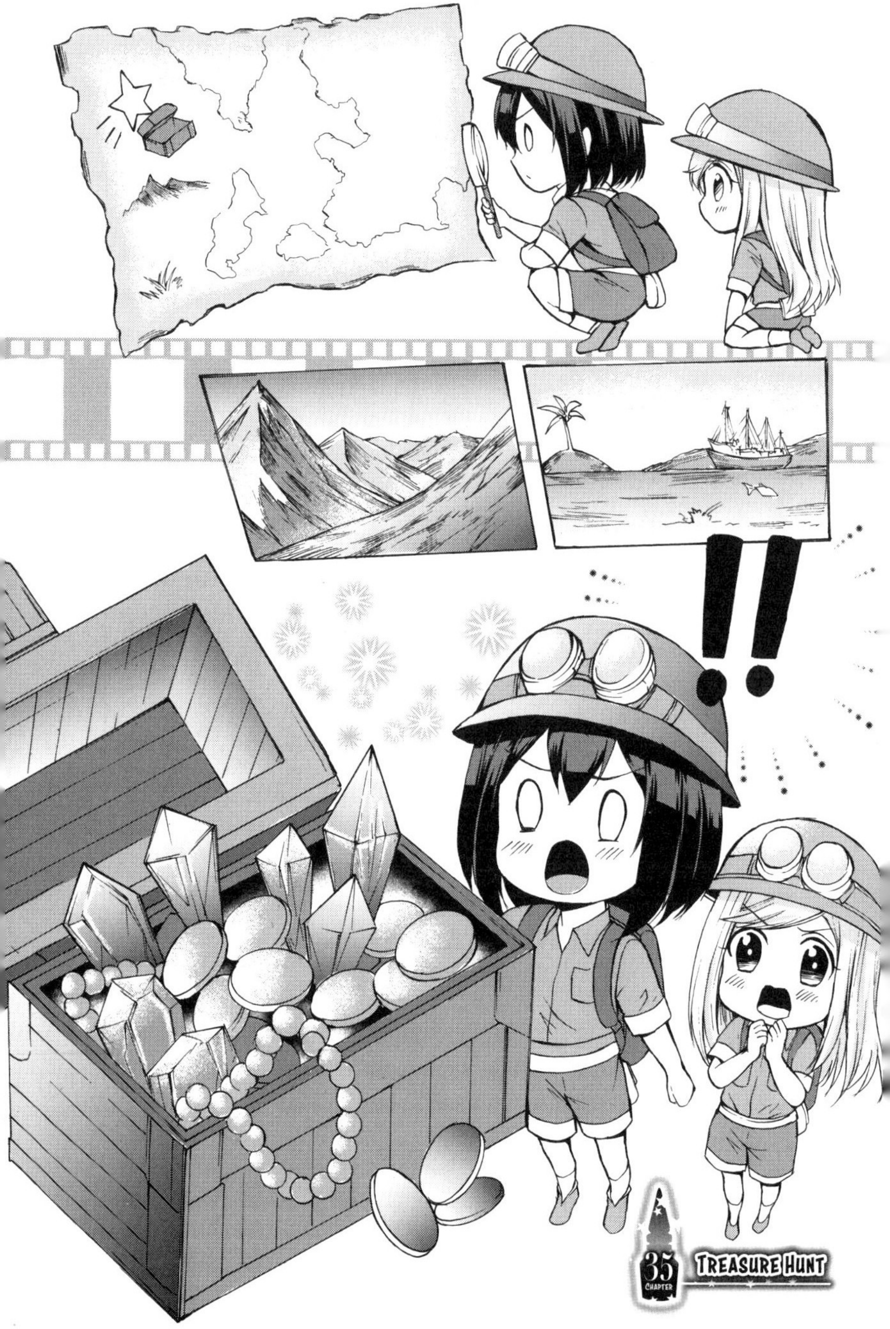

!!
35
CHAPTER
TREASURE HUNT

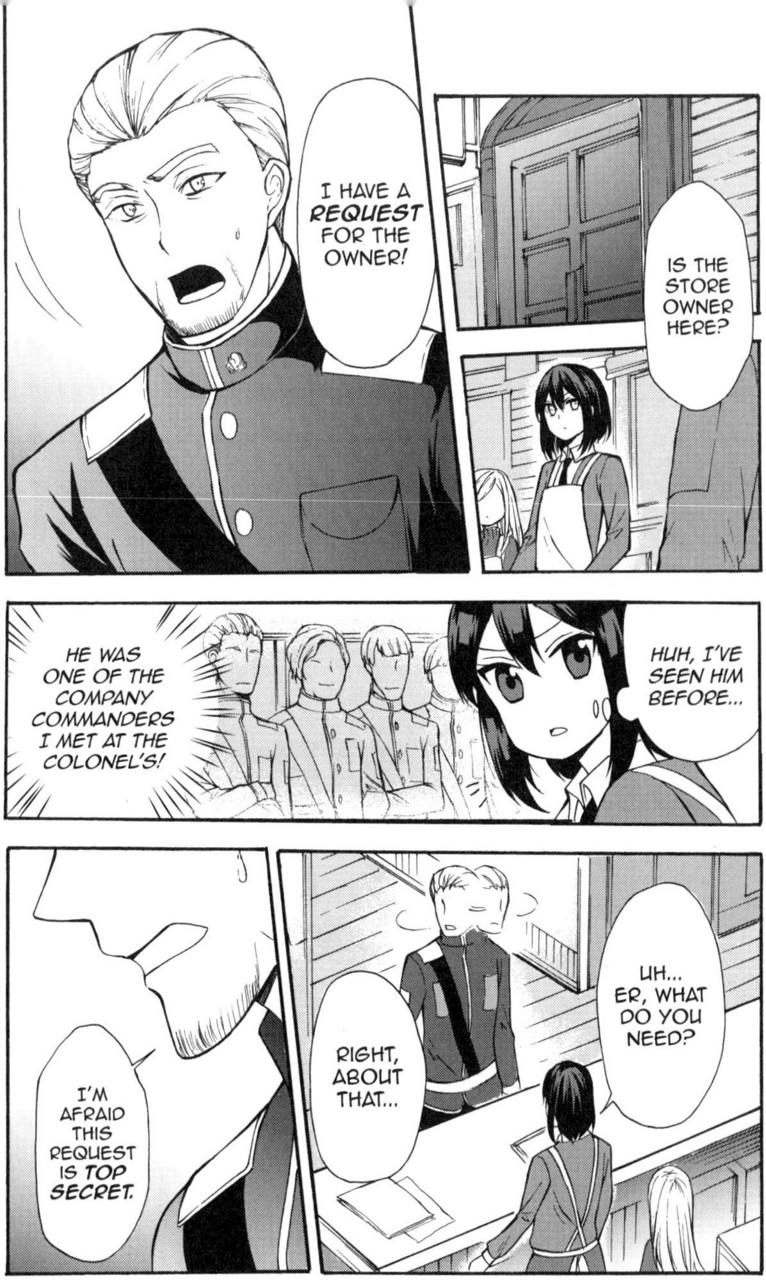
IS THE STORE OWNER HERE?
I HAVE A **REQUEST** FOR THE OWNER!
HUH, I'VE SEEN HIM BEFORE...
HE WAS ONE OF THE COMPANY COMMANDERS I MET AT THE COLONEL'S!
UH... ER, WHAT DO YOU NEED?
RIGHT, ABOUT THAT...
I'M AFRAID THIS REQUEST IS **TOP SECRET.**

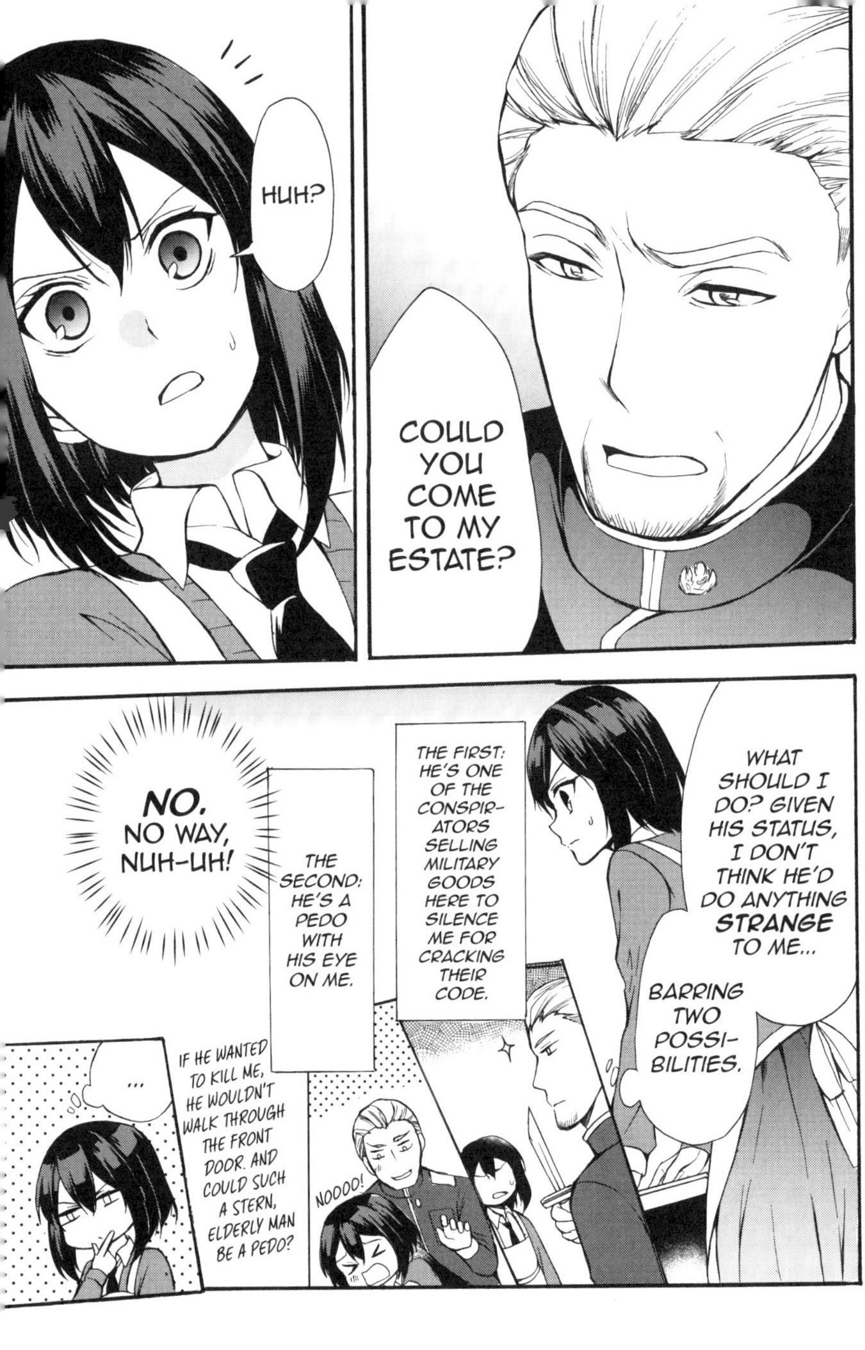
COULD YOU COME TO MY ESTATE?
HUH?
WHAT SHOULD I DO? GIVEN HIS STATUS, I DON'T THINK HE'D DO ANYTHING **STRANGE** TO ME...
BARRING TWO POSSIBILITIES.
THE FIRST: HE'S ONE OF THE CONSPIRATORS SELLING MILITARY GOODS HERE TO SILENCE ME FOR CRACKING THEIR CODE.
THE SECOND: HE'S A PEDO WITH HIS EYE ON ME.
NO. NO WAY, NUH-UH!
NOOOO!
...
IF HE WANTED TO KILL ME, HE WOULDN'T WALK THROUGH THE FRONT DOOR. AND COULD SUCH A STERN, ELDERLY MAN BE A PEDO?

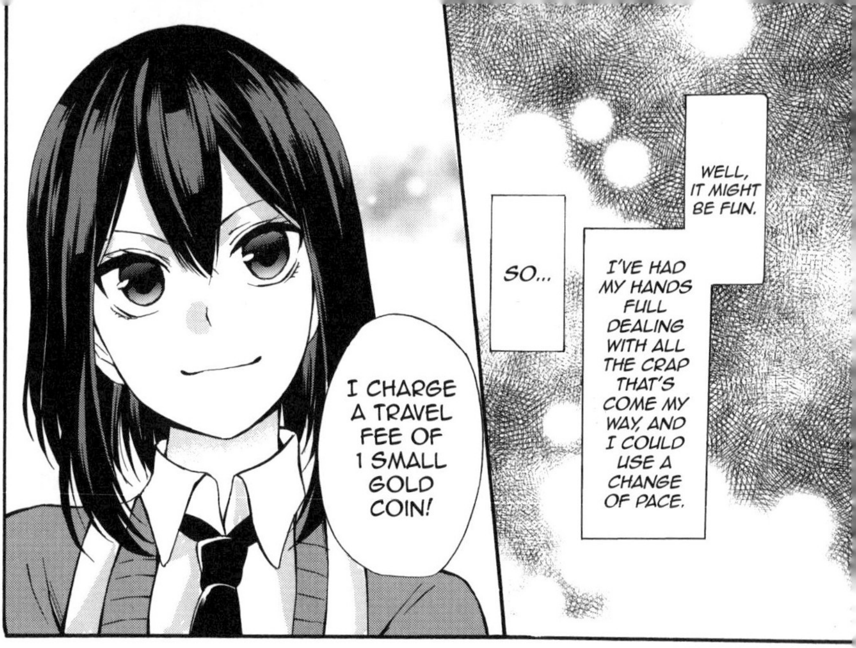
WELL, IT MIGHT BE FUN.
I'VE HAD MY HANDS FULL DEALING WITH ALL THE CRAP THAT'S COME MY WAY, AND I COULD USE A CHANGE OF PACE.
SO...
I CHARGE A TRAVEL FEE OF 1 SMALL GOLD COIN!

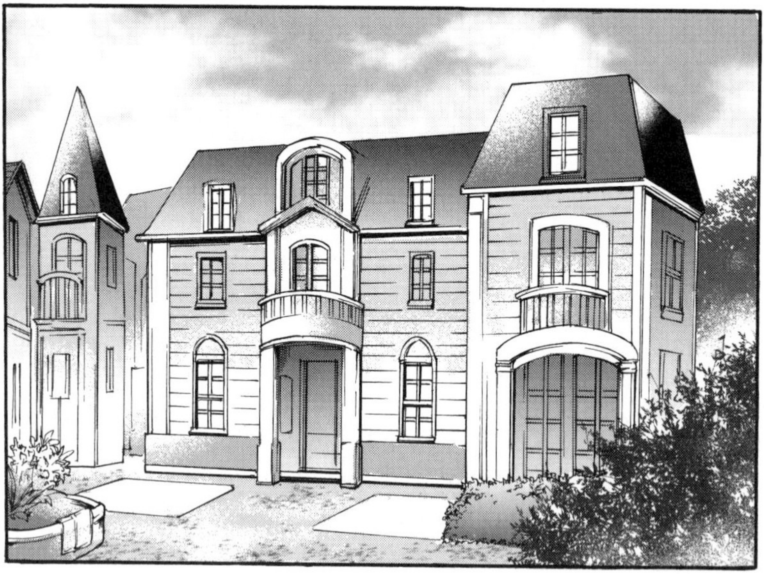

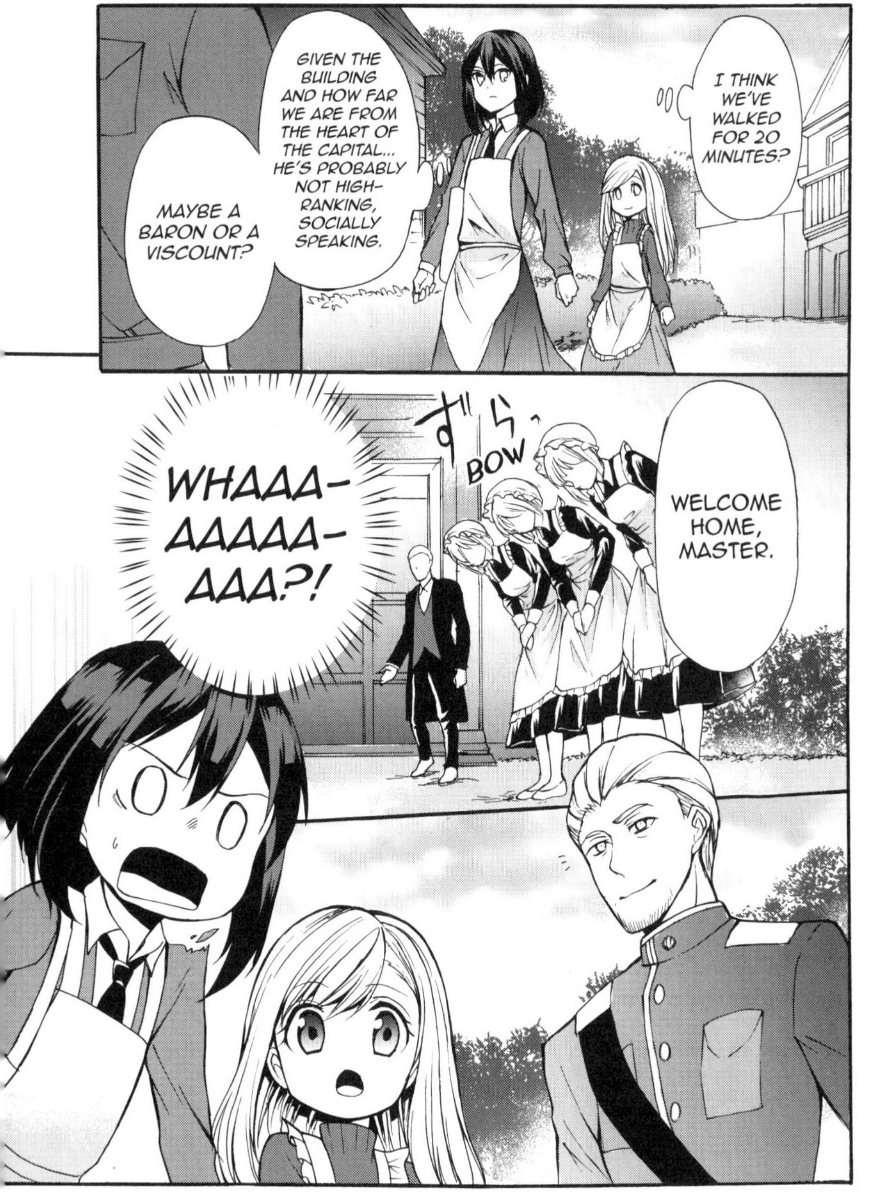

I THINK WE'VE WALKED FOR 20 MINUTES?
GIVEN THE BUILDING AND HOW FAR WE ARE FROM THE HEART OF THE CAPITAL... HE'S PROBABLY NOT HIGH-RANKING, SOCIALLY SPEAKING.
MAYBE A BARON OR A VISCOUNT?
WELCOME HOME, MASTER.
ずら、
BOW
WHAAA-AAAAA-AAA?!

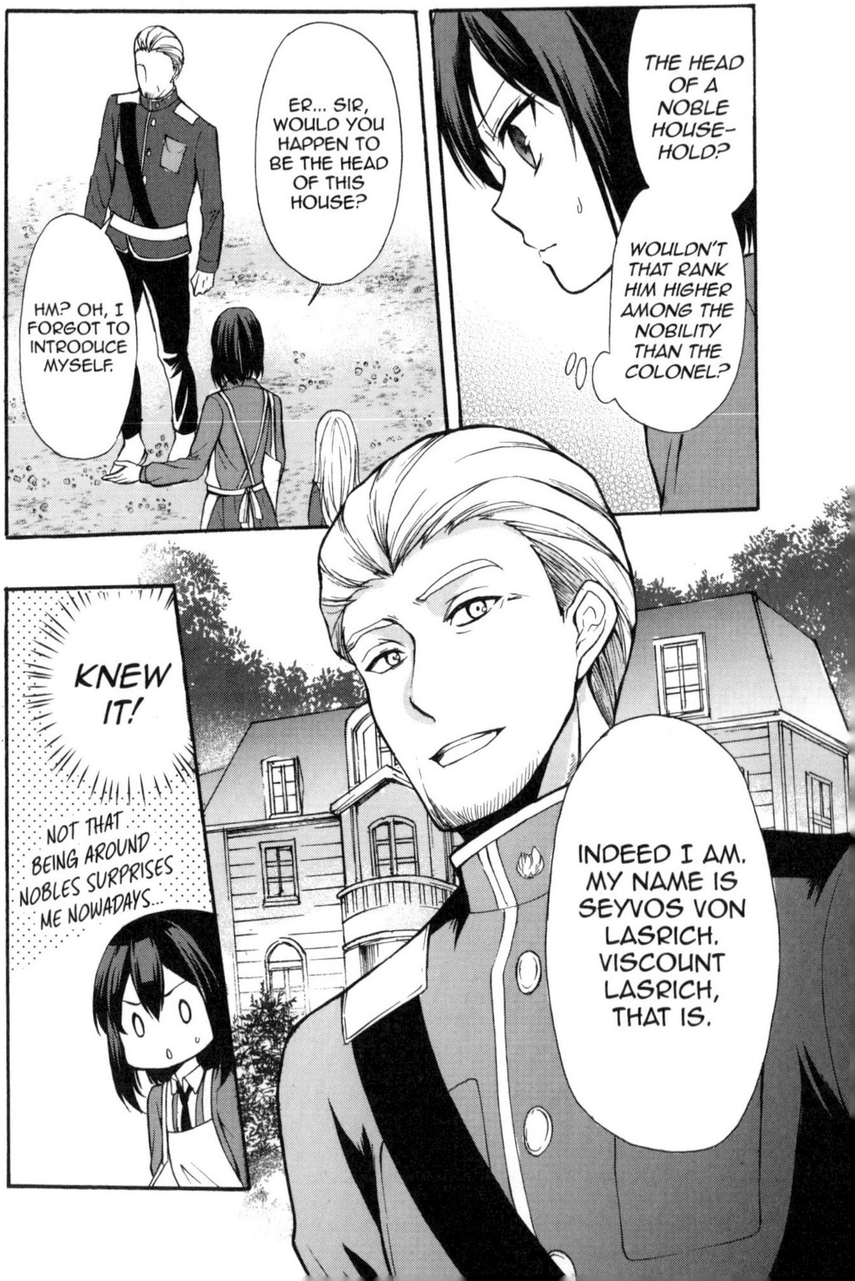
THE HEAD OF A NOBLE HOUSE-HOLD?
WOULDN'T THAT RANK HIM HIGHER AMONG THE NOBILITY THAN THE COLONEL?
ER... SIR, WOULD YOU HAPPEN TO BE THE HEAD OF THIS HOUSE?
HM? OH, I FORGOT TO INTRODUCE MYSELF.
INDEED I AM. MY NAME IS SEYVOS VON LASRICH. VISCOUNT LASRICH, THAT IS.
KNEW IT!
NOT THAT BEING AROUND NOBLES SURPRISES ME NOWADAYS...

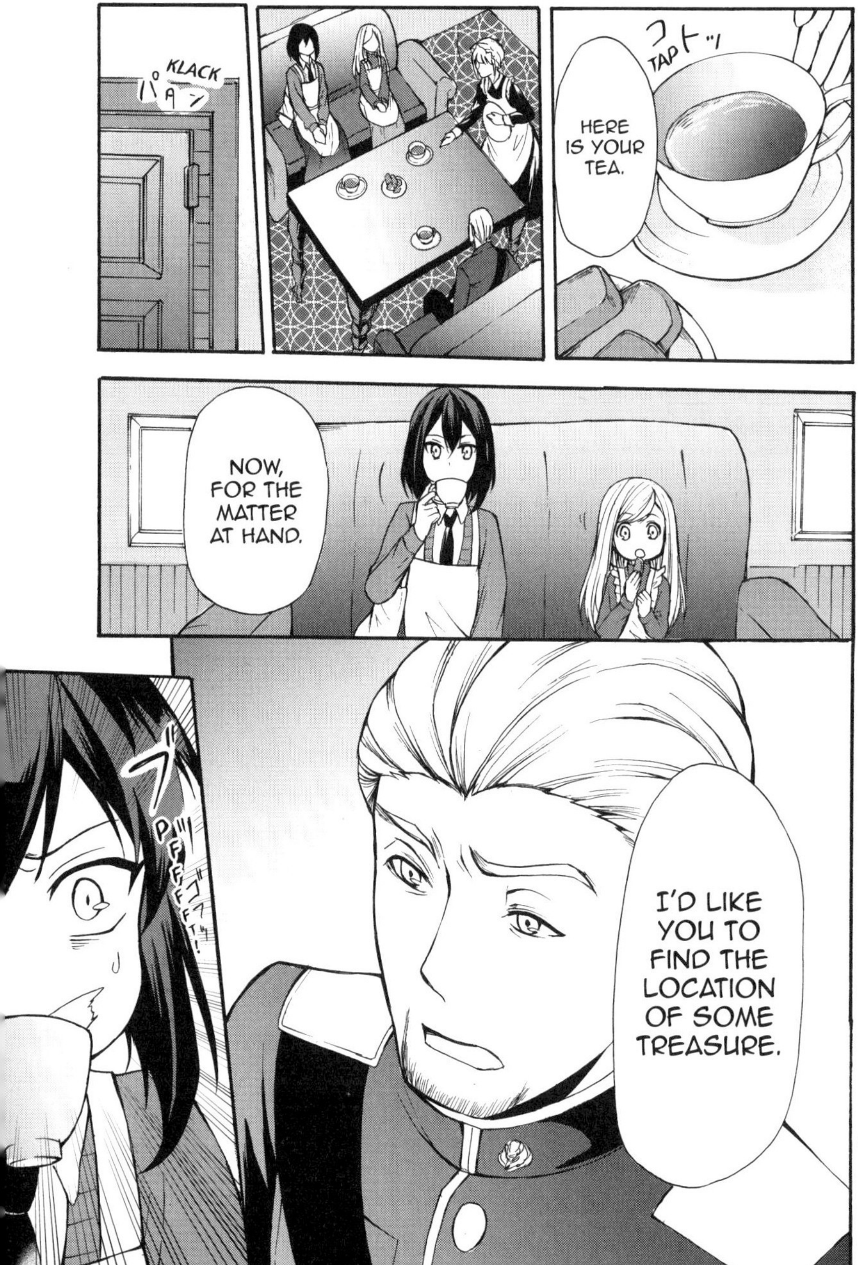
コトッ
TAP
HERE IS YOUR TEA.
パタン
KLACK
NOW, FOR THE MATTER AT HAND.
I'D LIKE YOU TO FIND THE LOCATION OF SOME TREASURE.
PFFFFT!

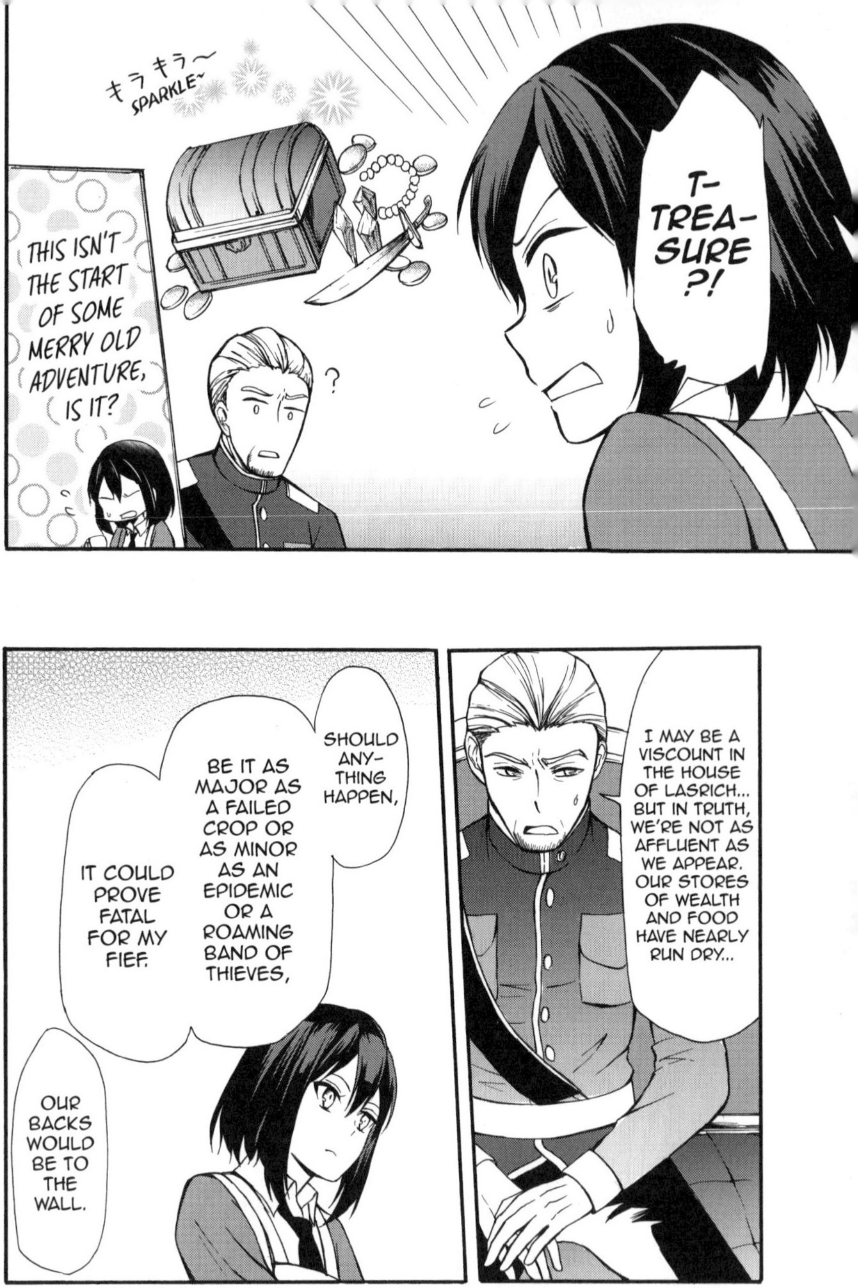
キラキラ~ SPARKLE~
T-TREASURE?!
THIS ISN'T THE START OF SOME MERRY OLD ADVENTURE, IS IT?
?
I MAY BE A VISCOUNT IN THE HOUSE OF LASRICH... BUT IN TRUTH, WE'RE NOT AS AFFLUENT AS WE APPEAR. OUR STORES OF WEALTH AND FOOD HAVE NEARLY RUN DRY...
SHOULD ANYTHING HAPPEN,
BE IT AS MAJOR AS A FAILED CROP OR AS MINOR AS AN EPIDEMIC OR A ROAMING BAND OF THIEVES,
IT COULD PROVE FATAL FOR MY FIEF.
OUR BACKS WOULD BE TO THE WALL.

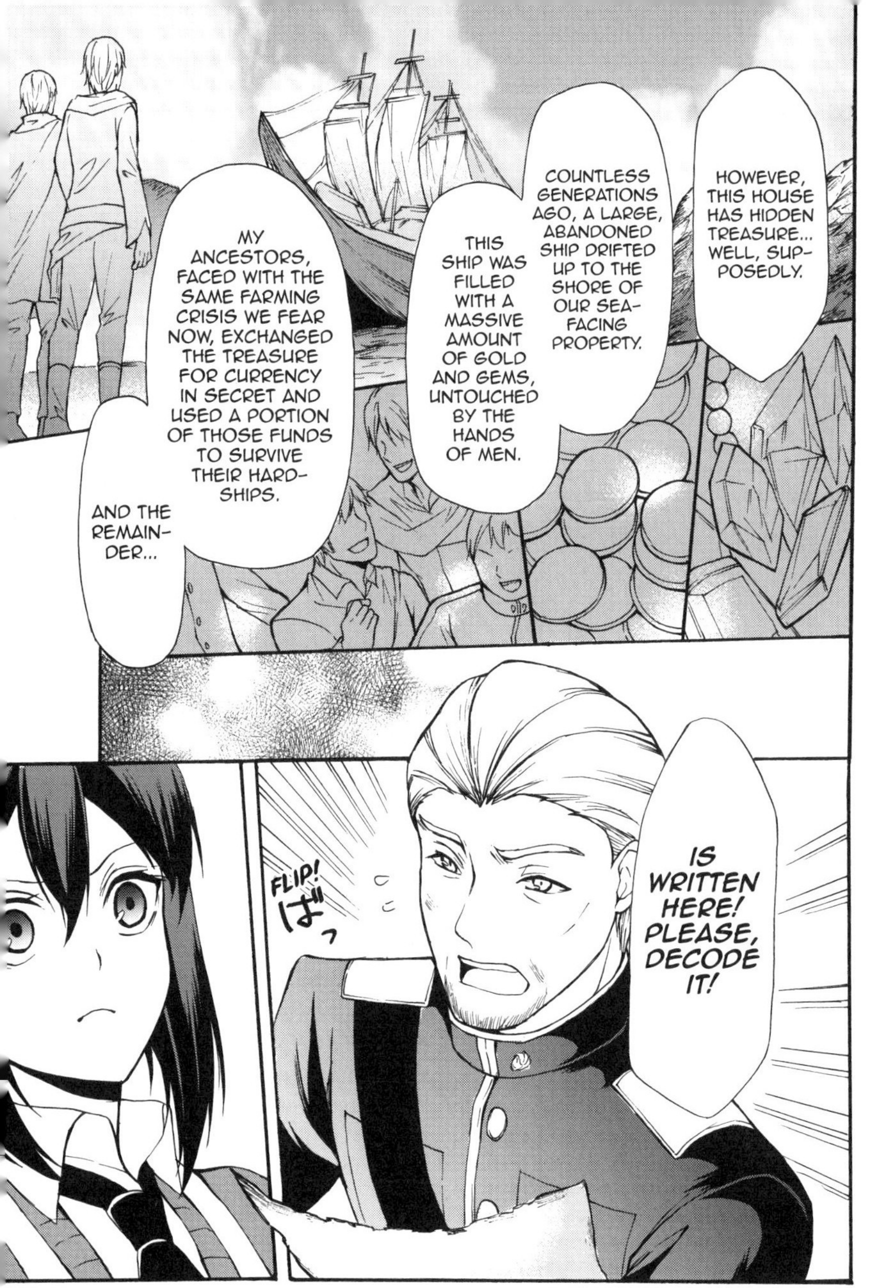

HOWEVER, THIS HOUSE HAS HIDDEN TREASURE... WELL, SUP-POSEDLY.
COUNTLESS GENERATIONS AGO, A LARGE, ABANDONED SHIP DRIFTED UP TO THE SHORE OF OUR SEA-FACING PROPERTY.
THIS SHIP WAS FILLED WITH A MASSIVE AMOUNT OF GOLD AND GEMS, UNTOUCHED BY THE HANDS OF MEN.
MY ANCESTORS, FACED WITH THE SAME FARMING CRISIS WE FEAR NOW, EXCHANGED THE TREASURE FOR CURRENCY IN SECRET AND USED A PORTION OF THOSE FUNDS TO SURVIVE THEIR HARD-SHIPS.
AND THE REMAIN-DER...
IS WRITTEN HERE! PLEASE, DECODE IT!
FLIP! ばっ

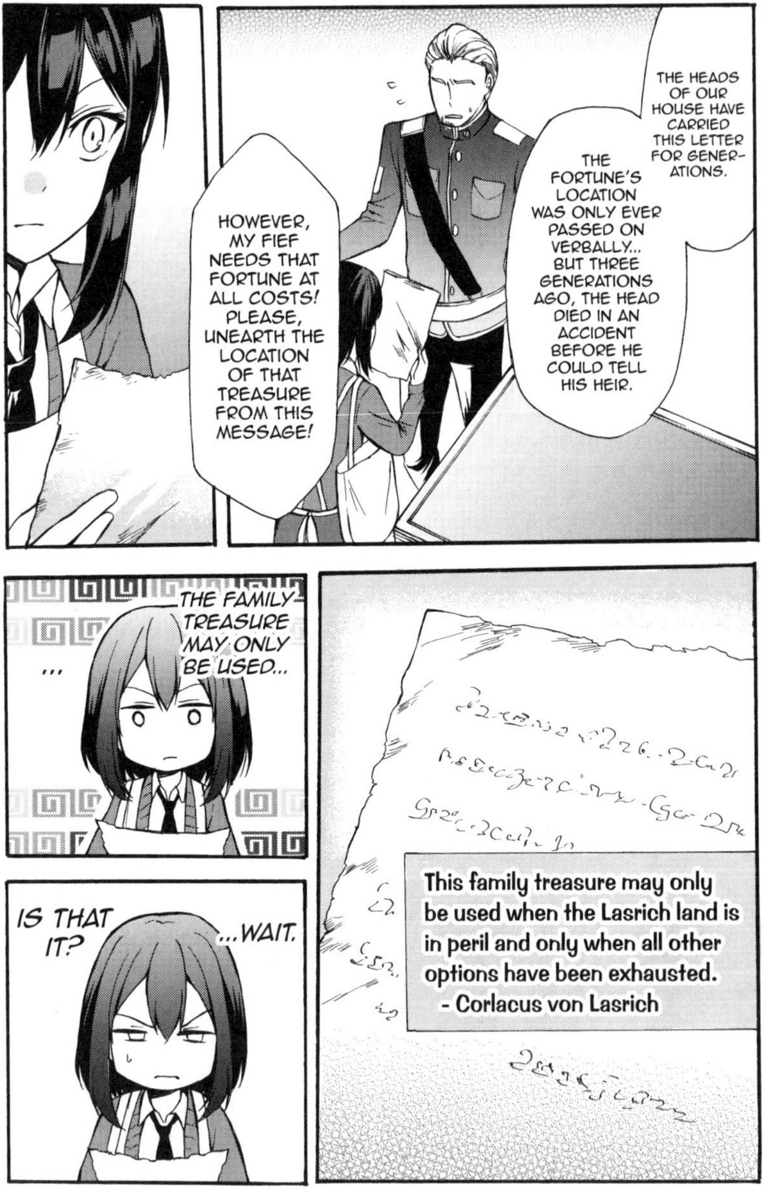
THE HEADS OF OUR HOUSE HAVE CARRIED THIS LETTER FOR GENERATIONS.
THE FORTUNE'S LOCATION WAS ONLY EVER PASSED ON VERBALLY... BUT THREE GENERATIONS AGO, THE HEAD DIED IN AN ACCIDENT BEFORE HE COULD TELL HIS HEIR.
HOWEVER, MY FIEF NEEDS THAT FORTUNE AT ALL COSTS! PLEASE, UNEARTH THE LOCATION OF THAT TREASURE FROM THIS MESSAGE!
This family treasure may only be used when the Lasrich land is in peril and only when all other options have been exhausted.
- Corlacus von Lasrich
THE FAMILY TREASURE MAY ONLY BE USED...
...
...WAIT.
IS THAT IT?

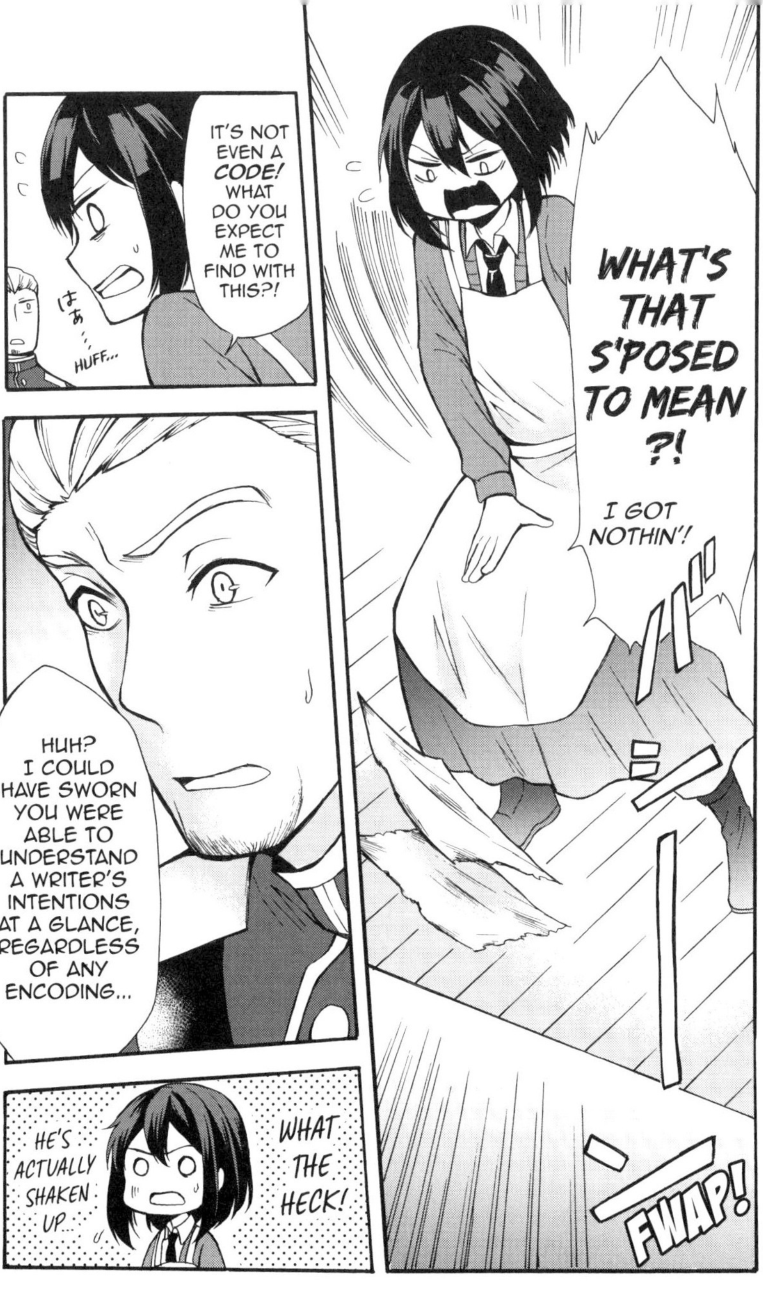
WHAT'S THAT S'POSED TO MEAN ?!
I GOT NOTHIN'!
FWAP!
IT'S NOT EVEN A CODE! WHAT DO YOU EXPECT ME TO FIND WITH THIS?!
はぁ…
HUFF...
HUH? I COULD HAVE SWORN YOU WERE ABLE TO UNDERSTAND A WRITER'S INTENTIONS AT A GLANCE, REGARDLESS OF ANY ENCODING...
WHAT THE HECK!
HE'S ACTUALLY SHAKEN UP...

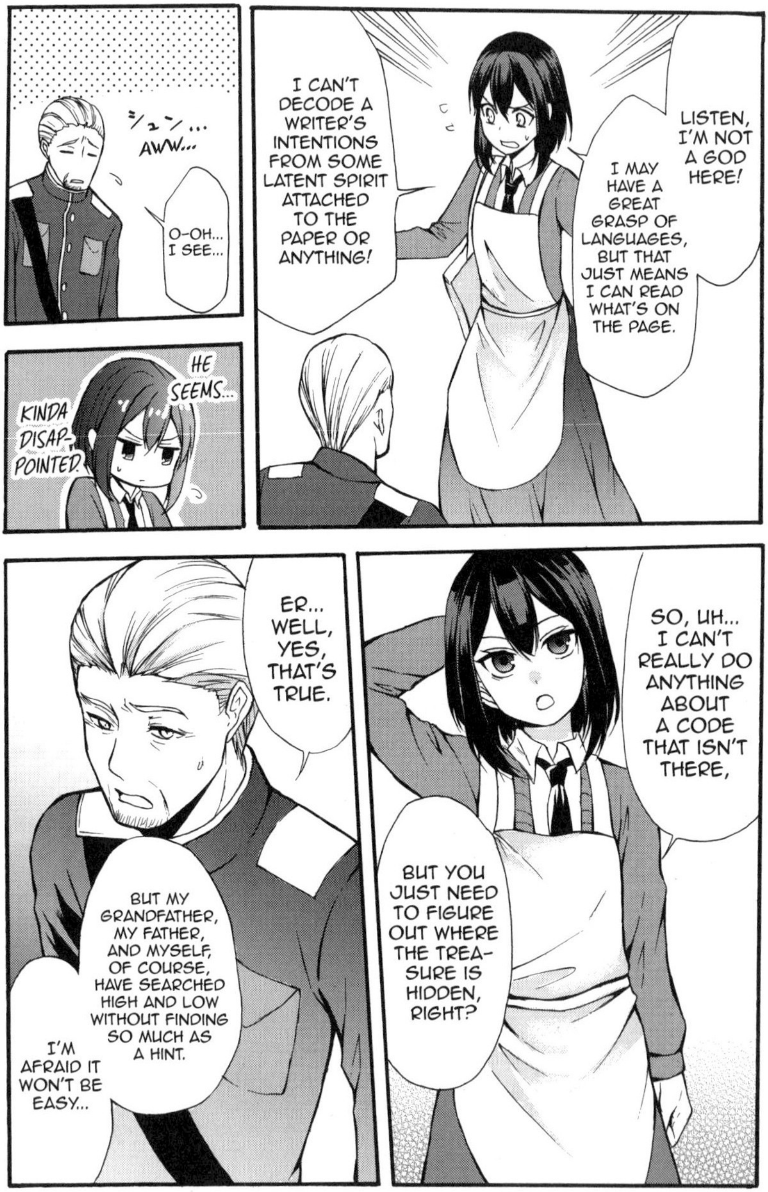
LISTEN, I'M NOT A GOD HERE!
I MAY HAVE A GREAT GRASP OF LANGUAGES, BUT THAT JUST MEANS I CAN READ WHAT'S ON THE PAGE.
I CAN'T DECODE A WRITER'S INTENTIONS FROM SOME LATENT SPIRIT ATTACHED TO THE PAPER OR ANYTHING!
シュン... AWW...
O-OH... I SEE...
HE SEEMS... KINDA DISAPPOINTED.
SO, UH... I CAN'T REALLY DO ANYTHING ABOUT A CODE THAT ISN'T THERE,
BUT YOU JUST NEED TO FIGURE OUT WHERE THE TREASURE IS HIDDEN, RIGHT?
ER... WELL, YES, THAT'S TRUE.
BUT MY GRANDFATHER, MY FATHER, AND MYSELF, OF COURSE, HAVE SEARCHED HIGH AND LOW WITHOUT FINDING SO MUCH AS A HINT.
I'M AFRAID IT WON'T BE EASY...

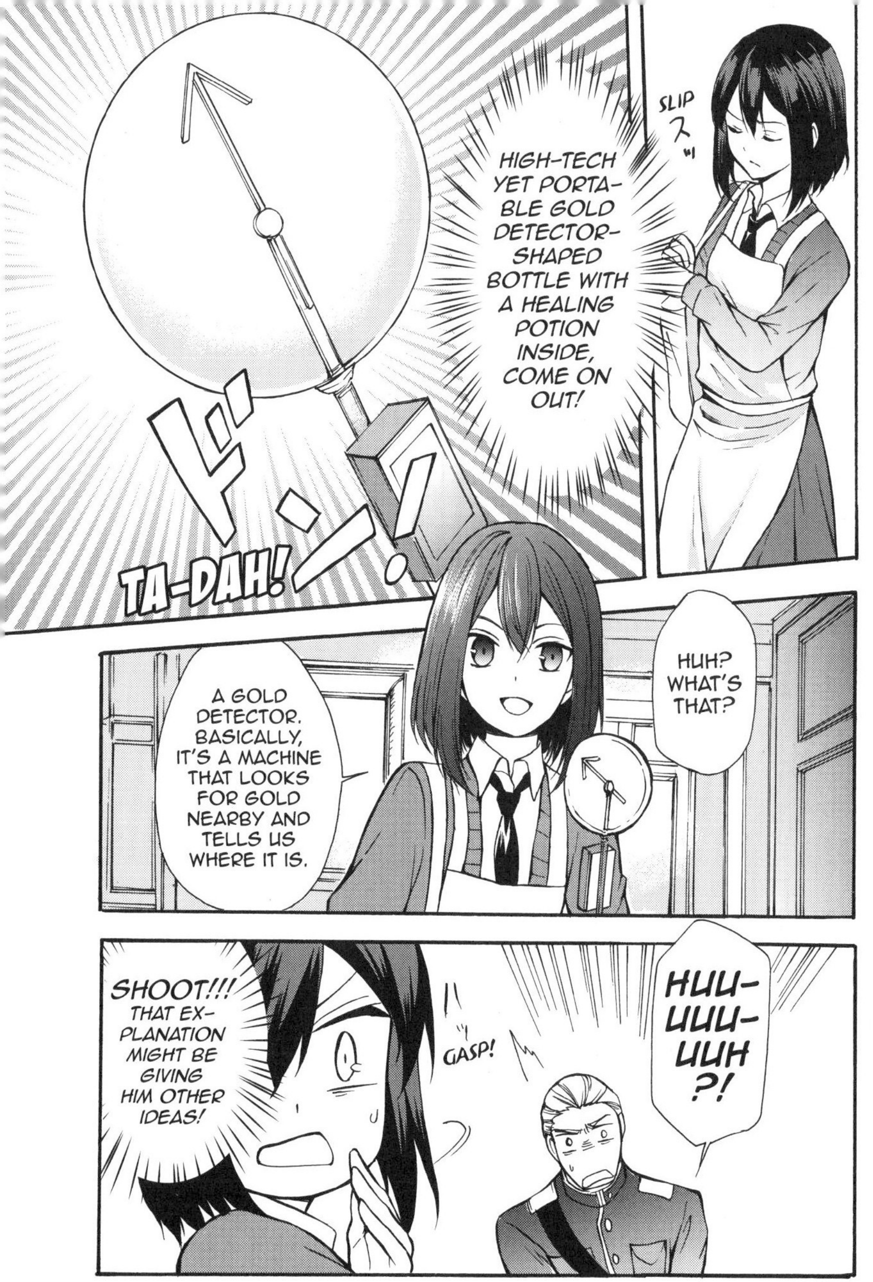
SLIP
HIGH-TECH YET PORTA-BLE GOLD DETECTOR-SHAPED BOTTLE WITH A HEALING POTION INSIDE, COME ON OUT!
TA-DAH!
HUH? WHAT'S THAT?
A GOLD DETECTOR. BASICALLY, IT'S A MACHINE THAT LOOKS FOR GOLD NEARBY AND TELLS US WHERE IT IS.
HUU-UUU-UUH?!
GASP!
SHOOT!!! THAT EX-PLANATION MIGHT BE GIVING HIM OTHER IDEAS!

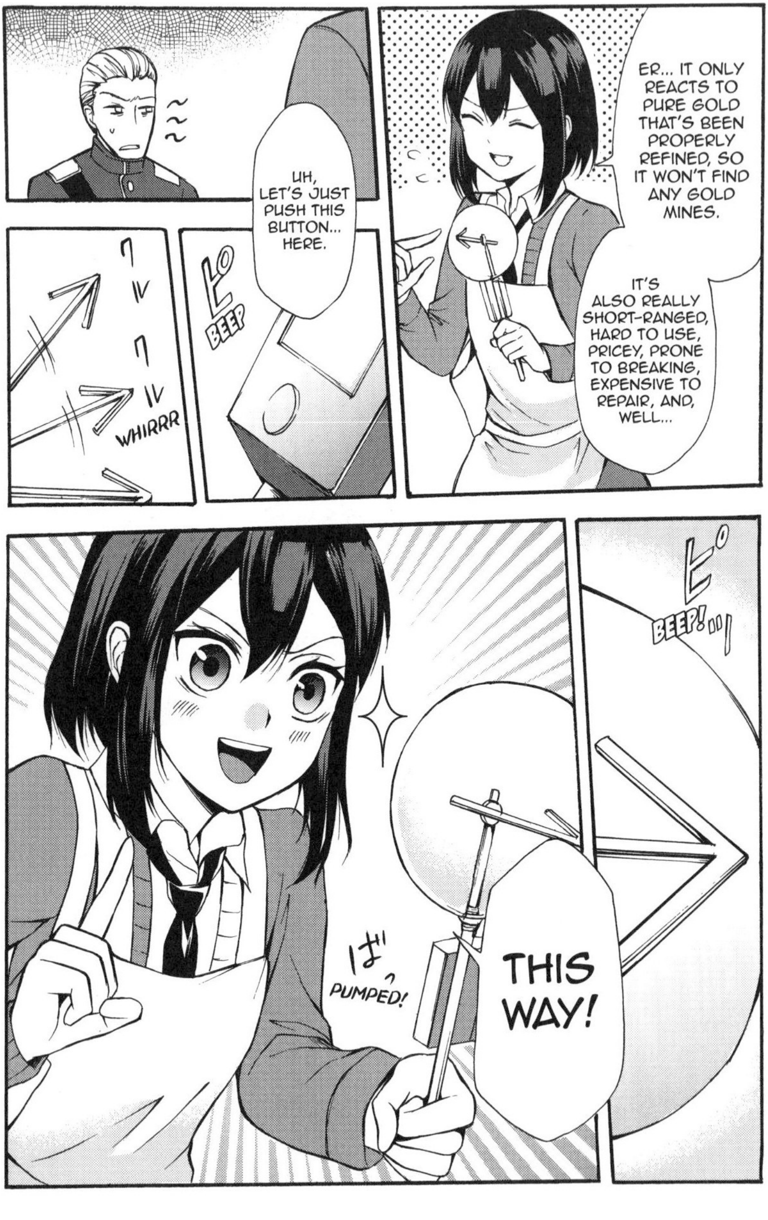
ER... IT ONLY REACTS TO PURE GOLD THAT'S BEEN PROPERLY REFINED, SO IT WON'T FIND ANY GOLD MINES.
IT'S ALSO REALLY SHORT-RANGED, HARD TO USE, PRICEY, PRONE TO BREAKING, EXPENSIVE TO REPAIR, AND, WELL...
UH, LET'S JUST PUSH THIS BUTTON... HERE.
ピ
BEEP
クル クル
WHIRRR
ピ
BEEP!
ぱっ
PUMPED!
THIS WAY!

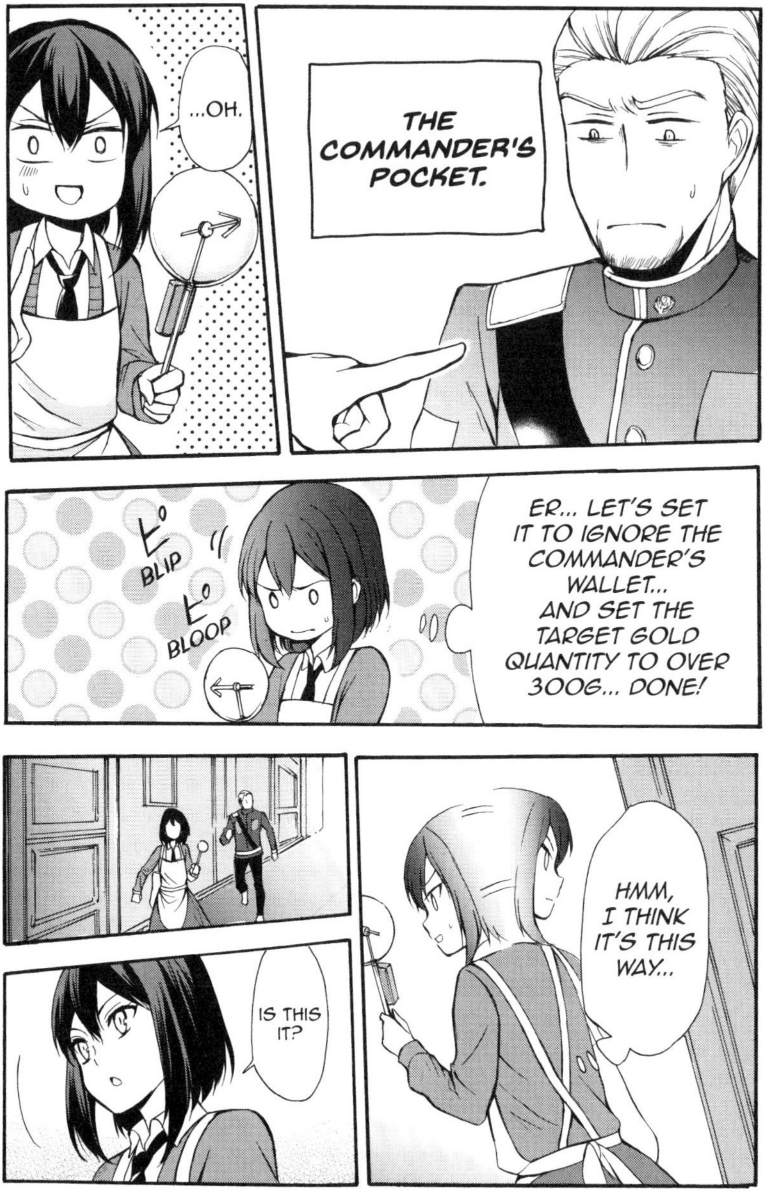
THE COMMANDER'S POCKET.
...OH.
ER... LET'S SET IT TO IGNORE THE COMMANDER'S WALLET... AND SET THE TARGET GOLD QUANTITY TO OVER 300G... DONE!
ピ BLIP
ピ BLOOP
HMM, I THINK IT'S THIS WAY...
IS THIS IT?

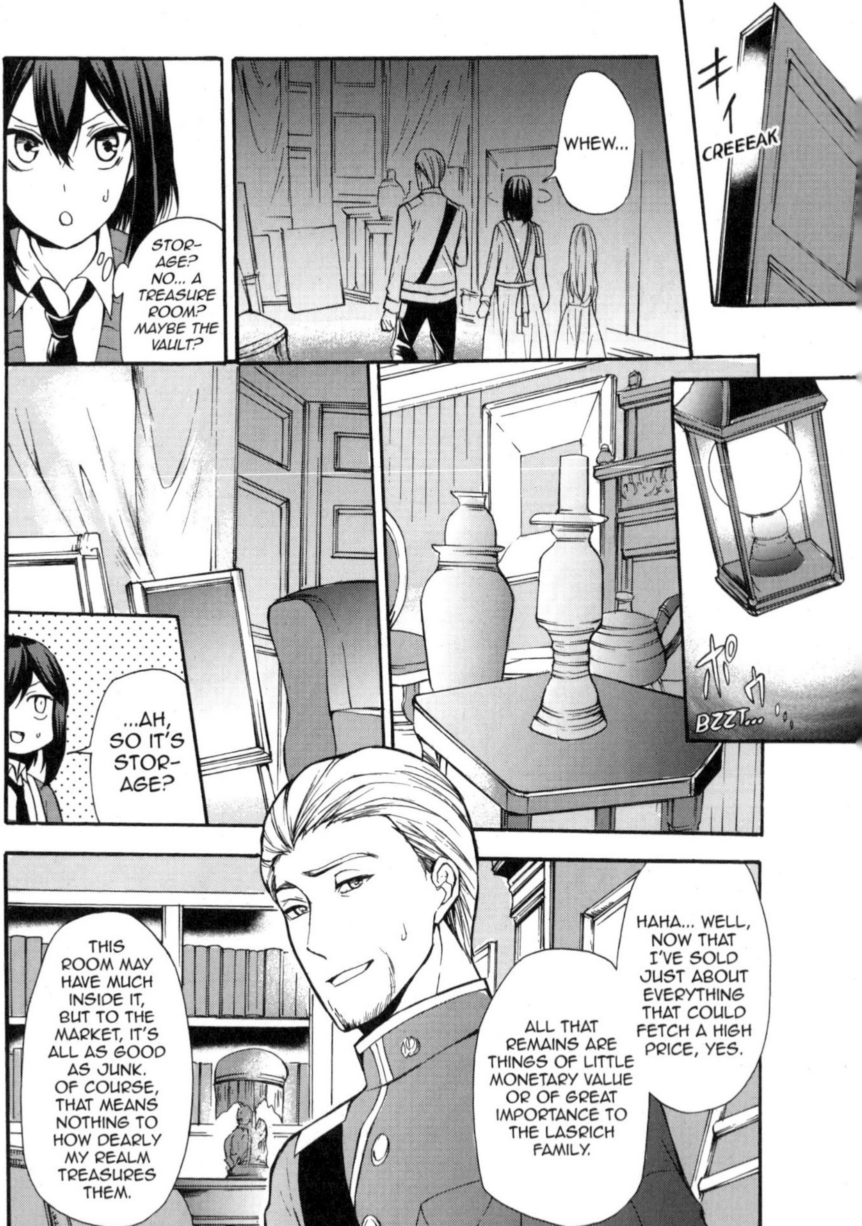

キィ
CREEEAK
WHEW...
STORAGE? NO... A TREASURE ROOM? MAYBE THE VAULT?
ポゥ
BZZT...
...AH, SO IT'S STORAGE?
HAHA... WELL, NOW THAT I'VE SOLD JUST ABOUT EVERYTHING THAT COULD FETCH A HIGH PRICE, YES.
ALL THAT REMAINS ARE THINGS OF LITTLE MONETARY VALUE OR OF GREAT IMPORTANCE TO THE LASRICH FAMILY.
THIS ROOM MAY HAVE MUCH INSIDE IT, BUT TO THE MARKET, IT'S ALL AS GOOD AS JUNK. OF COURSE, THAT MEANS NOTHING TO HOW DEARLY MY REALM TREASURES THEM.

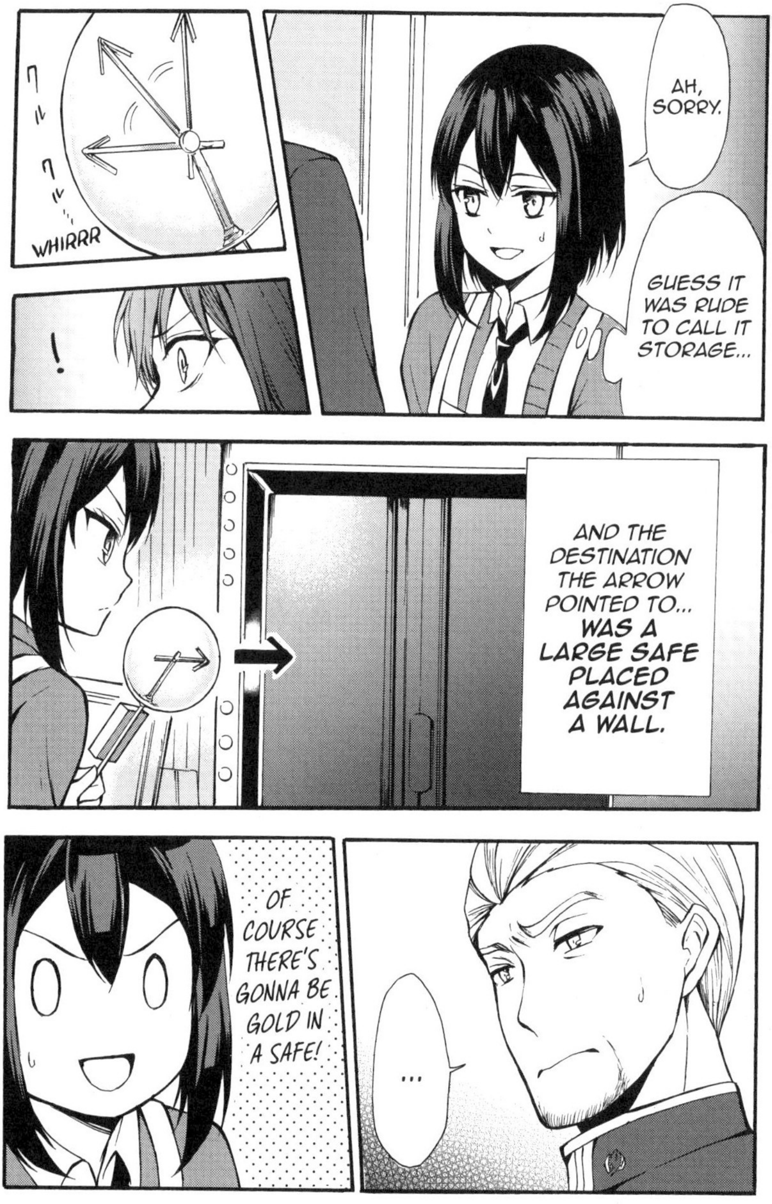

AH, SORRY.
GUESS IT WAS RUDE TO CALL IT STORAGE...
クル クル…
WHIRRR
!
AND THE DESTINATION THE ARROW POINTED TO... **WAS A LARGE SAFE PLACED AGAINST A WALL.**
...
OF COURSE THERE'S GONNA BE GOLD IN A SAFE!

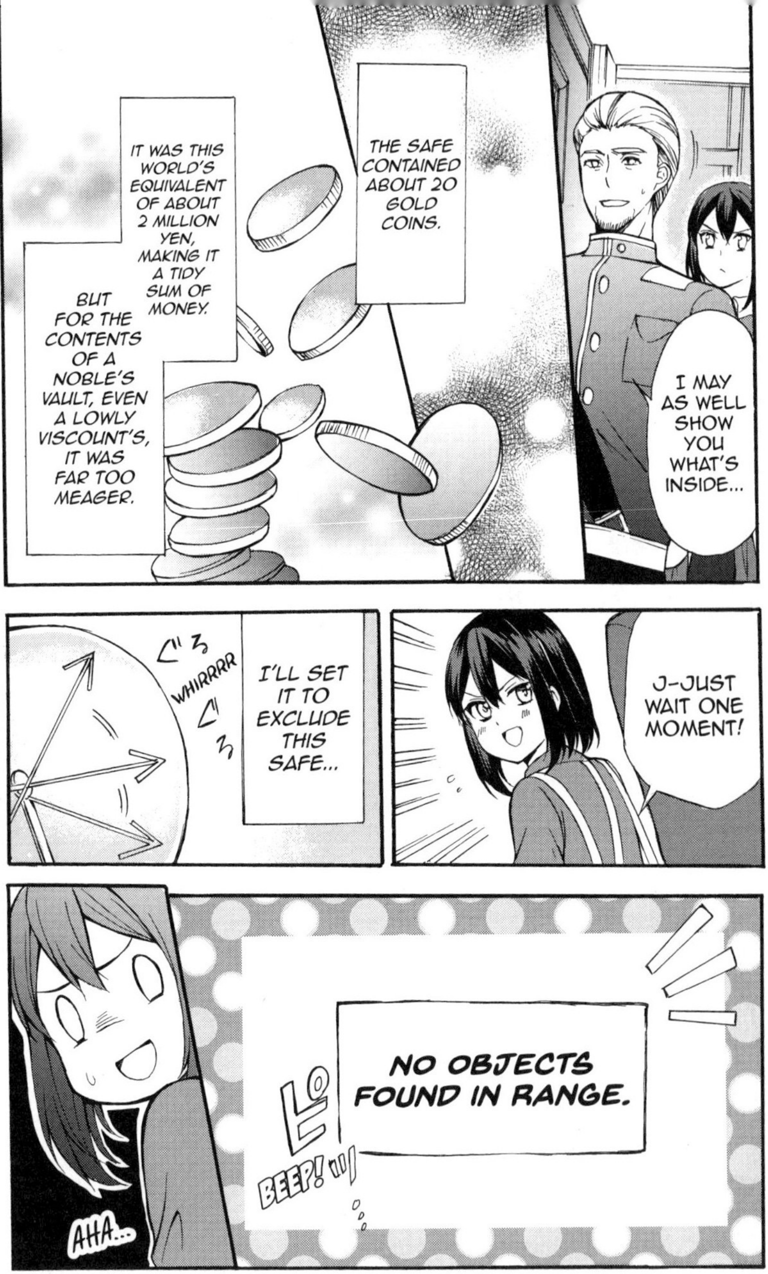
I MAY AS WELL SHOW YOU WHAT'S INSIDE...
THE SAFE CONTAINED ABOUT 20 GOLD COINS.
IT WAS THIS WORLD'S EQUIVALENT OF ABOUT 2 MILLION YEN, MAKING IT A TIDY SUM OF MONEY.
BUT FOR THE CONTENTS OF A NOBLE'S VAULT, EVEN A LOWLY VISCOUNT'S, IT WAS FAR TOO MEAGER.
J-JUST WAIT ONE MOMENT!
I'LL SET IT TO EXCLUDE THIS SAFE...
WHIRRRR
NO OBJECTS FOUND IN RANGE.
BEEP!
AHA...

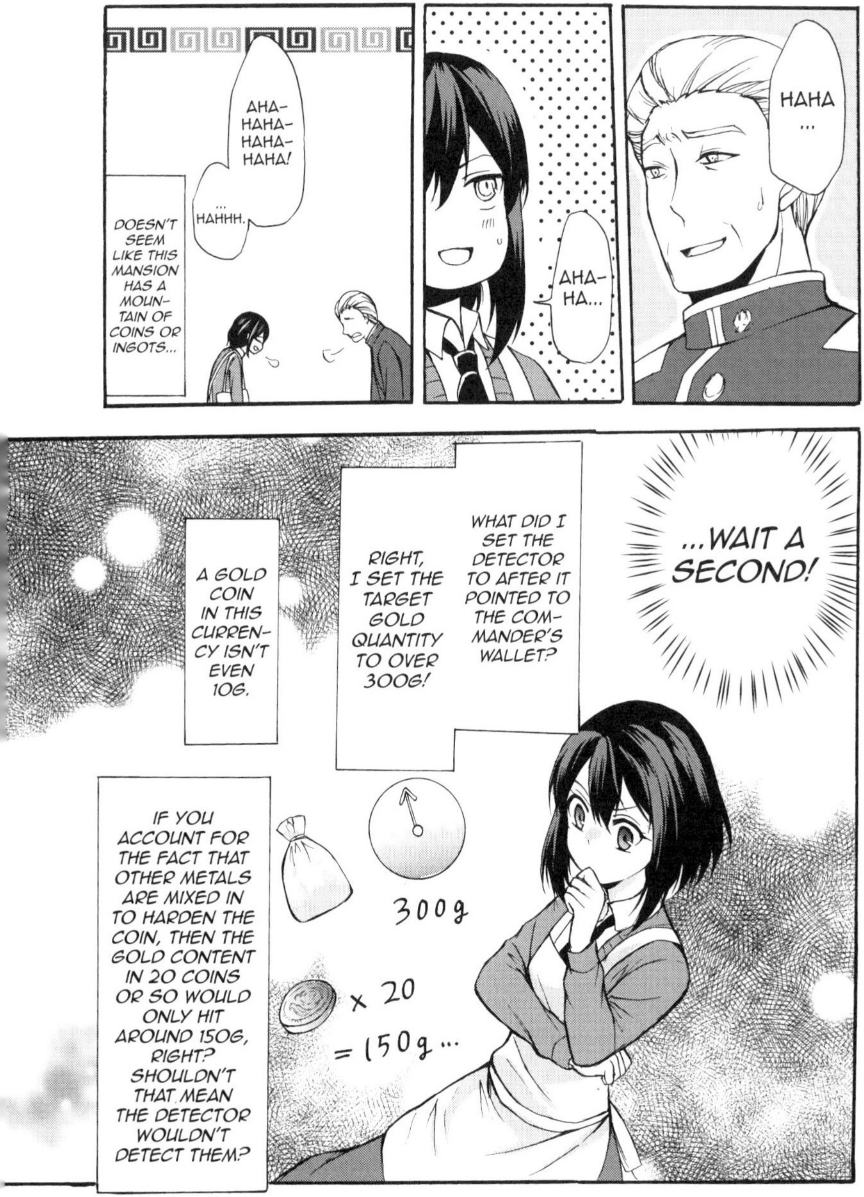
HAHA ...
AHA-HA...
AHA-HAHA-HAHA-HAHA!
... HAHHH.
DOESN'T SEEM LIKE THIS MANSION HAS A MOUN-TAIN OF COINS OR INGOTS...
...WAIT A SECOND!
WHAT DID I SET THE DETECTOR TO AFTER IT POINTED TO THE COM-MANDER'S WALLET?
RIGHT, I SET THE TARGET GOLD QUANTITY TO OVER 300G!
A GOLD COIN IN THIS CURREN-CY ISN'T EVEN 10G.
300g
x 20
= 150g ...
IF YOU ACCOUNT FOR THE FACT THAT OTHER METALS ARE MIXED IN TO HARDEN THE COIN, THEN THE GOLD CONTENT IN 20 COINS OR SO WOULD ONLY HIT AROUND 150G, RIGHT? SHOULDN'T THAT MEAN THE DETECTOR WOULDN'T DETECT THEM?

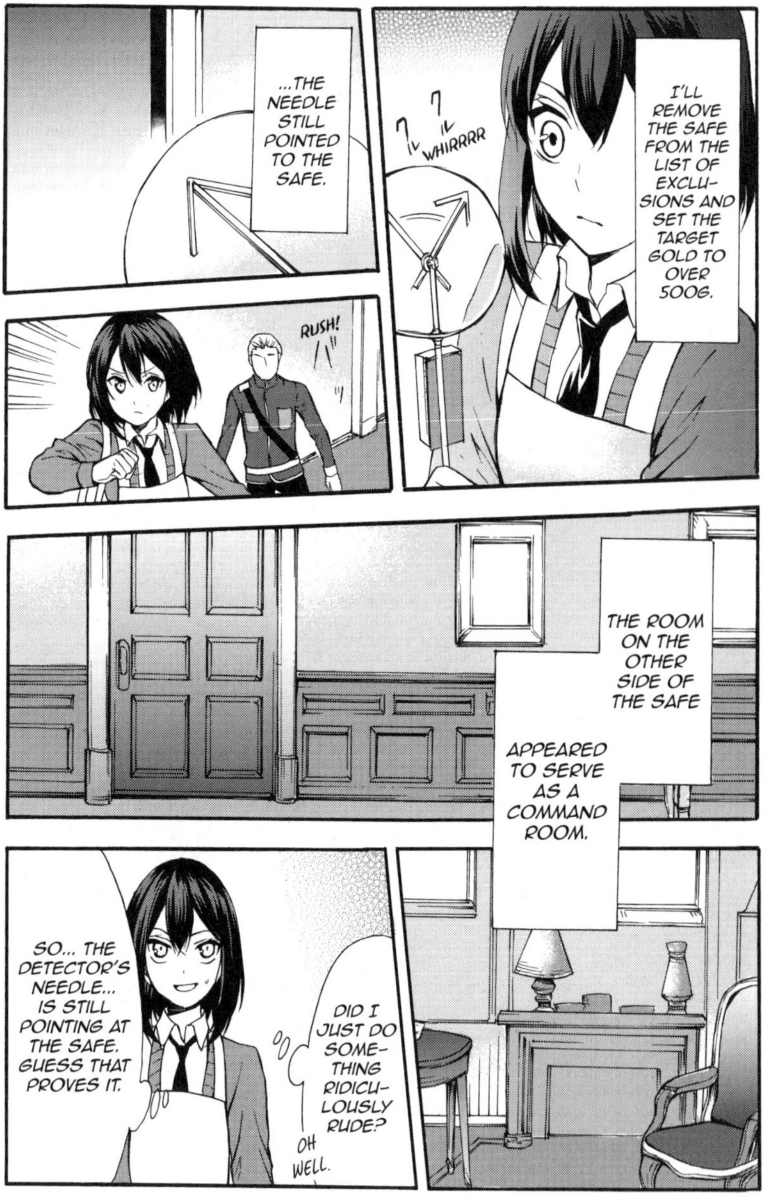

I'LL REMOVE THE SAFE FROM THE LIST OF EXCLUSIONS AND SET THE TARGET GOLD TO OVER 500G.
WHIRRRR
...THE NEEDLE STILL POINTED TO THE SAFE.
RUSH!
THE ROOM ON THE OTHER SIDE OF THE SAFE
APPEARED TO SERVE AS A COMMAND ROOM.
DID I JUST DO SOMETHING RIDICULOUSLY RUDE?
SO... THE DETECTOR'S NEEDLE... IS STILL POINTING AT THE SAFE. GUESS THAT PROVES IT.
OH WELL.

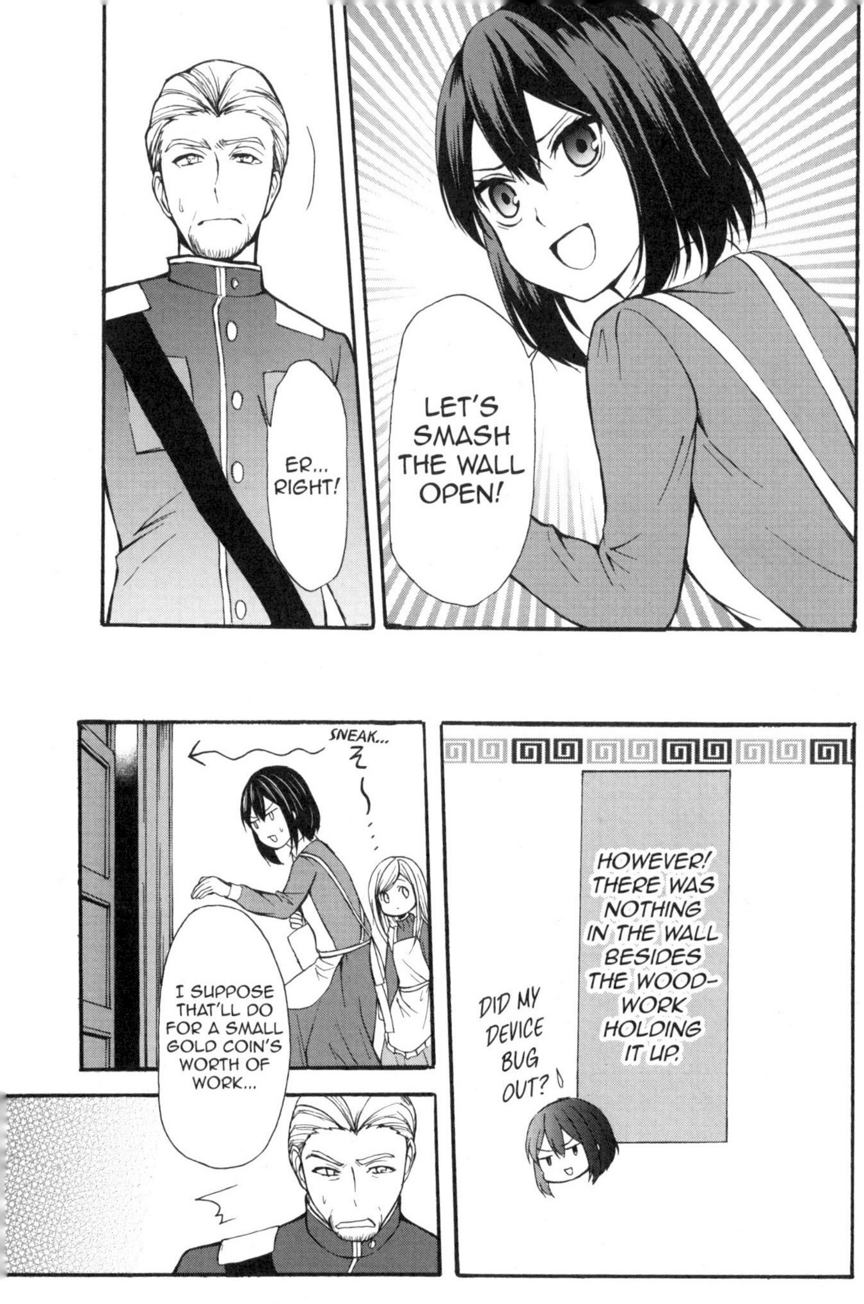
LET'S SMASH THE WALL OPEN!
ER... RIGHT!
HOWEVER! THERE WAS NOTHING IN THE WALL BESIDES THE WOOD-WORK HOLDING IT UP.
DID MY DEVICE BUG OUT?
SNEAK...
I SUPPOSE THAT'LL DO FOR A SMALL GOLD COIN'S WORTH OF WORK...

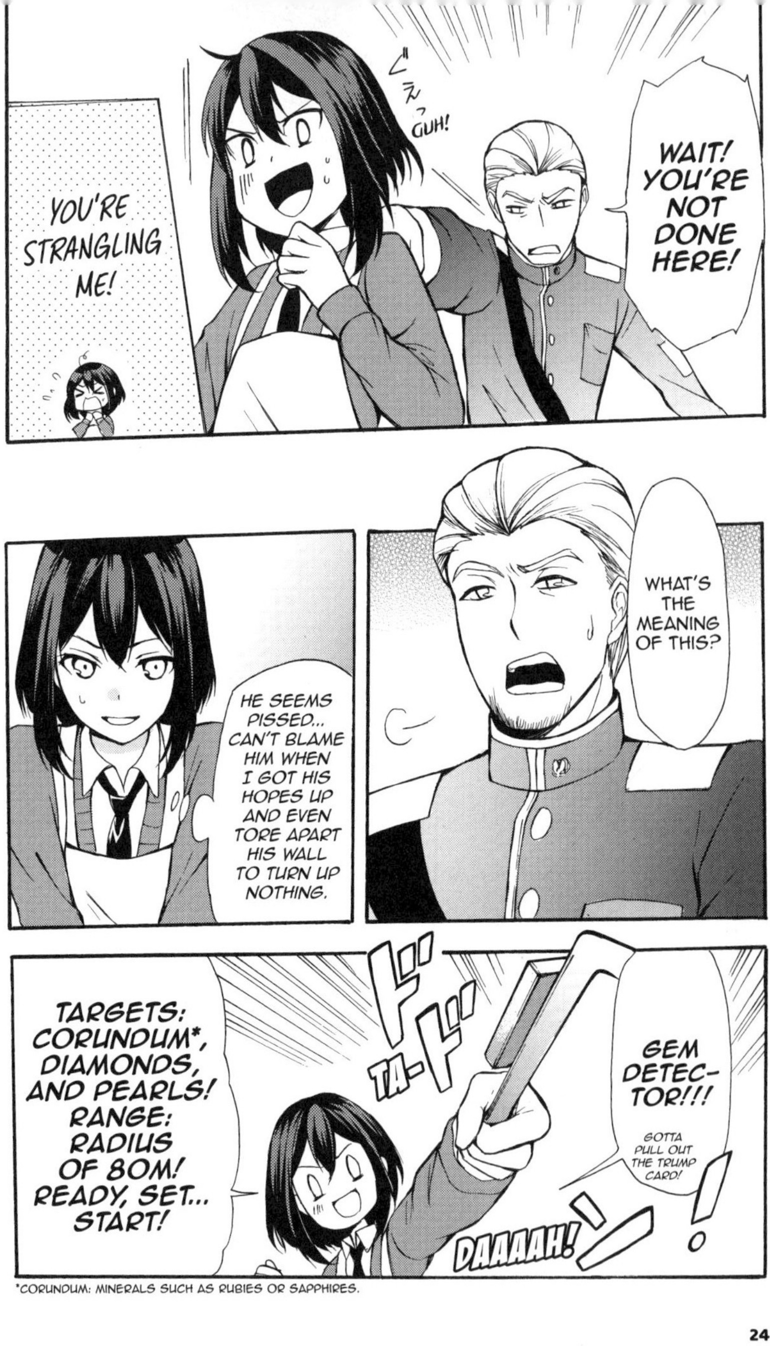
WAIT! YOU'RE NOT DONE HERE!
ぐえっ
GUH!
YOU'RE STRANGLING ME!
WHAT'S THE MEANING OF THIS?
HE SEEMS PISSED... CAN'T BLAME HIM WHEN I GOT HIS HOPES UP AND EVEN TORE APART HIS WALL TO TURN UP NOTHING.
GEM DETECTOR!!!
GOTTA PULL OUT THE TRUMP CARD!
TA-
DAAAAH!
TARGETS: CORUNDUM*, DIAMONDS, AND PEARLS! RANGE: RADIUS OF 80M! READY, SET... START!

*CORUNDUM: MINERALS SUCH AS RUBIES OR SAPPHIRES.

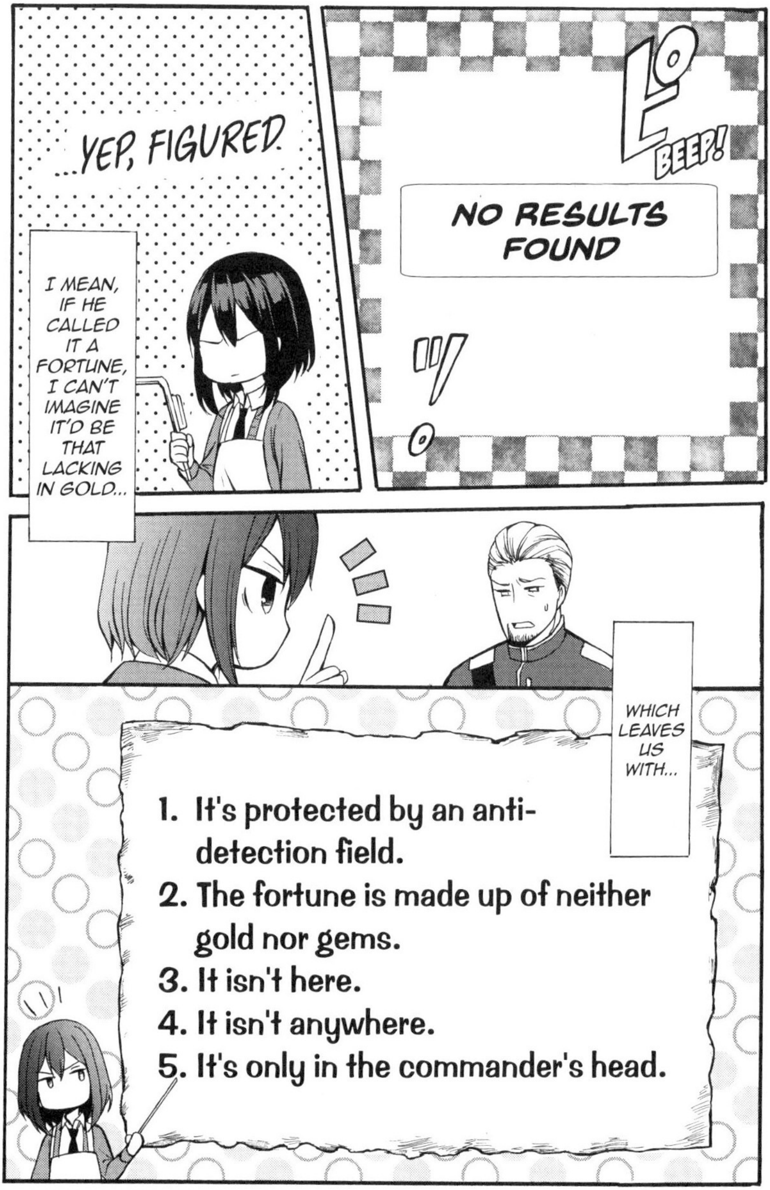
BEEP!
NO RESULTS FOUND
...YEP, FIGURED.
I MEAN, IF HE CALLED IT A FORTUNE, I CAN'T IMAGINE IT'D BE THAT LACKING IN GOLD...
WHICH LEAVES US WITH...
1. It's protected by an anti-detection field.
2. The fortune is made up of neither gold nor gems.
3. It isn't here.
4. It isn't anywhere.
5. It's only in the commander's head.

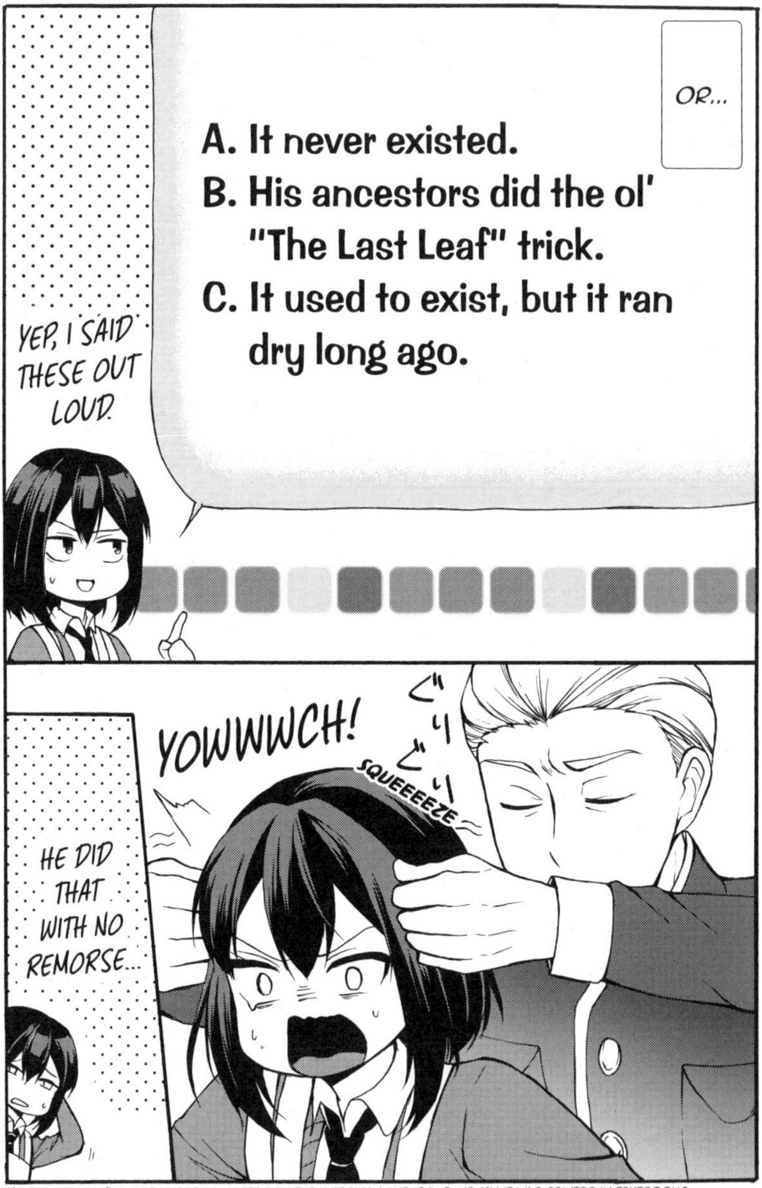
OR...
A. It never existed.
B. His ancestors did the ol' "The Last Leaf" trick.
C. It used to exist, but it ran dry long ago.
YEP, I SAID THESE OUT LOUD.
ぐりぐり
SQUEEEEEZE
YOWWWCH!
HE DID THAT WITH NO REMORSE...

*"THE LAST LEAF": A SHORT STORY WRITTEN BY THE AMERICAN AUTHOR, O. HENRY. IT WAS PRINTED IN TEXTBOOKS.

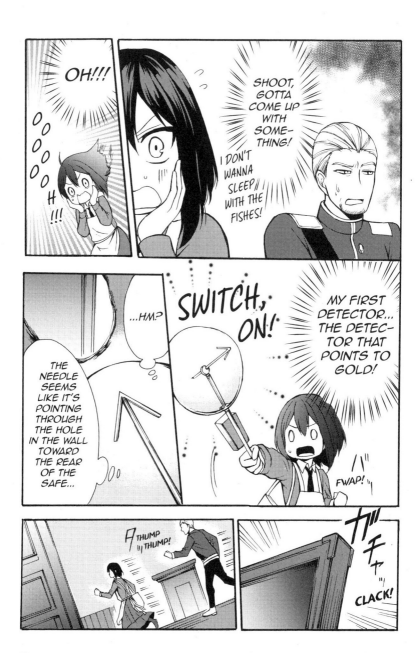

OH!!!

OOOOOH!!!

SHOOT, GOTTA COME UP WITH SOME-THING!

I DON'T WANNA SLEEP WITH THE FISHES!

...HM?

SWITCH, ON!

MY FIRST DETECTOR... THE DETECTOR THAT POINTS TO GOLD!

THE NEEDLE SEEMS LIKE IT'S POINTING THROUGH THE HOLE IN THE WALL TOWARD THE REAR OF THE SAFE...

FWAP!

THUMP THUMP!

CLACK!

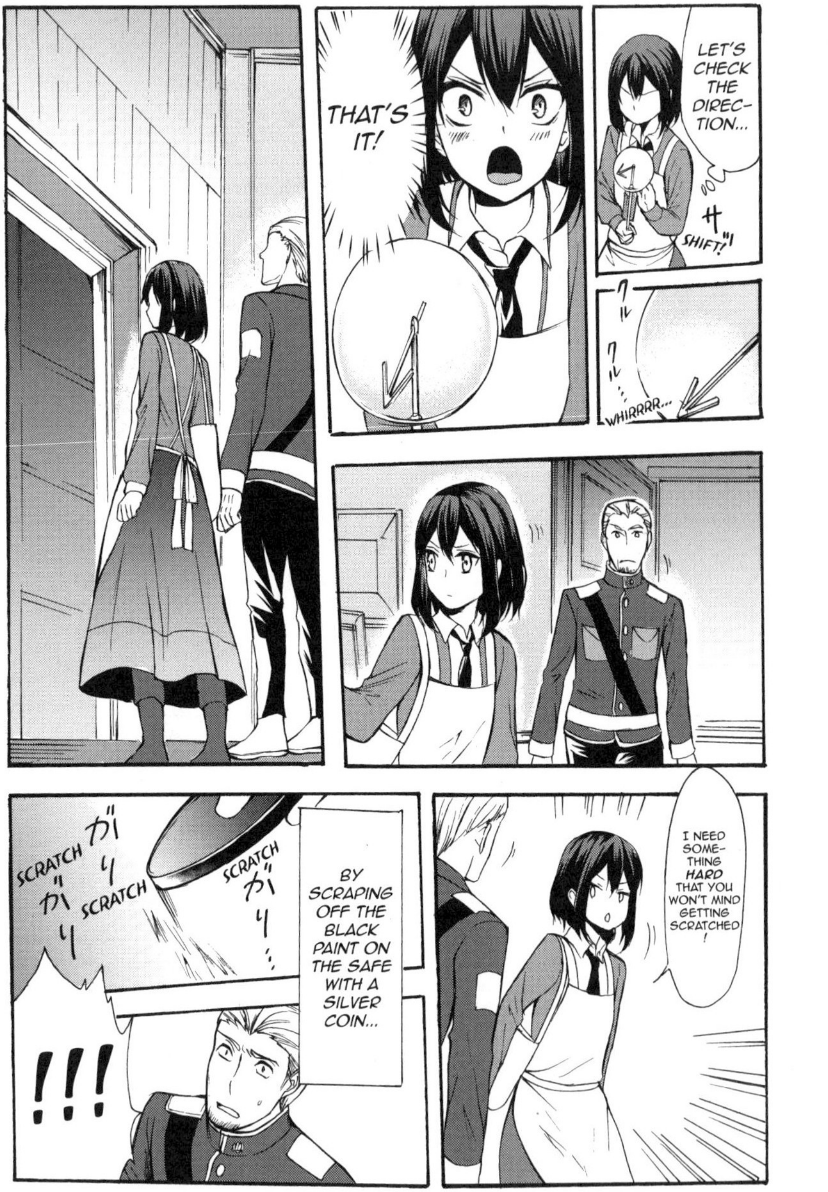
LET'S CHECK THE DIRECTION...
サ
SHIFT!
クル クル…
WHIRRRR...
THAT'S IT!
I NEED SOMETHING **HARD** THAT YOU WON'T MIND GETTING SCRATCHED!
がり がり
SCRATCH SCRATCH
がり…
SCRATCH
BY SCRAPING OFF THE BLACK PAINT ON THE SAFE WITH A SILVER COIN...
!!!

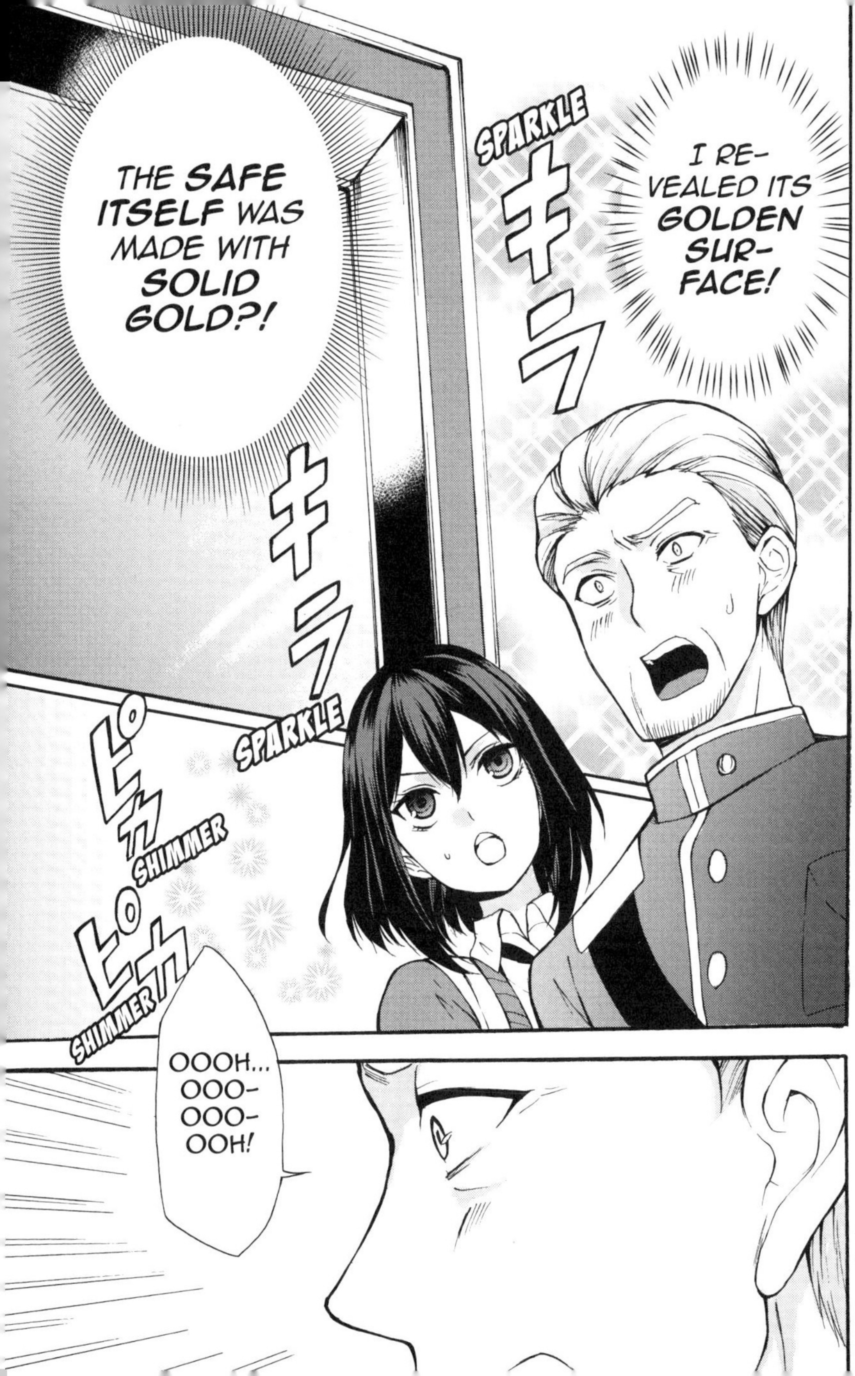
I RE-VEALED ITS GOLDEN SUR-FACE!
SPARKLE
THE SAFE ITSELF WAS MADE WITH SOLID GOLD?!
SPARKLE
SHIMMER
SHIMMER
OOOH... OOO-OOO-OOH!

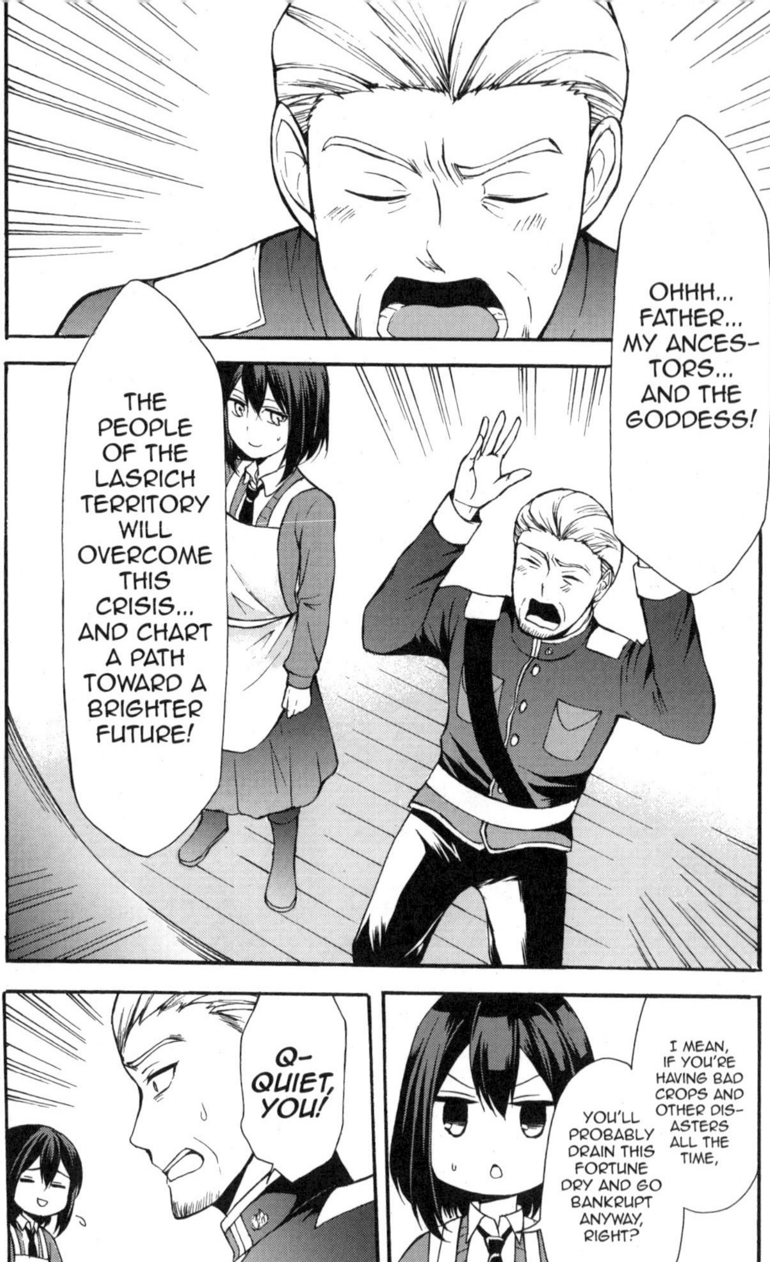
OHHH... FATHER... MY ANCESTORS... AND THE GODDESS!
THE PEOPLE OF THE LASRICH TERRITORY WILL OVERCOME THIS CRISIS... AND CHART A PATH TOWARD A BRIGHTER FUTURE!
I MEAN, IF YOU'RE HAVING BAD CROPS AND OTHER DISASTERS ALL THE TIME,
YOU'LL PROBABLY DRAIN THIS FORTUNE DRY AND GO BANKRUPT ANYWAY, RIGHT?
Q-QUIET, YOU!

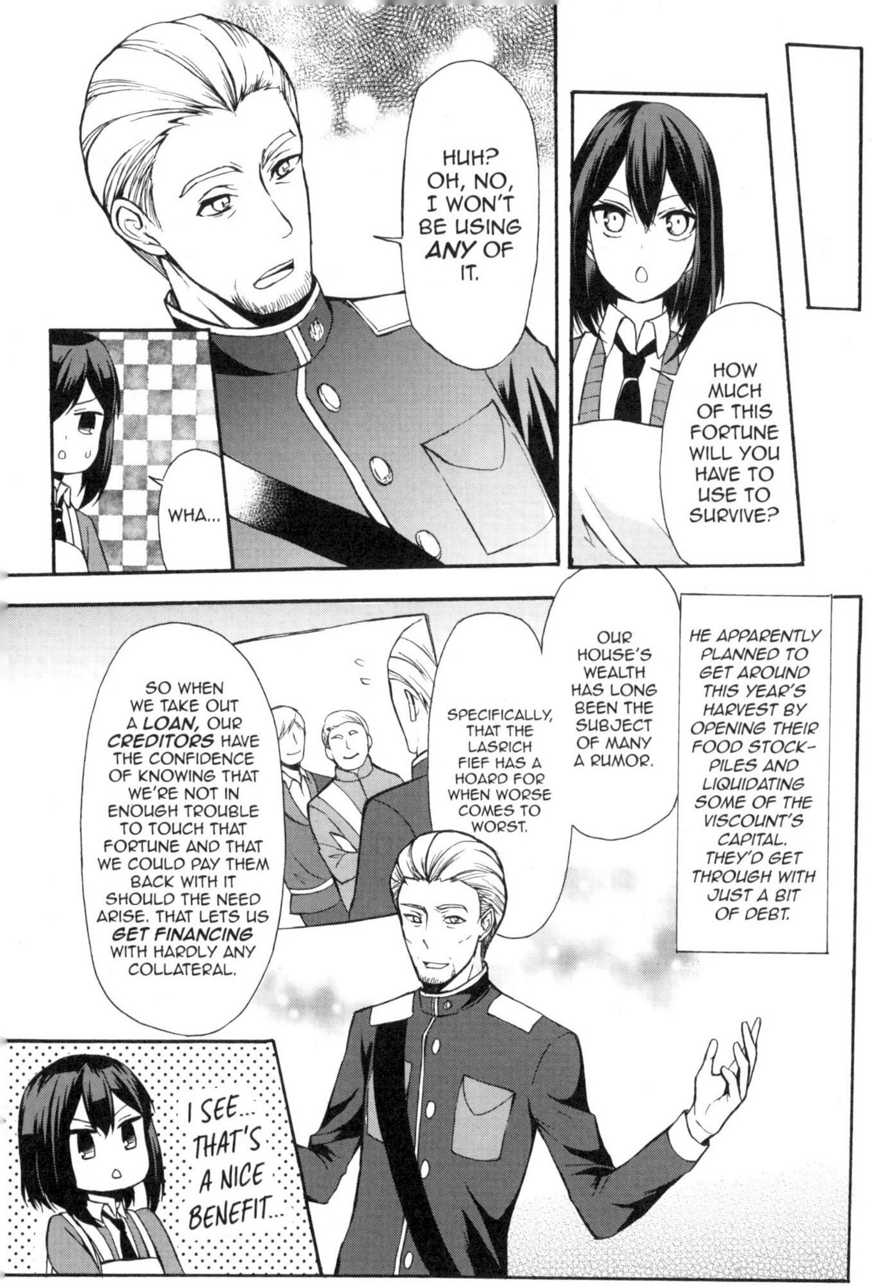
HOW MUCH OF THIS FORTUNE WILL YOU HAVE TO USE TO SURVIVE?
HUH? OH, NO, I WON'T BE USING ANY OF IT.
WHA...
HE APPARENTLY PLANNED TO GET AROUND THIS YEAR'S HARVEST BY OPENING THEIR FOOD STOCK-PILES AND LIQUIDATING SOME OF THE VISCOUNT'S CAPITAL. THEY'D GET THROUGH WITH JUST A BIT OF DEBT.
OUR HOUSE'S WEALTH HAS LONG BEEN THE SUBJECT OF MANY A RUMOR.
SPECIFICALLY, THAT THE LASRICH FIEF HAS A HOARD FOR WHEN WORSE COMES TO WORST.
SO WHEN WE TAKE OUT A LOAN, OUR CREDITORS HAVE THE CONFIDENCE OF KNOWING THAT WE'RE NOT IN ENOUGH TROUBLE TO TOUCH THAT FORTUNE AND THAT WE COULD PAY THEM BACK WITH IT SHOULD THE NEED ARISE. THAT LETS US GET FINANCING WITH HARDLY ANY COLLATERAL.
I SEE... THAT'S A NICE BENEFIT...

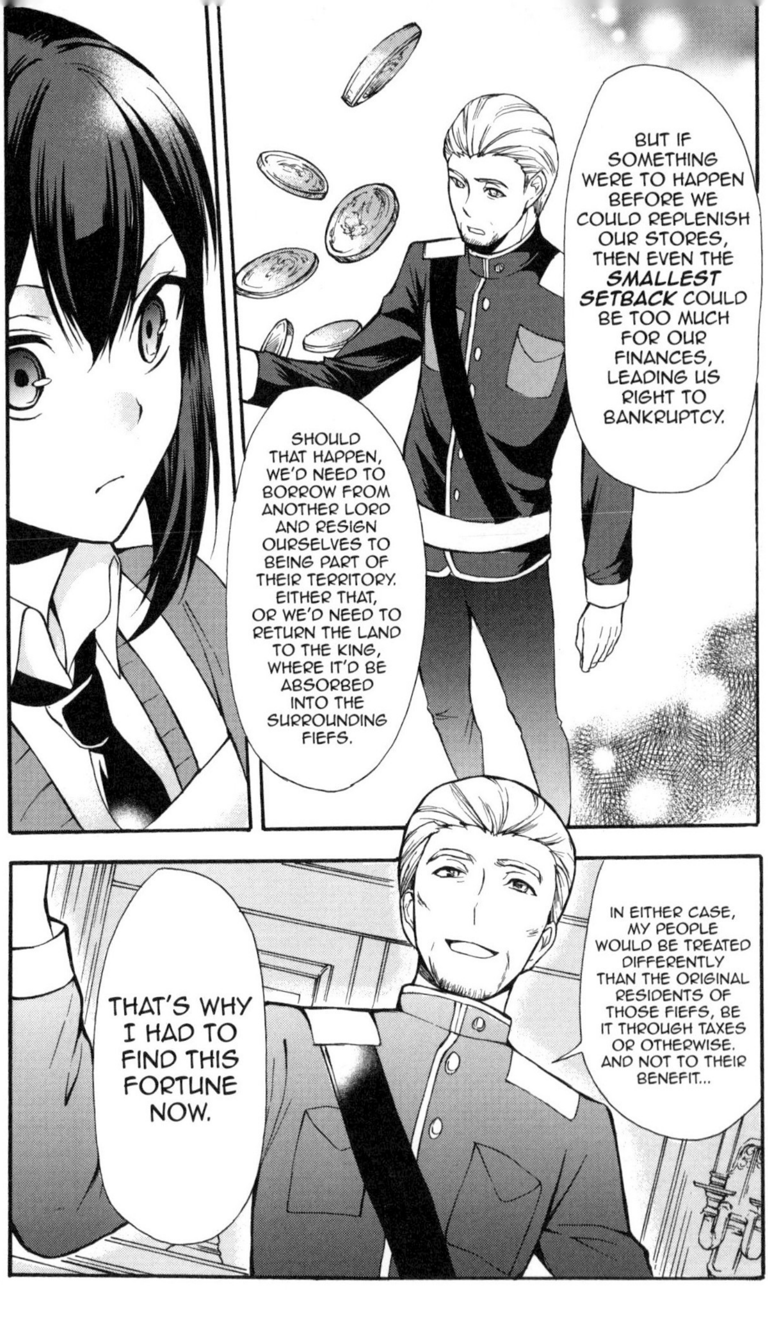
BUT IF SOMETHING WERE TO HAPPEN BEFORE WE COULD REPLENISH OUR STORES, THEN EVEN THE **SMALLEST SETBACK** COULD BE TOO MUCH FOR OUR FINANCES, LEADING US RIGHT TO BANKRUPTCY.
SHOULD THAT HAPPEN, WE'D NEED TO BORROW FROM ANOTHER LORD AND RESIGN OURSELVES TO BEING PART OF THEIR TERRITORY. EITHER THAT, OR WE'D NEED TO RETURN THE LAND TO THE KING, WHERE IT'D BE ABSORBED INTO THE SURROUNDING FIEFS.
IN EITHER CASE, MY PEOPLE WOULD BE TREATED DIFFERENTLY THAN THE ORIGINAL RESIDENTS OF THOSE FIEFS, BE IT THROUGH TAXES OR OTHERWISE. AND NOT TO THEIR BENEFIT...
THAT'S WHY I HAD TO FIND THIS FORTUNE NOW.

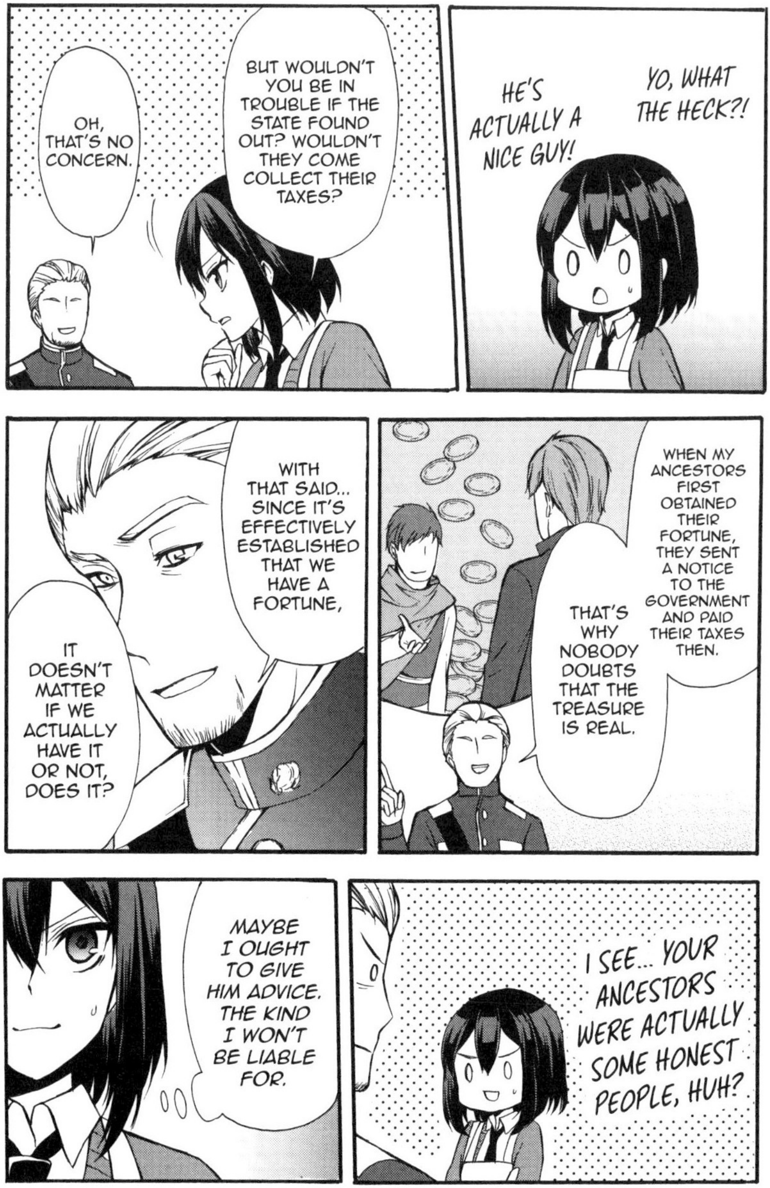
YO, WHAT THE HECK?!
HE'S ACTUALLY A NICE GUY!
BUT WOULDN'T YOU BE IN TROUBLE IF THE STATE FOUND OUT? WOULDN'T THEY COME COLLECT THEIR TAXES?
OH, THAT'S NO CONCERN.
WHEN MY ANCESTORS FIRST OBTAINED THEIR FORTUNE, THEY SENT A NOTICE TO THE GOVERNMENT AND PAID THEIR TAXES THEN.
THAT'S WHY NOBODY DOUBTS THAT THE TREASURE IS REAL.
WITH THAT SAID... SINCE IT'S EFFECTIVELY ESTABLISHED THAT WE HAVE A FORTUNE,
IT DOESN'T MATTER IF WE ACTUALLY HAVE IT OR NOT, DOES IT?
I SEE... YOUR ANCESTORS WERE ACTUALLY SOME HONEST PEOPLE, HUH?
MAYBE I OUGHT TO GIVE HIM ADVICE. THE KIND I WON'T BE LIABLE FOR.

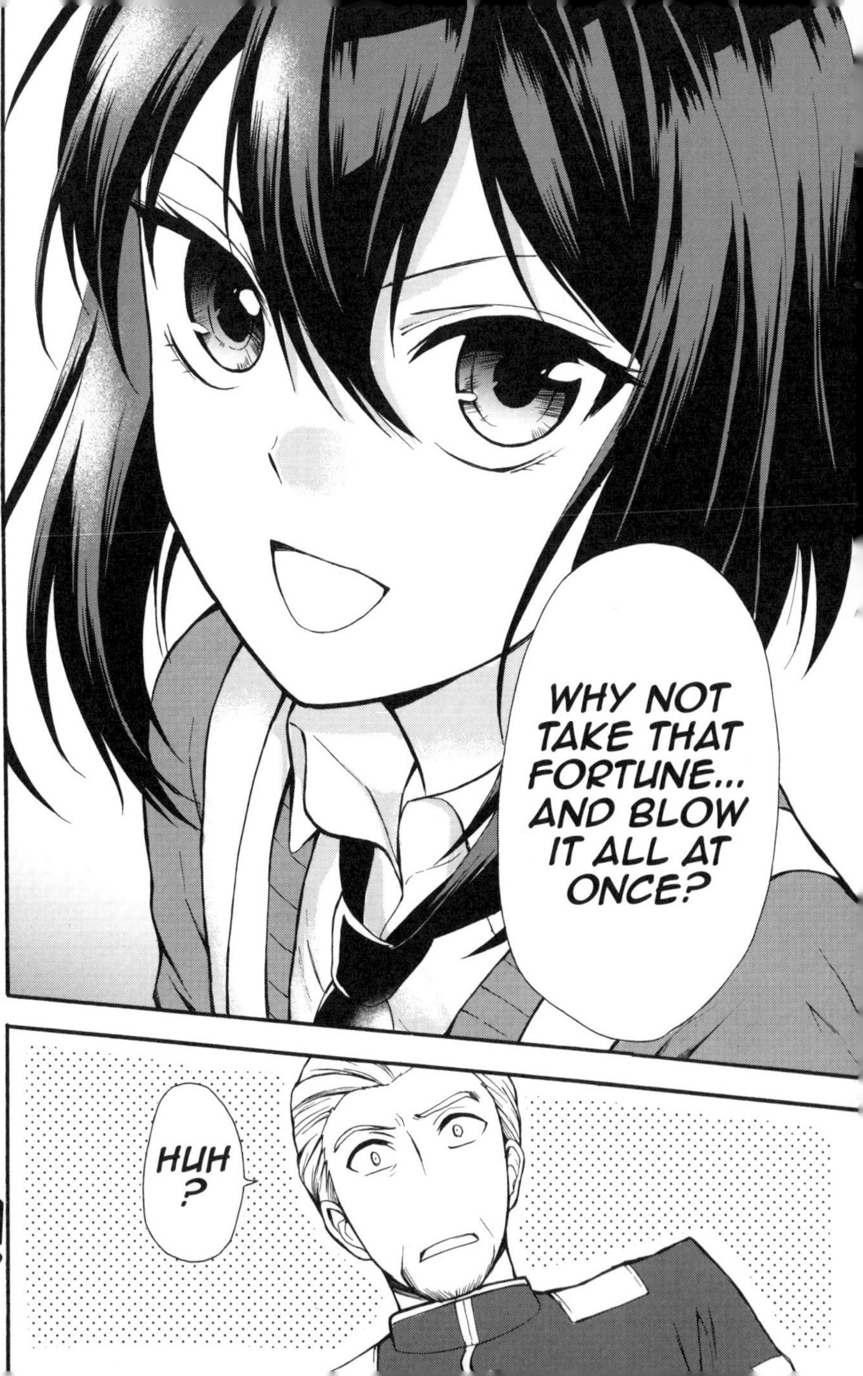
WHY NOT TAKE THAT FORTUNE... AND BLOW IT ALL AT ONCE?
HUH ?

35 CHAPTER END

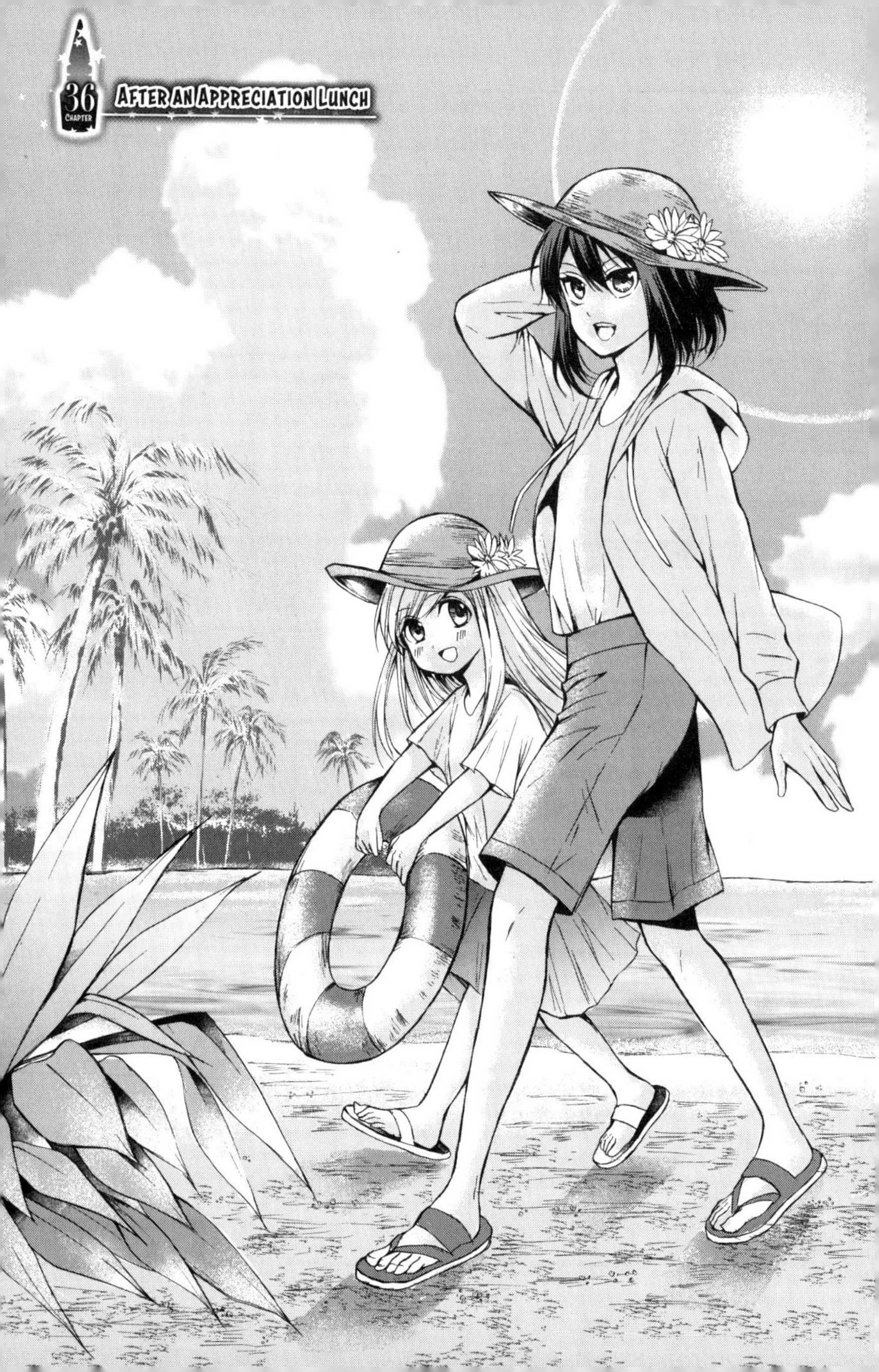
36
CHAPTER
AFTER AN APPRECIATION LUNCH

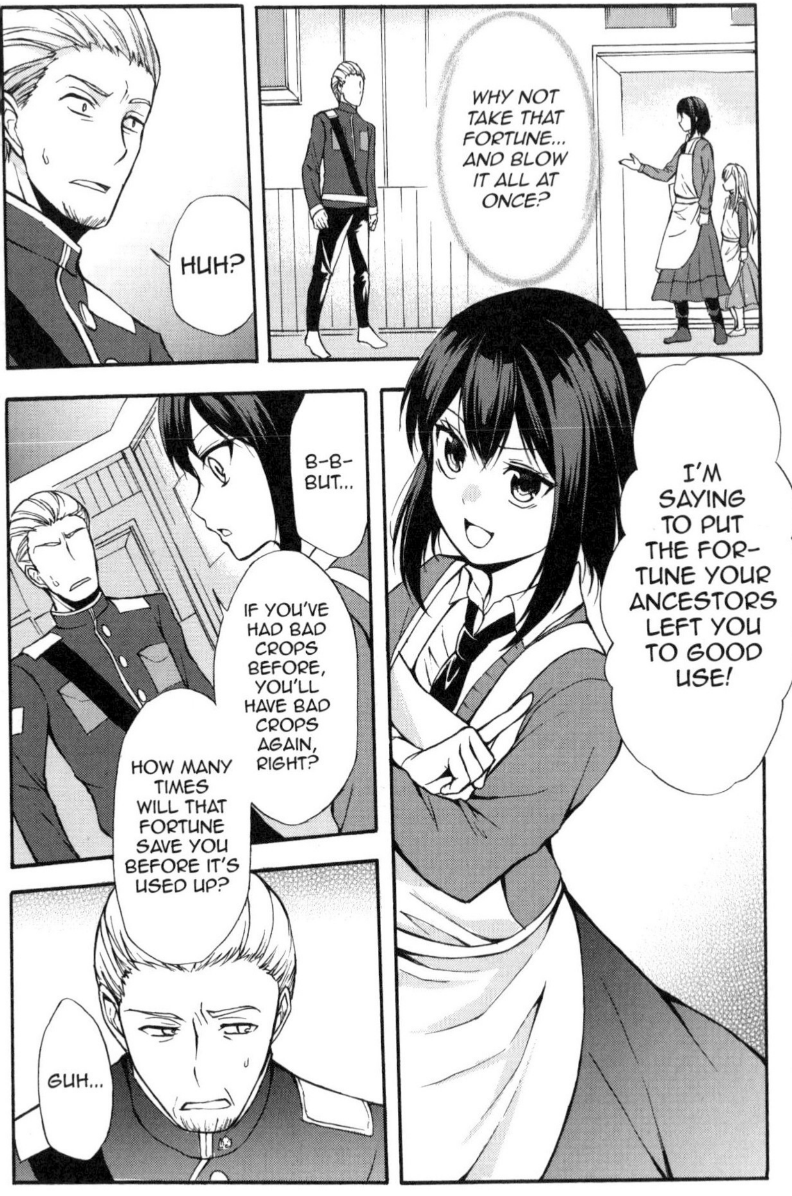
WHY NOT TAKE THAT FORTUNE... AND BLOW IT ALL AT ONCE?
HUH?
I'M SAYING TO PUT THE FOR-TUNE YOUR ANCESTORS LEFT YOU TO GOOD USE!
B-B-BUT...
IF YOU'VE HAD BAD CROPS BEFORE, YOU'LL HAVE BAD CROPS AGAIN, RIGHT?
HOW MANY TIMES WILL THAT FORTUNE SAVE YOU BEFORE IT'S USED UP?
GUH...

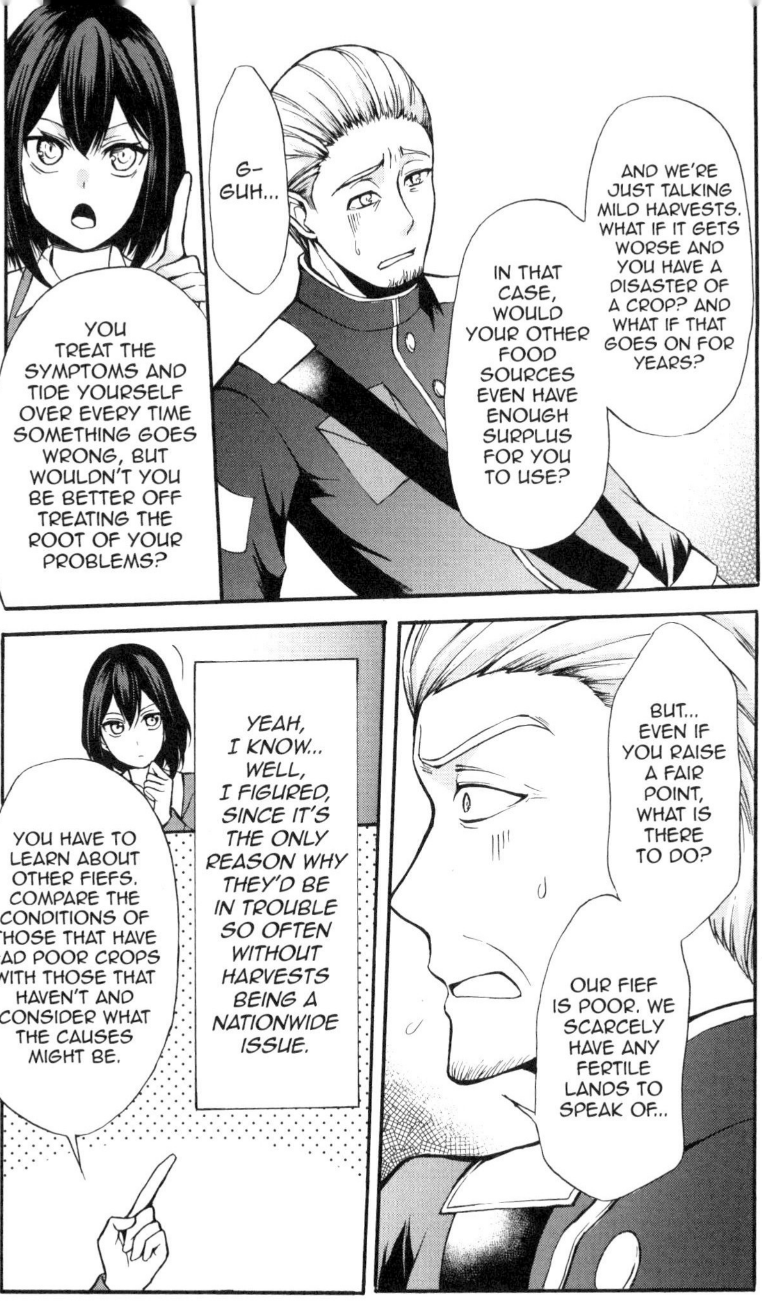
AND WE'RE JUST TALKING MILD HARVESTS. WHAT IF IT GETS WORSE AND YOU HAVE A DISASTER OF A CROP? AND WHAT IF THAT GOES ON FOR YEARS?
IN THAT CASE, WOULD YOUR OTHER FOOD SOURCES EVEN HAVE ENOUGH SURPLUS FOR YOU TO USE?
G-GUH...
YOU TREAT THE SYMPTOMS AND TIDE YOURSELF OVER EVERY TIME SOMETHING GOES WRONG, BUT WOULDN'T YOU BE BETTER OFF TREATING THE ROOT OF YOUR PROBLEMS?
BUT... EVEN IF YOU RAISE A FAIR POINT, WHAT IS THERE TO DO?
OUR FIEF IS POOR. WE SCARCELY HAVE ANY FERTILE LANDS TO SPEAK OF...
YEAH, I KNOW... WELL, I FIGURED, SINCE IT'S THE ONLY REASON WHY THEY'D BE IN TROUBLE SO OFTEN WITHOUT HARVESTS BEING A NATIONWIDE ISSUE.
YOU HAVE TO LEARN ABOUT OTHER FIEFS. COMPARE THE CONDITIONS OF THOSE THAT HAVE HAD POOR CROPS WITH THOSE THAT HAVEN'T AND CONSIDER WHAT THE CAUSES MIGHT BE.

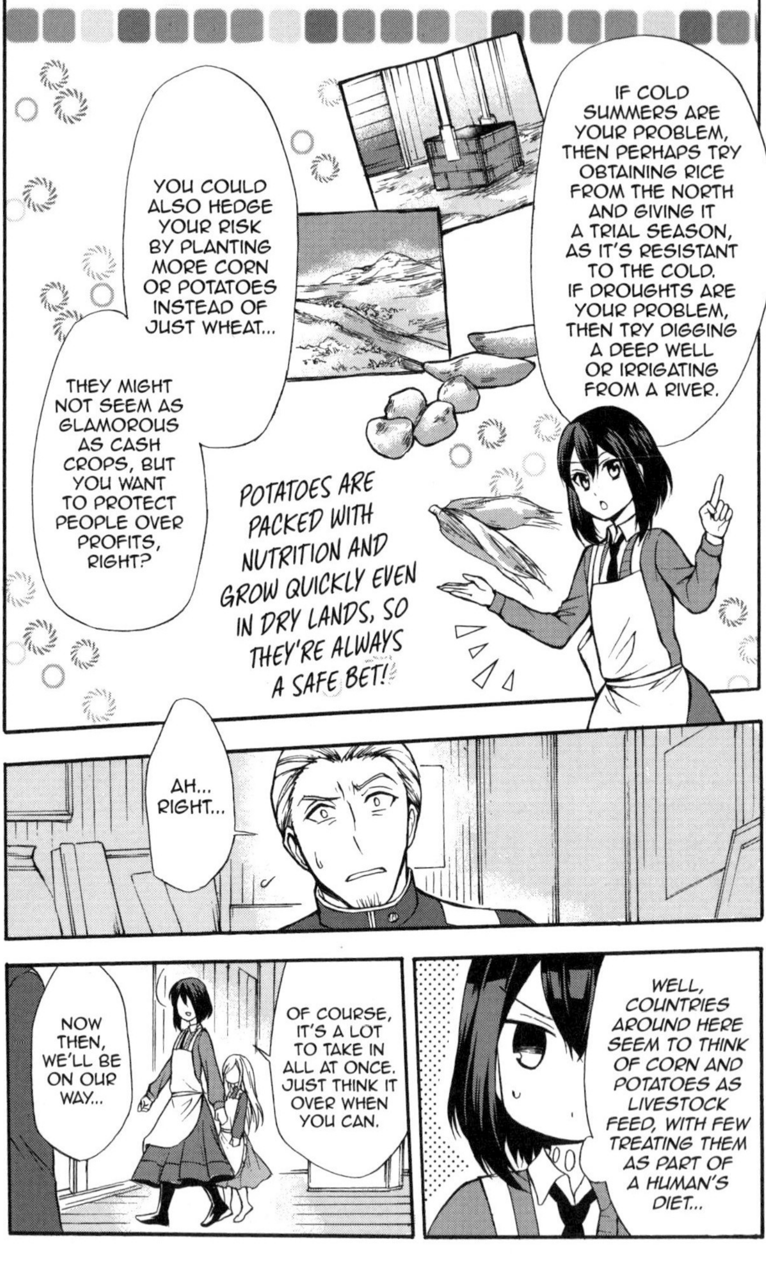
IF COLD SUMMERS ARE YOUR PROBLEM, THEN PERHAPS TRY OBTAINING RICE FROM THE NORTH AND GIVING IT A TRIAL SEASON, AS IT'S RESISTANT TO THE COLD. IF DROUGHTS ARE YOUR PROBLEM, THEN TRY DIGGING A DEEP WELL OR IRRIGATING FROM A RIVER.
YOU COULD ALSO HEDGE YOUR RISK BY PLANTING MORE CORN OR POTATOES INSTEAD OF JUST WHEAT...
THEY MIGHT NOT SEEM AS GLAMOROUS AS CASH CROPS, BUT YOU WANT TO PROTECT PEOPLE OVER PROFITS, RIGHT?
POTATOES ARE PACKED WITH NUTRITION AND GROW QUICKLY EVEN IN DRY LANDS, SO THEY'RE ALWAYS A SAFE BET!
AH... RIGHT...
WELL, COUNTRIES AROUND HERE SEEM TO THINK OF CORN AND POTATOES AS LIVESTOCK FEED, WITH FEW TREATING THEM AS PART OF A HUMAN'S DIET...
OF COURSE, IT'S A LOT TO TAKE IN ALL AT ONCE. JUST THINK IT OVER WHEN YOU CAN.
NOW THEN, WE'LL BE ON OUR WAY...

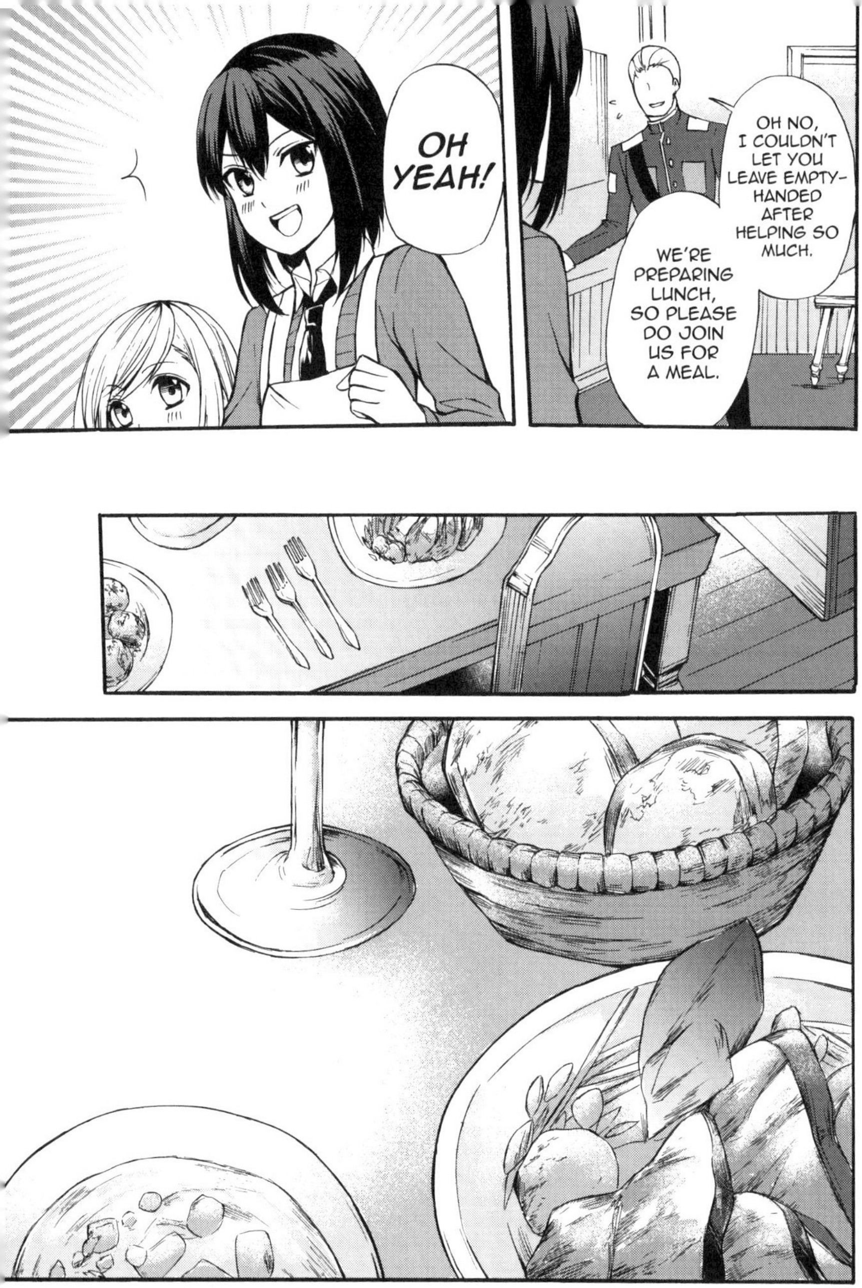
OH NO, I COULDN'T LET YOU LEAVE EMPTY-HANDED AFTER HELPING SO MUCH.
WE'RE PREPARING LUNCH, SO PLEASE DO JOIN US FOR A MEAL.
OH YEAH!

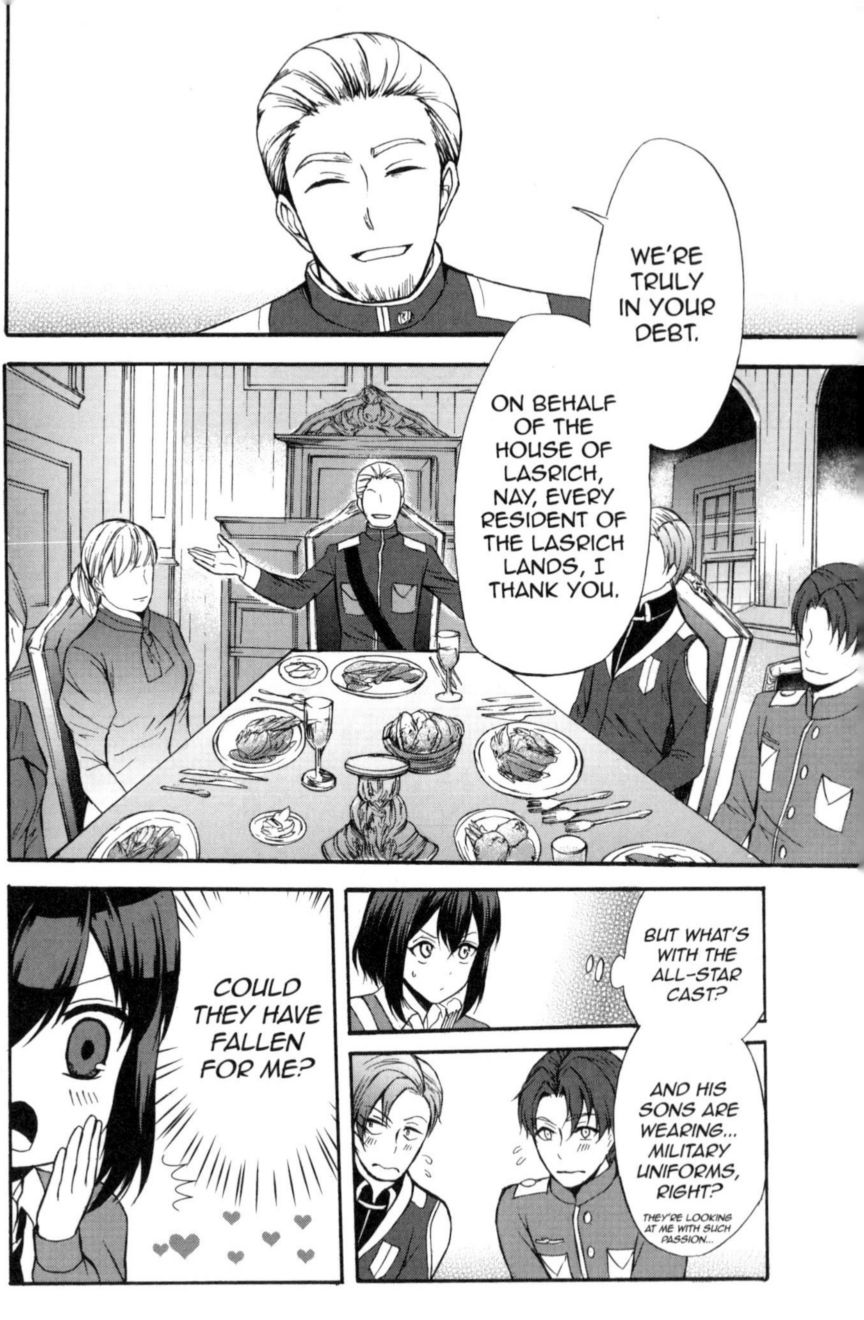

WE'RE TRULY IN YOUR DEBT.
ON BEHALF OF THE HOUSE OF LASRICH, NAY, EVERY RESIDENT OF THE LASRICH LANDS, I THANK YOU.
BUT WHAT'S WITH THE ALL-STAR CAST?
AND HIS SONS ARE WEARING... MILITARY UNIFORMS, RIGHT?
THEY'RE LOOKING AT ME WITH SUCH PASSION...
COULD THEY HAVE FALLEN FOR ME?

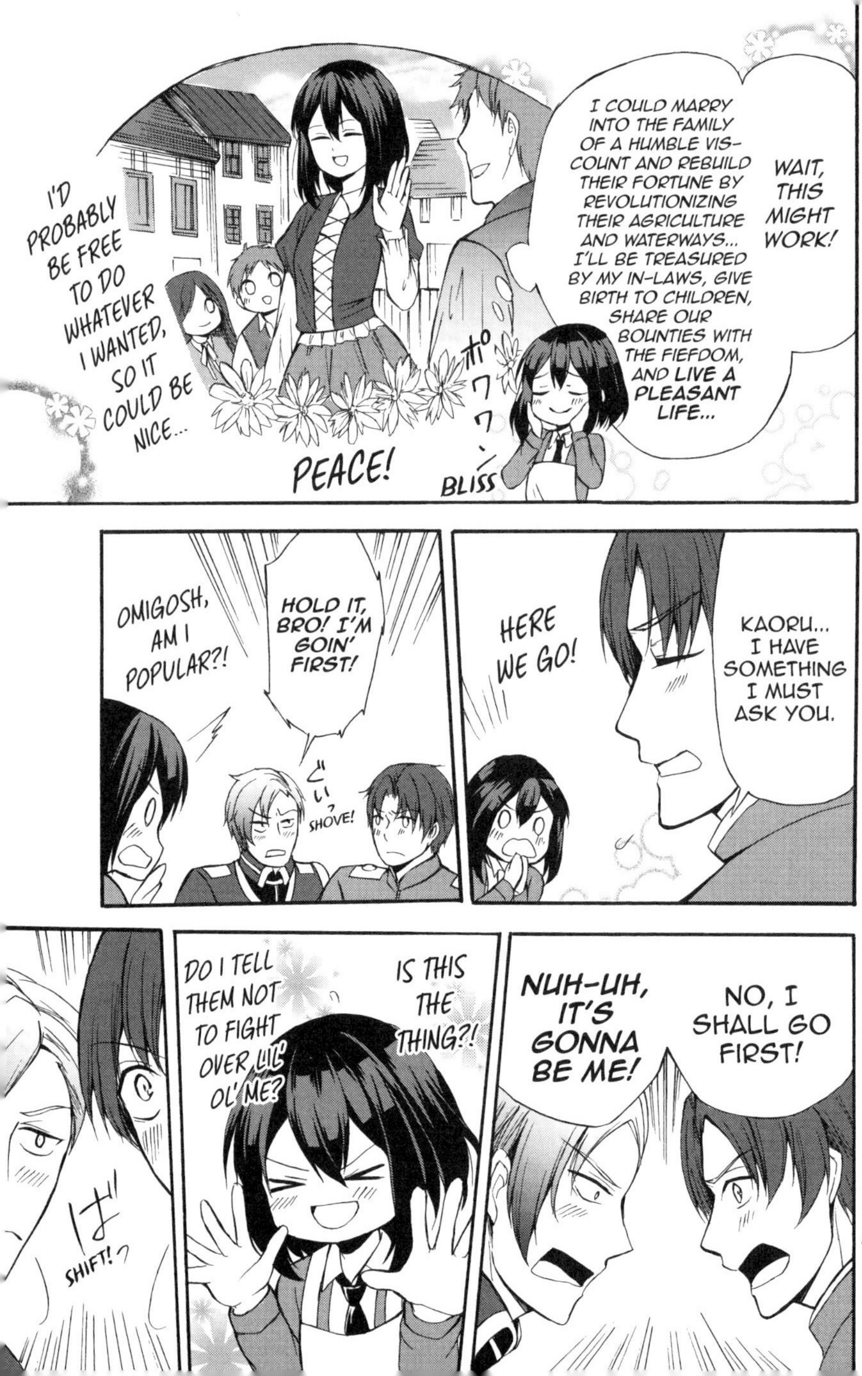
WAIT, THIS MIGHT WORK!
I COULD MARRY INTO THE FAMILY OF A HUMBLE VIS-COUNT AND REBUILD THEIR FORTUNE BY REVOLUTIONIZING THEIR AGRICULTURE AND WATERWAYS... I'LL BE TREASURED BY MY IN-LAWS, GIVE BIRTH TO CHILDREN, SHARE OUR BOUNTIES WITH THE FIEFDOM, AND LIVE A PLEASANT LIFE...
ポワワン
BLISS
I'D PROBABLY BE FREE TO DO WHATEVER I WANTED, SO IT COULD BE NICE...
PEACE!
KAORU... I HAVE SOMETHING I MUST ASK YOU.
HERE WE GO!
HOLD IT, BRO! I'M GOIN' FIRST!
ぐいっ
SHOVE!
OMIGOSH, AM I POPULAR?!
NO, I SHALL GO FIRST!
NUH-UH, IT'S GONNA BE ME!
IS THIS THE THING?!
DO I TELL THEM NOT TO FIGHT OVER LIL' OL' ME?
は
SHIFT!

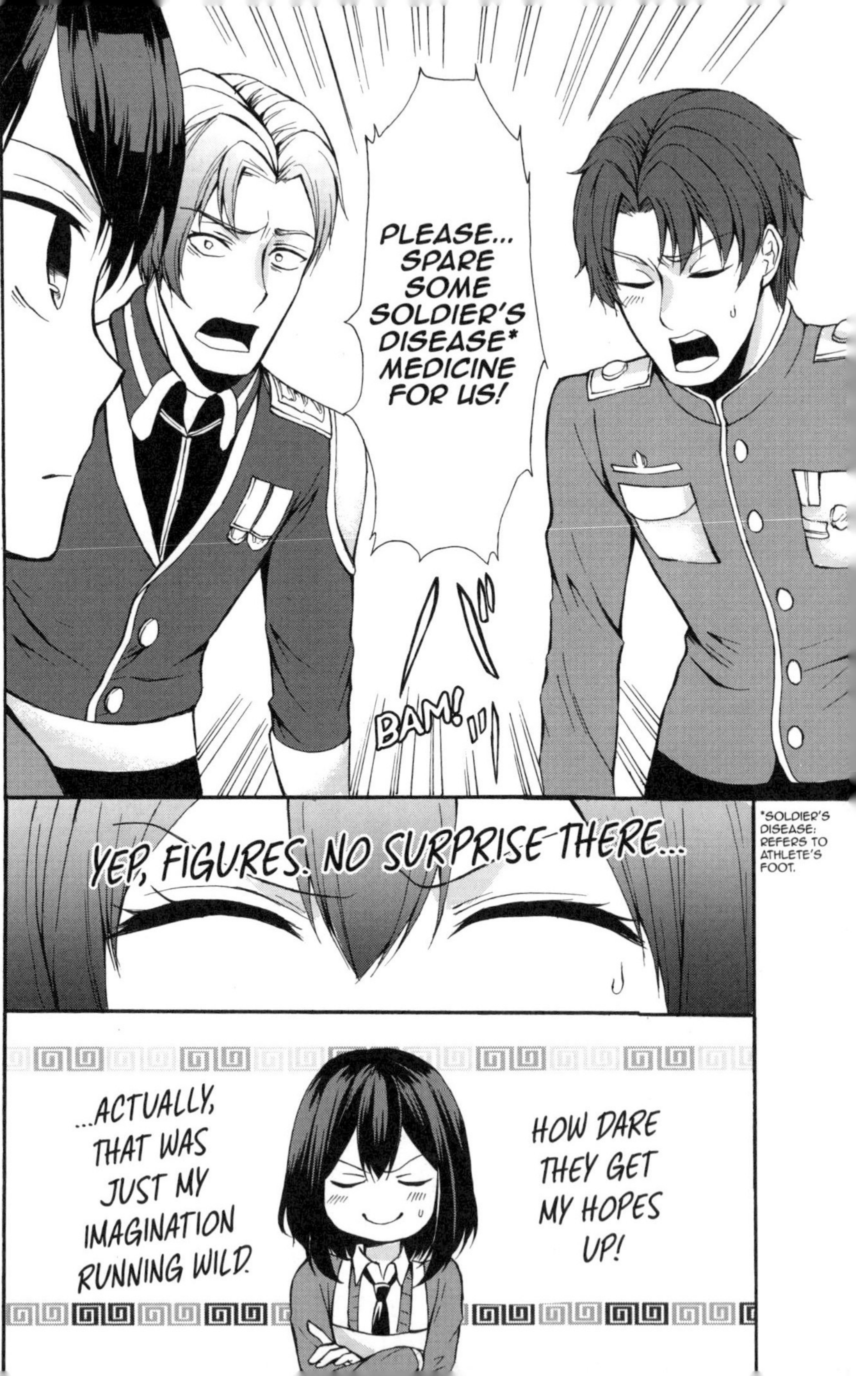
PLEASE... SPARE SOME SOLDIER'S DISEASE* MEDICINE FOR US!
BAM!
YEP, FIGURES. NO SURPRISE THERE...
...ACTUALLY, THAT WAS JUST MY IMAGINATION RUNNING WILD.
HOW DARE THEY GET MY HOPES UP!

*SOLDIER'S DISEASE: REFERS TO ATHLETE'S FOOT.

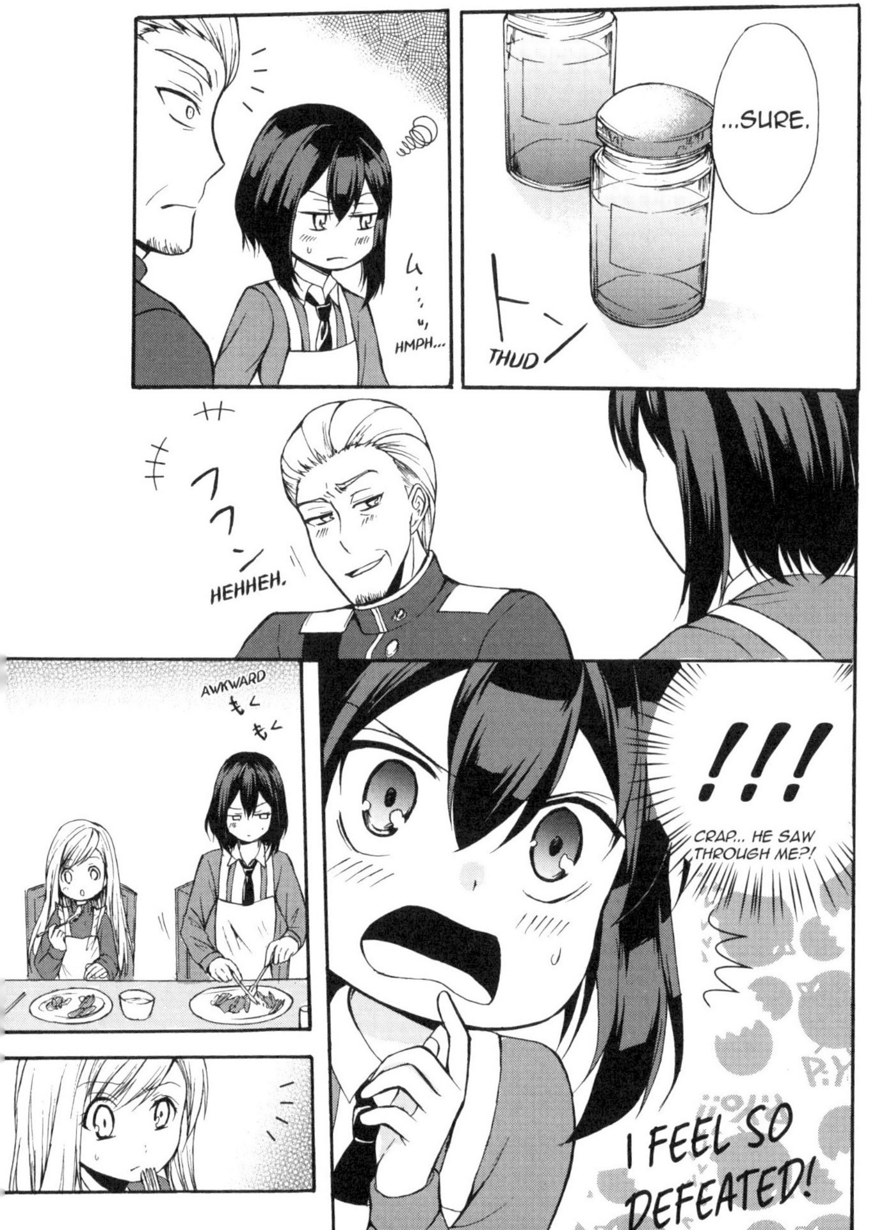

...SURE.
THUD
HMPH...
HEHHEH.
!!!
CRAP... HE SAW THROUGH ME?!
I FEEL SO DEFEATED!
AWKWARD
もく もく

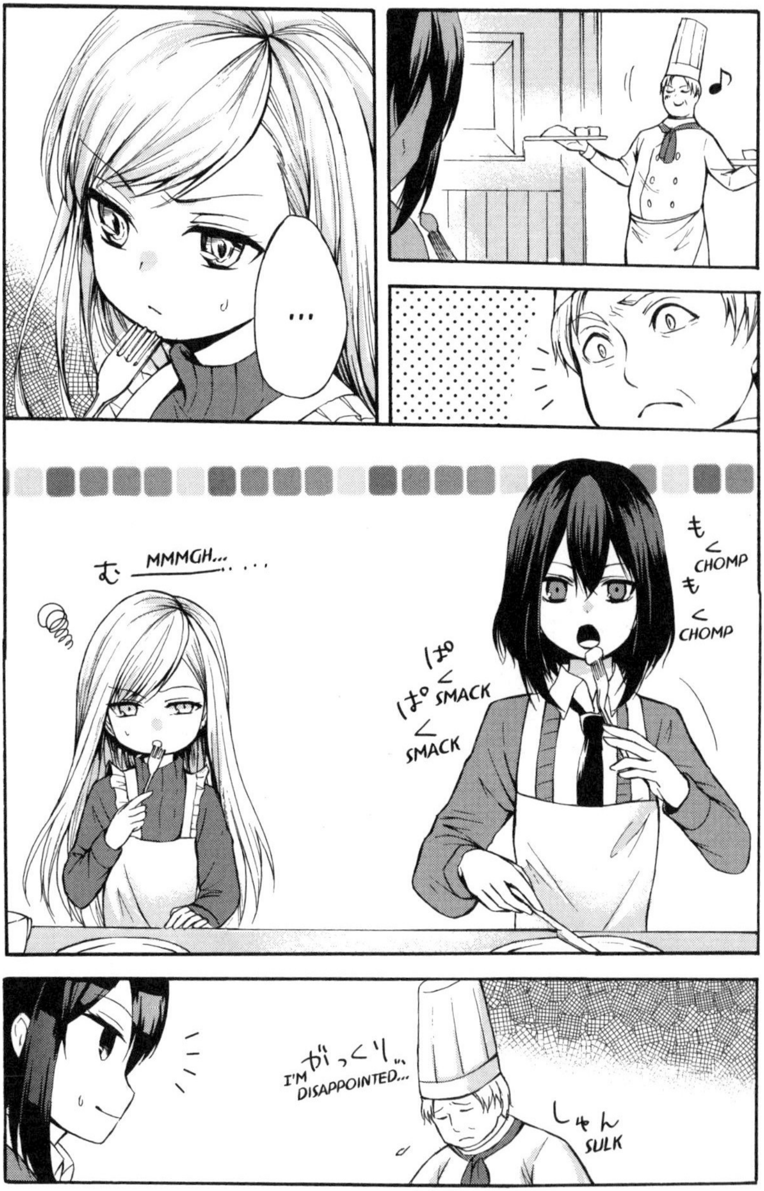
...
もくCHOMP
もくCHOMP
ぱくSMACK
ぱくSMACK
むMMMGH.......
しゅん SULK
がっくり I'M DISAPPOINTED...

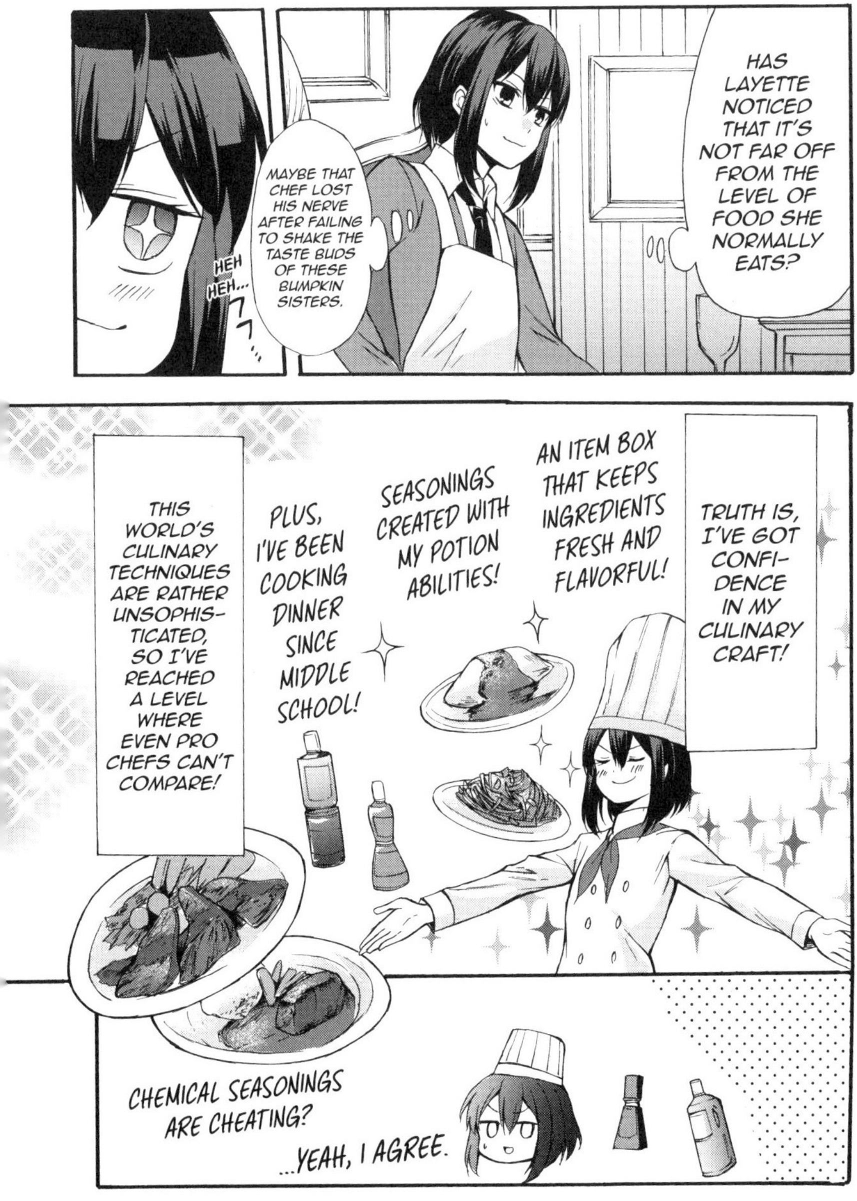
HAS LAYETTE NOTICED THAT IT'S NOT FAR OFF FROM THE LEVEL OF FOOD SHE NORMALLY EATS?
MAYBE THAT CHEF LOST HIS NERVE AFTER FAILING TO SHAKE THE TASTE BUDS OF THESE BUMPKIN SISTERS.
HEH HEH...
TRUTH IS, I'VE GOT CONFI-DENCE IN MY CULINARY CRAFT!
AN ITEM BOX THAT KEEPS INGREDIENTS FRESH AND FLAVORFUL!
SEASONINGS CREATED WITH MY POTION ABILITIES!
PLUS, I'VE BEEN COOKING DINNER SINCE MIDDLE SCHOOL!
THIS WORLD'S CULINARY TECHNIQUES ARE RATHER UNSOPHIS-TICATED, SO I'VE REACHED A LEVEL WHERE EVEN PRO CHEFS CAN'T COMPARE!
CHEMICAL SEASONINGS ARE CHEATING?
...YEAH, I AGREE.

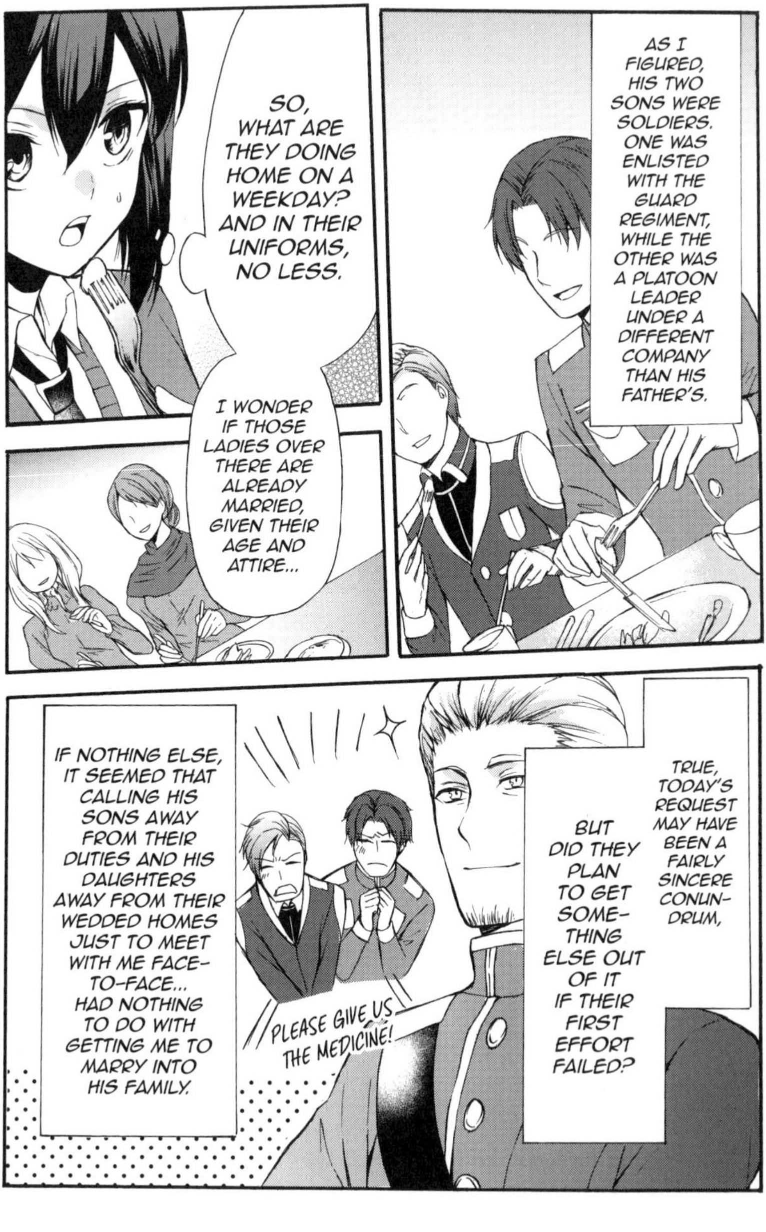
AS I FIGURED, HIS TWO SONS WERE SOLDIERS. ONE WAS ENLISTED WITH THE GUARD REGIMENT, WHILE THE OTHER WAS A PLATOON LEADER UNDER A DIFFERENT COMPANY THAN HIS FATHER'S.
SO, WHAT ARE THEY DOING HOME ON A WEEKDAY? AND IN THEIR UNIFORMS, NO LESS.
I WONDER IF THOSE LADIES OVER THERE ARE ALREADY MARRIED, GIVEN THEIR AGE AND ATTIRE...
TRUE, TODAY'S REQUEST MAY HAVE BEEN A FAIRLY SINCERE CONUN-DRUM,
BUT DID THEY PLAN TO GET SOME-THING ELSE OUT OF IT IF THEIR FIRST EFFORT FAILED?
PLEASE GIVE US THE MEDICINE!
IF NOTHING ELSE, IT SEEMED THAT CALLING HIS SONS AWAY FROM THEIR DUTIES AND HIS DAUGHTERS AWAY FROM THEIR WEDDED HOMES JUST TO MEET WITH ME FACE-TO-FACE... HAD NOTHING TO DO WITH GETTING ME TO MARRY INTO HIS FAMILY.

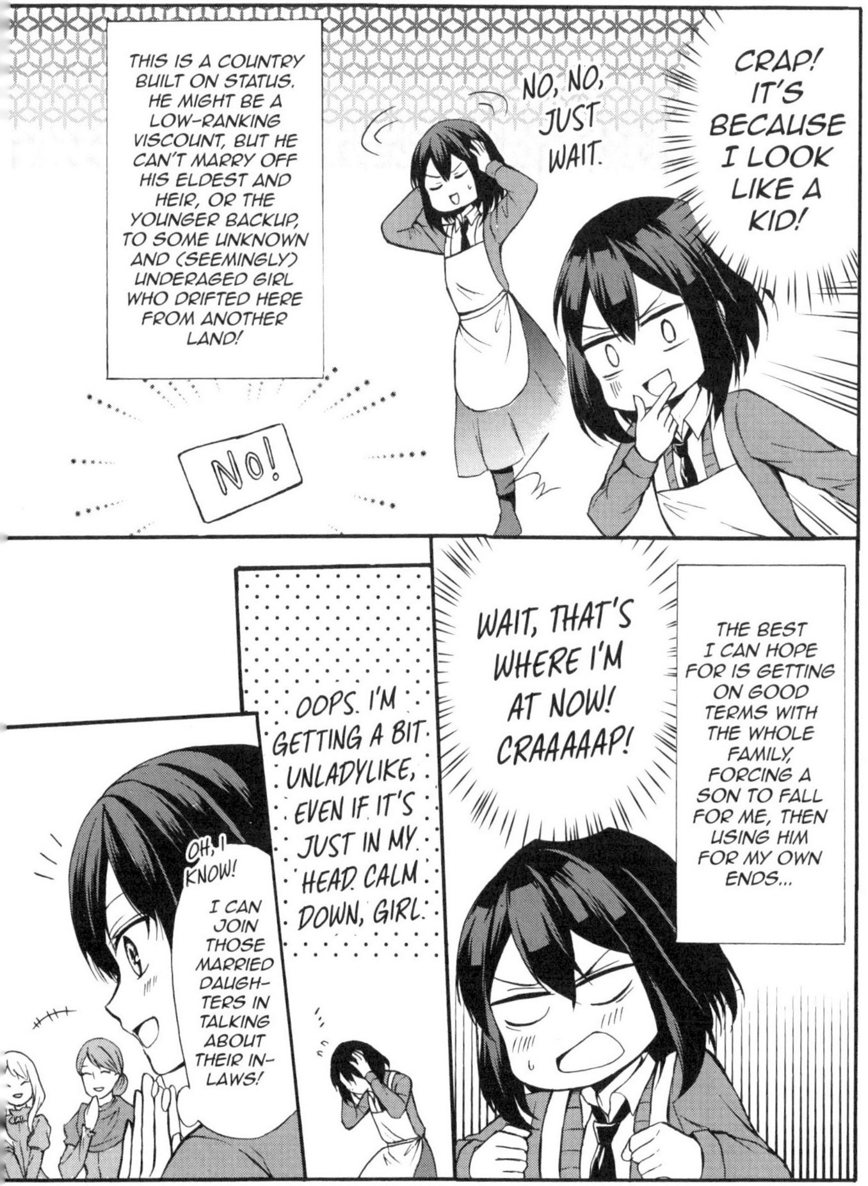
CRAP! IT'S BECAUSE I LOOK LIKE A KID!
NO, NO, JUST WAIT.
THIS IS A COUNTRY BUILT ON STATUS. HE MIGHT BE A LOW-RANKING VISCOUNT, BUT HE CAN'T MARRY OFF HIS ELDEST AND HEIR, OR THE YOUNGER BACKUP, TO SOME UNKNOWN AND (SEEMINGLY) UNDERAGED GIRL WHO DRIFTED HERE FROM ANOTHER LAND!
No!
THE BEST I CAN HOPE FOR IS GETTING ON GOOD TERMS WITH THE WHOLE FAMILY, FORCING A SON TO FALL FOR ME, THEN USING HIM FOR MY OWN ENDS...
WAIT, THAT'S WHERE I'M AT NOW! CRAAAAAP!
OOPS. I'M GETTING A BIT UNLADYLIKE, EVEN IF IT'S JUST IN MY HEAD. CALM DOWN, GIRL.
OH, I KNOW!
I CAN JOIN THOSE MARRIED DAUGHTERS IN TALKING ABOUT THEIR IN-LAWS!

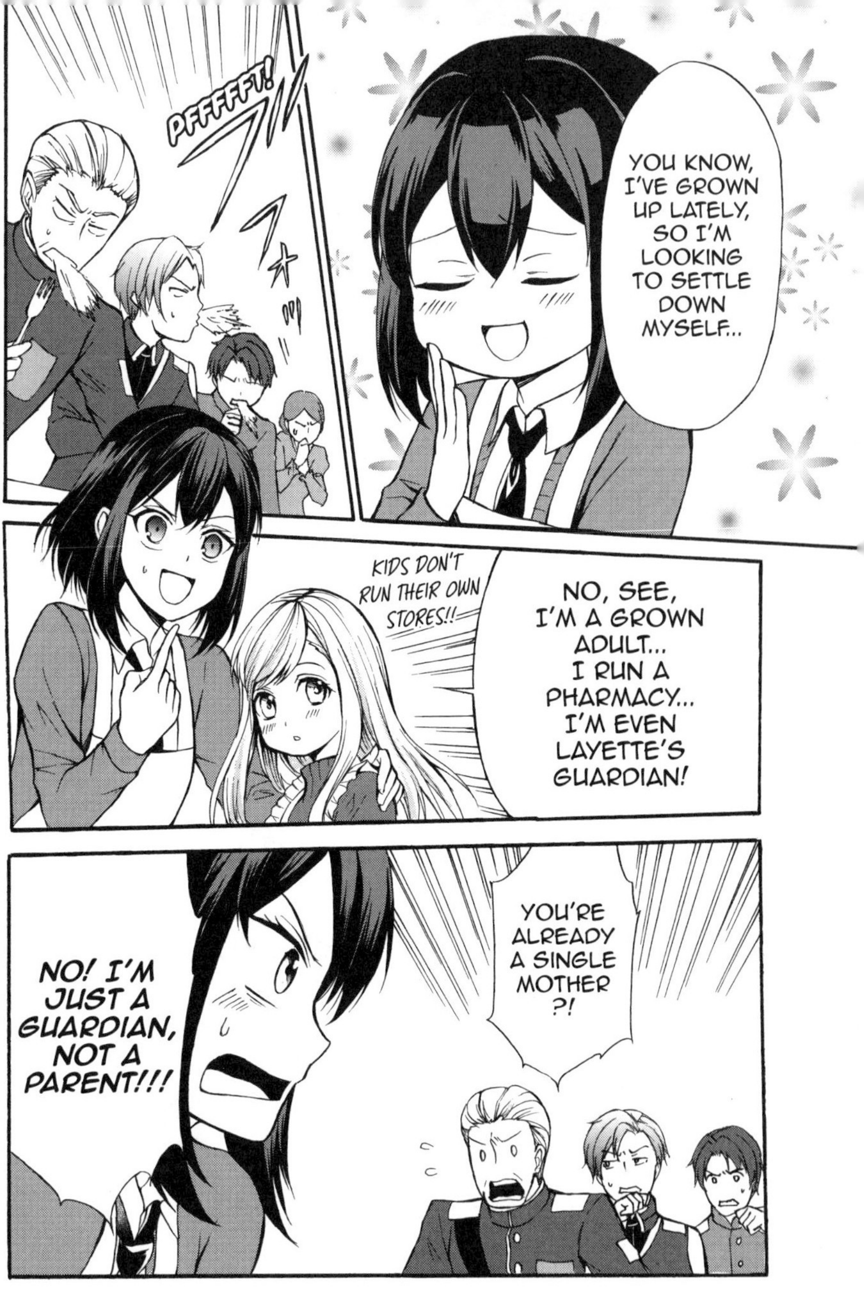
YOU KNOW, I'VE GROWN UP LATELY, SO I'M LOOKING TO SETTLE DOWN MYSELF...
PFFFFFT!
NO, SEE, I'M A GROWN ADULT... I RUN A PHARMACY... I'M EVEN LAYETTE'S SINGLE GUARDIAN!
KIDS DON'T RUN THEIR OWN STORES!!
YOU'RE ALREADY A SINGLE MOTHER ?!
NO! I'M JUST A GUARDIAN, NOT A PARENT!!!

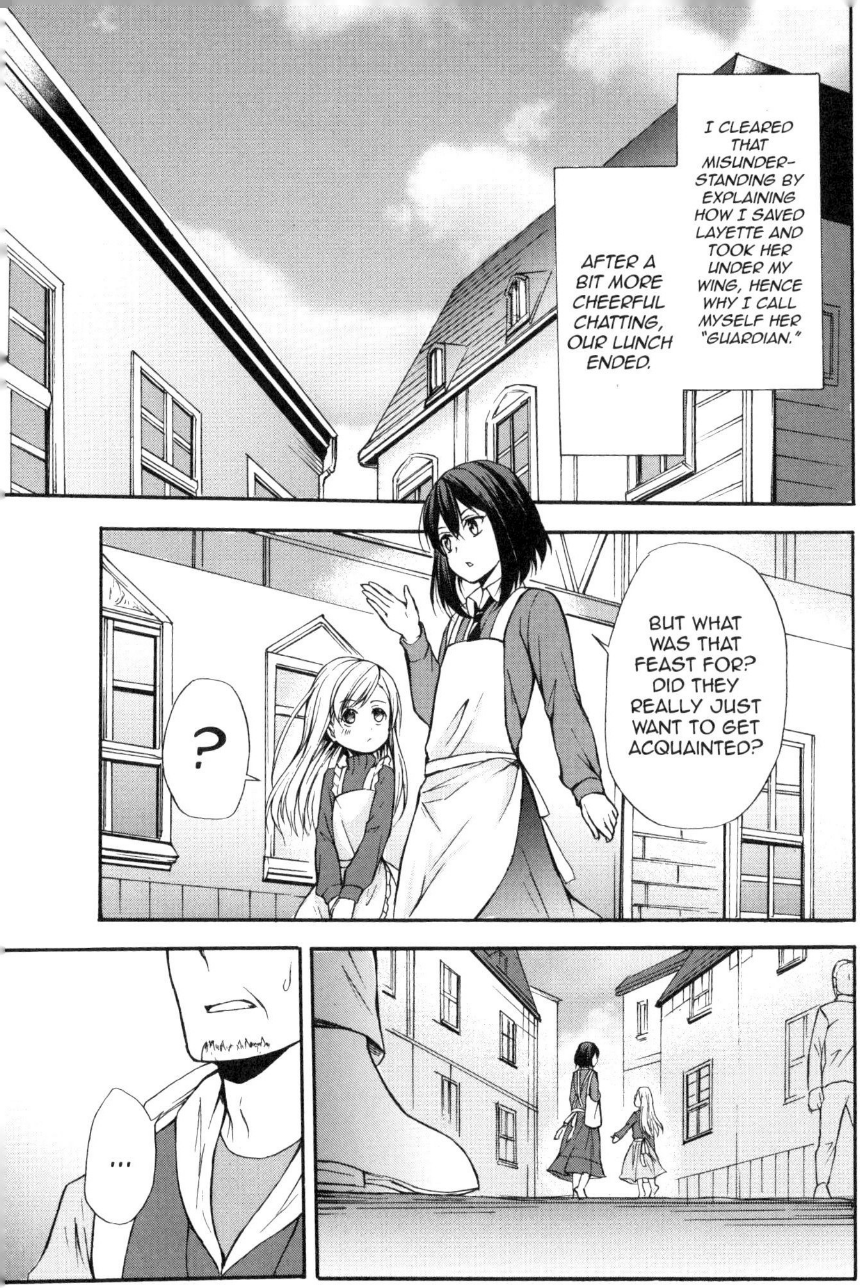
I CLEARED THAT MISUNDERSTANDING BY EXPLAINING HOW I SAVED LAYETTE AND TOOK HER UNDER MY WING, HENCE WHY I CALL MYSELF HER "GUARDIAN."
AFTER A BIT MORE CHEERFUL CHATTING, OUR LUNCH ENDED.
BUT WHAT WAS THAT FEAST FOR? DID THEY REALLY JUST WANT TO GET ACQUAINTED?
?
...

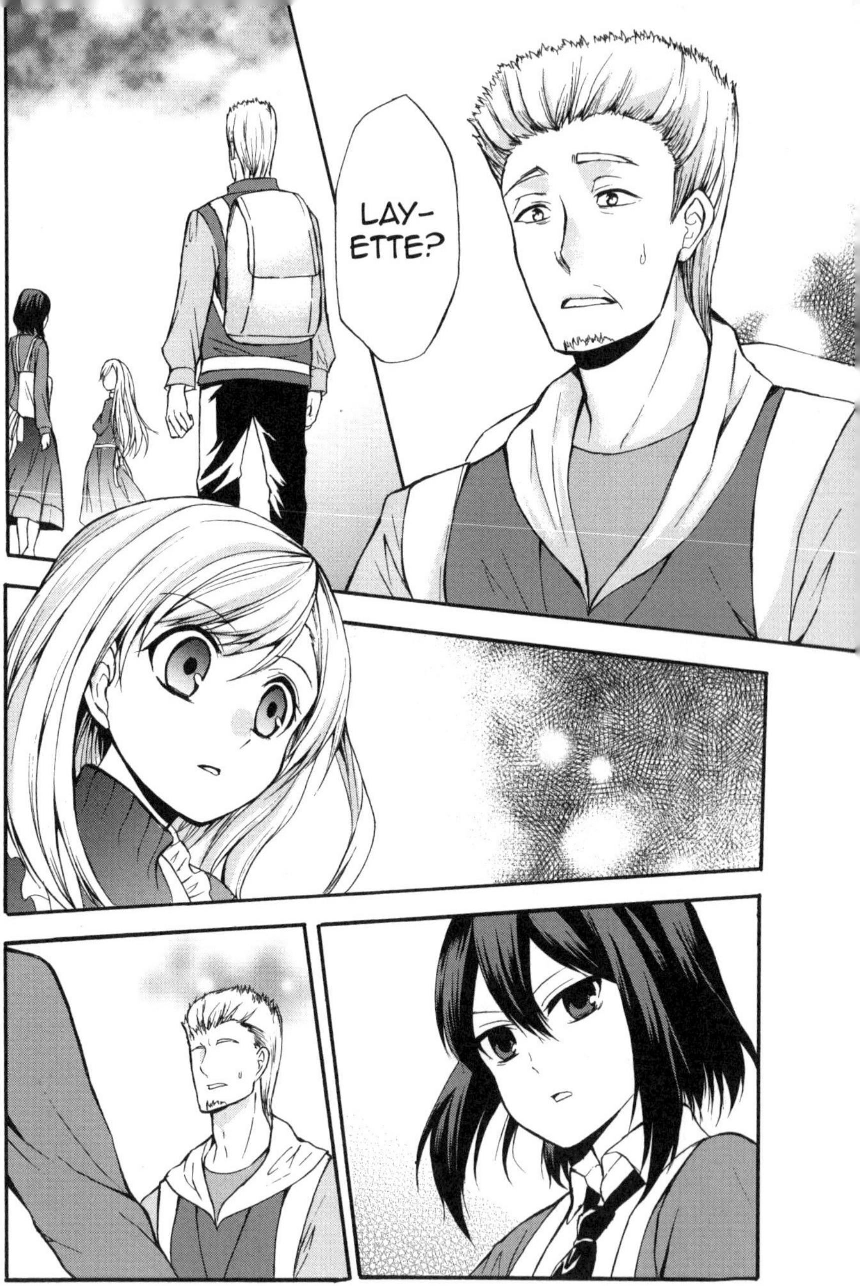
LAY-
ETTE?

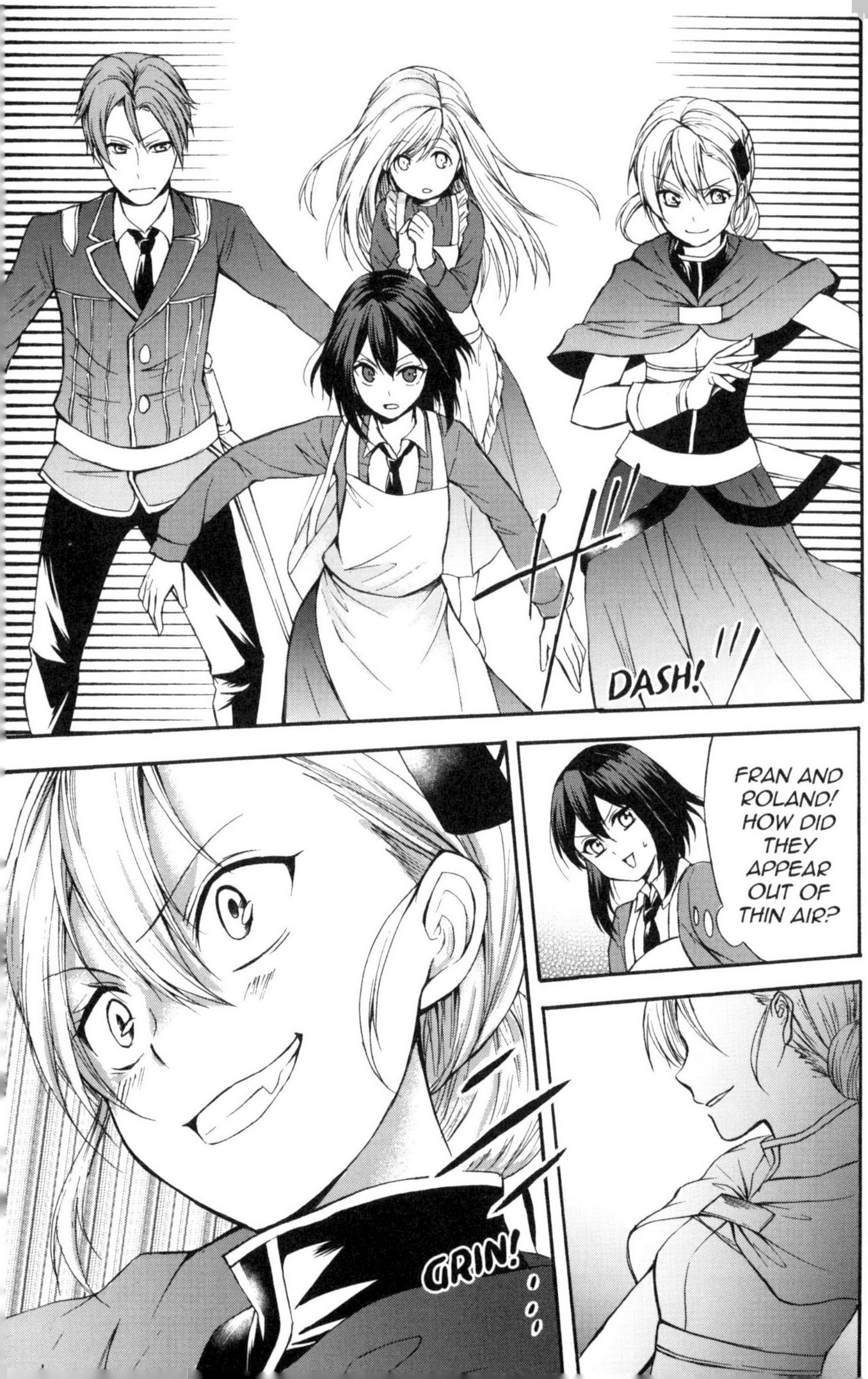
DASH!
FRAN AND ROLAND! HOW DID THEY APPEAR OUT OF THIN AIR?
GRIN!

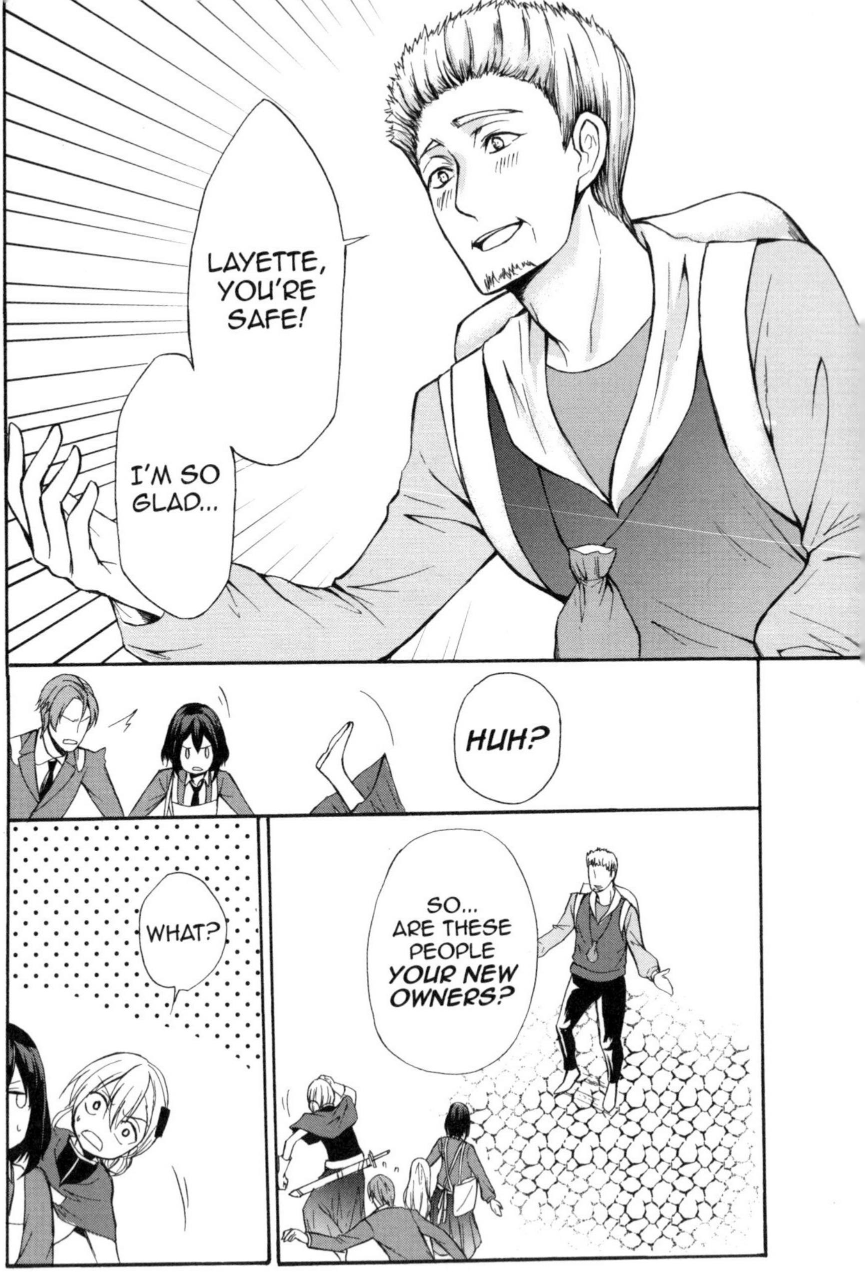
LAYETTE, YOU'RE SAFE!
I'M SO GLAD...
HUH?
SO... ARE THESE PEOPLE YOUR NEW OWNERS?
WHAT?

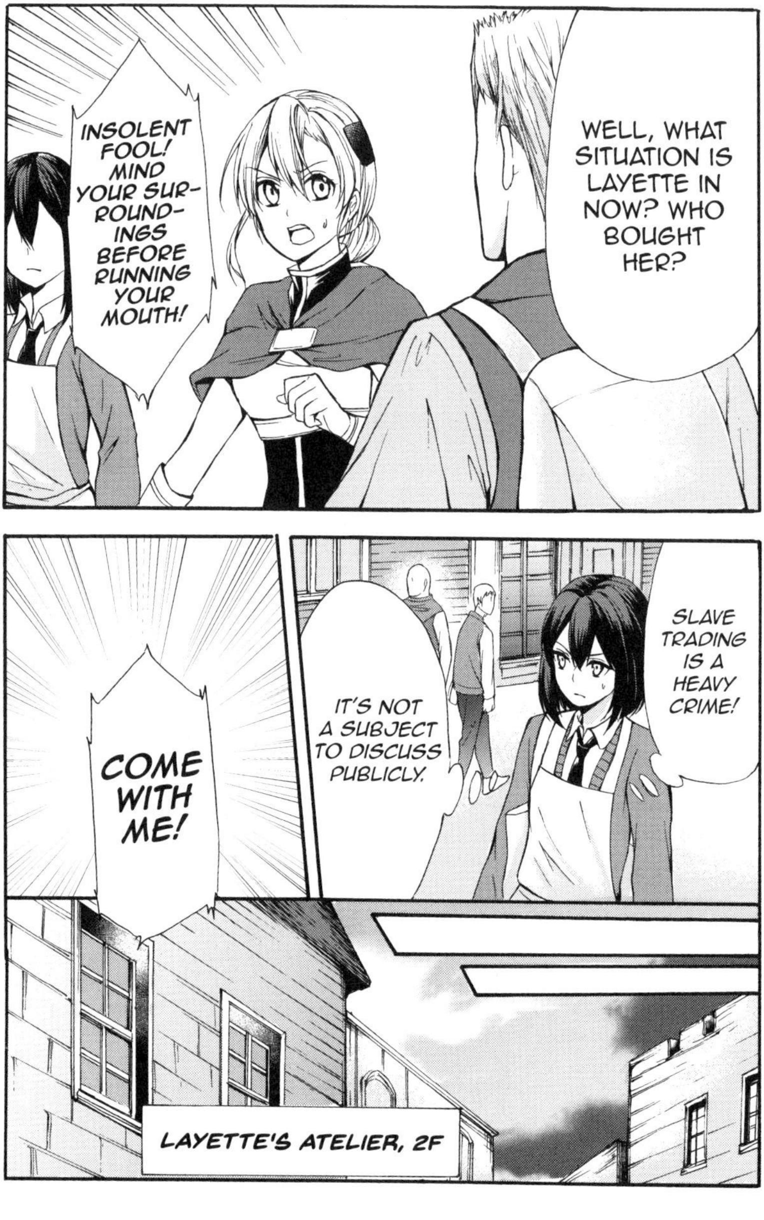
WELL, WHAT SITUATION IS LAYETTE IN NOW? WHO BOUGHT HER?
INSOLENT FOOL! MIND YOUR SUR-ROUND-INGS BEFORE RUNNING YOUR MOUTH!
SLAVE TRADING IS A HEAVY CRIME!
IT'S NOT A SUBJECT TO DISCUSS PUBLICLY.
COME WITH ME!
LAYETTE'S ATELIER, 2F

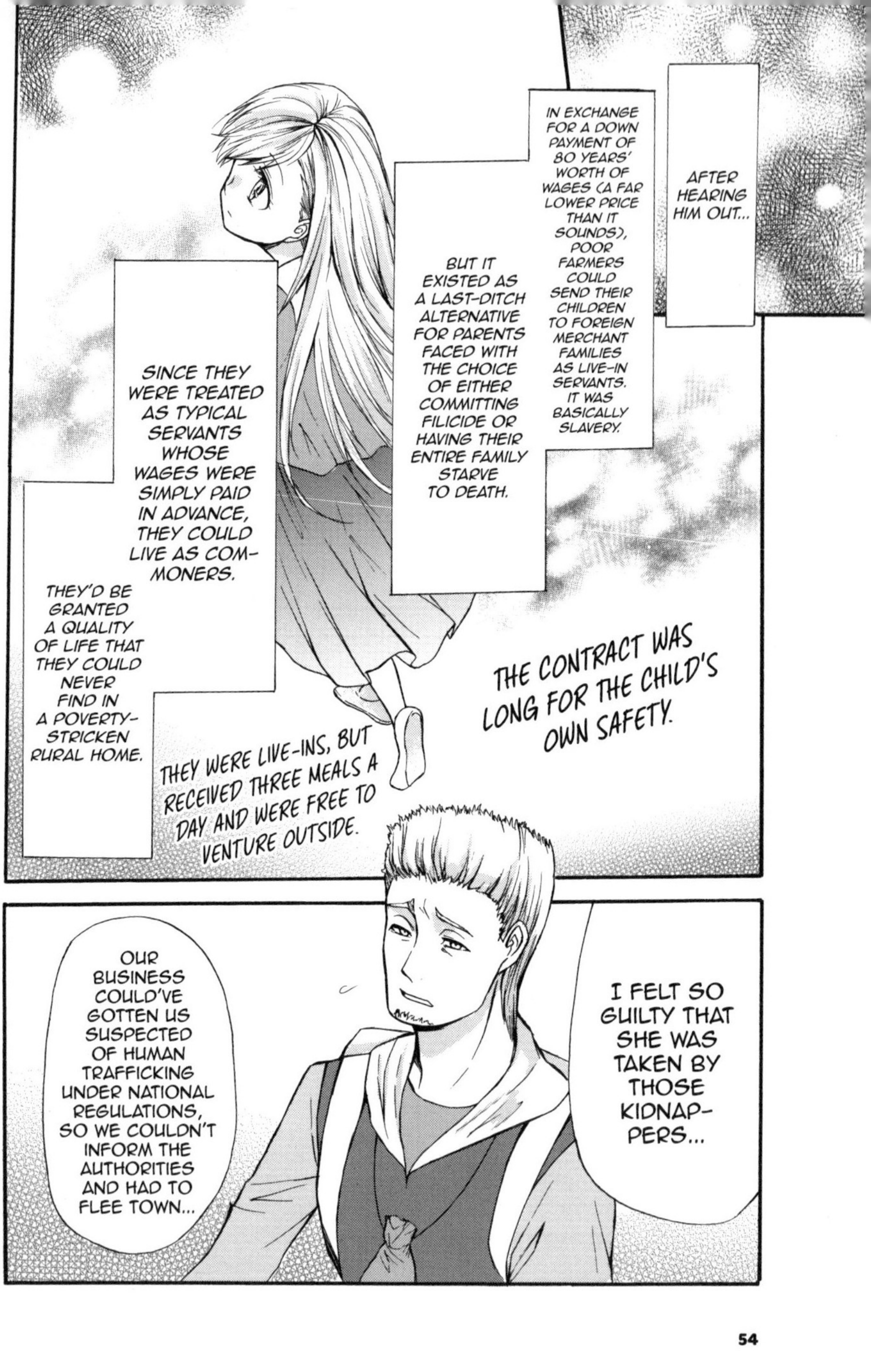

AFTER HEARING HIM OUT...
IN EXCHANGE FOR A DOWN PAYMENT OF 80 YEARS' WORTH OF WAGES (A FAR LOWER PRICE THAN IT SOUNDS), POOR FARMERS COULD SEND THEIR CHILDREN TO FOREIGN MERCHANT FAMILIES AS LIVE-IN SERVANTS. IT WAS BASICALLY SLAVERY.
BUT IT EXISTED AS A LAST-DITCH ALTERNATIVE FOR PARENTS FACED WITH THE CHOICE OF EITHER COMMITTING FILICIDE OR HAVING THEIR ENTIRE FAMILY STARVE TO DEATH.
SINCE THEY WERE TREATED AS TYPICAL SERVANTS WHOSE WAGES WERE SIMPLY PAID IN ADVANCE, THEY COULD LIVE AS COM-MONERS.
THE CONTRACT WAS LONG FOR THE CHILD'S OWN SAFETY.
THEY'D BE GRANTED A QUALITY OF LIFE THAT THEY COULD NEVER FIND IN A POVERTY-STRICKEN RURAL HOME.
THEY WERE LIVE-INS, BUT RECEIVED THREE MEALS A DAY AND WERE FREE TO VENTURE OUTSIDE.
I FELT SO GUILTY THAT SHE WAS TAKEN BY THOSE KIDNAP-PERS...
OUR BUSINESS COULD'VE GOTTEN US SUSPECTED OF HUMAN TRAFFICKING UNDER NATIONAL REGULATIONS, SO WE COULDN'T INFORM THE AUTHORITIES AND HAD TO FLEE TOWN...

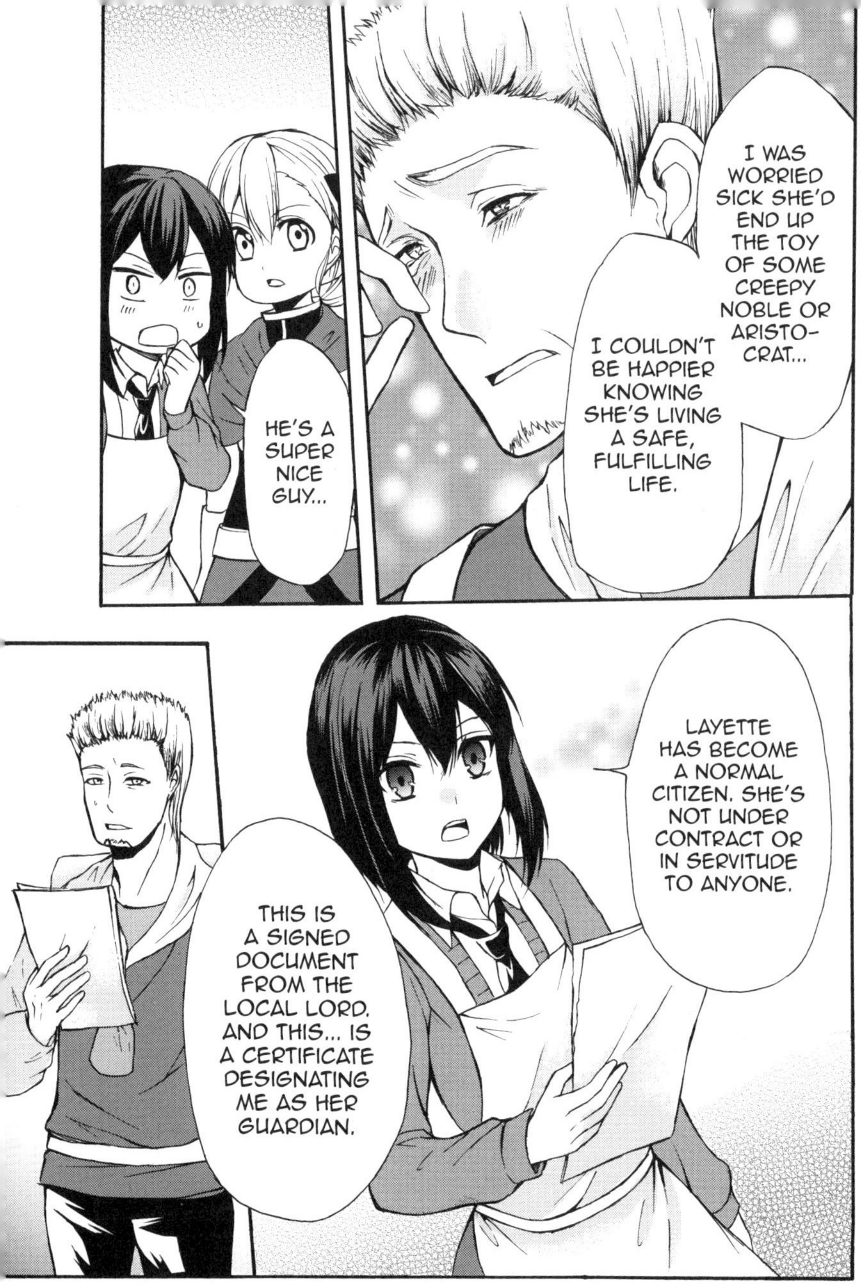

I WAS WORRIED SICK SHE'D END UP THE TOY OF SOME CREEPY NOBLE OR ARISTO-CRAT...
I COULDN'T BE HAPPIER KNOWING SHE'S LIVING A SAFE, FULFILLING LIFE.
HE'S A SUPER NICE GUY...
LAYETTE HAS BECOME A NORMAL CITIZEN. SHE'S NOT UNDER CONTRACT OR IN SERVITUDE TO ANYONE.
THIS IS A SIGNED DOCUMENT FROM THE LOCAL LORD. AND THIS... IS A CERTIFICATE DESIGNATING ME AS HER GUARDIAN.

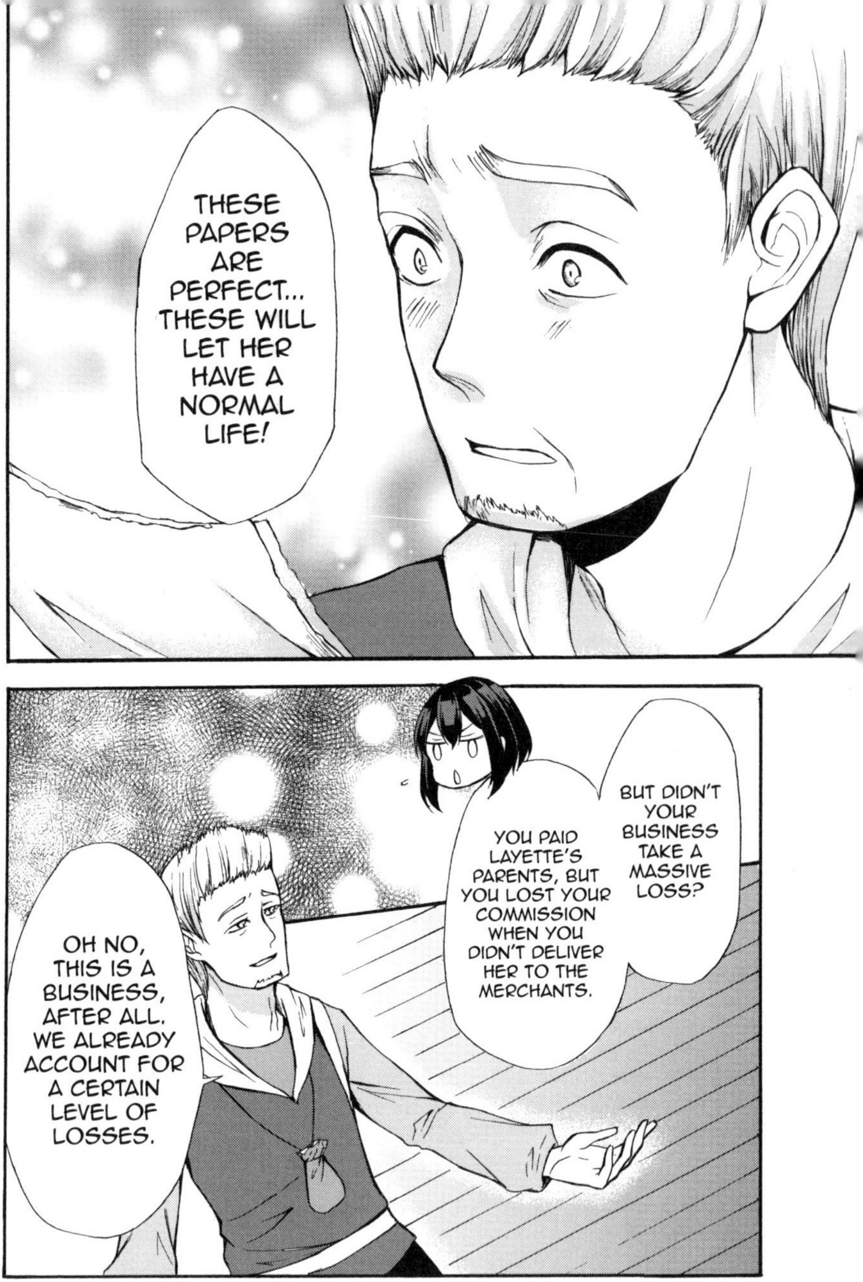
THESE PAPERS ARE PERFECT... THESE WILL LET HER HAVE A NORMAL LIFE!
BUT DIDN'T YOUR BUSINESS TAKE A MASSIVE LOSS?
YOU PAID LAYETTE'S PARENTS, BUT YOU LOST YOUR COMMISSION WHEN YOU DIDN'T DELIVER HER TO THE MERCHANTS.
OH NO, THIS IS A BUSINESS, AFTER ALL. WE ALREADY ACCOUNT FOR A CERTAIN LEVEL OF LOSSES.

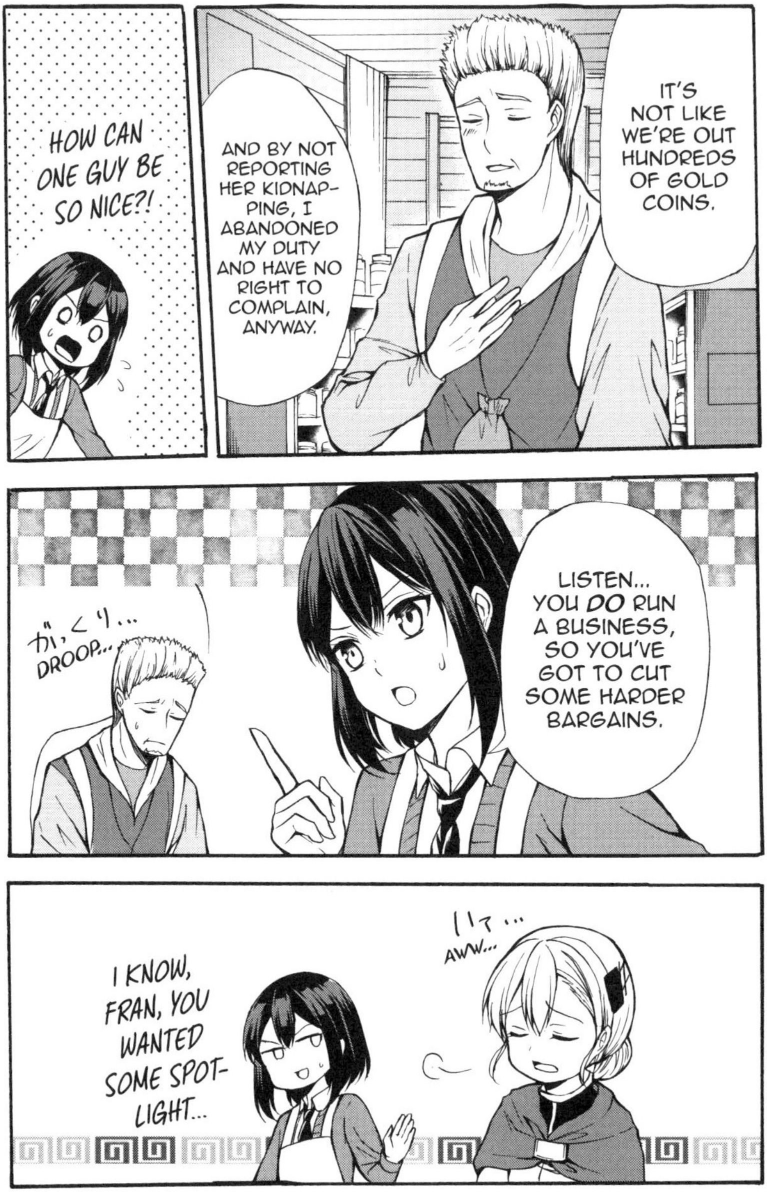
IT'S NOT LIKE WE'RE OUT HUNDREDS OF GOLD COINS.
AND BY NOT REPORTING HER KIDNAP-PING, I ABANDONED MY DUTY AND HAVE NO RIGHT TO COMPLAIN, ANYWAY.
HOW CAN ONE GUY BE SO NICE?!
LISTEN... YOU DO RUN A BUSINESS, SO YOU'VE GOT TO CUT SOME HARDER BARGAINS.
がっくり…
DROOP...
はァ…
AWW...
I KNOW, FRAN, YOU WANTED SOME SPOT-LIGHT...

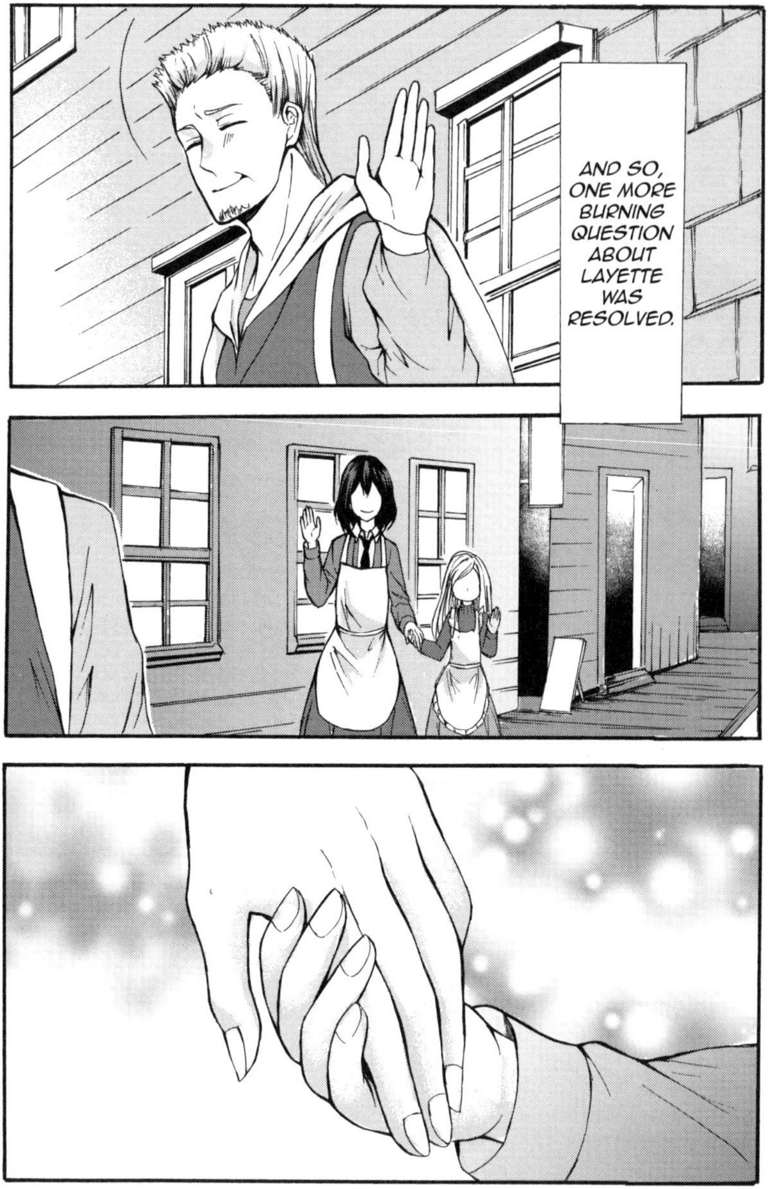
AND SO, ONE MORE BURNING QUESTION ABOUT LAYETTE WAS RESOLVED.

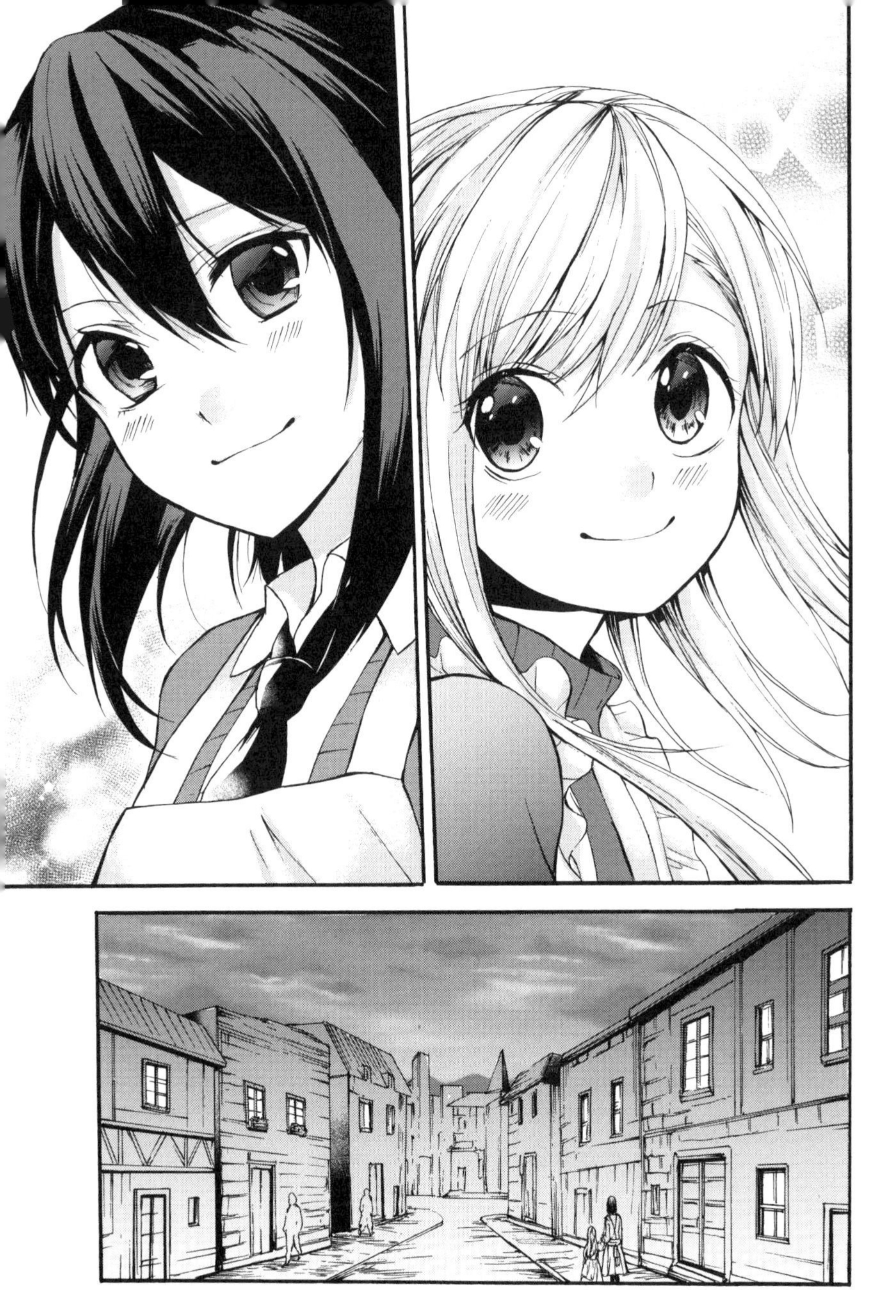

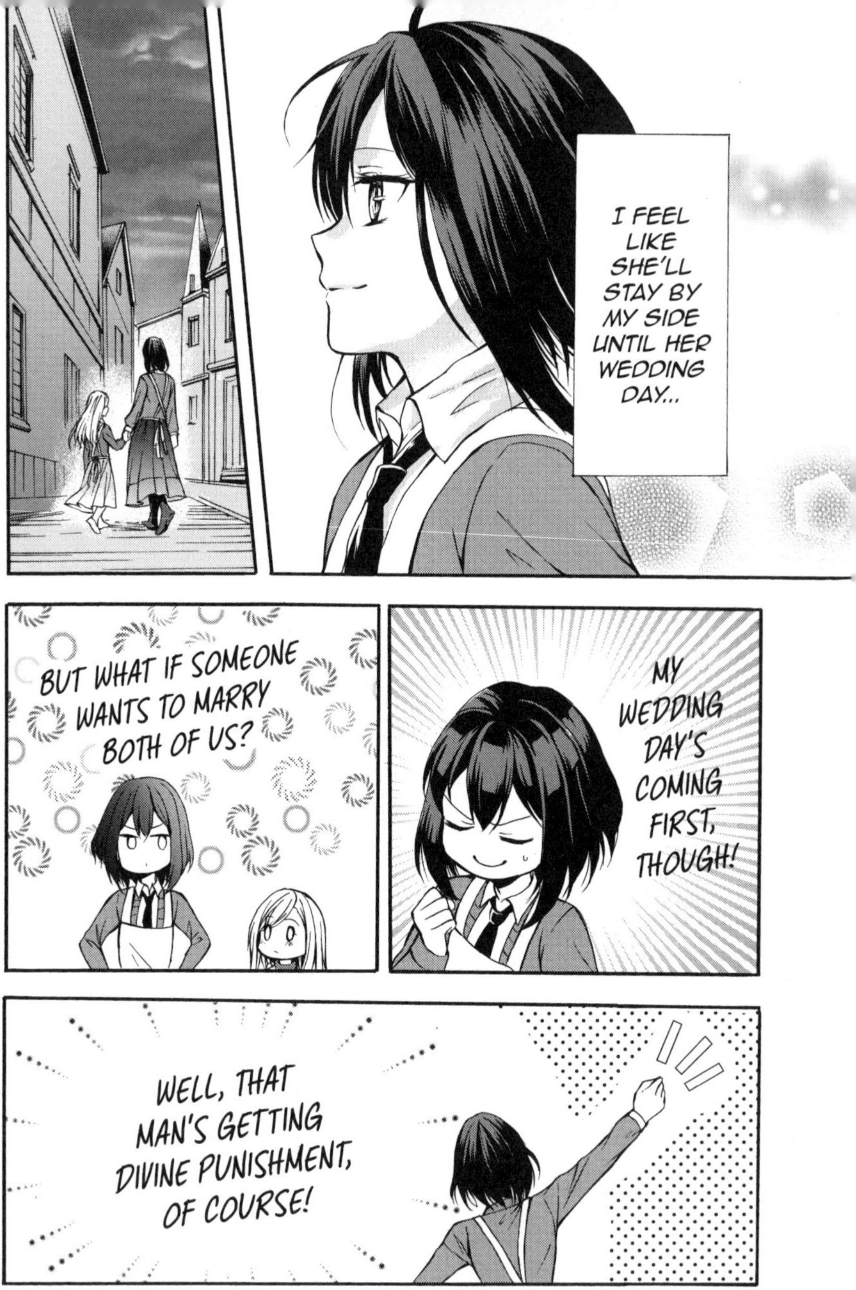
I FEEL LIKE SHE'LL STAY BY MY SIDE UNTIL HER WEDDING DAY...
MY WEDDING DAY'S COMING FIRST, THOUGH!
BUT WHAT IF SOMEONE WANTS TO MARRY BOTH OF US?
WELL, THAT MAN'S GETTING DIVINE PUNISHMENT, OF COURSE!

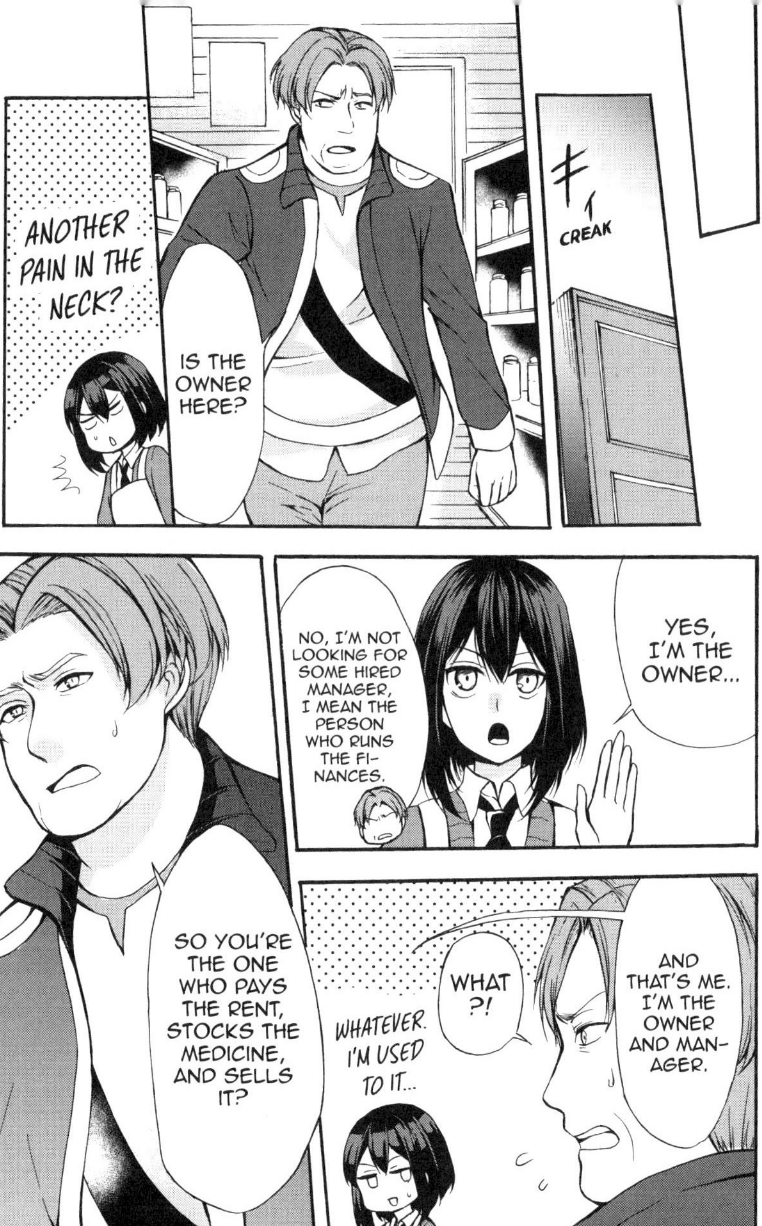

CREAK
IS THE OWNER HERE?
ANOTHER PAIN IN THE NECK?
YES, I'M THE OWNER...
NO, I'M NOT LOOKING FOR SOME HIRED MANAGER, I MEAN THE PERSON WHO RUNS THE FI- NANCES.
AND THAT'S ME. I'M THE OWNER AND MAN- AGER.
WHAT ?!
WHATEVER. I'M USED TO IT...
SO YOU'RE THE ONE WHO PAYS THE RENT, STOCKS THE MEDICINE, AND SELLS IT?

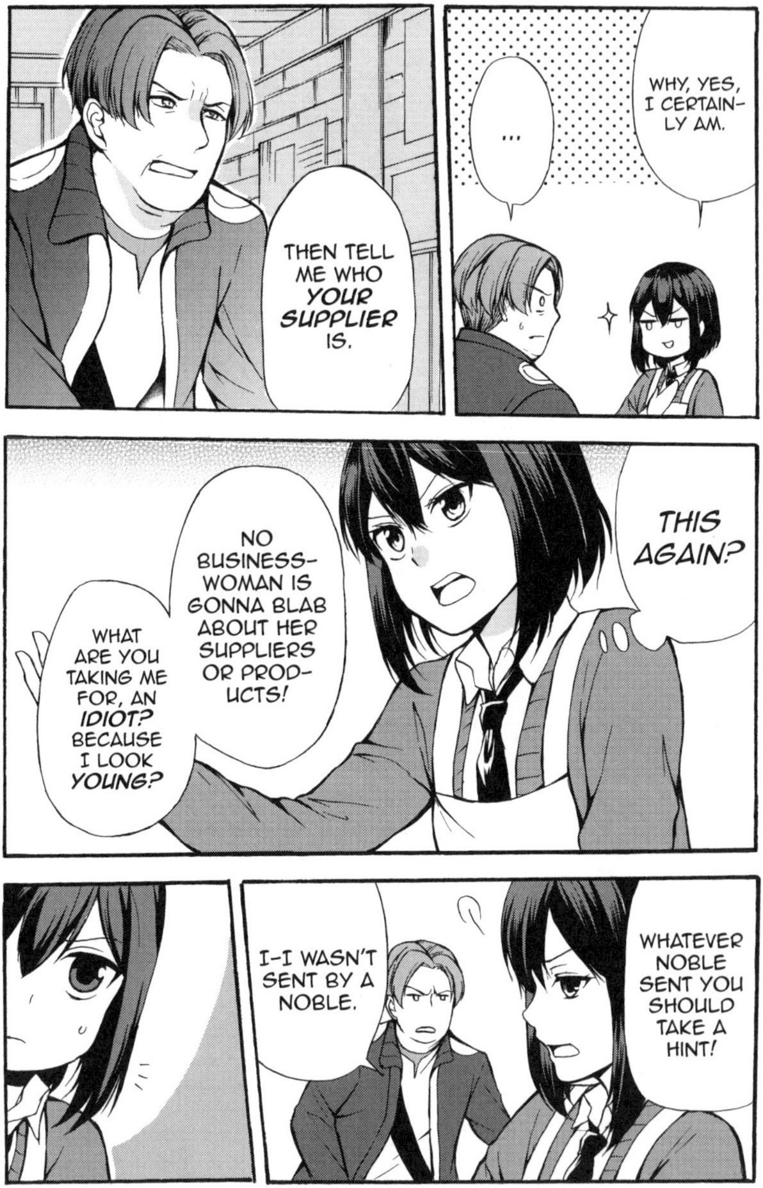
WHY, YES, I CERTAIN-LY AM.
...
THEN TELL ME WHO YOUR SUPPLIER IS.
THIS AGAIN?
NO BUSINESS-WOMAN IS GONNA BLAB ABOUT HER SUPPLIERS OR PROD-UCTS!
WHAT ARE YOU TAKING ME FOR, AN IDIOT? BECAUSE I LOOK YOUNG?
WHATEVER NOBLE SENT YOU SHOULD TAKE A HINT!
I-I WASN'T SENT BY A NOBLE.

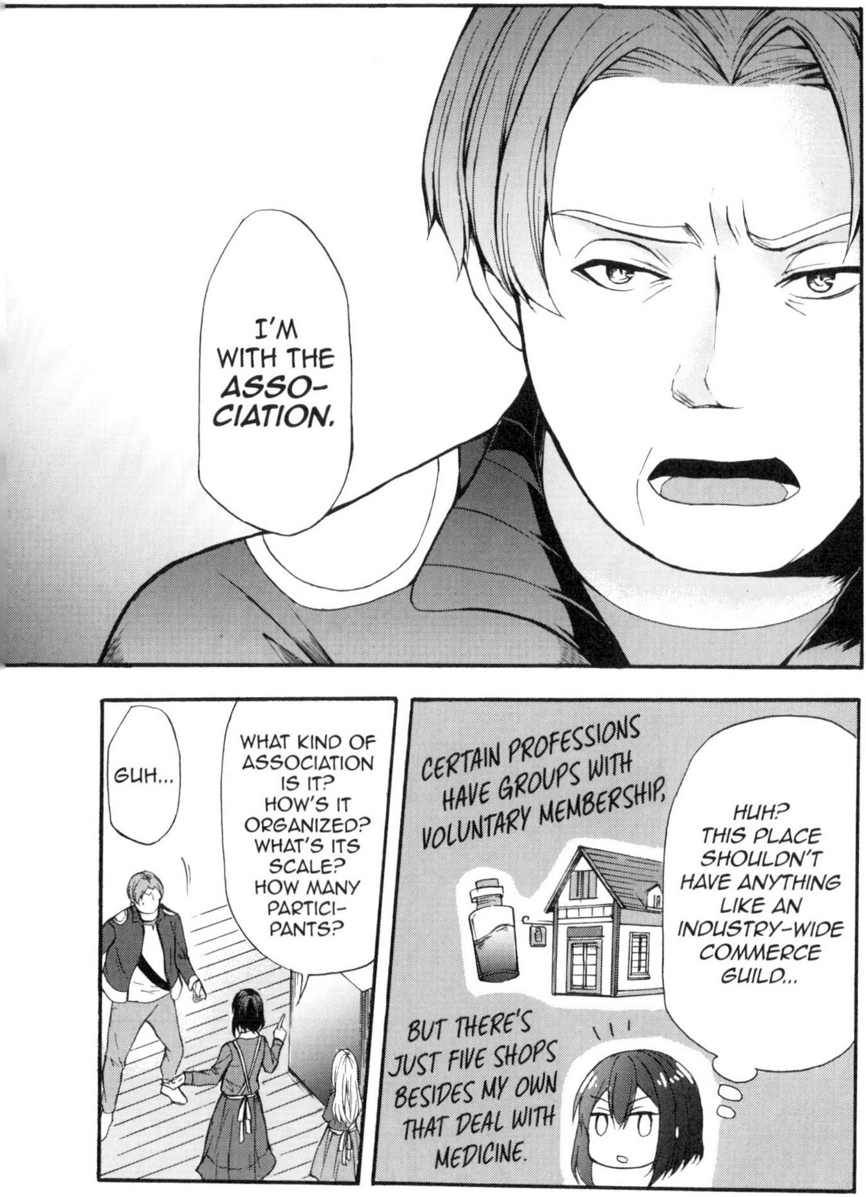
I'M WITH THE ASSOCIATION.
HUH? THIS PLACE SHOULDN'T HAVE ANYTHING LIKE AN INDUSTRY-WIDE COMMERCE GUILD...
CERTAIN PROFESSIONS HAVE GROUPS WITH VOLUNTARY MEMBERSHIP,
BUT THERE'S JUST FIVE SHOPS BESIDES MY OWN THAT DEAL WITH MEDICINE.
WHAT KIND OF ASSOCIATION IS IT? HOW'S IT ORGANIZED? WHAT'S ITS SCALE? HOW MANY PARTICIPANTS?
GUH...

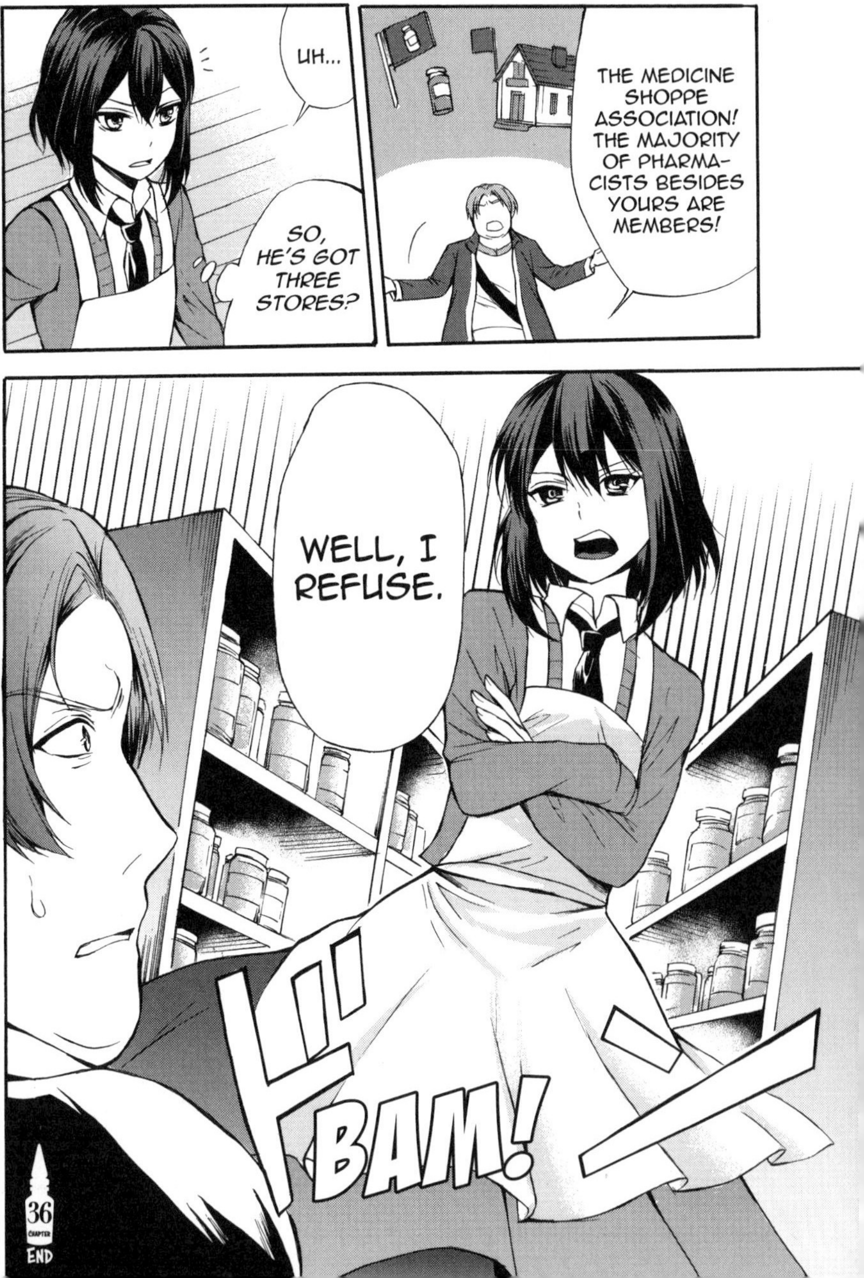
THE MEDICINE SHOPPE ASSOCIATION! THE MAJORITY OF PHARMA-CISTS BESIDES YOURS ARE MEMBERS!
UH...
SO, HE'S GOT THREE STORES?
WELL, I REFUSE.
BAM!
36
CHAPTER
END

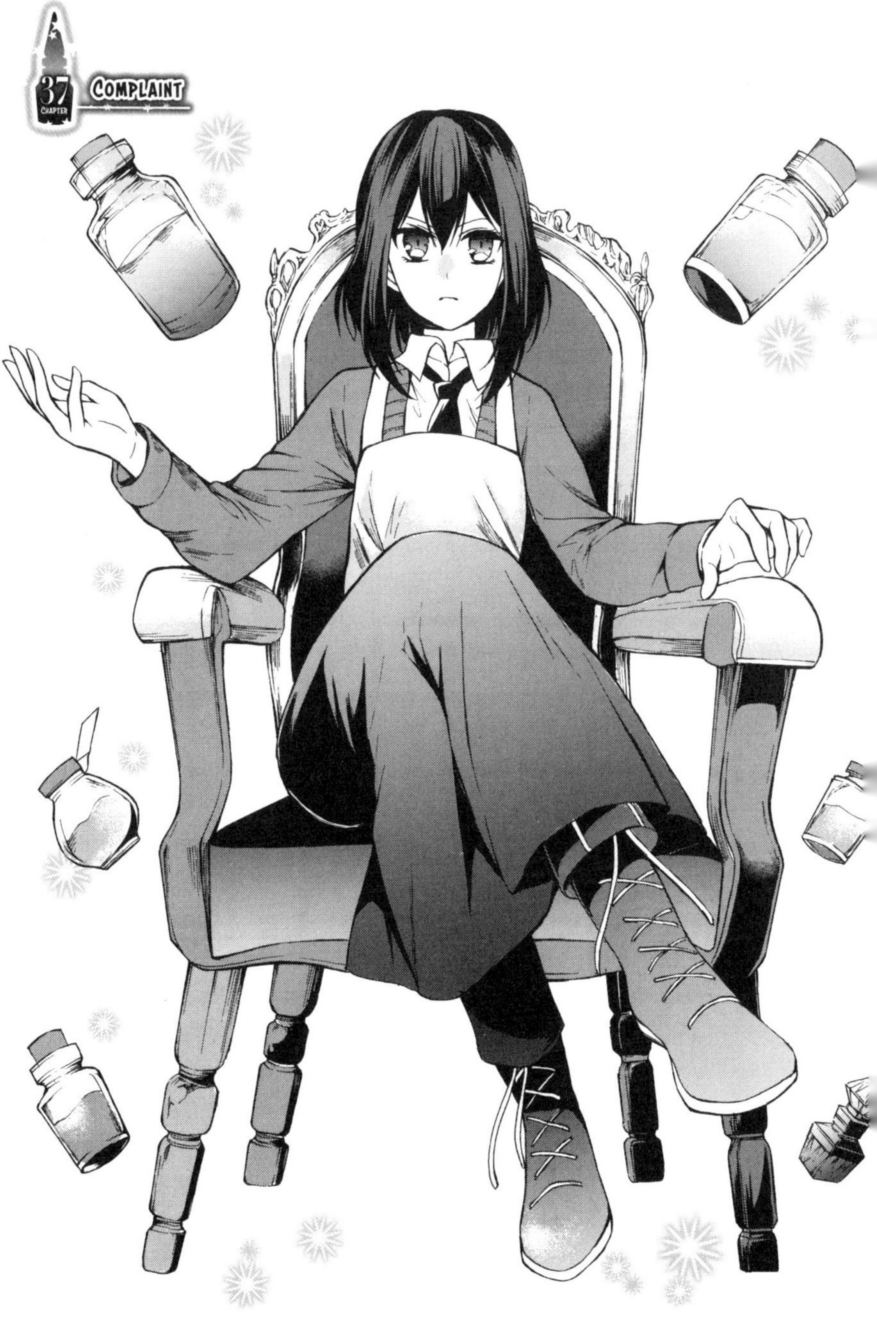
37
CHAPTER
COMPLAINT

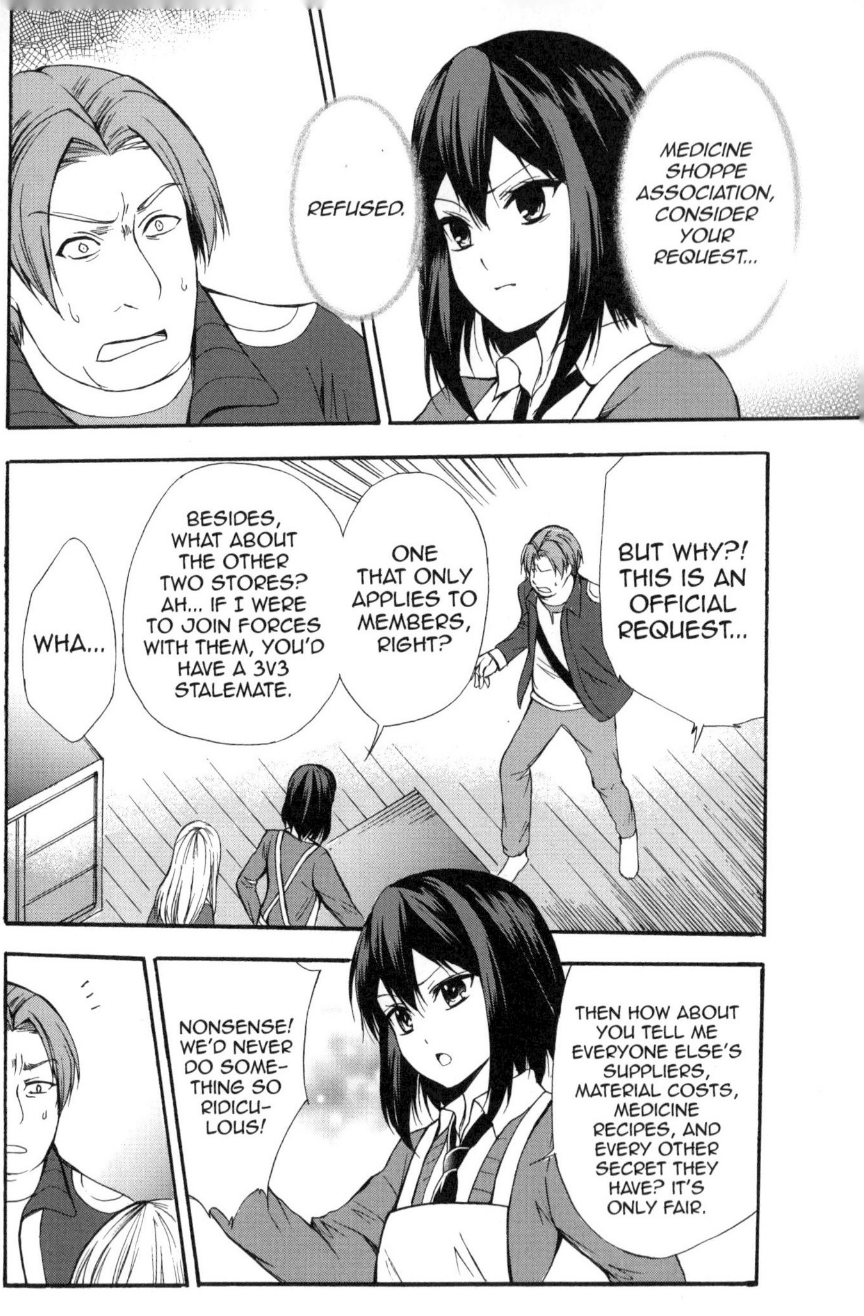
MEDICINE SHOPPE ASSOCIATION, CONSIDER YOUR REQUEST...
REFUSED.
BUT WHY?! THIS IS AN OFFICIAL REQUEST...
ONE THAT ONLY APPLIES TO MEMBERS, RIGHT?
BESIDES, WHAT ABOUT THE OTHER TWO STORES? AH... IF I WERE TO JOIN FORCES WITH THEM, YOU'D HAVE A 3V3 STALEMATE.
WHA...
THEN HOW ABOUT YOU TELL ME EVERYONE ELSE'S SUPPLIERS, MATERIAL COSTS, MEDICINE RECIPES, AND EVERY OTHER SECRET THEY HAVE? IT'S ONLY FAIR.
NONSENSE! WE'D NEVER DO SOME-THING SO RIDICU-LOUS!

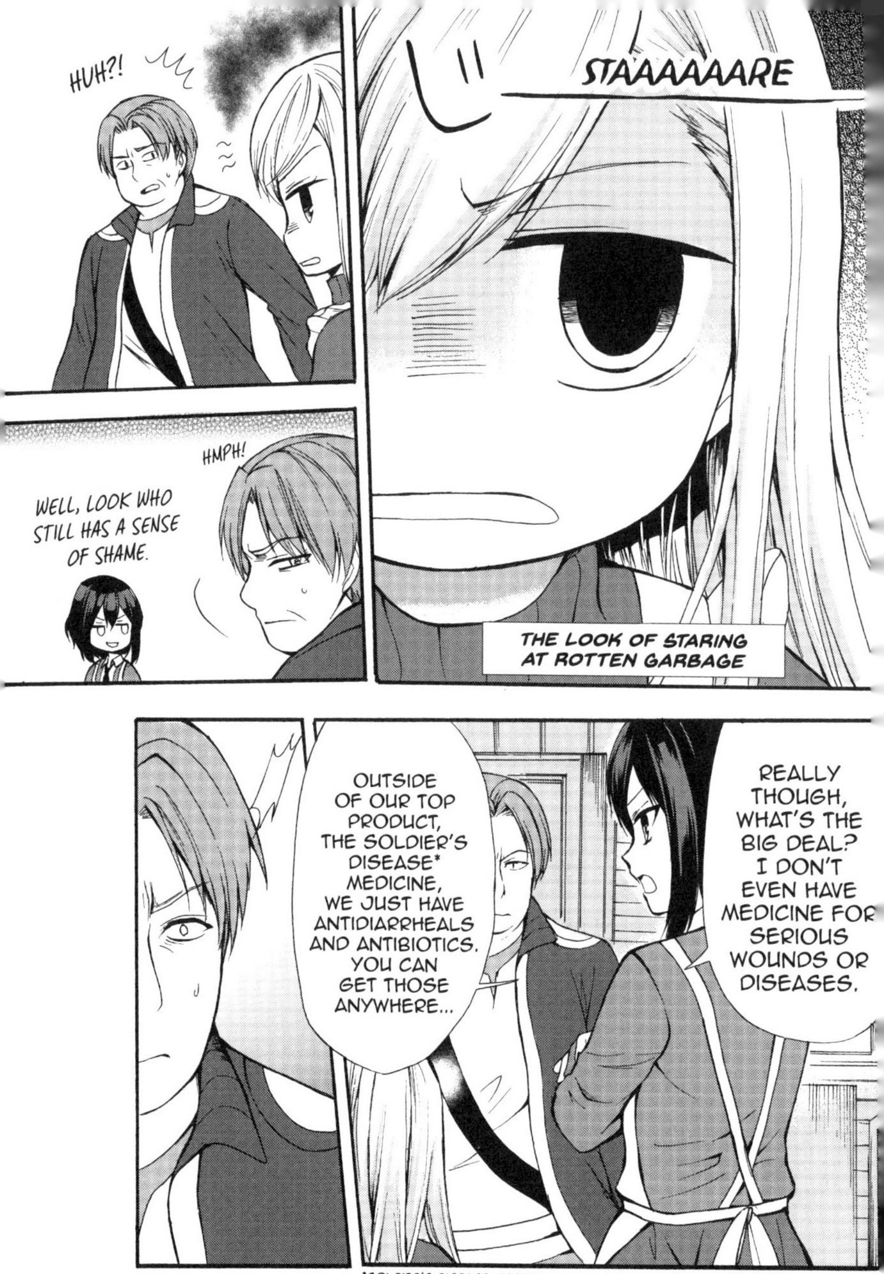
STAAAAAARE
THE LOOK OF STARING AT ROTTEN GARBAGE
HUH?!
HMPH!
WELL, LOOK WHO STILL HAS A SENSE OF SHAME.
REALLY THOUGH, WHAT'S THE BIG DEAL? I DON'T EVEN HAVE MEDICINE FOR SERIOUS WOUNDS OR DISEASES.
OUTSIDE OF OUR TOP PRODUCT, THE SOLDIER'S DISEASE* MEDICINE, WE JUST HAVE ANTIDIARRHEALS AND ANTIBIOTICS. YOU CAN GET THOSE ANYWHERE...

*SOLDIER'S DISEASE: REFERS TO ATHLETE'S FOOT.

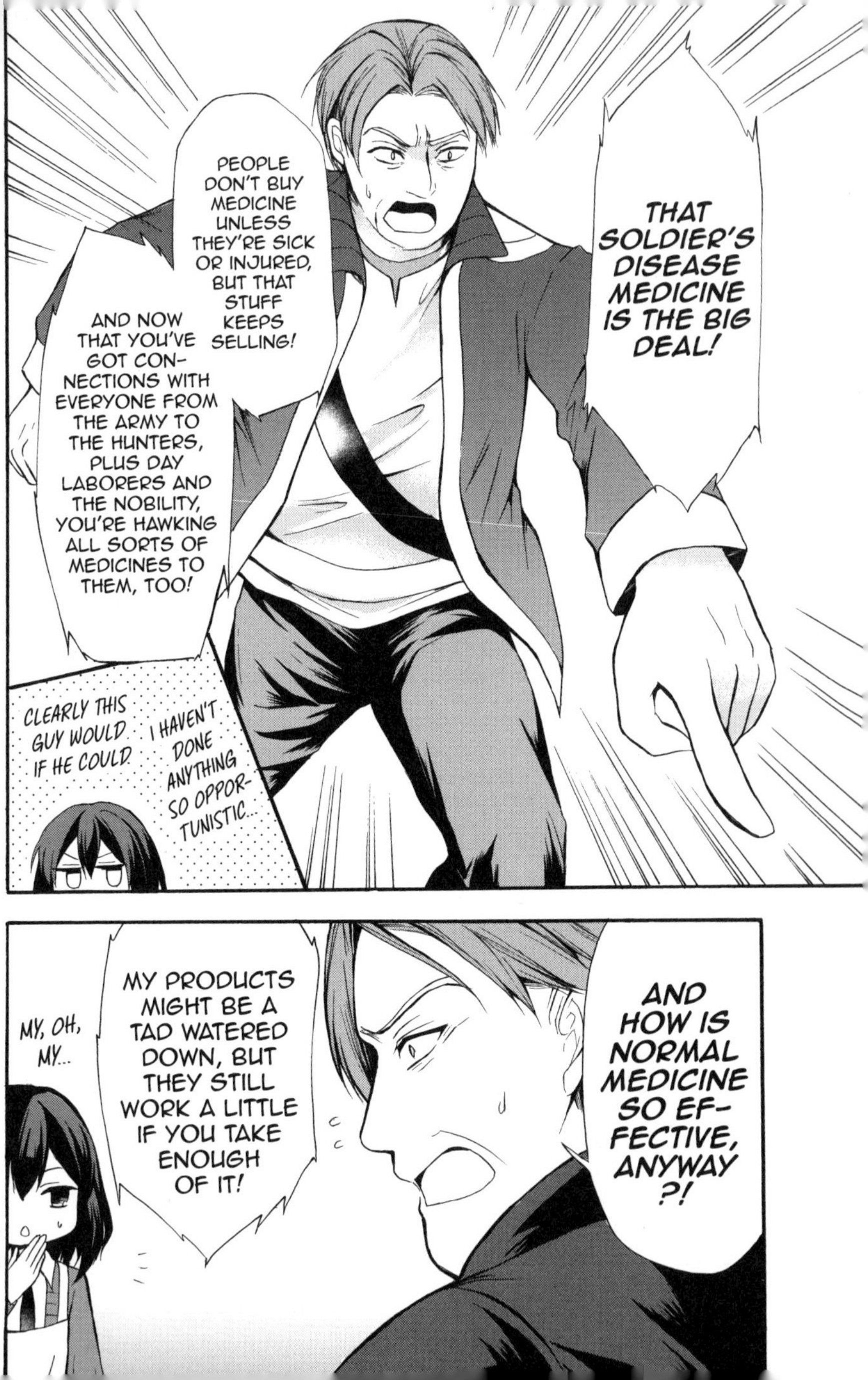
THAT SOLDIER'S DISEASE MEDICINE IS THE BIG DEAL!
PEOPLE DON'T BUY MEDICINE UNLESS THEY'RE SICK OR INJURED, BUT THAT STUFF KEEPS SELLING!
AND NOW THAT YOU'VE GOT CON-NECTIONS WITH EVERYONE FROM THE ARMY TO THE HUNTERS, PLUS DAY LABORERS AND THE NOBILITY, YOU'RE HAWKING ALL SORTS OF MEDICINES TO THEM, TOO!
I HAVEN'T DONE ANYTHING SO OPPOR-TUNISTIC...
CLEARLY THIS GUY WOULD IF HE COULD.
AND HOW IS NORMAL MEDICINE SO EF-FECTIVE, ANYWAY?!
MY PRODUCTS MIGHT BE A TAD WATERED DOWN, BUT THEY STILL WORK A LITTLE IF YOU TAKE ENOUGH OF IT!
MY, OH, MY...

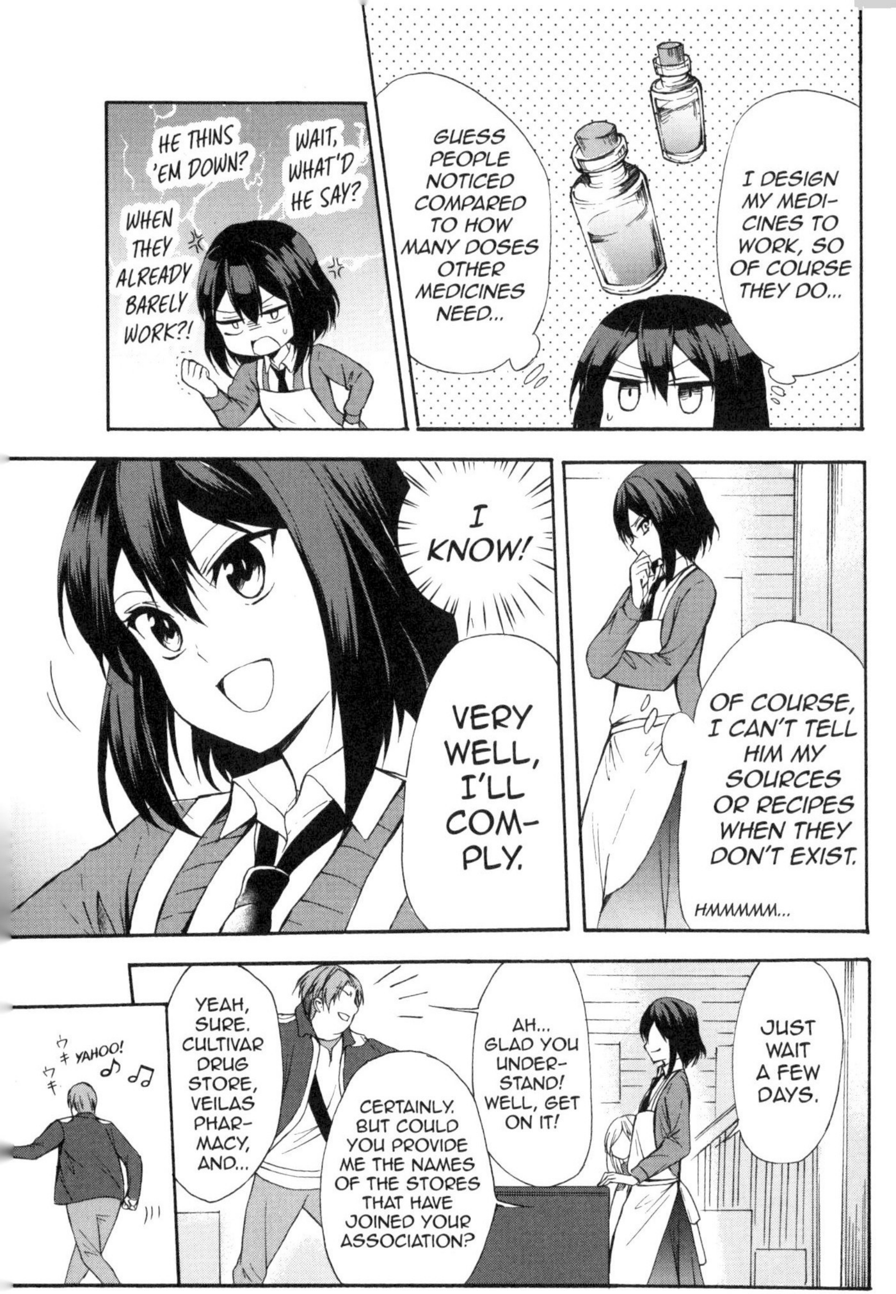
I DESIGN MY MEDI-CINES TO WORK, SO OF COURSE THEY DO...
GUESS PEOPLE NOTICED COMPARED TO HOW MANY DOSES OTHER MEDICINES NEED...
WAIT, WHAT'D HE SAY?
HE THINS 'EM DOWN?
WHEN THEY ALREADY BARELY WORK?!
OF COURSE, I CAN'T TELL HIM MY SOURCES OR RECIPES WHEN THEY DON'T EXIST.
HMMMMM...
I KNOW!
VERY WELL, I'LL COM-PLY.
JUST WAIT A FEW DAYS.
AH... GLAD YOU UNDER-STAND! WELL, GET ON IT!
CERTAINLY. BUT COULD YOU PROVIDE ME THE NAMES OF THE STORES THAT HAVE JOINED YOUR ASSOCIATION?
YEAH, SURE. CULTIVAR DRUG STORE, VEILAS PHAR-MACY, AND...
ウキ ウキ YAHOO! ♪ ♫

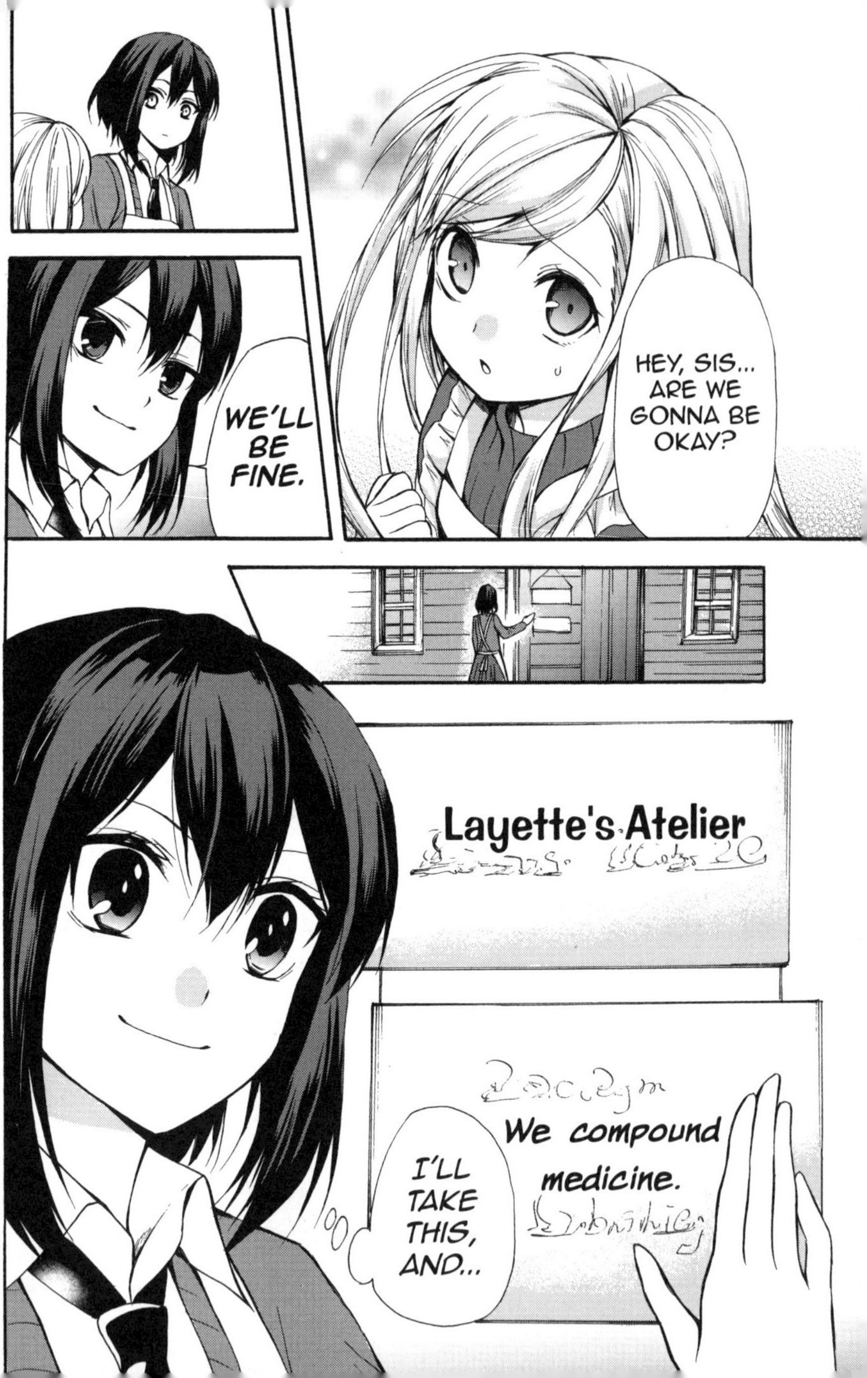
HEY, SIS... ARE WE GONNA BE OKAY?
WE'LL BE FINE.
Layette's Atelier
We compound medicine.
I'LL TAKE THIS, AND...

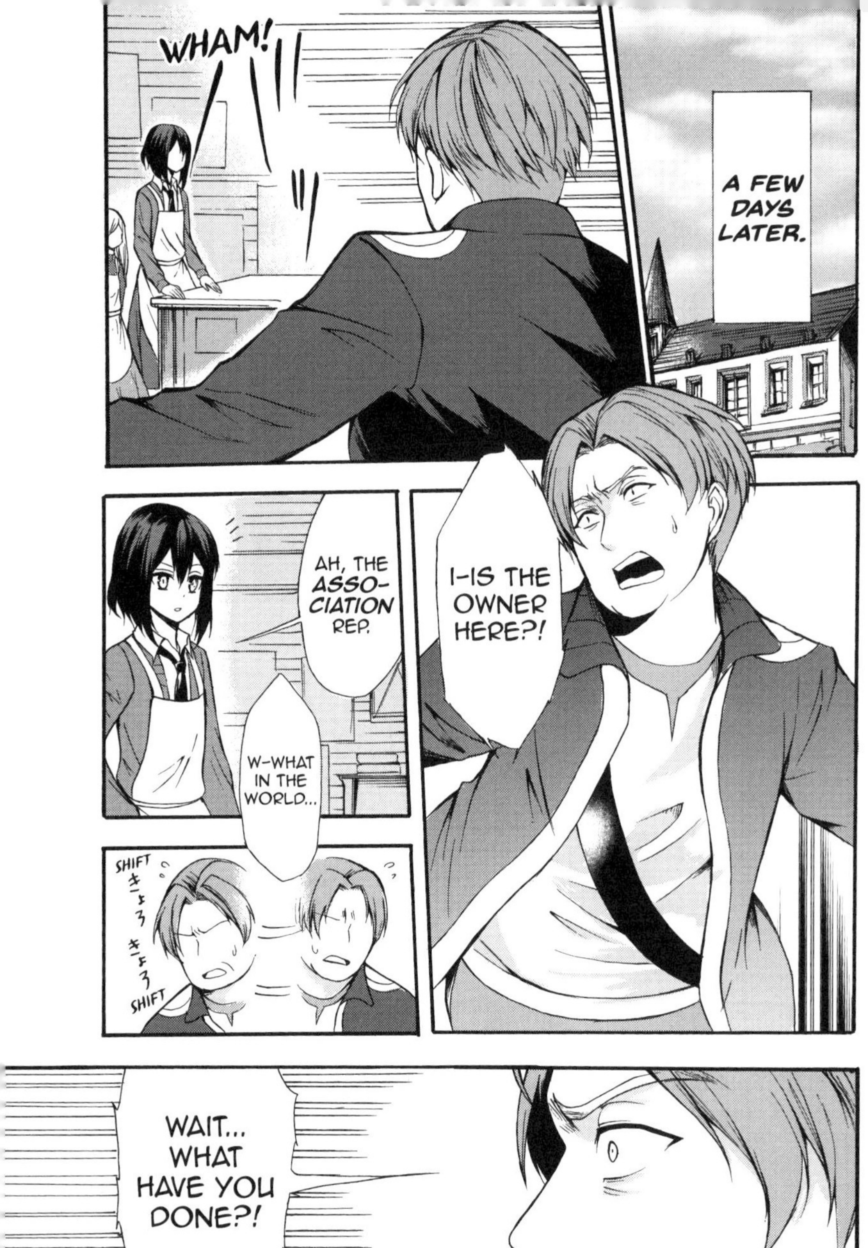
A FEW DAYS LATER.
WHAM!
I-IS THE OWNER HERE?!
AH, THE ASSOCIATION REP.
W-WHAT IN THE WORLD...
SHIFT
きょろ
きょろ
SHIFT
WAIT... WHAT HAVE YOU DONE?!

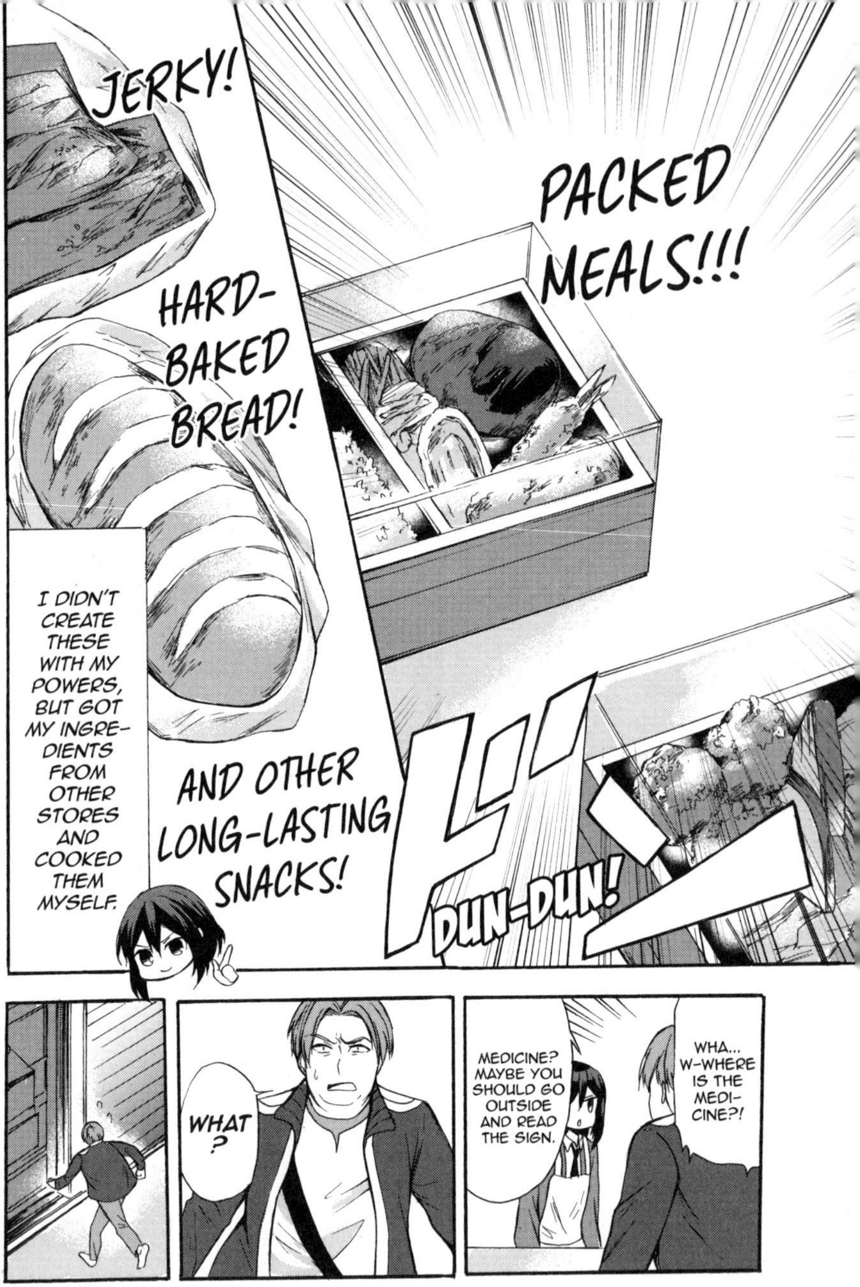
PACKED MEALS!!!
DUN-DUN!
JERKY!
HARD-BAKED BREAD!
AND OTHER LONG-LASTING SNACKS!
I DIDN'T CREATE THESE WITH MY POWERS, BUT GOT MY INGREDIENTS FROM OTHER STORES AND COOKED THEM MYSELF.
WHA... W-WHERE IS THE MEDICINE?!
MEDICINE? MAYBE YOU SHOULD GO OUTSIDE AND READ THE SIGN.
WHAT?

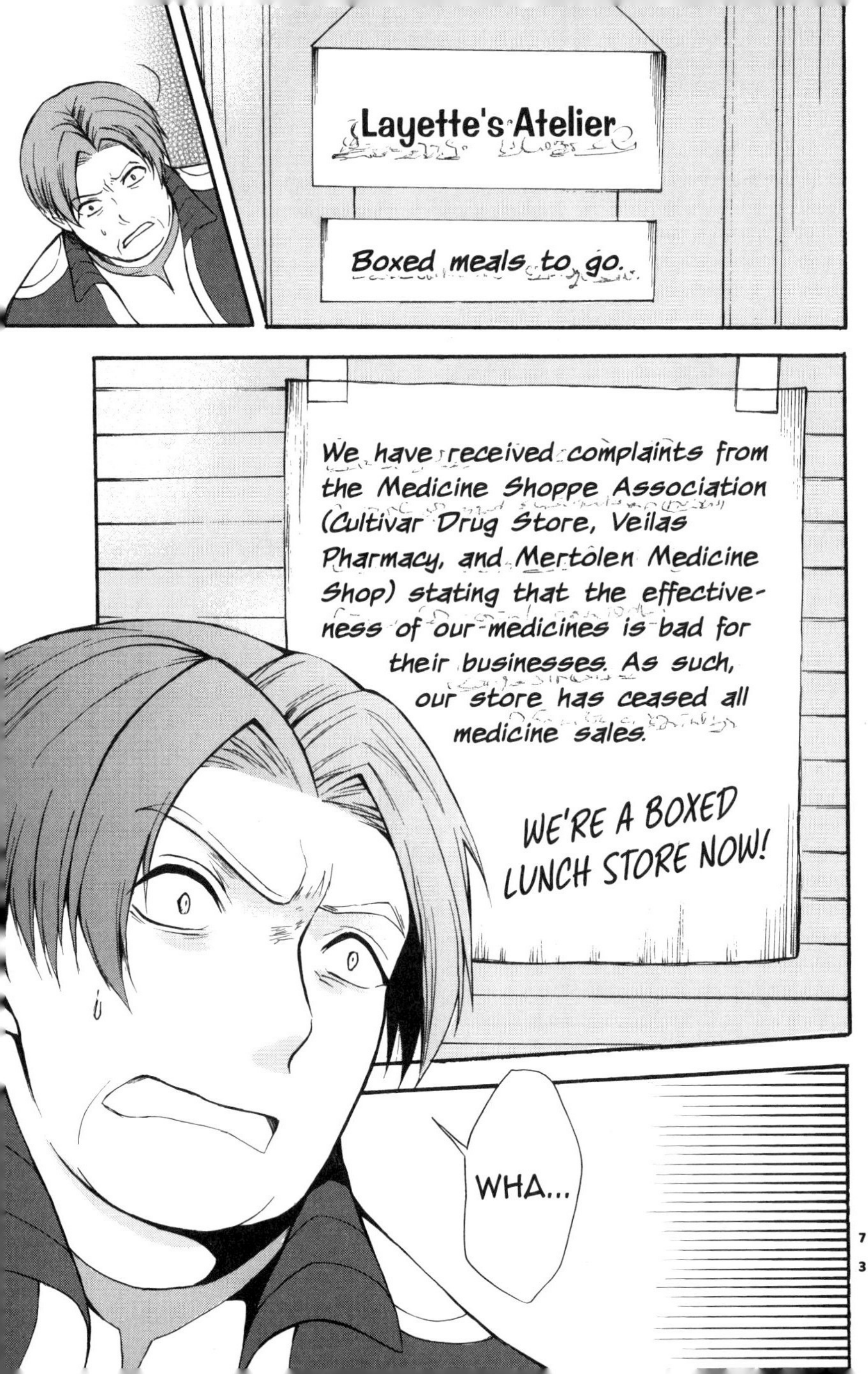

Layette's Atelier
Boxed meals to go.
We have received complaints from the Medicine Shoppe Association (Cultivar Drug Store, Veilas Pharmacy, and Mertolen Medicine Shop) stating that the effective-ness of our medicines is bad for their businesses. As such, our store has ceased all medicine sales.
WE'RE A BOXED LUNCH STORE NOW!
WHA...

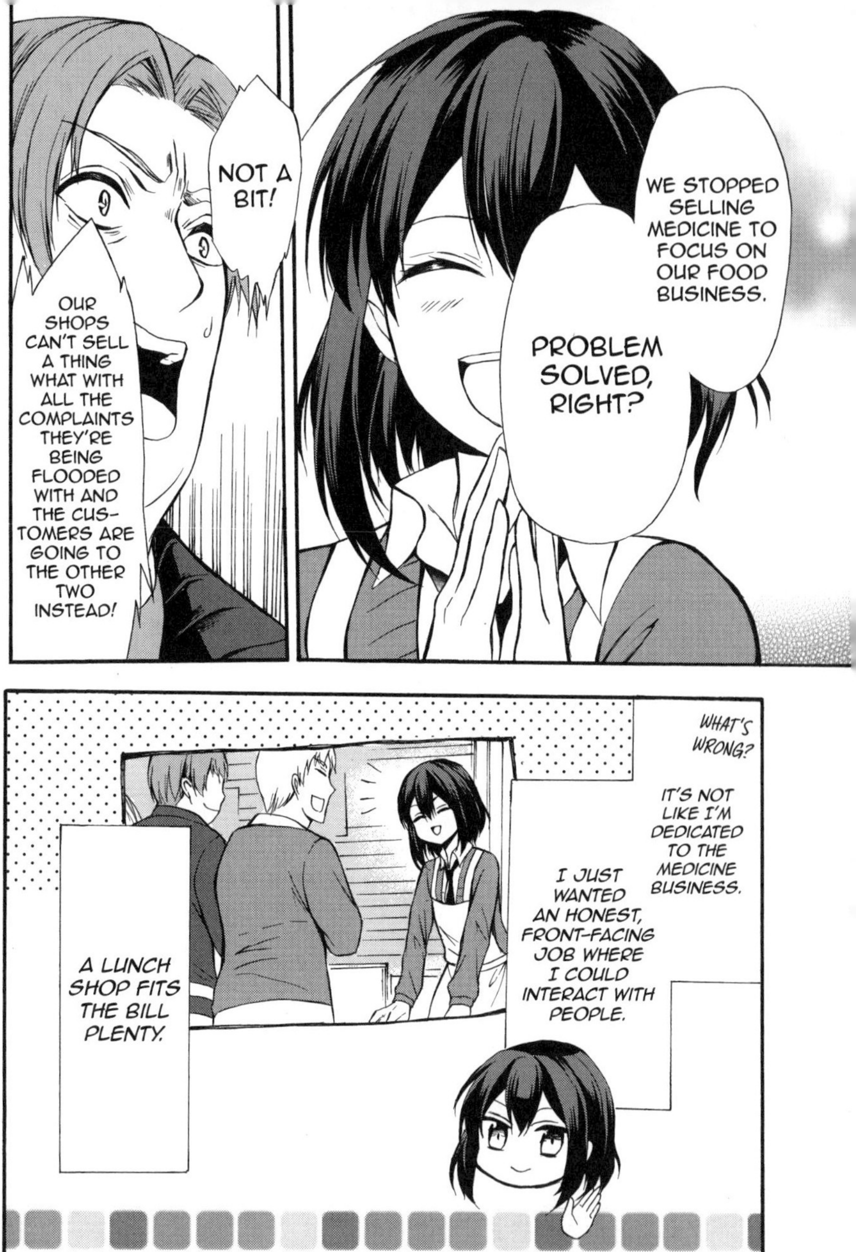
WE STOPPED SELLING MEDICINE TO FOCUS ON OUR FOOD BUSINESS.
PROBLEM SOLVED, RIGHT?
NOT A BIT!
OUR SHOPS CAN'T SELL A THING WHAT WITH ALL THE COMPLAINTS THEY'RE BEING FLOODED WITH AND THE CUS-TOMERS ARE GOING TO THE OTHER TWO INSTEAD!
WHAT'S WRONG?
IT'S NOT LIKE I'M DEDICATED TO THE MEDICINE BUSINESS.
I JUST WANTED AN HONEST, FRONT-FACING JOB WHERE I COULD INTERACT WITH PEOPLE.
A LUNCH SHOP FITS THE BILL PLENTY.

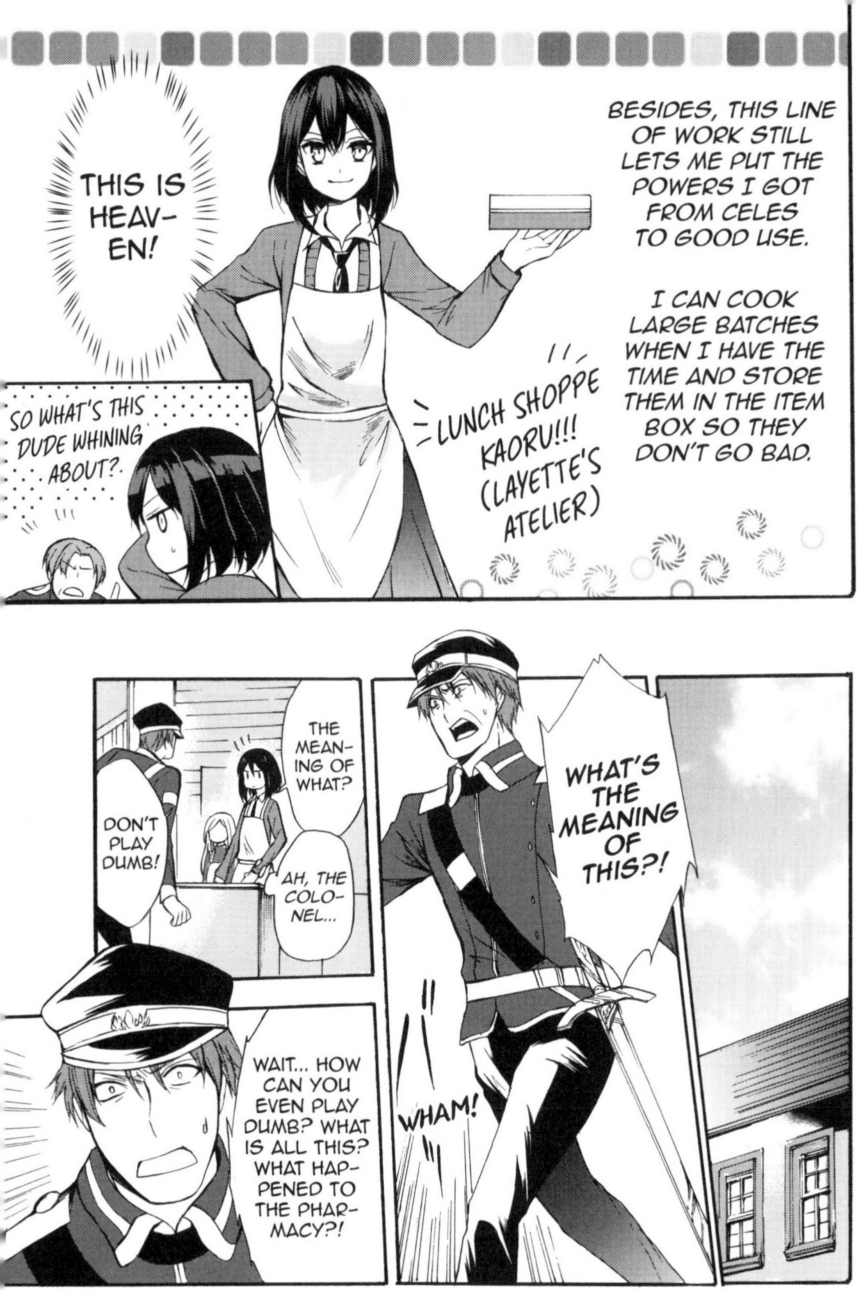
BESIDES, THIS LINE OF WORK STILL LETS ME PUT THE POWERS I GOT FROM CELES TO GOOD USE.
I CAN COOK LARGE BATCHES WHEN I HAVE THE TIME AND STORE THEM IN THE ITEM BOX SO THEY DON'T GO BAD.
LUNCH SHOPPE KAORU!!! (LAYETTE'S ATELIER)
THIS IS HEAV-EN!
SO WHAT'S THIS DUDE WHINING ABOUT?
WHAT'S THE MEANING OF THIS?!
WHAM!
THE MEAN-ING OF WHAT?
AH, THE COLO-NEL...
DON'T PLAY DUMB!
WAIT... HOW CAN YOU EVEN PLAY DUMB? WHAT IS ALL THIS? WHAT HAP-PENED TO THE PHAR-MACY?!

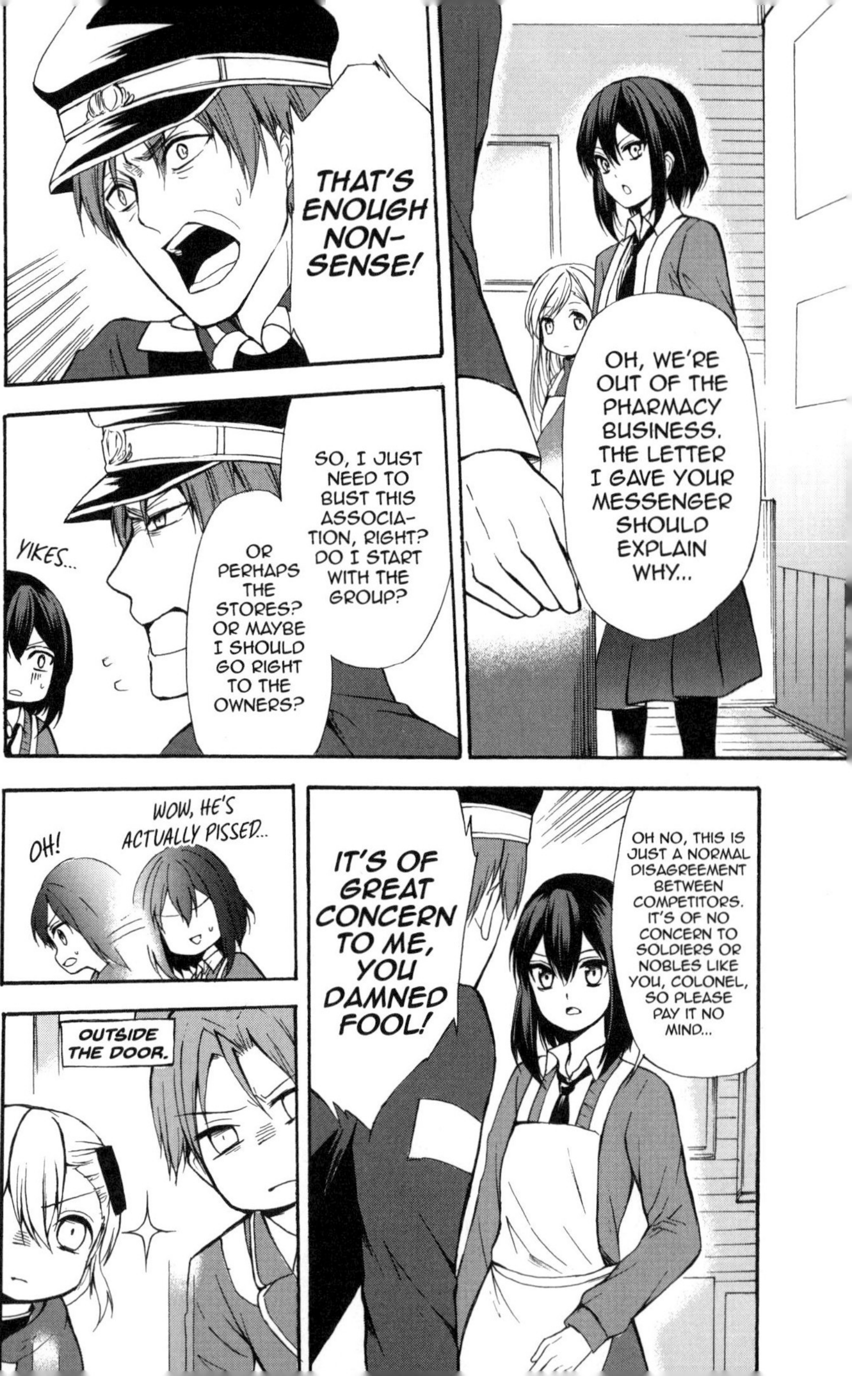
OH, WE'RE OUT OF THE PHARMACY BUSINESS. THE LETTER I GAVE YOUR MESSENGER SHOULD EXPLAIN WHY...
THAT'S ENOUGH NON-SENSE!
SO, I JUST NEED TO BUST THIS ASSOCIA-TION, RIGHT? DO I START WITH THE GROUP?
OR PERHAPS THE STORES? OR MAYBE I SHOULD GO RIGHT TO THE OWNERS?
YIKES...
OH NO, THIS IS JUST A NORMAL DISAGREEMENT BETWEEN COMPETITORS. IT'S OF NO CONCERN TO SOLDIERS OR NOBLES LIKE YOU, COLONEL, SO PLEASE PAY IT NO MIND...
IT'S OF GREAT CONCERN TO ME, YOU DAMNED FOOL!
WOW, HE'S ACTUALLY PISSED...
OH!
OUTSIDE THE DOOR.

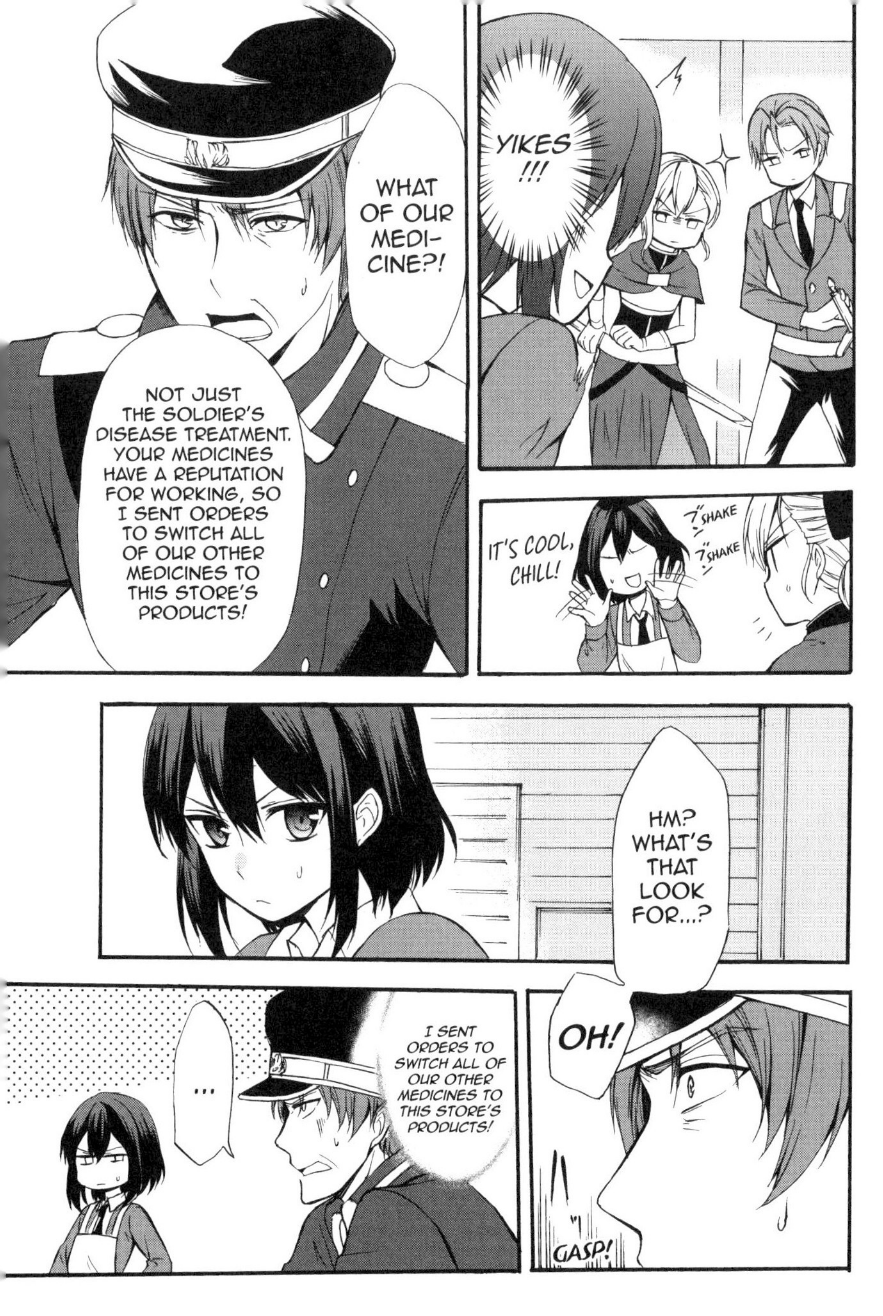
YIKES !!!
IT'S COOL, CHILL!
SHAKE
SHAKE
WHAT OF OUR MEDICINE?!
NOT JUST THE SOLDIER'S DISEASE TREATMENT. YOUR MEDICINES HAVE A REPUTATION FOR WORKING, SO I SENT ORDERS TO SWITCH ALL OF OUR OTHER MEDICINES TO THIS STORE'S PRODUCTS!
HM? WHAT'S THAT LOOK FOR...?
OH!
GASP!
I SENT ORDERS TO SWITCH ALL OF OUR OTHER MEDICINES TO THIS STORE'S PRODUCTS!
...

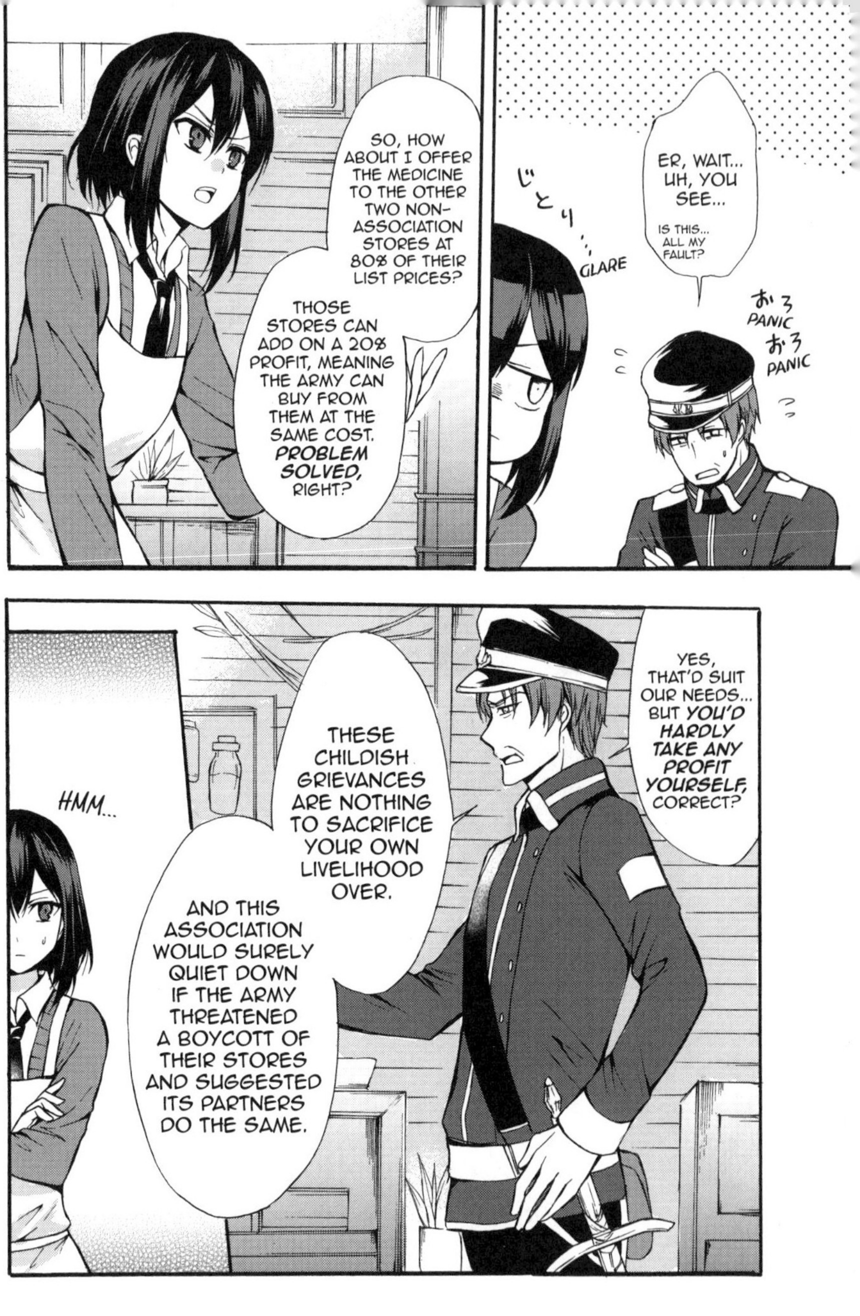
ER, WAIT... UH, YOU SEE...
IS THIS... ALL MY FAULT?
じとり... GLARE
おろ PANIC おろ PANIC
SO, HOW ABOUT I OFFER THE MEDICINE TO THE OTHER TWO NON-ASSOCIATION STORES AT 80% OF THEIR LIST PRICES?
THOSE STORES CAN ADD ON A 20% PROFIT, MEANING THE ARMY CAN BUY FROM THEM AT THE SAME COST. *PROBLEM SOLVED,* RIGHT?
YES, THAT'D SUIT OUR NEEDS... BUT *YOU'D HARDLY TAKE ANY PROFIT YOURSELF,* CORRECT?
THESE CHILDISH GRIEVANCES ARE NOTHING TO SACRIFICE YOUR OWN LIVELIHOOD OVER.
AND THIS ASSOCIATION WOULD SURELY QUIET DOWN IF THE ARMY THREATENED A BOYCOTT OF THEIR STORES AND SUGGESTED ITS PARTNERS DO THE SAME.
HMM...

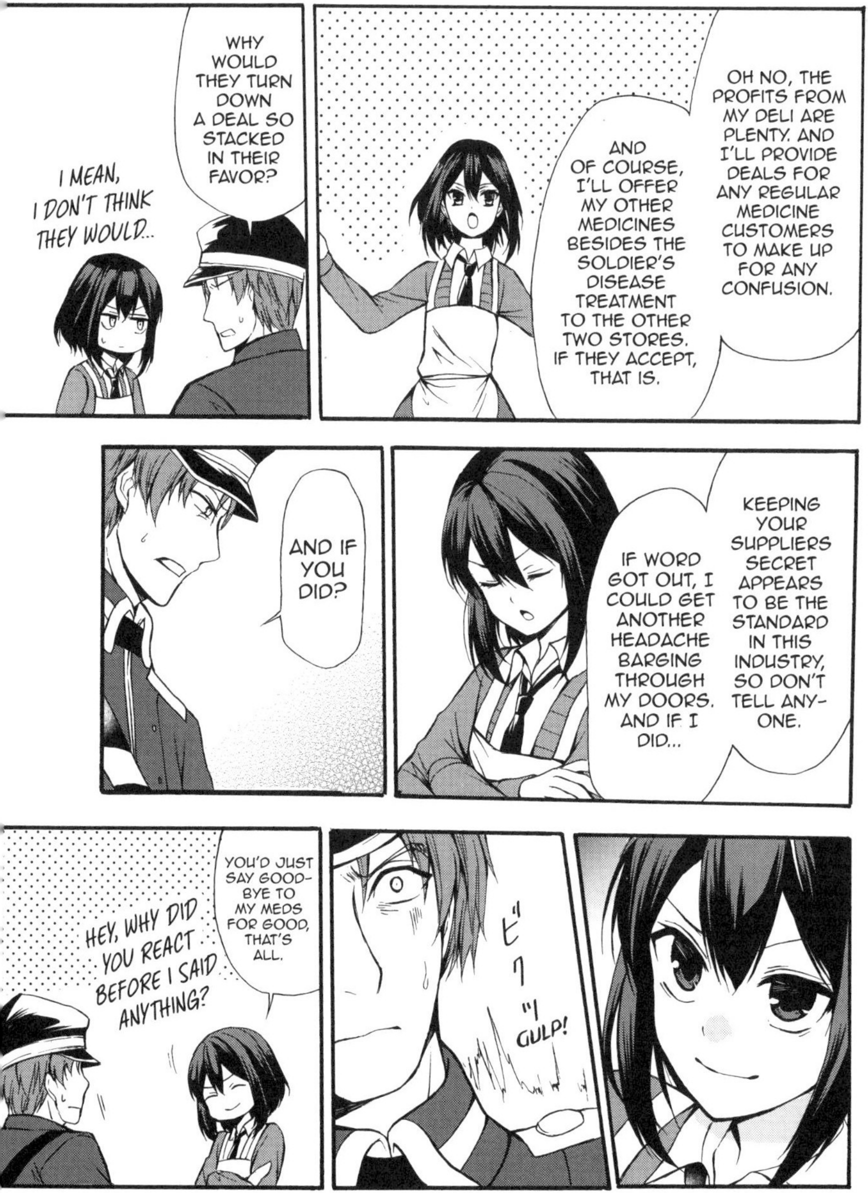
OH NO, THE PROFITS FROM MY DELI ARE PLENTY. AND I'LL PROVIDE DEALS FOR ANY REGULAR MEDICINE CUSTOMERS TO MAKE UP FOR ANY CONFUSION.
AND OF COURSE, I'LL OFFER MY OTHER MEDICINES BESIDES THE SOLDIER'S DISEASE TREATMENT TO THE OTHER TWO STORES. IF THEY ACCEPT, THAT IS.
WHY WOULD THEY TURN DOWN A DEAL SO STACKED IN THEIR FAVOR?
I MEAN, I DON'T THINK THEY WOULD...
KEEPING YOUR SUPPLIERS SECRET APPEARS TO BE THE STANDARD IN THIS INDUSTRY, SO DON'T TELL ANY-ONE.
IF WORD GOT OUT, I COULD GET ANOTHER HEADACHE BARGING THROUGH MY DOORS. AND IF I DID...
AND IF YOU DID?
ビクッ
GULP!
YOU'D JUST SAY GOOD-BYE TO MY MEDS FOR GOOD, THAT'S ALL.
HEY, WHY DID YOU REACT BEFORE I SAID ANYTHING?

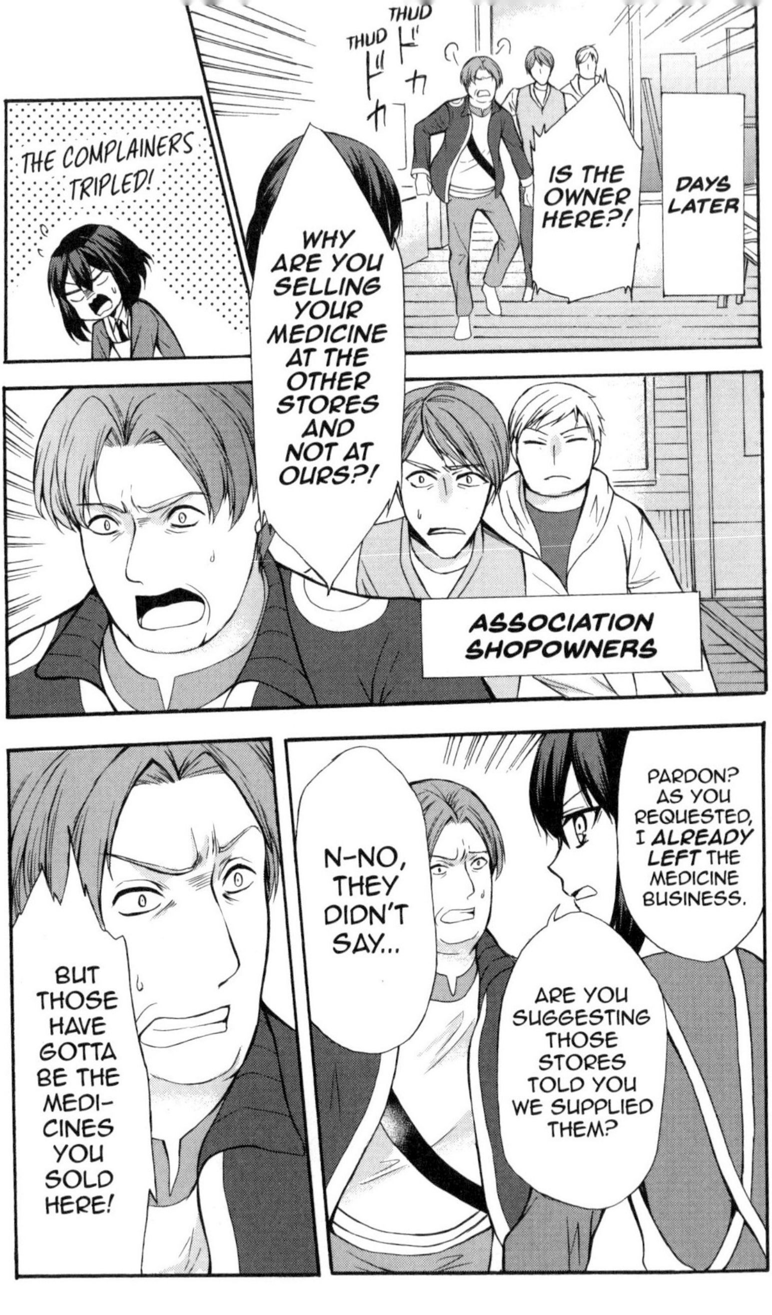
DAYS LATER
THUD THUD
IS THE OWNER HERE?!
THE COMPLAINERS TRIPLED!
WHY ARE YOU SELLING YOUR MEDICINE AT THE OTHER STORES AND NOT AT OURS?!
ASSOCIATION SHOPOWNERS
PARDON? AS YOU REQUESTED, I ALREADY LEFT THE MEDICINE BUSINESS.
ARE YOU SUGGESTING THOSE STORES TOLD YOU WE SUPPLIED THEM?
N-NO, THEY DIDN'T SAY...
BUT THOSE HAVE GOTTA BE THE MEDI- CINES YOU SOLD HERE!

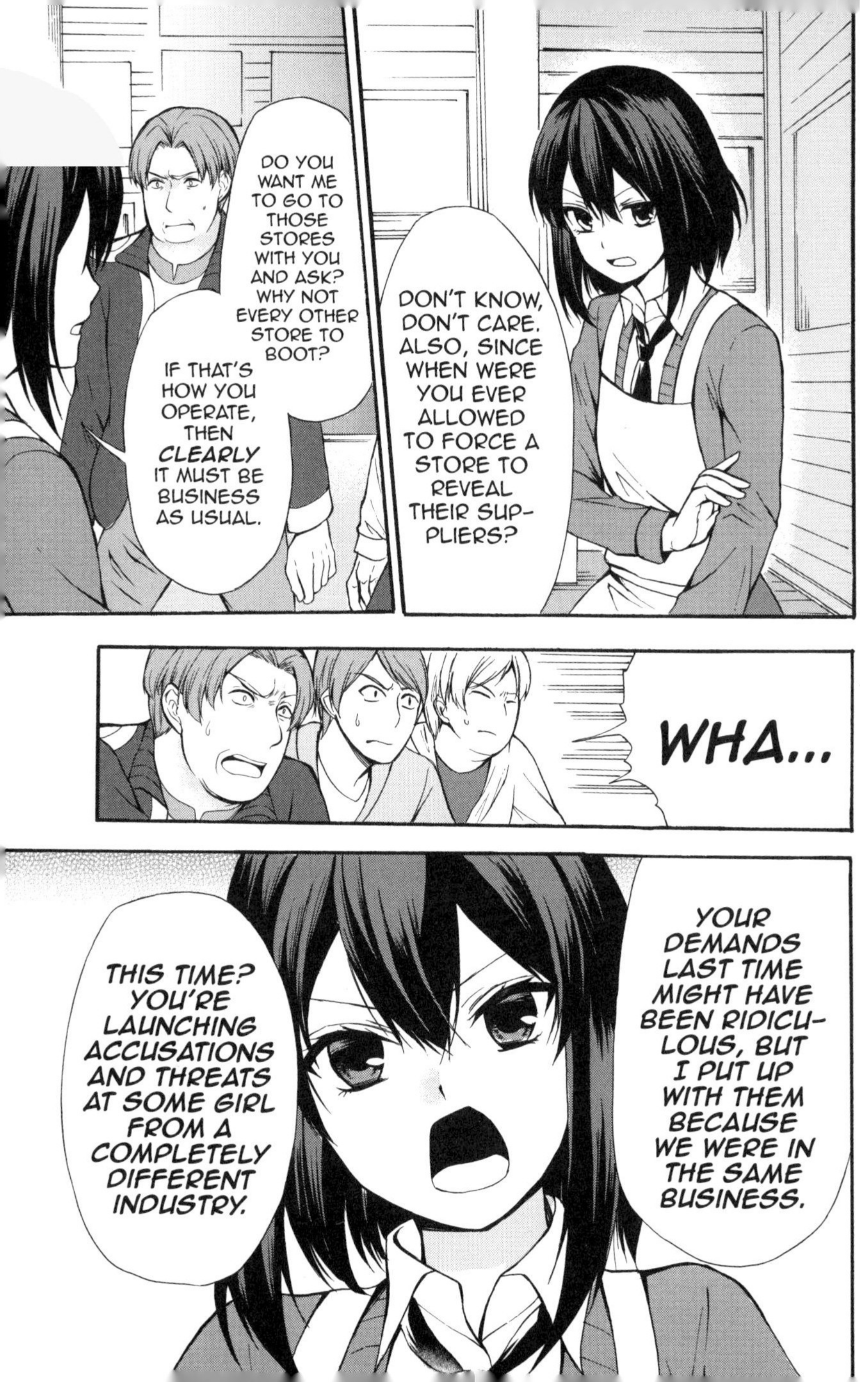
DON'T KNOW, DON'T CARE. ALSO, SINCE WHEN WERE YOU EVER ALLOWED TO FORCE A STORE TO REVEAL THEIR SUP-PLIERS?
DO YOU WANT ME TO GO TO THOSE STORES WITH YOU AND ASK? WHY NOT EVERY OTHER STORE TO BOOT?
IF THAT'S HOW YOU OPERATE, THEN *CLEARLY* IT MUST BE BUSINESS AS USUAL.
WHA...
YOUR DEMANDS LAST TIME MIGHT HAVE BEEN RIDICU-LOUS, BUT I PUT UP WITH THEM BECAUSE WE WERE IN THE SAME BUSINESS.
THIS TIME? YOU'RE LAUNCHING ACCUSATIONS AND THREATS AT SOME GIRL FROM A COMPLETELY DIFFERENT INDUSTRY.

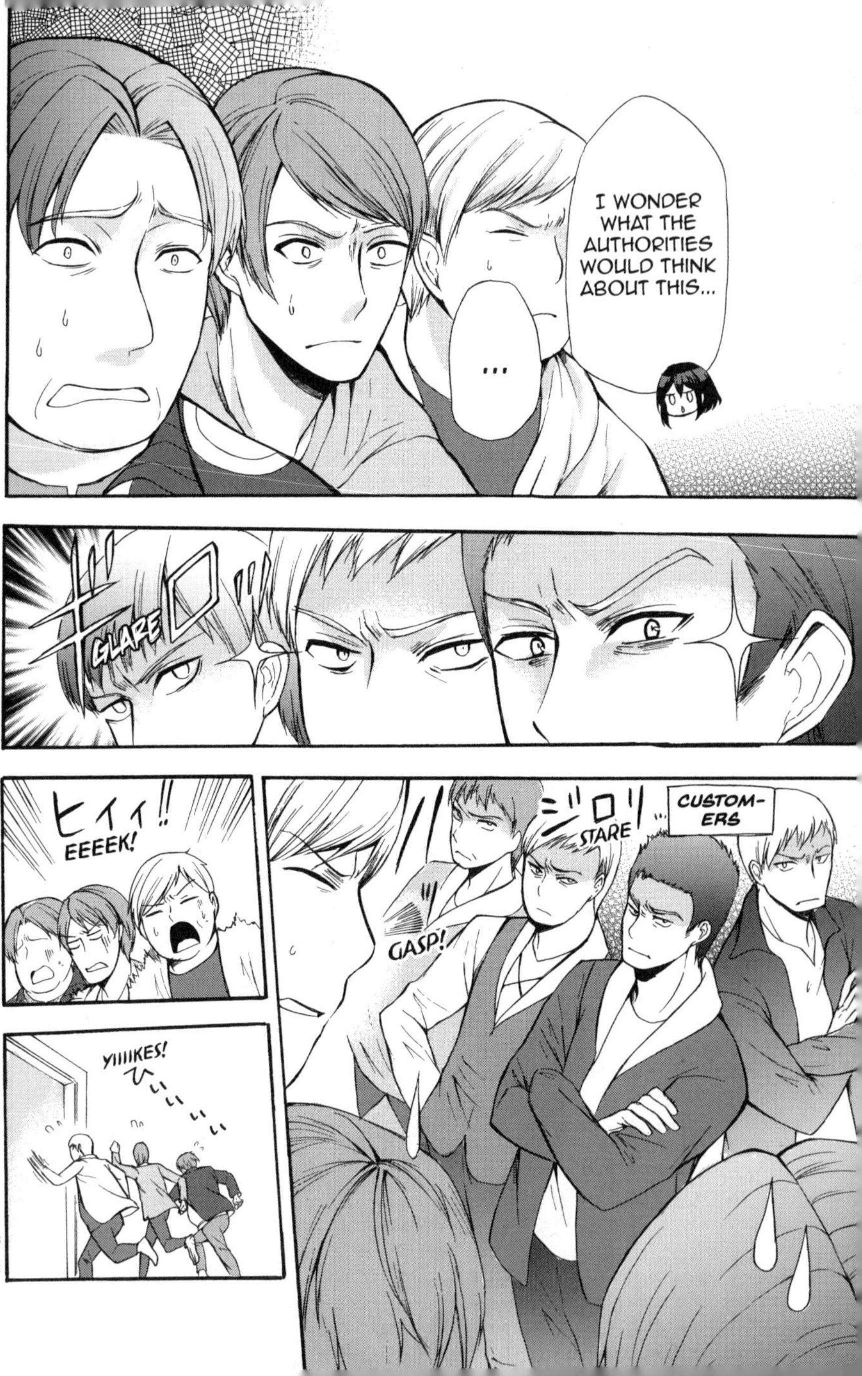
I WONDER WHAT THE AUTHORITIES WOULD THINK ABOUT THIS...
...
ギロッ
GLARE
CUSTOMERS
ジロリ
STARE
GASP!
ヒィィ!!
EEEEK!
YIIIIKES!
ひぃぃぃぃ

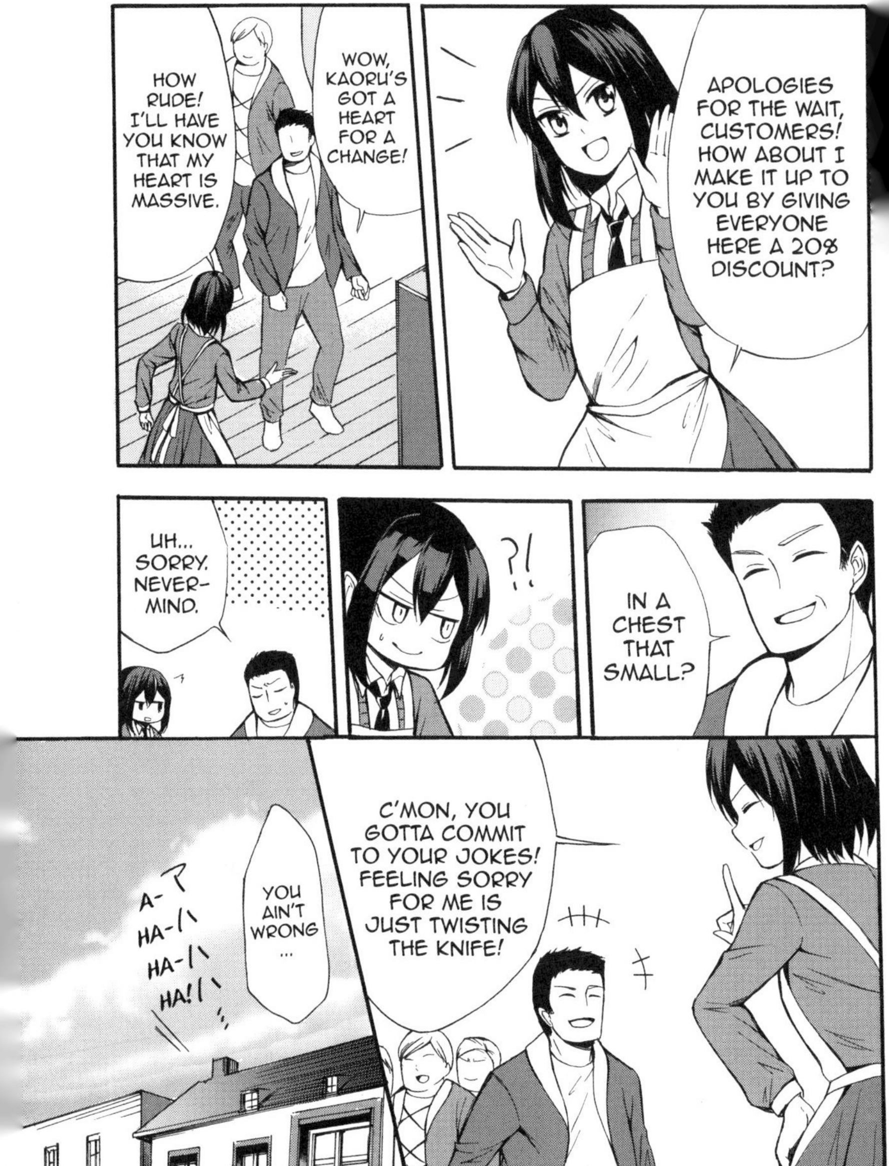
APOLOGIES FOR THE WAIT, CUSTOMERS! HOW ABOUT I MAKE IT UP TO YOU BY GIVING EVERYONE HERE A 20% DISCOUNT?
WOW, KAORU'S GOT A HEART FOR A CHANGE!
HOW RUDE! I'LL HAVE YOU KNOW THAT MY HEART IS MASSIVE.
IN A CHEST THAT SMALL?
?!
UH... SORRY. NEVER-MIND.
C'MON, YOU GOTTA COMMIT TO YOUR JOKES! FEELING SORRY FOR ME IS JUST TWISTING THE KNIFE!
YOU AIN'T WRONG ...
A-HA-HA-HA!

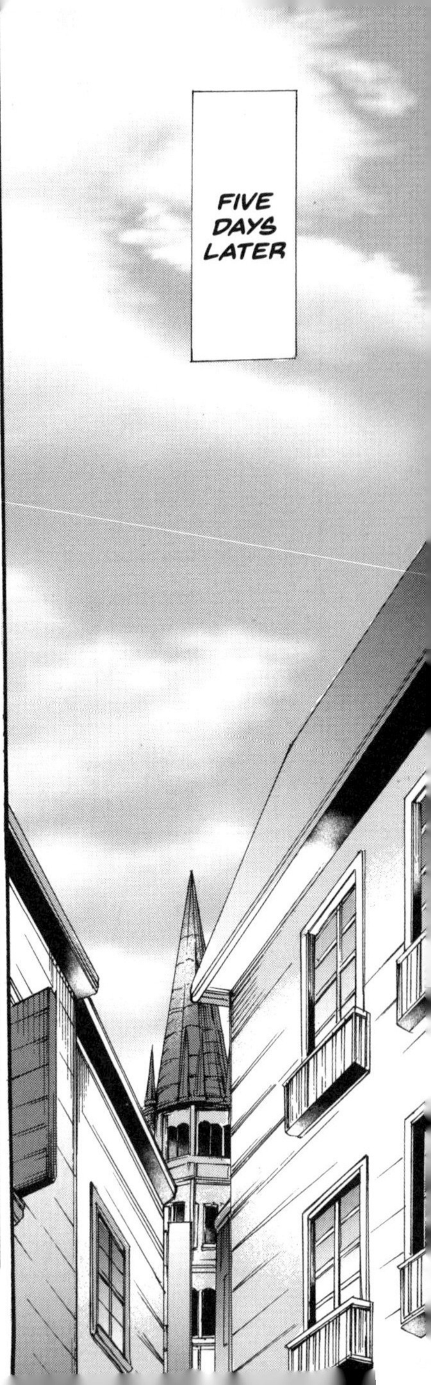
FIVE DAYS LATER

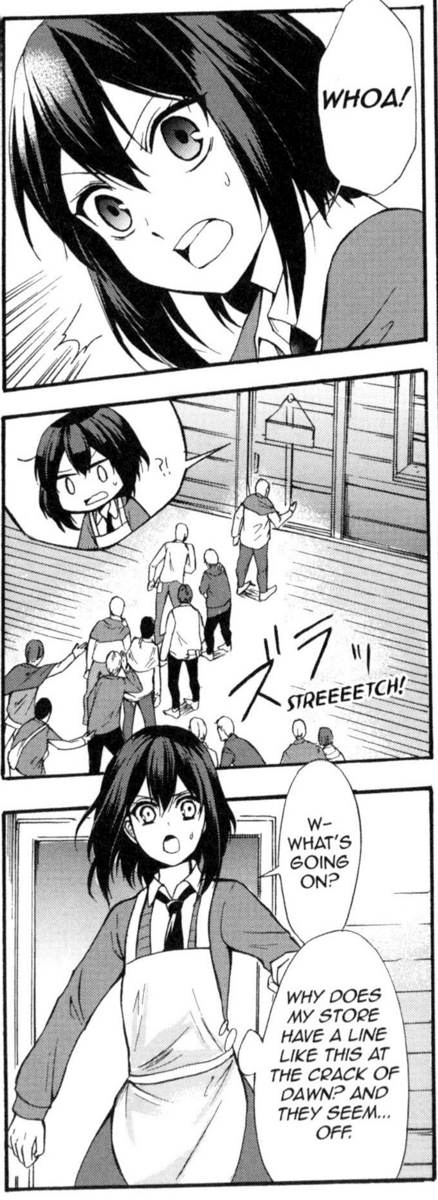
WHOA!
?!
ズラッ
STREEEETCH!
W-WHAT'S GOING ON?
WHY DOES MY STORE HAVE A LINE LIKE THIS AT THE CRACK OF DAWN? AND THEY SEEM... OFF.

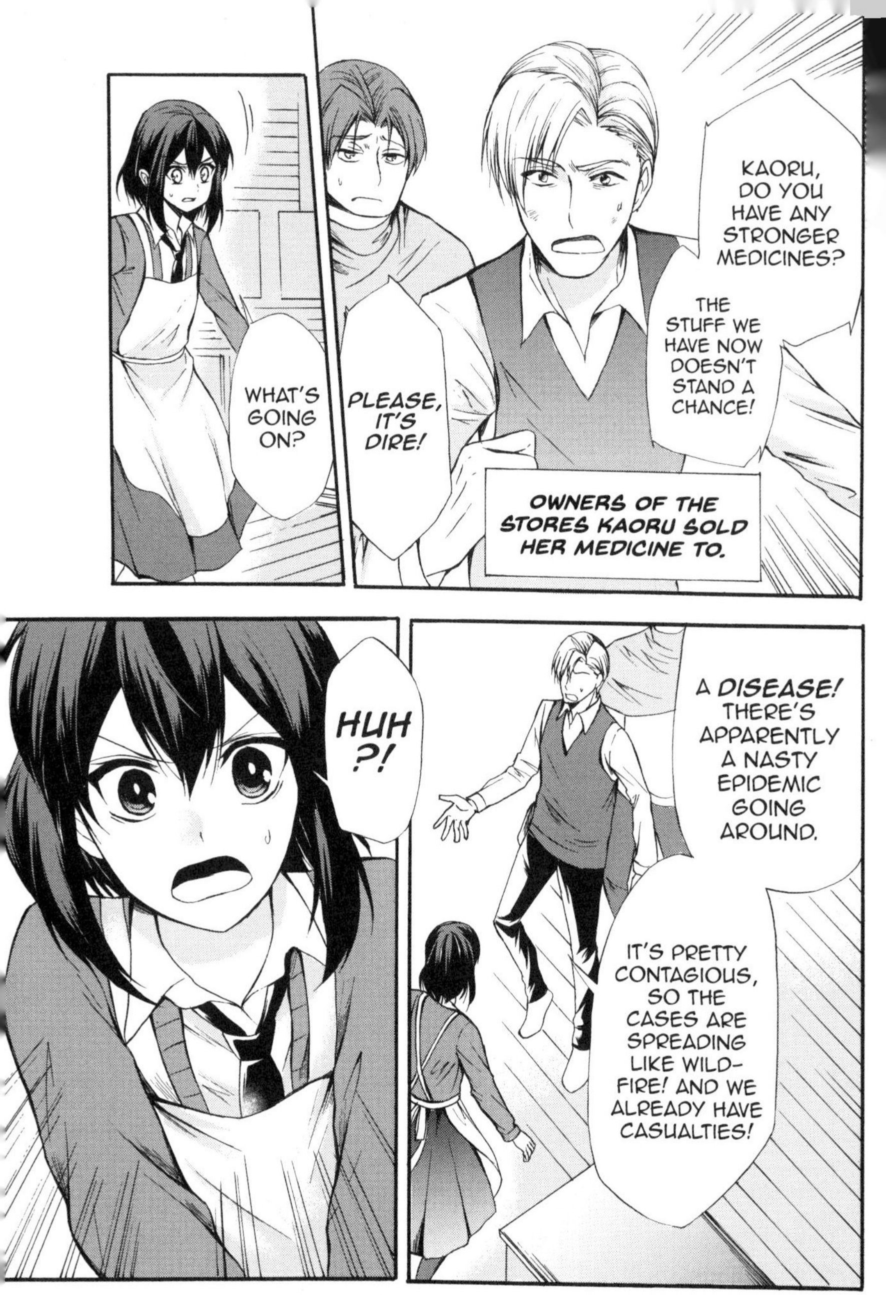
KAORU, DO YOU HAVE ANY STRONGER MEDICINES?
THE STUFF WE HAVE NOW DOESN'T STAND A CHANCE!
PLEASE, IT'S DIRE!
OWNERS OF THE STORES KAORU SOLD HER MEDICINE TO.
WHAT'S GOING ON?
A DISEASE! THERE'S APPARENTLY A NASTY EPIDEMIC GOING AROUND.
IT'S PRETTY CONTAGIOUS, SO THE CASES ARE SPREADING LIKE WILD-FIRE! AND WE ALREADY HAVE CASUALTIES!
HUH ?!

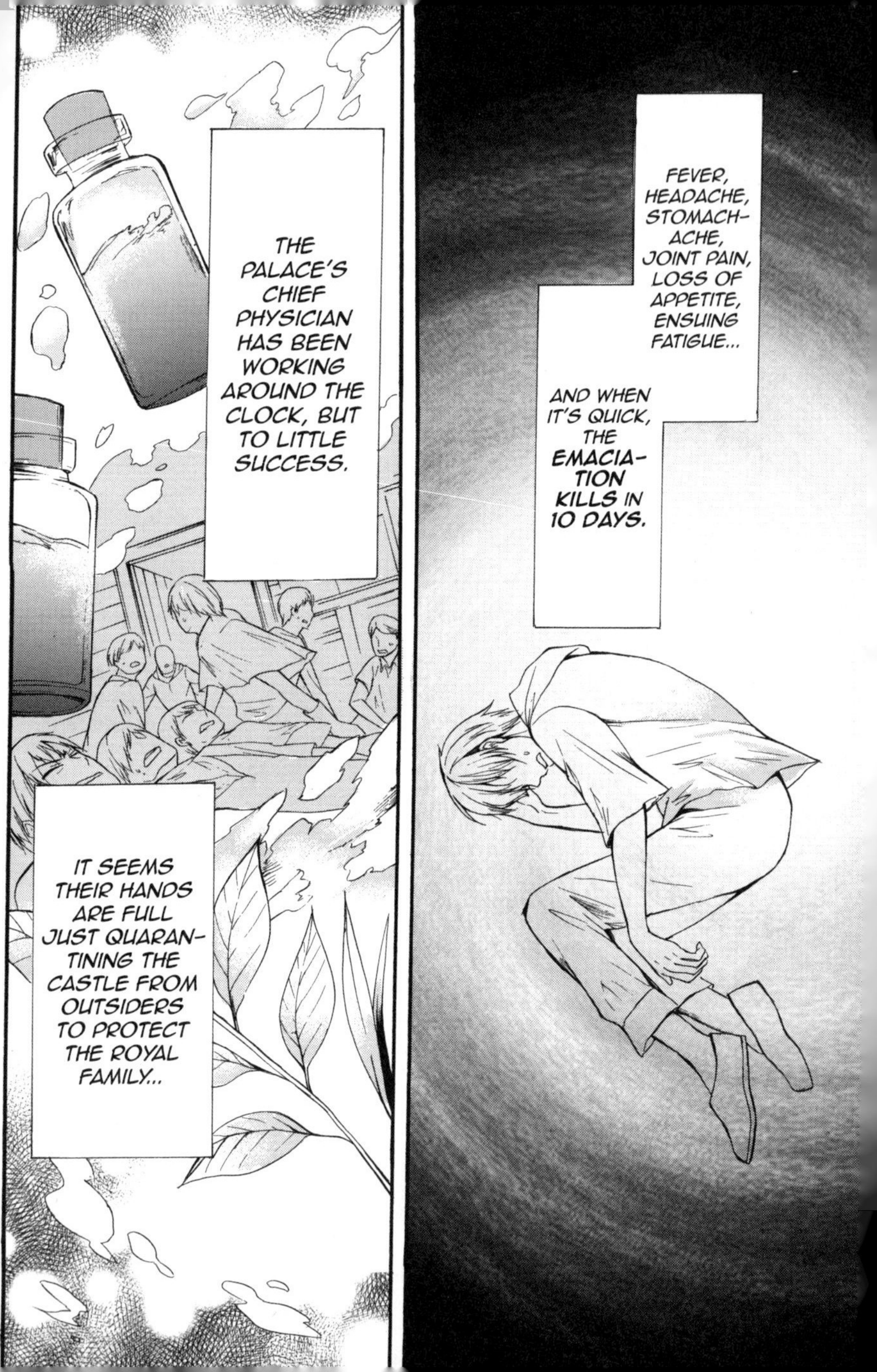
FEVER, HEADACHE, STOMACH-ACHE, JOINT PAIN, LOSS OF APPETITE, ENSUING FATIGUE...
AND WHEN IT'S QUICK, THE EMACIATION KILLS IN 10 DAYS.
THE PALACE'S CHIEF PHYSICIAN HAS BEEN WORKING AROUND THE CLOCK, BUT TO LITTLE SUCCESS.
IT SEEMS THEIR HANDS ARE FULL JUST QUARANTINING THE CASTLE FROM OUTSIDERS TO PROTECT THE ROYAL FAMILY...

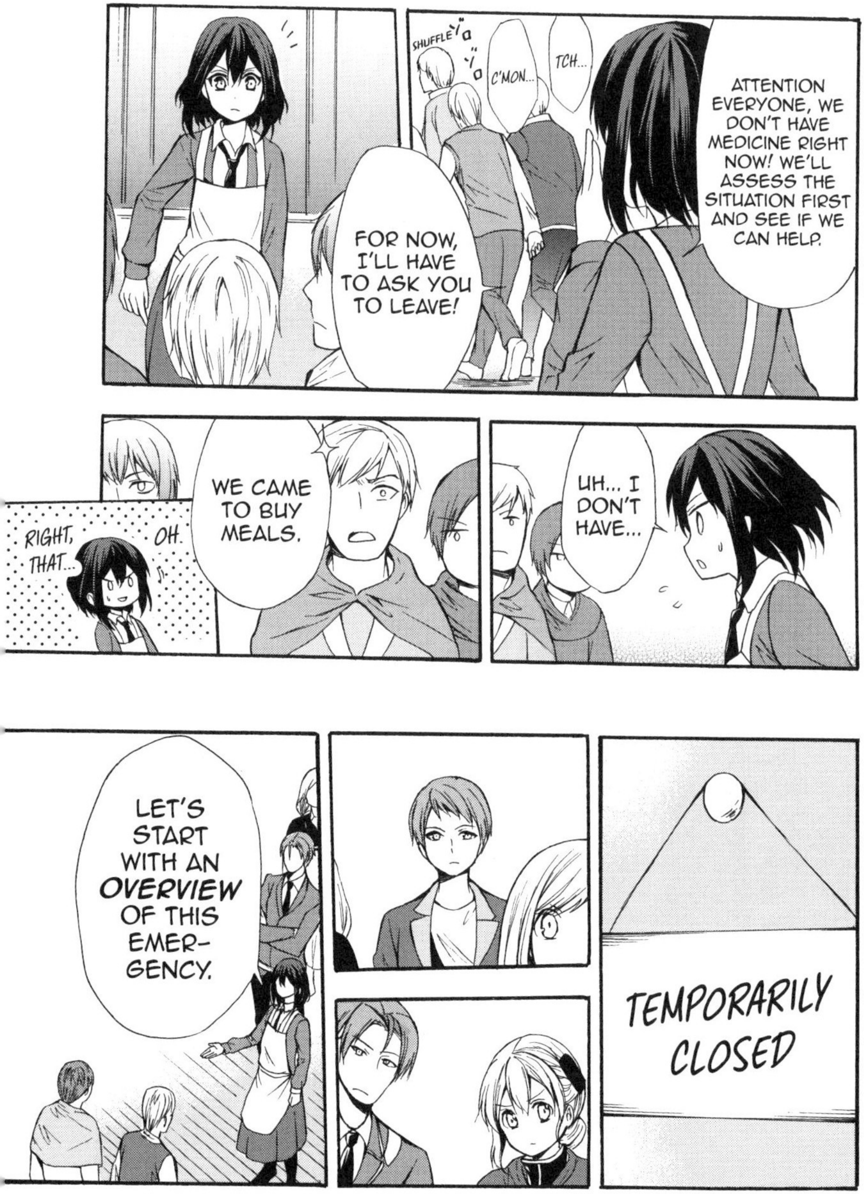
ATTENTION EVERYONE, WE DON'T HAVE MEDICINE RIGHT NOW! WE'LL ASSESS THE SITUATION FIRST AND SEE IF WE CAN HELP.
TCH...
C'MON...
SHUFFLE
FOR NOW, I'LL HAVE TO ASK YOU TO LEAVE!
UH... I DON'T HAVE...
WE CAME TO BUY MEALS.
OH.
RIGHT, THAT...
TEMPORARILY CLOSED
LET'S START WITH AN OVERVIEW OF THIS EMER- GENCY.

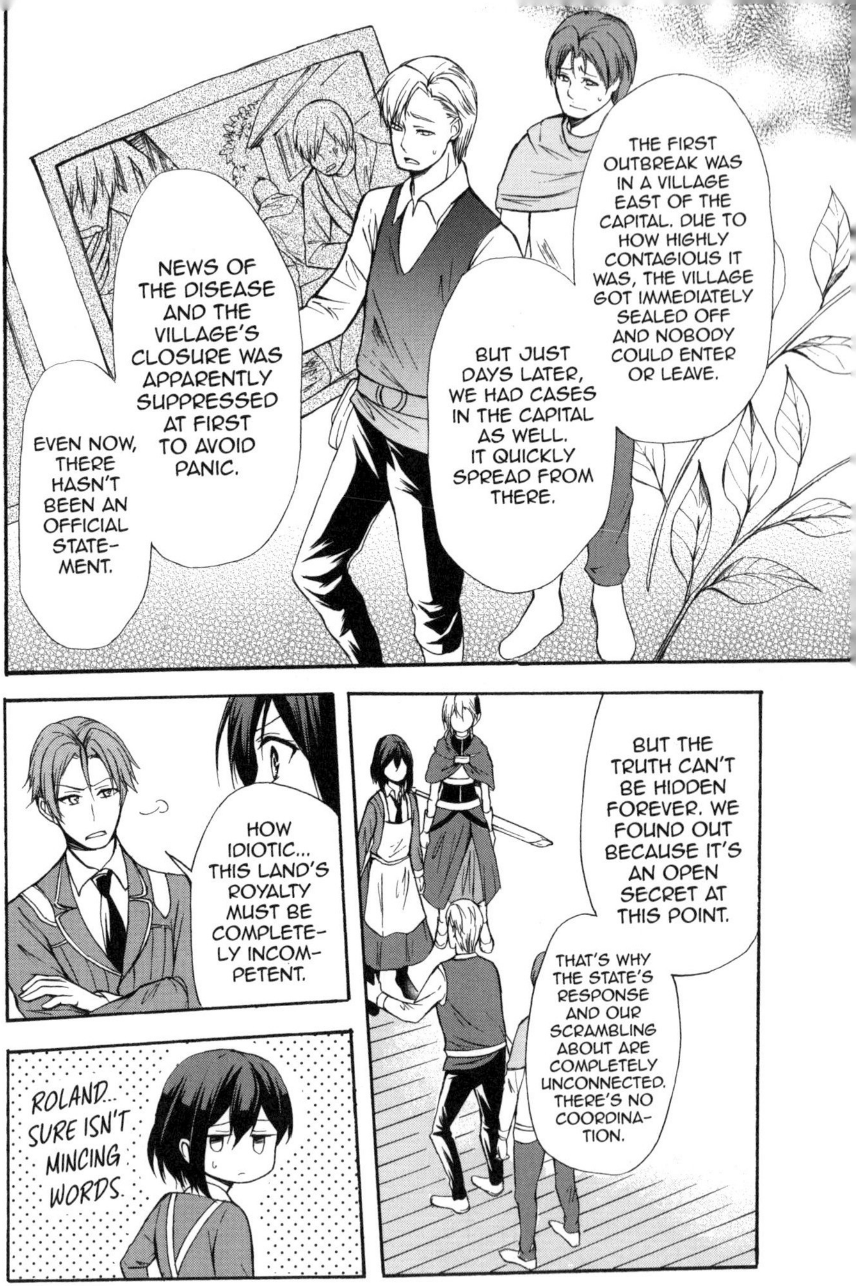
THE FIRST OUTBREAK WAS IN A VILLAGE EAST OF THE CAPITAL. DUE TO HOW HIGHLY CONTAGIOUS IT WAS, THE VILLAGE GOT IMMEDIATELY SEALED OFF AND NOBODY COULD ENTER OR LEAVE.
BUT JUST DAYS LATER, WE HAD CASES IN THE CAPITAL AS WELL. IT QUICKLY SPREAD FROM THERE.
NEWS OF THE DISEASE AND THE VILLAGE'S CLOSURE WAS APPARENTLY SUPPRESSED AT FIRST TO AVOID PANIC.
EVEN NOW, THERE HASN'T BEEN AN OFFICIAL STATE-MENT.
BUT THE TRUTH CAN'T BE HIDDEN FOREVER. WE FOUND OUT BECAUSE IT'S AN OPEN SECRET AT THIS POINT.
THAT'S WHY THE STATE'S RESPONSE AND OUR SCRAMBLING ABOUT ARE COMPLETELY UNCONNECTED. THERE'S NO COORDINA-TION.
HOW IDIOTIC... THIS LAND'S ROYALTY MUST BE COMPLETE-LY INCOM-PETENT.
ROLAND... SURE ISN'T MINCING WORDS.

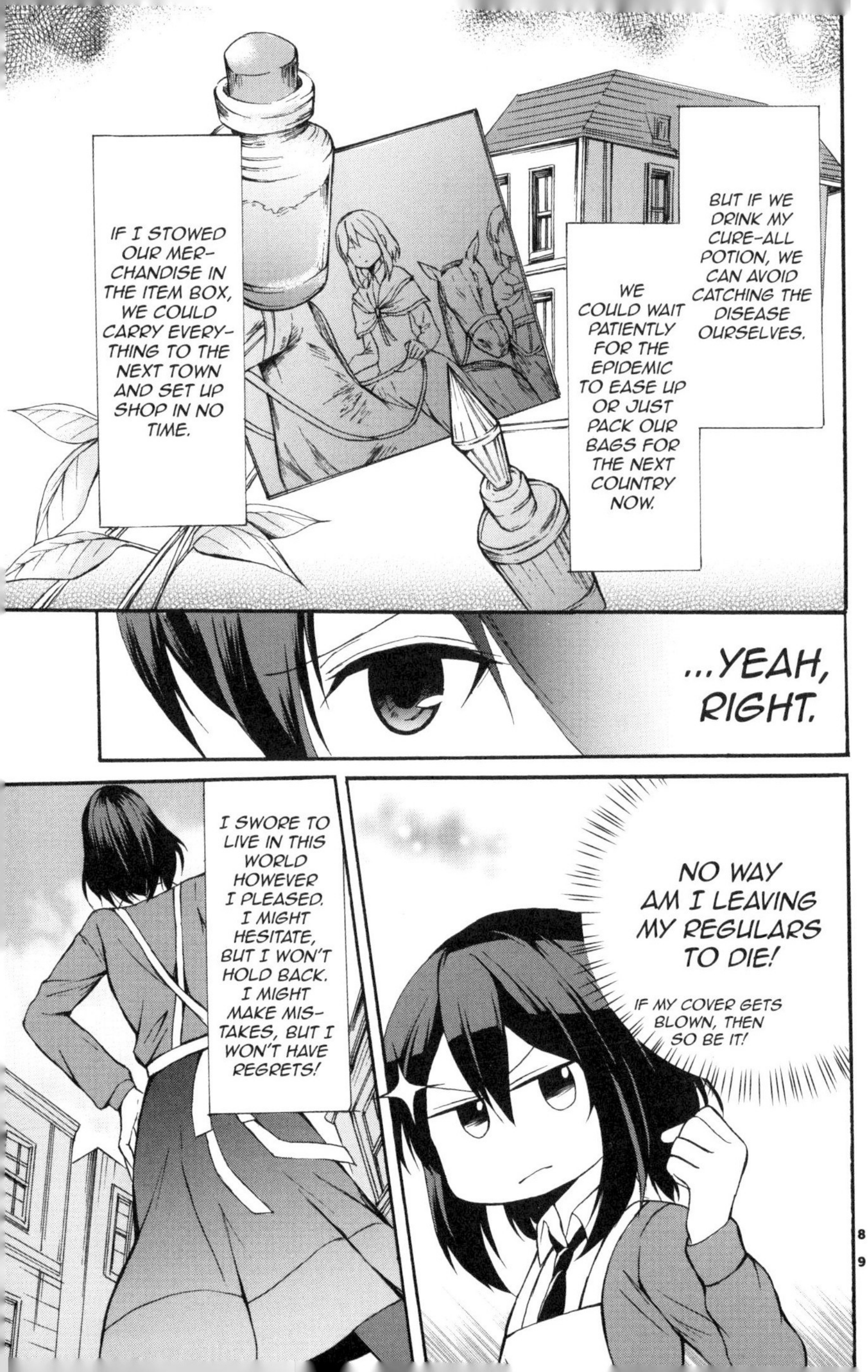
BUT IF WE DRINK MY CURE-ALL POTION, WE CAN AVOID CATCHING THE DISEASE OURSELVES.
WE COULD WAIT PATIENTLY FOR THE EPIDEMIC TO EASE UP OR JUST PACK OUR BAGS FOR THE NEXT COUNTRY NOW.
IF I STOWED OUR MER-CHANDISE IN THE ITEM BOX, WE COULD CARRY EVERY-THING TO THE NEXT TOWN AND SET UP SHOP IN NO TIME.
...YEAH, RIGHT.
NO WAY AM I LEAVING MY REGULARS TO DIE!
IF MY COVER GETS BLOWN, THEN SO BE IT!
I SWORE TO LIVE IN THIS WORLD HOWEVER I PLEASED. I MIGHT HESITATE, BUT I WON'T HOLD BACK. I MIGHT MAKE MIS-TAKES, BUT I WON'T HAVE REGRETS!

*FOR DETAILS, SEE VOLUME 6, PAGE 36.

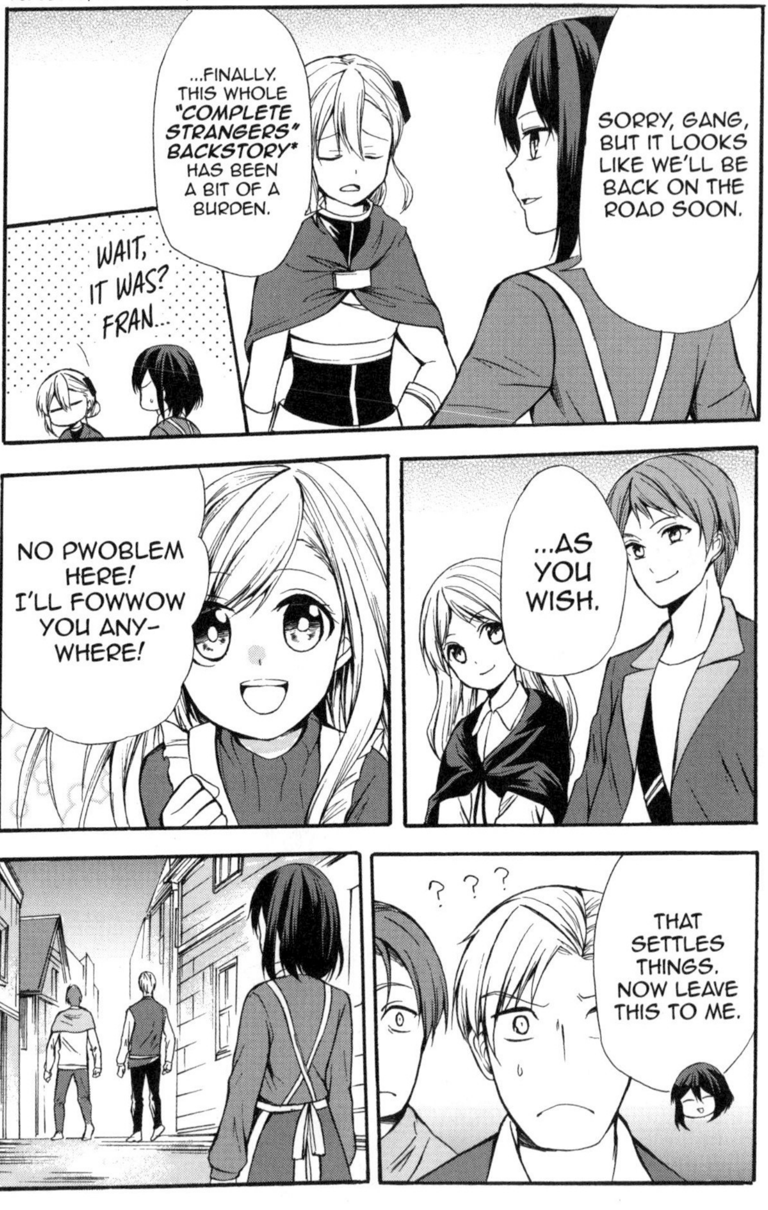
SORRY, GANG, BUT IT LOOKS LIKE WE'LL BE BACK ON THE ROAD SOON.
...FINALLY. THIS WHOLE "COMPLETE STRANGERS" BACKSTORY* HAS BEEN A BIT OF A BURDEN.
WAIT, IT WAS? FRAN...
...AS YOU WISH.
NO PWOBLEM HERE! I'LL FOWWOW YOU ANY-WHERE!
???
THAT SETTLES THINGS. NOW LEAVE THIS TO ME.

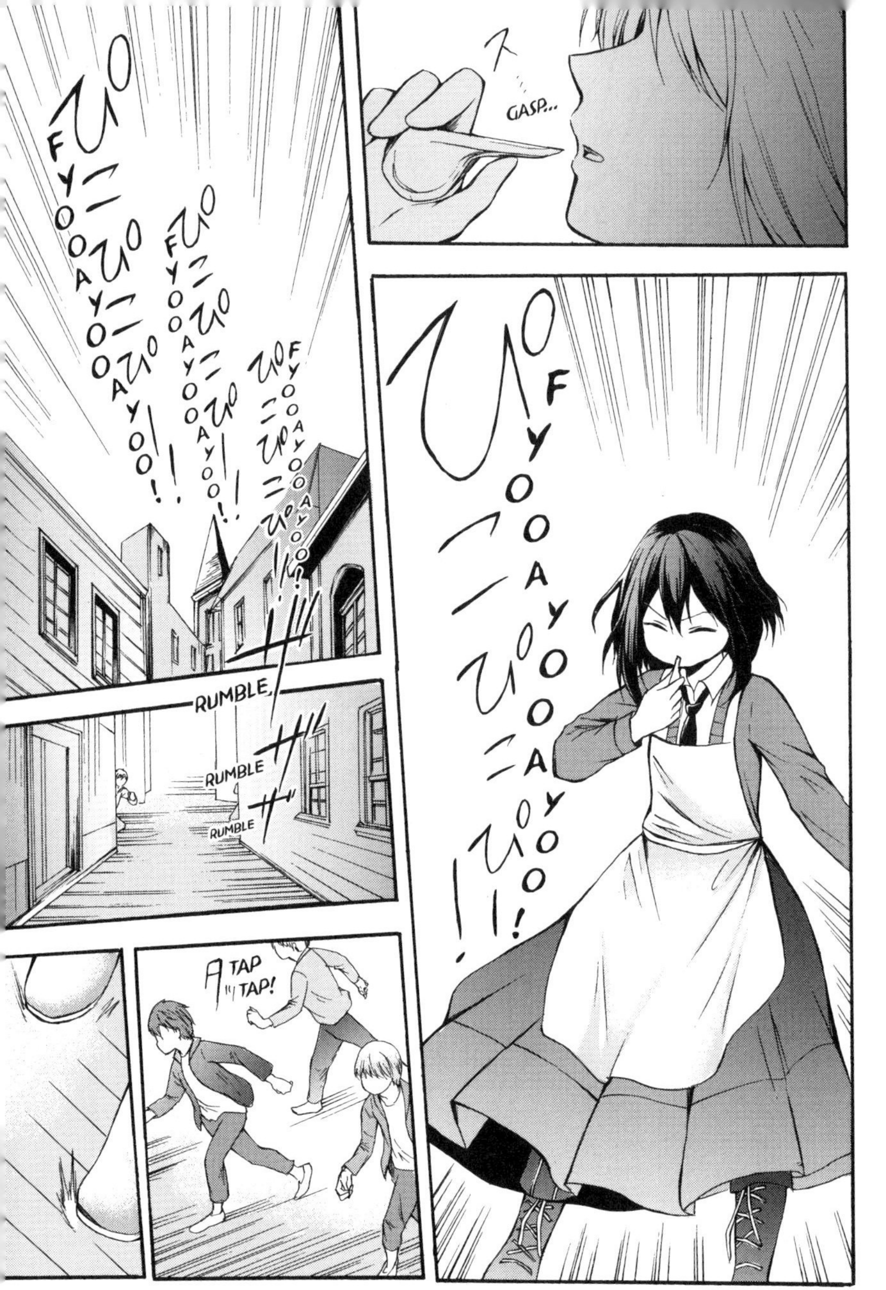
GASP...
FYOOOAYOOOAYOO!!
FYOOAYOOOAYOO!!
FYOOAYOOAYOOO!!
FYOOAYOOAYOOO!!
RUMBLE
RUMBLE
RUMBLE
TAP TAP!

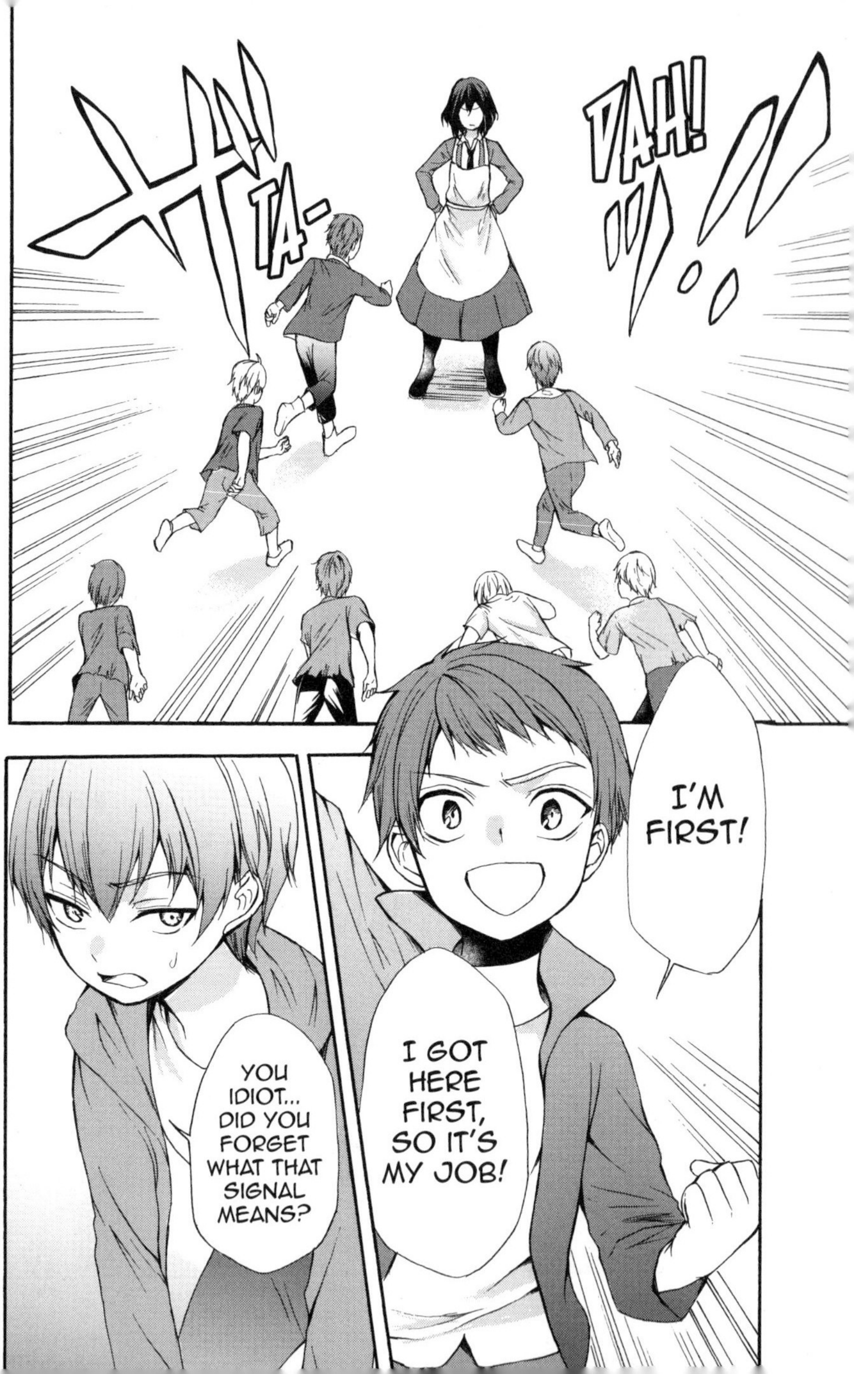
TA-
DAH!
I'M FIRST!
I GOT HERE FIRST, SO IT'S MY JOB!
YOU IDIOT... DID YOU FORGET WHAT THAT SIGNAL MEANS?

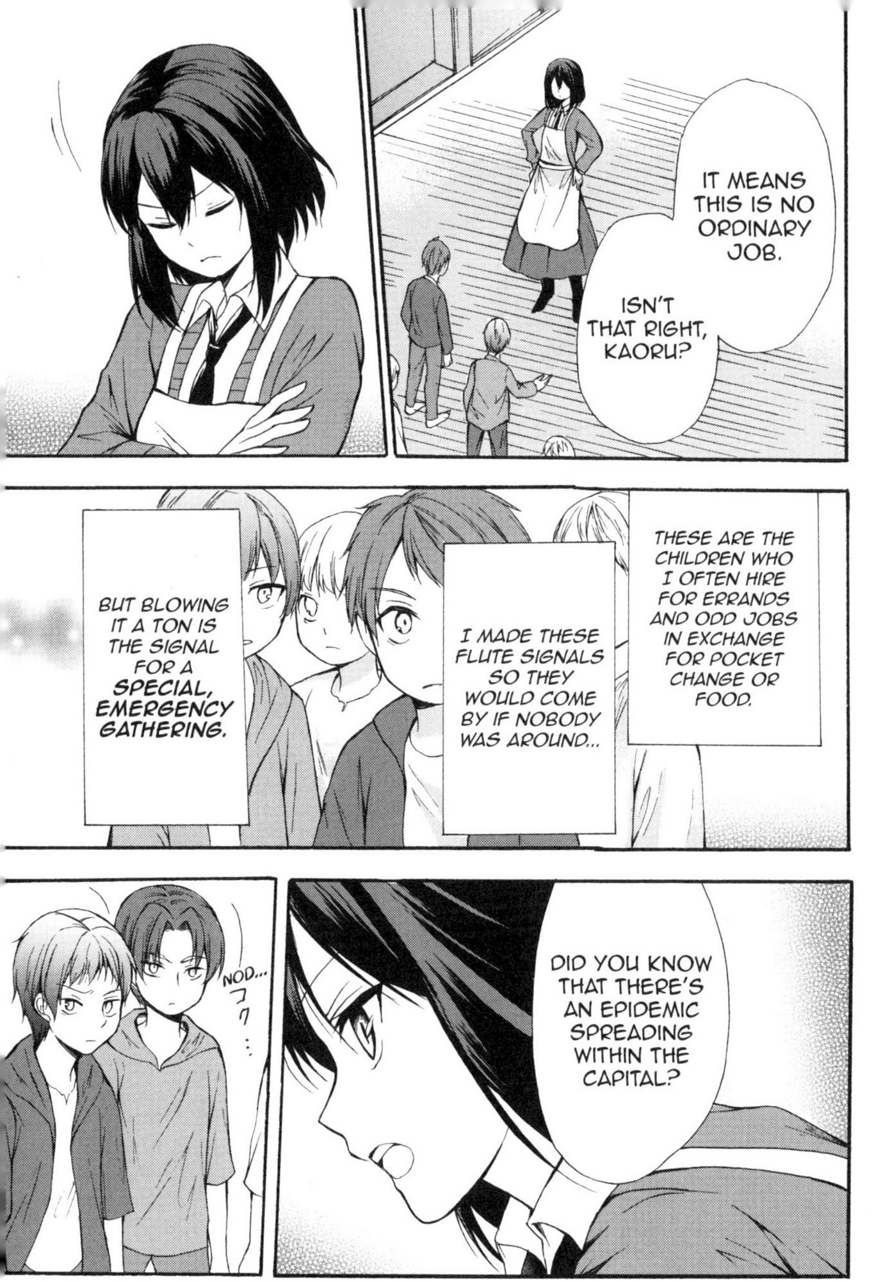
IT MEANS THIS IS NO ORDINARY JOB.
ISN'T THAT RIGHT, KAORU?
THESE ARE THE CHILDREN WHO I OFTEN HIRE FOR ERRANDS AND ODD JOBS IN EXCHANGE FOR POCKET CHANGE OR FOOD.
I MADE THESE FLUTE SIGNALS SO THEY WOULD COME BY IF NOBODY WAS AROUND...
BUT BLOWING IT A TON IS THE SIGNAL FOR A SPECIAL, EMERGENCY GATHERING.
DID YOU KNOW THAT THERE'S AN EPIDEMIC SPREADING WITHIN THE CAPITAL?
NOD...
コク…

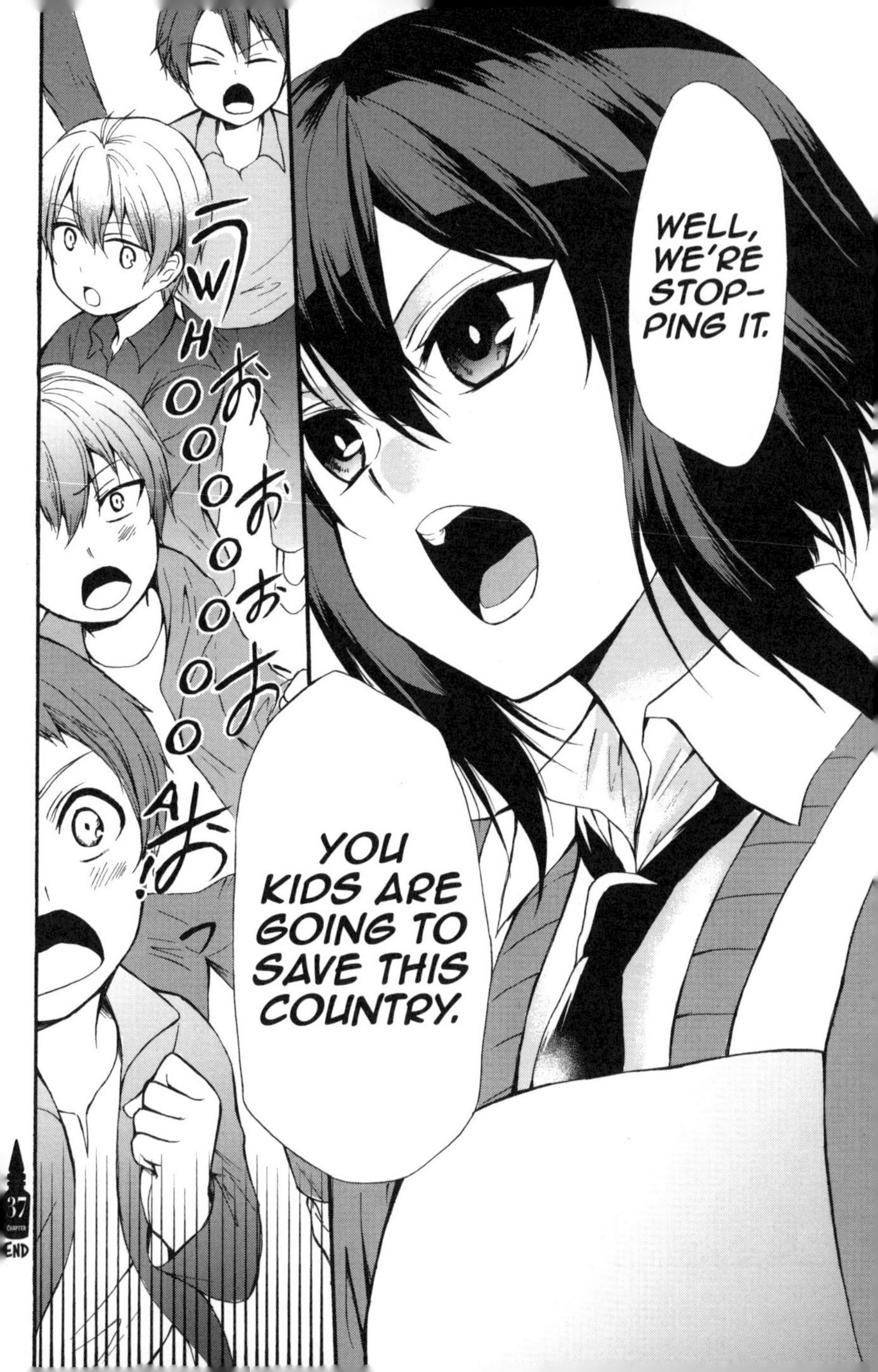
WELL, WE'RE STOPPING IT.
YOU KIDS ARE GOING TO SAVE THIS COUNTRY.
うおおおおお
WHOOOOOOOOA!!
37 CHAPTER END

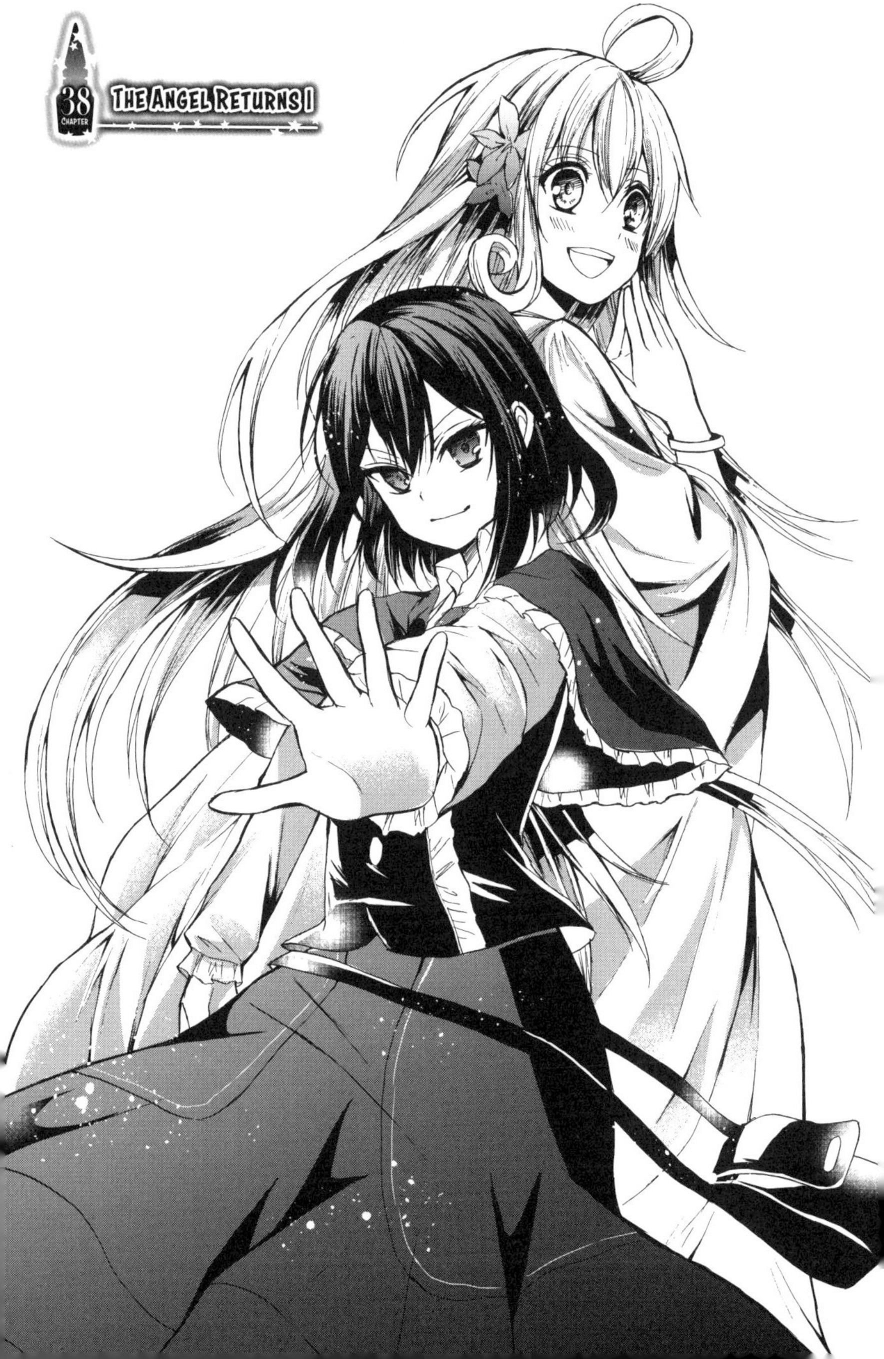
38
CHAPTER
THE ANGEL RETURNS I

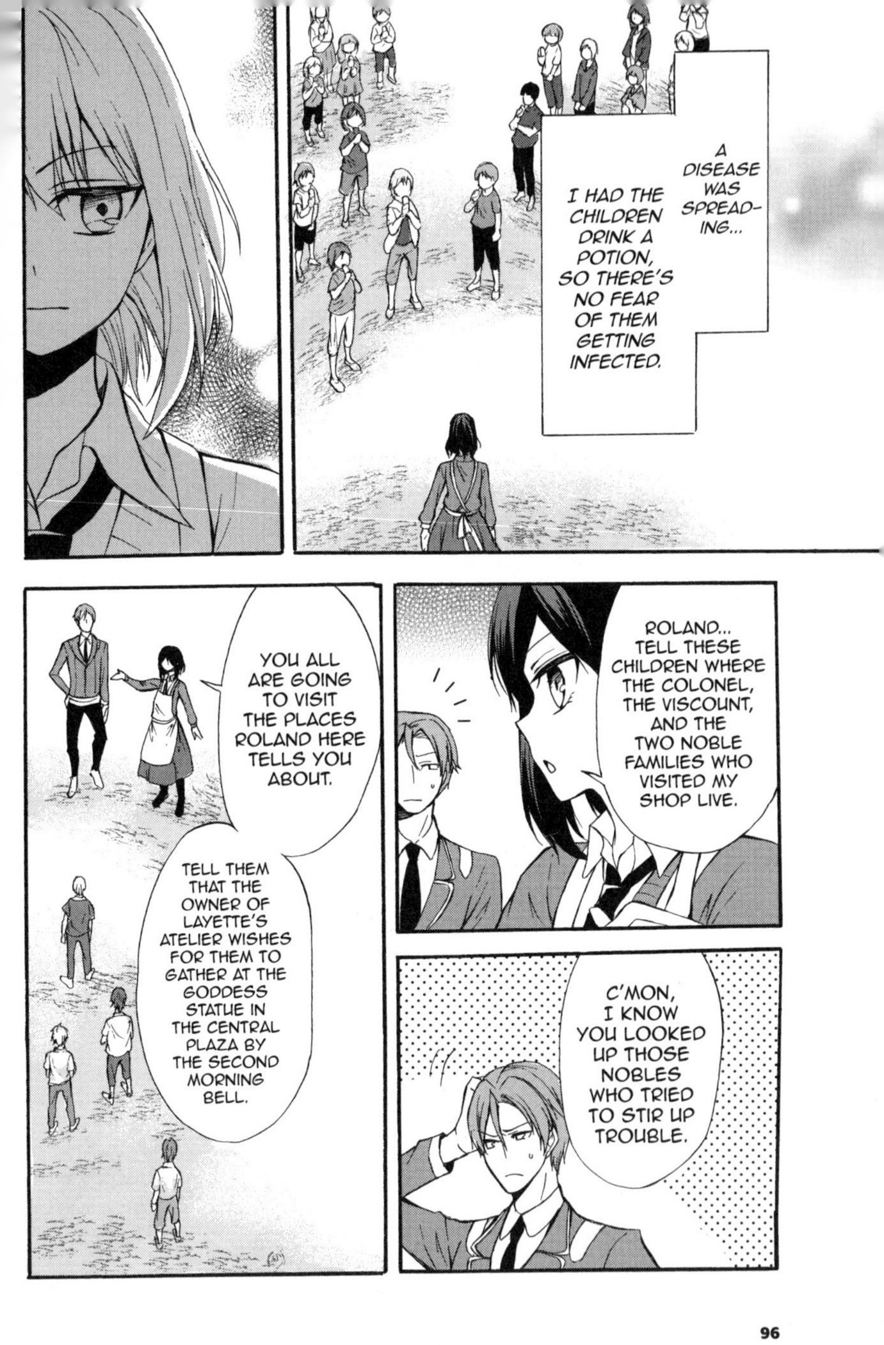
A DISEASE WAS SPREAD-ING...
I HAD THE CHILDREN DRINK A POTION, SO THERE'S NO FEAR OF THEM GETTING INFECTED.
ROLAND... TELL THESE CHILDREN WHERE THE COLONEL, THE VISCOUNT, AND THE TWO NOBLE FAMILIES WHO VISITED MY SHOP LIVE.
C'MON, I KNOW YOU LOOKED UP THOSE NOBLES WHO TRIED TO STIR UP TROUBLE.
YOU ALL ARE GOING TO VISIT THE PLACES ROLAND HERE TELLS YOU ABOUT.
TELL THEM THAT THE OWNER OF LAYETTE'S ATELIER WISHES FOR THEM TO GATHER AT THE GODDESS STATUE IN THE CENTRAL PLAZA BY THE SECOND MORNING BELL.

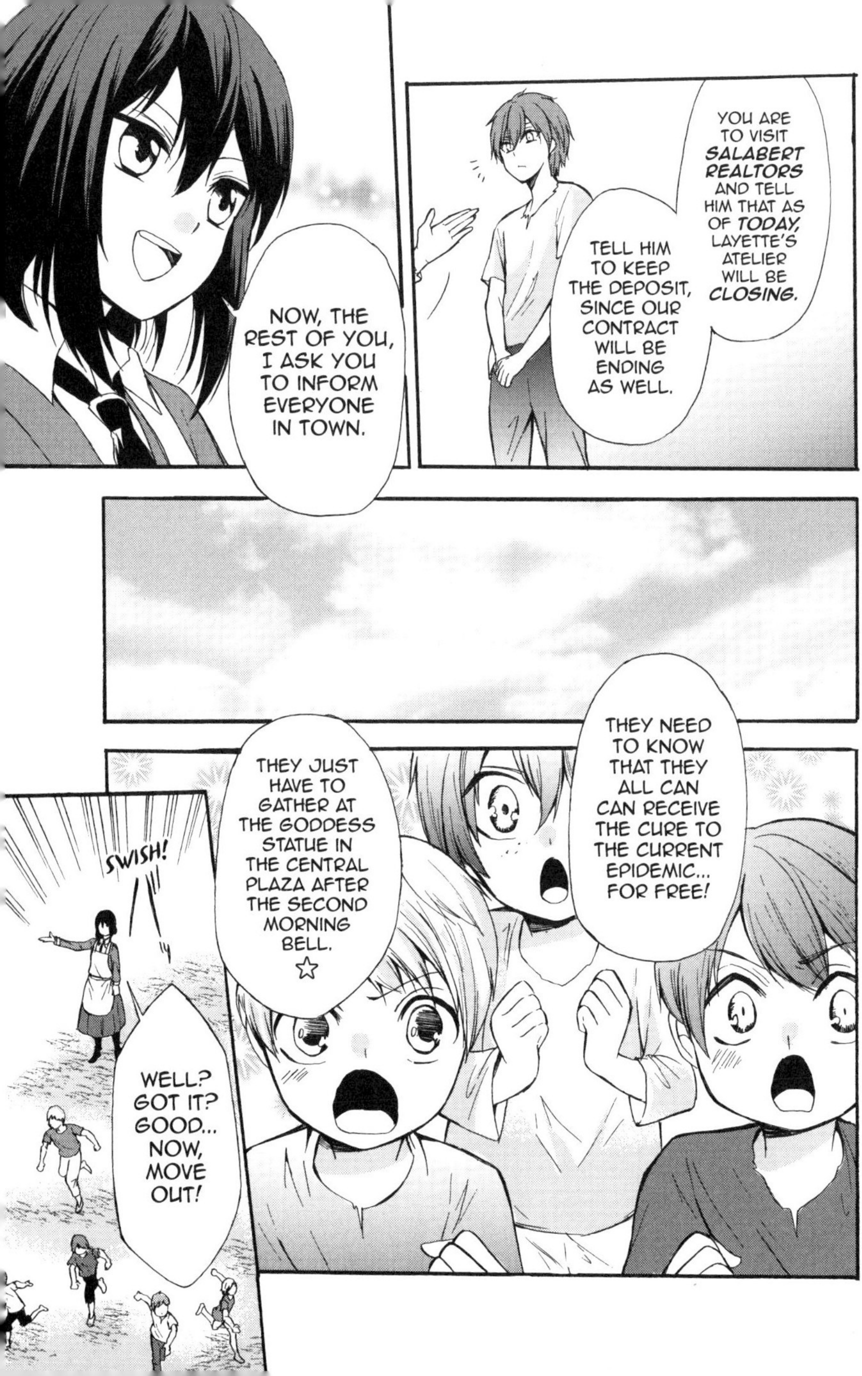
YOU ARE TO VISIT SALABERT REALTORS AND TELL HIM THAT AS OF TODAY, LAYETTE'S ATELIER WILL BE CLOSING.
TELL HIM TO KEEP THE DEPOSIT, SINCE OUR CONTRACT WILL BE ENDING AS WELL.
NOW, THE REST OF YOU, I ASK YOU TO INFORM EVERYONE IN TOWN.
THEY NEED TO KNOW THAT THEY ALL CAN CAN RECEIVE THE CURE TO THE CURRENT EPIDEMIC... FOR FREE!
THEY JUST HAVE TO GATHER AT THE GODDESS STATUE IN THE CENTRAL PLAZA AFTER THE SECOND MORNING BELL. ☆
SWISH!
WELL? GOT IT? GOOD... NOW, MOVE OUT!

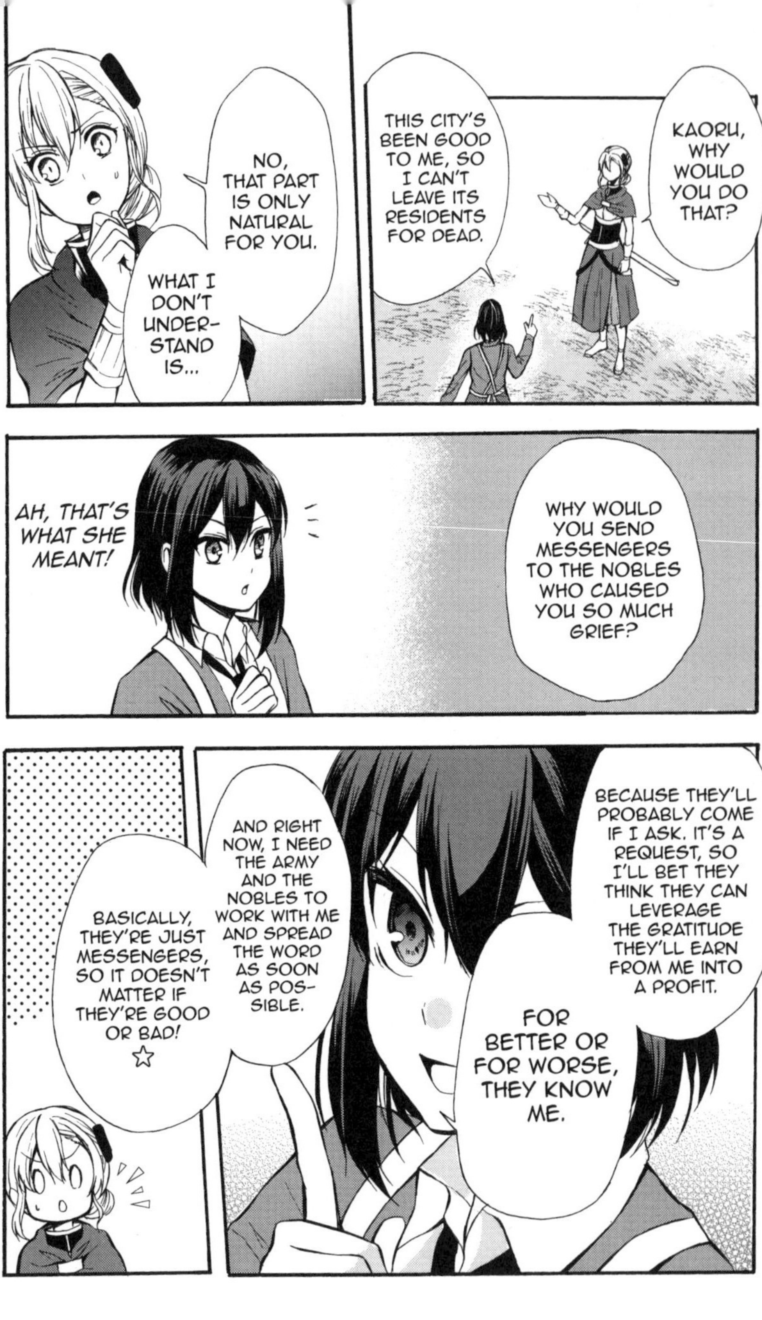
KAORU, WHY WOULD YOU DO THAT?
THIS CITY'S BEEN GOOD TO ME, SO I CAN'T LEAVE ITS RESIDENTS FOR DEAD.
NO, THAT PART IS ONLY NATURAL FOR YOU.
WHAT I DON'T UNDER-STAND IS...
WHY WOULD YOU SEND MESSENGERS TO THE NOBLES WHO CAUSED YOU SO MUCH GRIEF?
AH, THAT'S WHAT SHE MEANT!
BECAUSE THEY'LL PROBABLY COME IF I ASK. IT'S A REQUEST, SO I'LL BET THEY THINK THEY CAN LEVERAGE THE GRATITUDE THEY'LL EARN FROM ME INTO A PROFIT.
FOR BETTER OR FOR WORSE, THEY KNOW ME.
AND RIGHT NOW, I NEED THE ARMY AND THE NOBLES TO WORK WITH ME AND SPREAD THE WORD AS SOON AS POS-SIBLE.
BASICALLY, THEY'RE JUST MESSENGERS, SO IT DOESN'T MATTER IF THEY'RE GOOD OR BAD! ☆

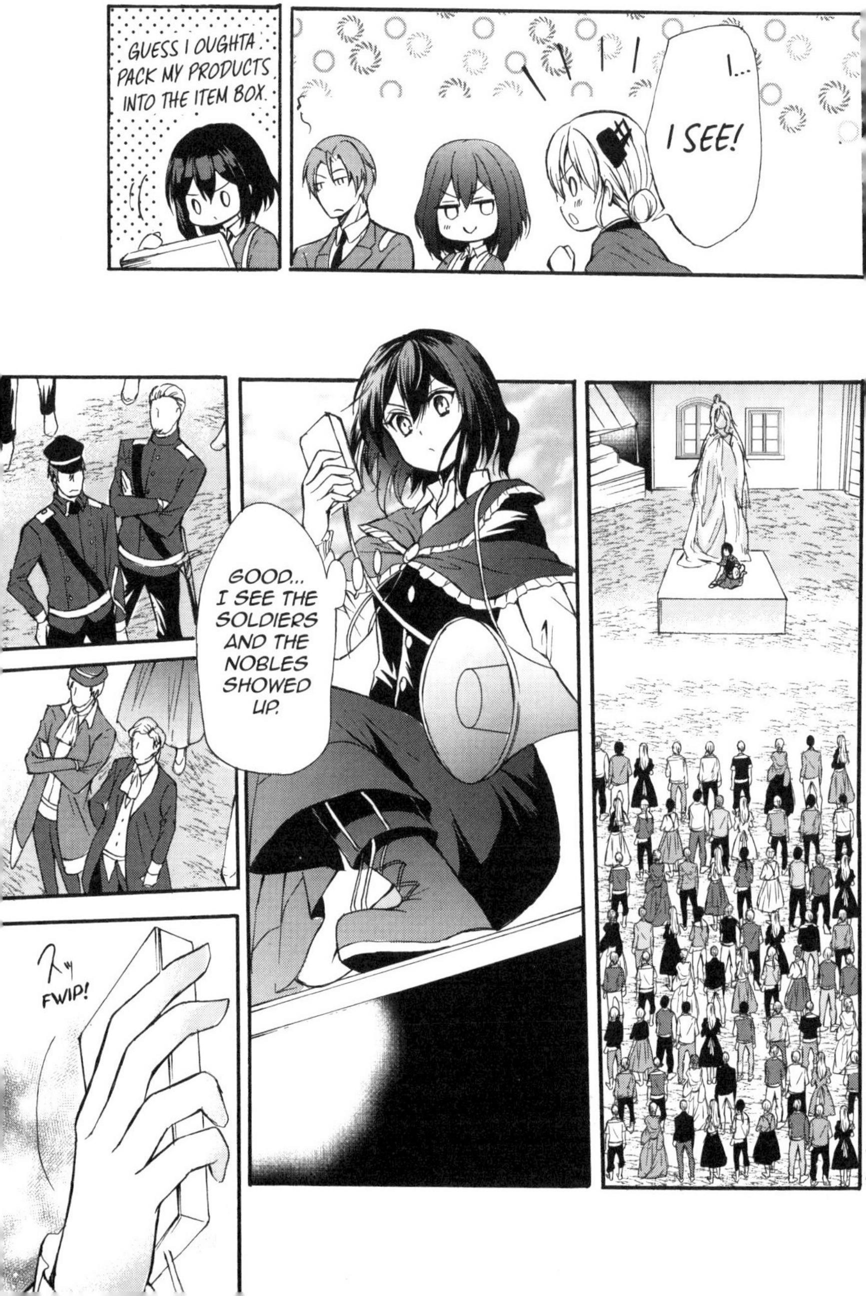
I...
I SEE!
GUESS I OUGHTA PACK MY PRODUCTS INTO THE ITEM BOX.
GOOD... I SEE THE SOLDIERS AND THE NOBLES SHOWED UP.
スッ
FWIP!

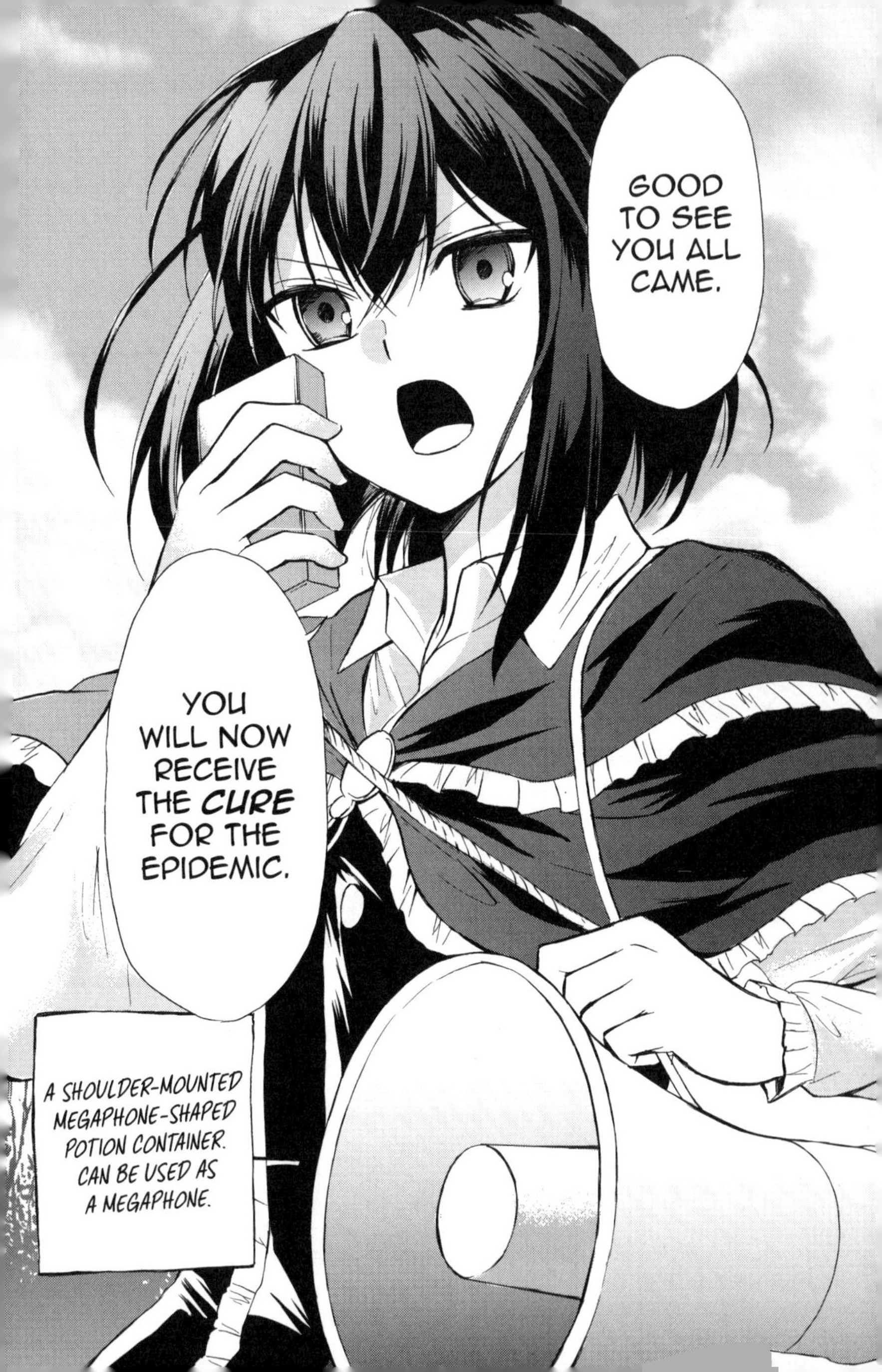
GOOD TO SEE YOU ALL CAME.
YOU WILL NOW RECEIVE THE CURE FOR THE EPIDEMIC.
A SHOULDER-MOUNTED MEGAPHONE-SHAPED POTION CONTAINER. CAN BE USED AS A MEGAPHONE.

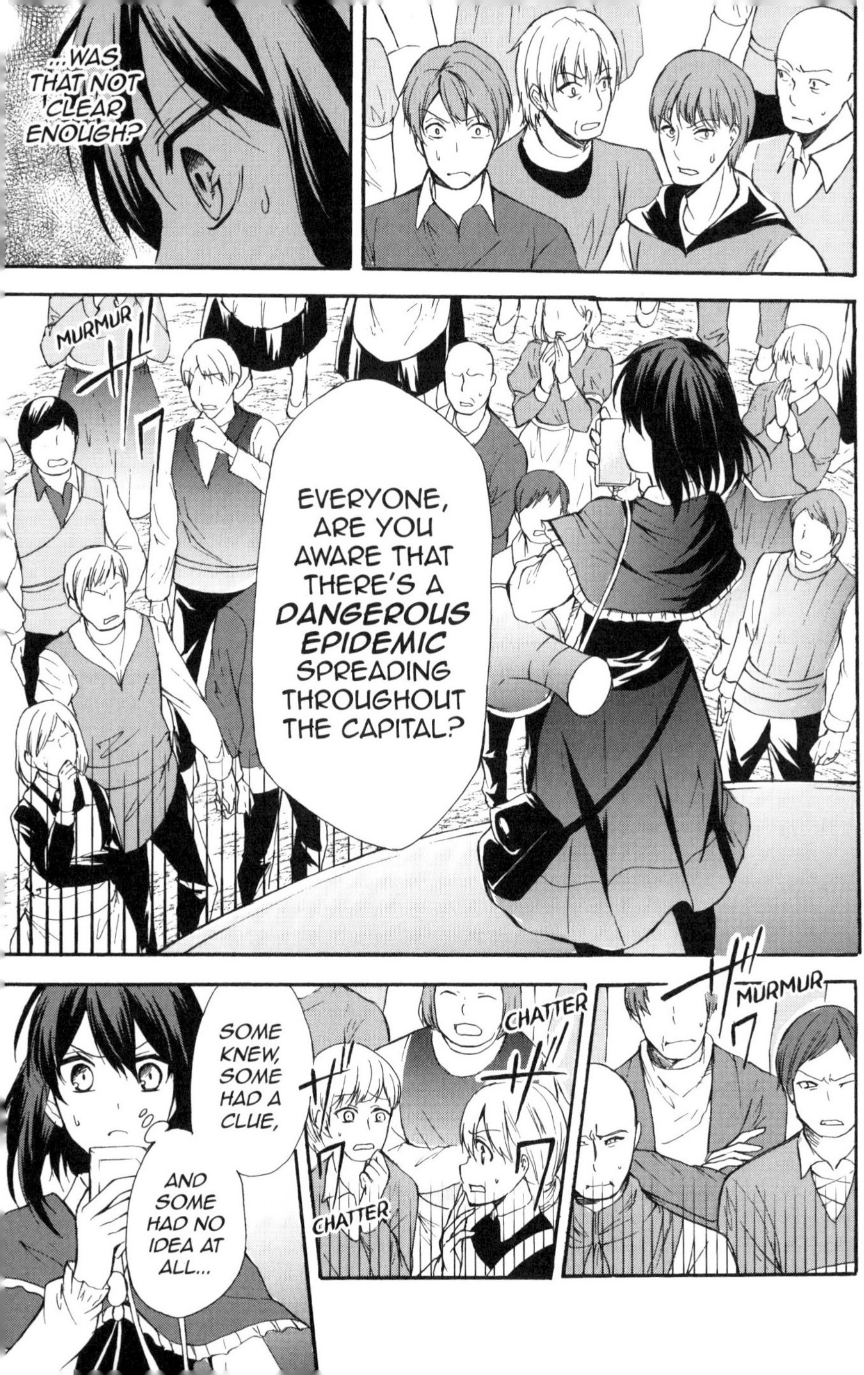
...WAS THAT NOT CLEAR ENOUGH?
MURMUR
EVERYONE, ARE YOU AWARE THAT THERE'S A DANGEROUS EPIDEMIC SPREADING THROUGHOUT THE CAPITAL?
MURMUR
CHATTER
CHATTER
SOME KNEW, SOME HAD A CLUE,
AND SOME HAD NO IDEA AT ALL...

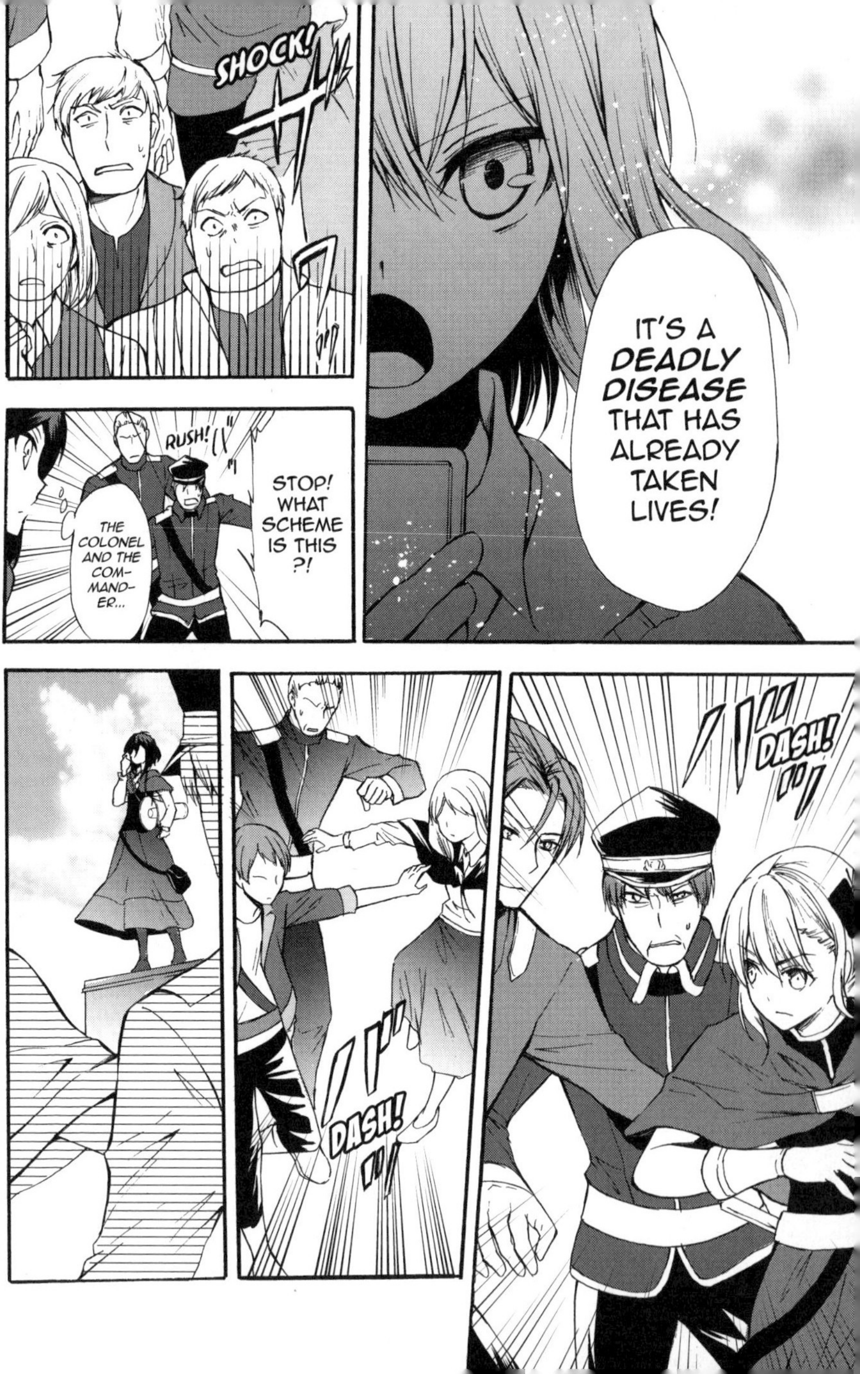
IT'S A DEADLY DISEASE THAT HAS ALREADY TAKEN LIVES!
SHOCK!
RUSH!
STOP! WHAT SCHEME IS THIS?!
THE COLONEL AND THE COM-MAND-ER...
DASH!
DASH!

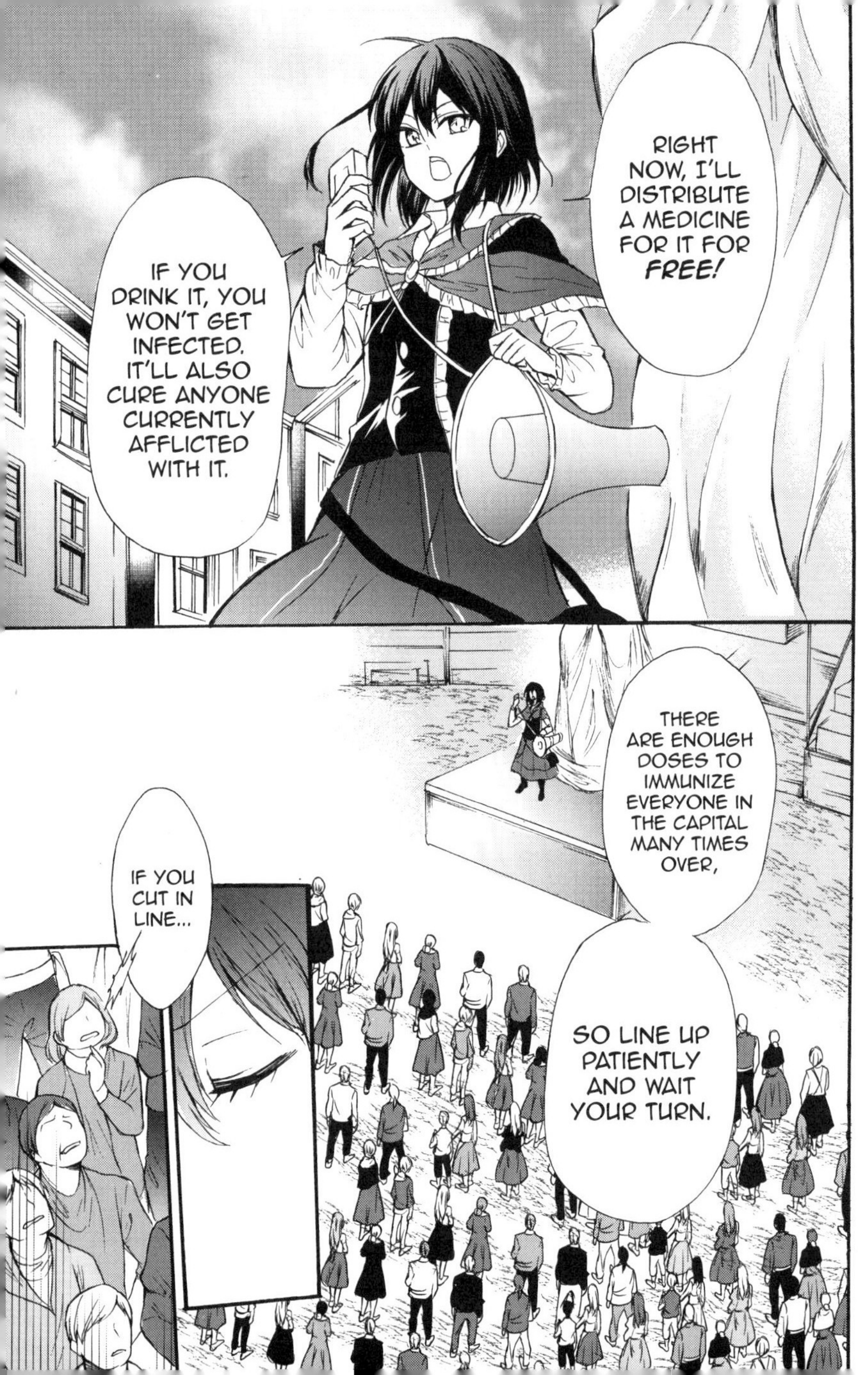
RIGHT NOW, I'LL DISTRIBUTE A MEDICINE FOR IT FOR *FREE!*
IF YOU DRINK IT, YOU WON'T GET INFECTED. IT'LL ALSO CURE ANYONE CURRENTLY AFFLICTED WITH IT.
THERE ARE ENOUGH DOSES TO IMMUNIZE EVERYONE IN THE CAPITAL MANY TIMES OVER,
SO LINE UP PATIENTLY AND WAIT YOUR TURN.
IF YOU CUT IN LINE...

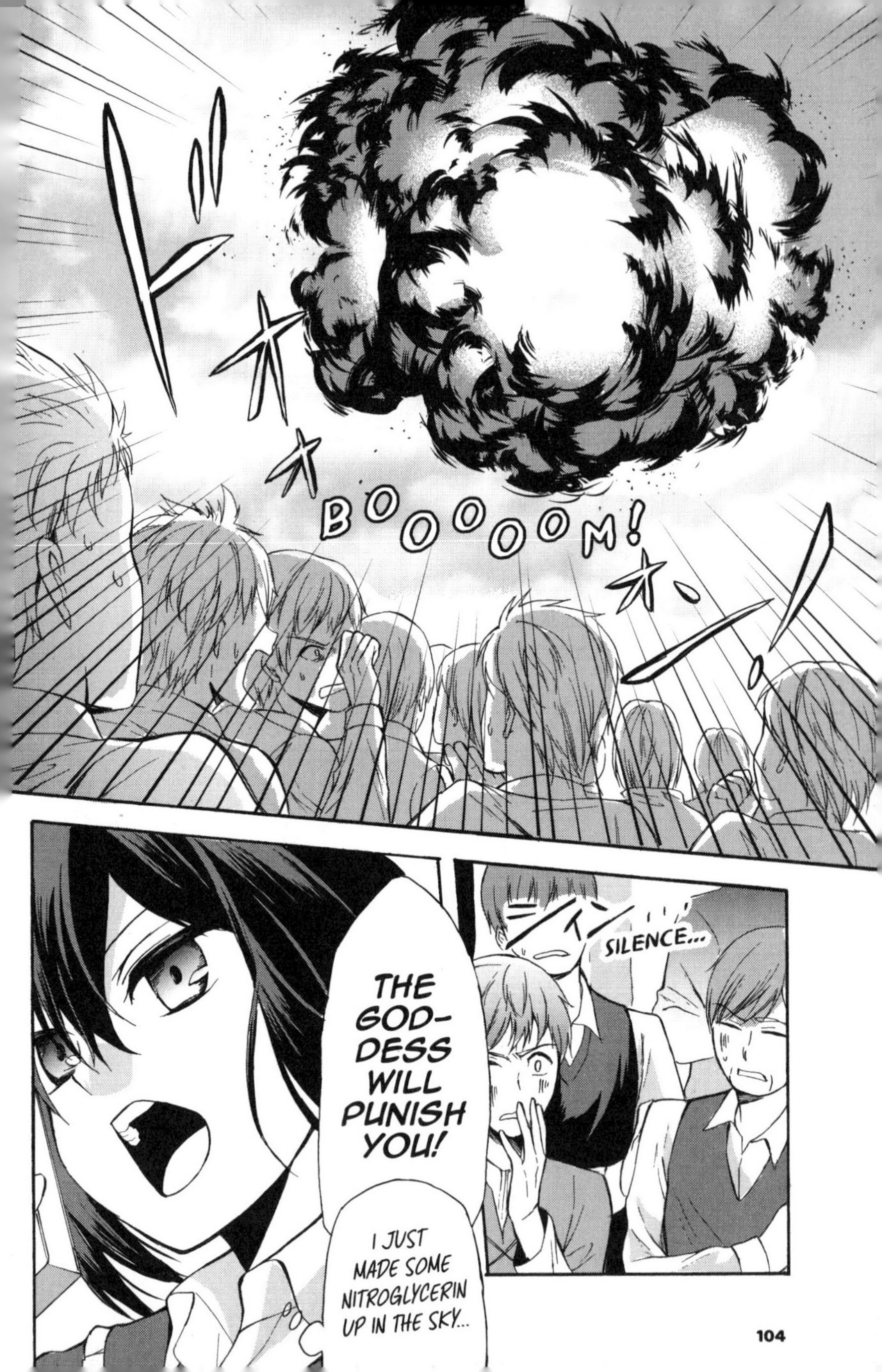
BOOOOOM!
SILENCE...
THE GODDESS WILL PUNISH YOU!
I JUST MADE SOME NITROGLYCERIN UP IN THE SKY...

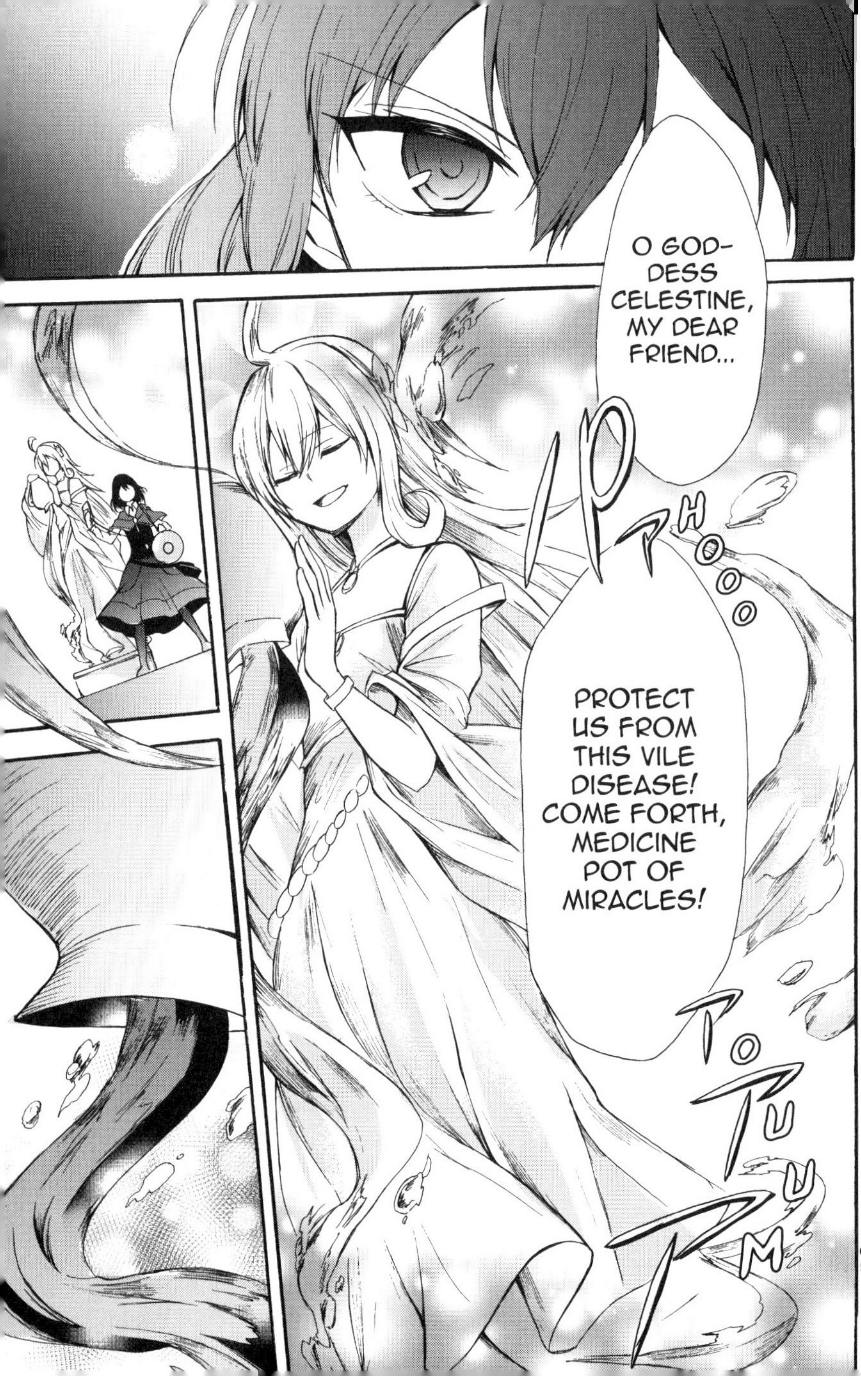
O GOD-DESS CELESTINE, MY DEAR FRIEND...
PHOOOO
PROTECT US FROM THIS VILE DISEASE! COME FORTH, MEDICINE POT OF MIRACLES!
POUUUM

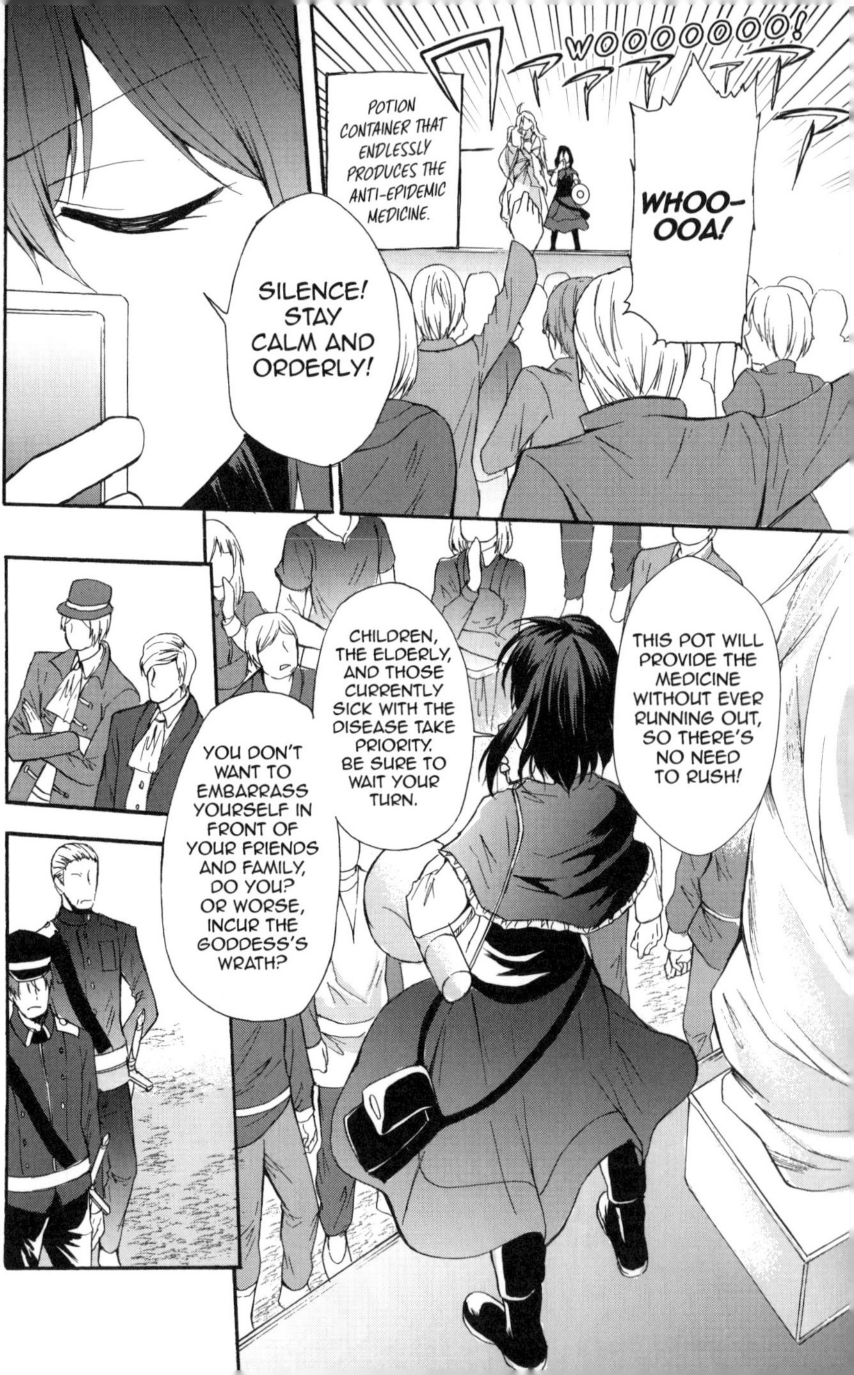
WOOOOOOO!
WHOO-OOA!
POTION CONTAINER THAT ENDLESSLY PRODUCES THE ANTI-EPIDEMIC MEDICINE.
SILENCE! STAY CALM AND ORDERLY!
THIS POT WILL PROVIDE THE MEDICINE WITHOUT EVER RUNNING OUT, SO THERE'S NO NEED TO RUSH!
CHILDREN, THE ELDERLY, AND THOSE CURRENTLY SICK WITH THE DISEASE TAKE PRIORITY. BE SURE TO WAIT YOUR TURN.
YOU DON'T WANT TO EMBARRASS YOURSELF IN FRONT OF YOUR FRIENDS AND FAMILY, DO YOU? OR WORSE, INCUR THE GODDESS'S WRATH?

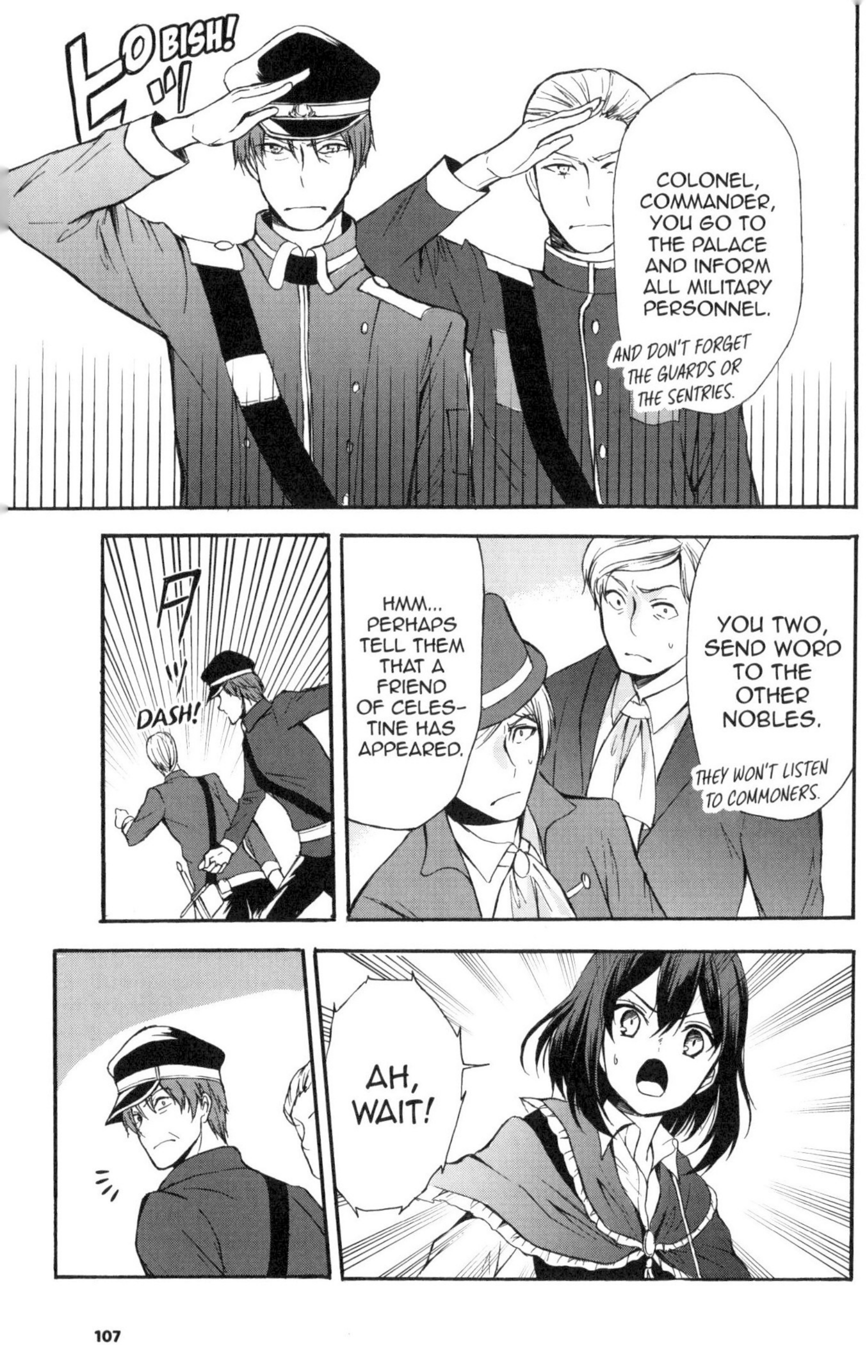

COLONEL, COMMANDER, YOU GO TO THE PALACE AND INFORM ALL MILITARY PERSONNEL.
AND DON'T FORGET THE GUARDS OR THE SENTRIES.
BISH!
YOU TWO, SEND WORD TO THE OTHER NOBLES.
THEY WON'T LISTEN TO COMMONERS.
HMM... PERHAPS TELL THEM THAT A FRIEND OF CELES-TINE HAS APPEARED.
DASH!
AH, WAIT!

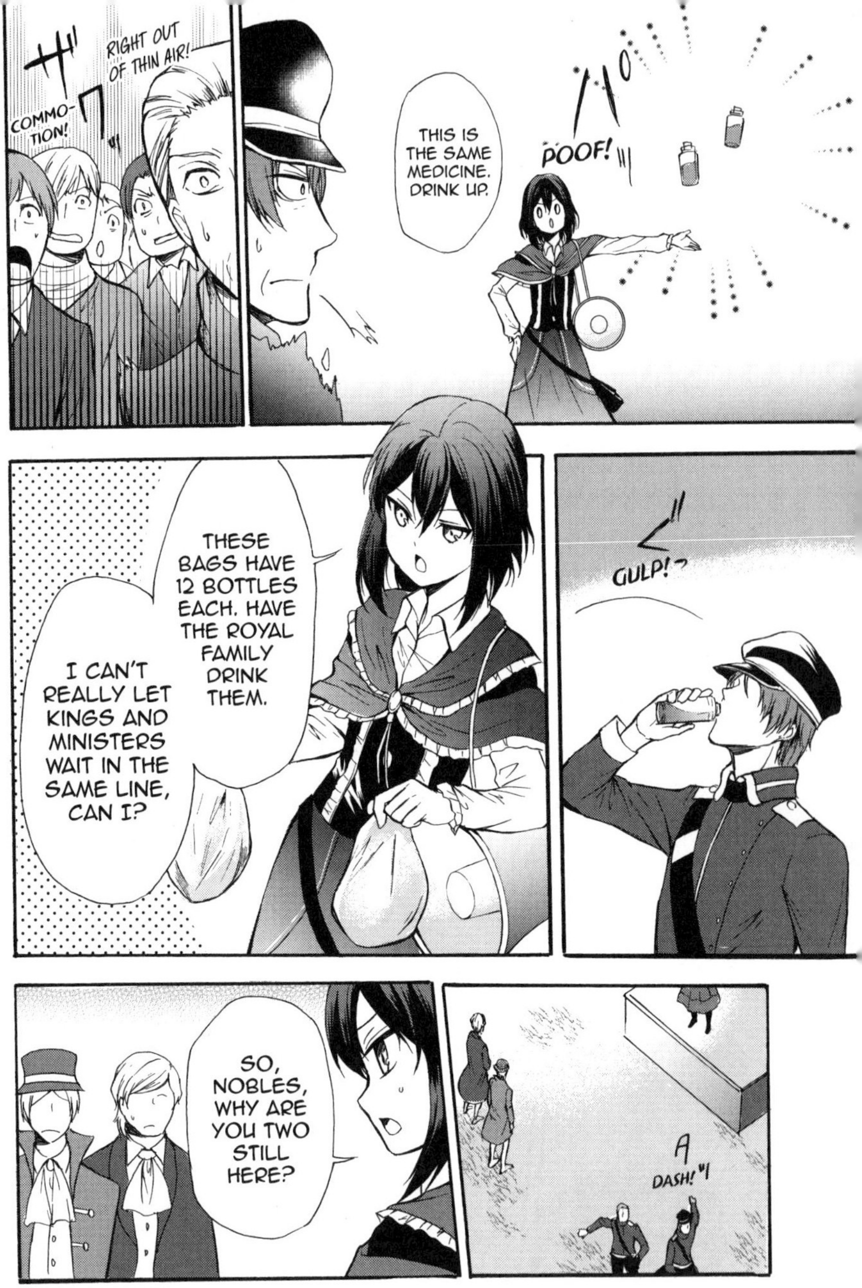
POOF!
THIS IS THE SAME MEDICINE. DRINK UP.
COMMOTION!
RIGHT OUT OF THIN AIR!
GULP!
THESE BAGS HAVE 12 BOTTLES EACH. HAVE THE ROYAL FAMILY DRINK THEM.
I CAN'T REALLY LET KINGS AND MINISTERS WAIT IN THE SAME LINE, CAN I?
DASH!
SO, NOBLES, WHY ARE YOU TWO STILL HERE?

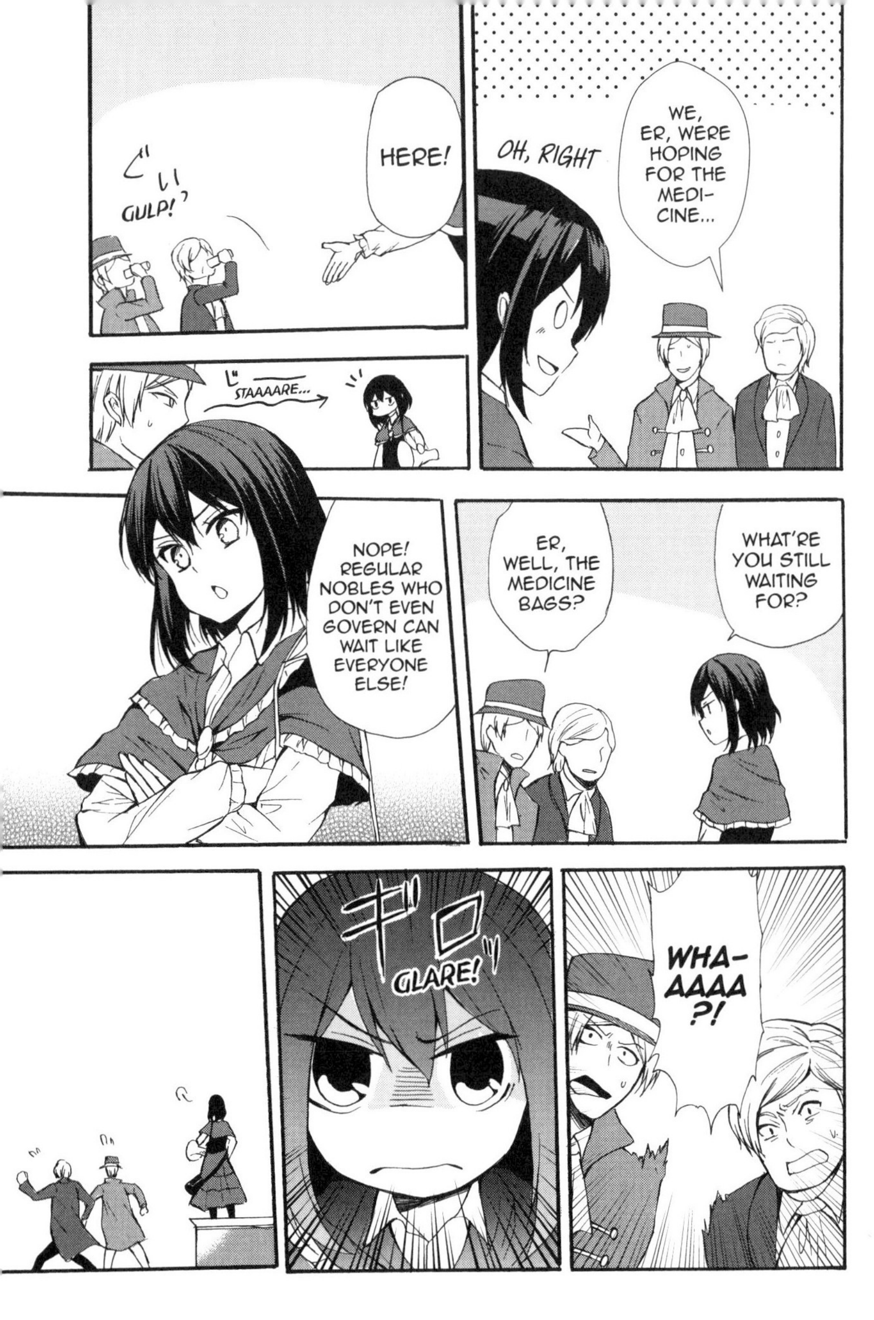
WE, ER, WERE HOPING FOR THE MEDICINE...
OH, RIGHT
HERE!
ぐい
GULP!
じー
STAAAARE...
WHAT'RE YOU STILL WAITING FOR?
ER, WELL, THE MEDICINE BAGS?
NOPE! REGULAR NOBLES WHO DON'T EVEN GOVERN CAN WAIT LIKE EVERYONE ELSE!
WHA-AAAA?!
ギロ
GLARE!

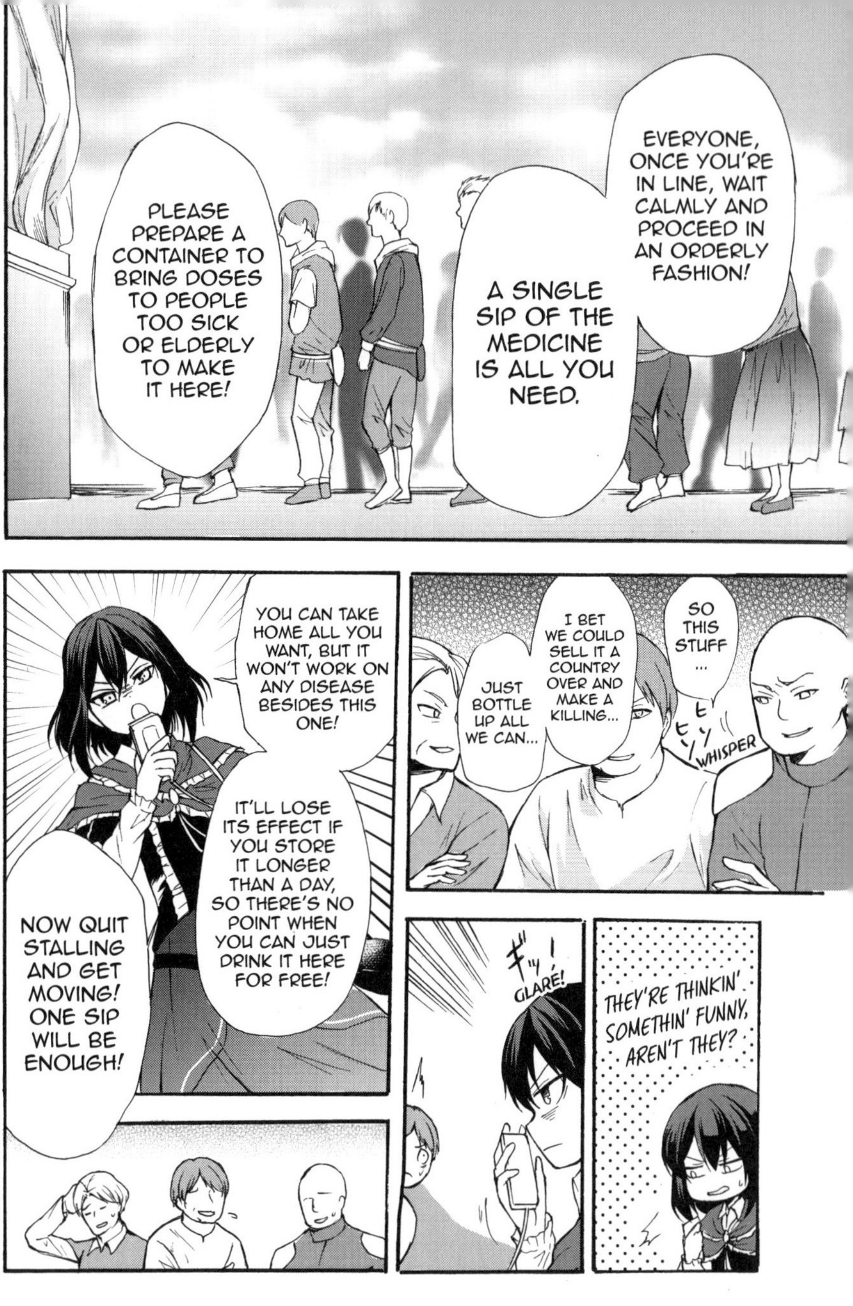
EVERYONE, ONCE YOU'RE IN LINE, WAIT CALMLY AND PROCEED IN AN ORDERLY FASHION!
A SINGLE SIP OF THE MEDICINE IS ALL YOU NEED.
PLEASE PREPARE A CONTAINER TO BRING DOSES TO PEOPLE TOO SICK OR ELDERLY TO MAKE IT HERE!
SO THIS STUFF ...
ヒソヒソ
WHISPER
I BET WE COULD SELL IT A COUNTRY OVER AND MAKE A KILLING...
JUST BOTTLE UP ALL WE CAN...
YOU CAN TAKE HOME ALL YOU WANT, BUT IT WON'T WORK ON ANY DISEASE BESIDES THIS ONE!
IT'LL LOSE ITS EFFECT IF YOU STORE IT LONGER THAN A DAY, SO THERE'S NO POINT WHEN YOU CAN JUST DRINK IT HERE FOR FREE!
NOW QUIT STALLING AND GET MOVING! ONE SIP WILL BE ENOUGH!
THEY'RE THINKIN' SOMETHIN' FUNNY, AREN'T THEY?
ギッ!
GLARE!

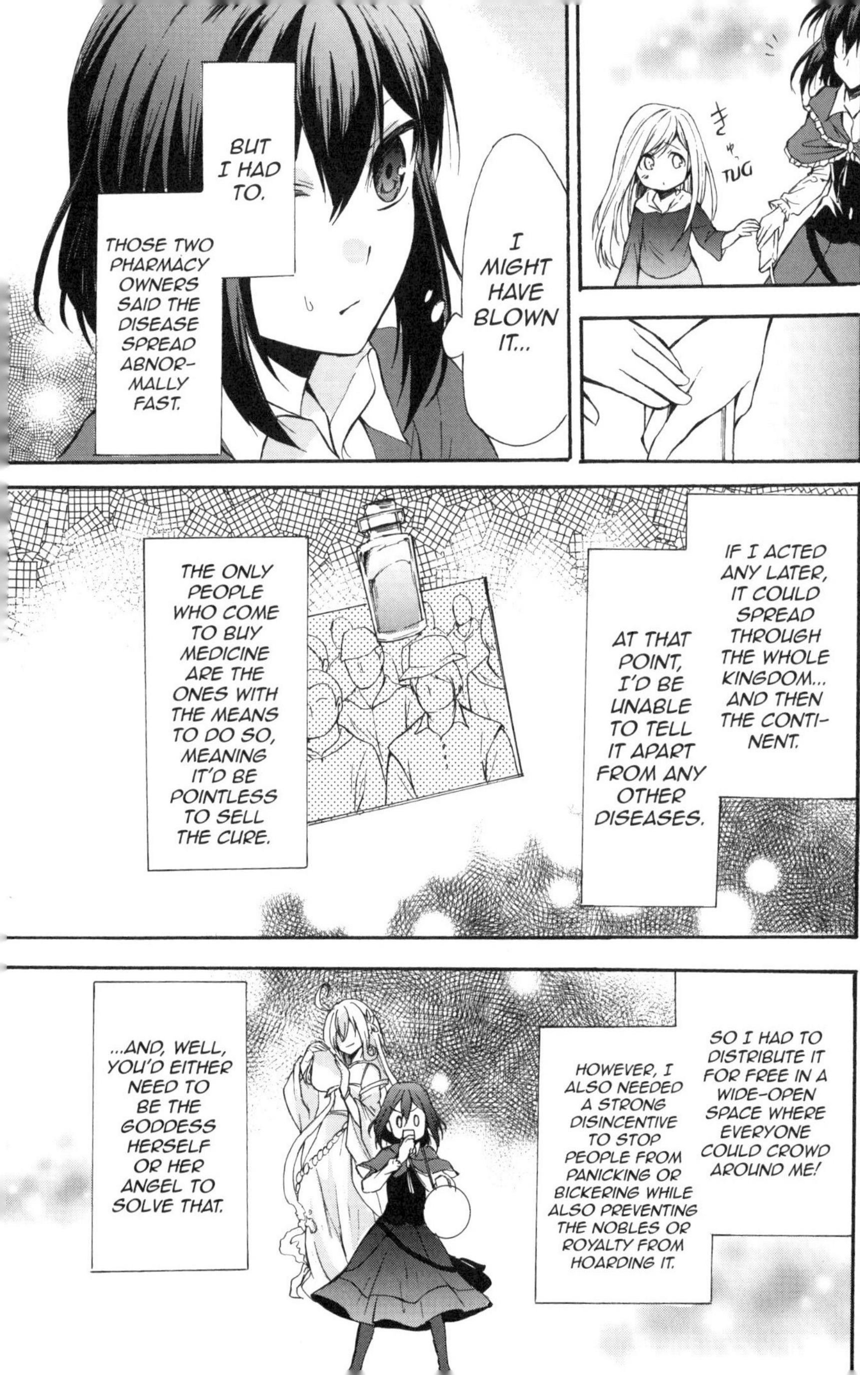
きゅっ
TUG
I MIGHT HAVE BLOWN IT...
BUT I HAD TO.
THOSE TWO PHARMACY OWNERS SAID THE DISEASE SPREAD ABNORMALLY FAST.
IF I ACTED ANY LATER, IT COULD SPREAD THROUGH THE WHOLE KINGDOM... AND THEN THE CONTINENT.
AT THAT POINT, I'D BE UNABLE TO TELL IT APART FROM ANY OTHER DISEASES.
THE ONLY PEOPLE WHO COME TO BUY MEDICINE ARE THE ONES WITH THE MEANS TO DO SO, MEANING IT'D BE POINTLESS TO SELL THE CURE.
SO I HAD TO DISTRIBUTE IT FOR FREE IN A WIDE-OPEN SPACE WHERE EVERYONE COULD CROWD AROUND ME!
HOWEVER, I ALSO NEEDED A STRONG DISINCENTIVE TO STOP PEOPLE FROM PANICKING OR BICKERING WHILE ALSO PREVENTING THE NOBLES OR ROYALTY FROM HOARDING IT.
...AND, WELL, YOU'D EITHER NEED TO BE THE GODDESS HERSELF OR HER ANGEL TO SOLVE THAT.

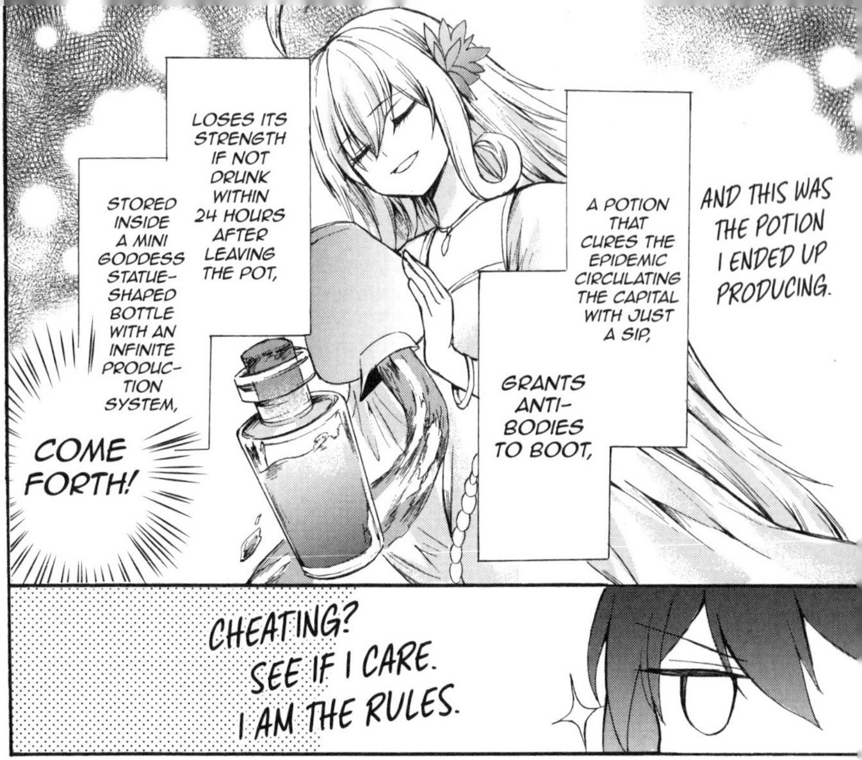
AND THIS WAS THE POTION I ENDED UP PRODUCING.
A POTION THAT CURES THE EPIDEMIC CIRCULATING THE CAPITAL WITH JUST A SIP,
GRANTS ANTI-BODIES TO BOOT,
LOSES ITS STRENGTH IF NOT DRUNK WITHIN 24 HOURS AFTER LEAVING THE POT,
STORED INSIDE A MINI GODDESS STATUE-SHAPED BOTTLE WITH AN INFINITE PRODUC-TION SYSTEM,
COME FORTH!
CHEATING? SEE IF I CARE. I AM THE RULES.

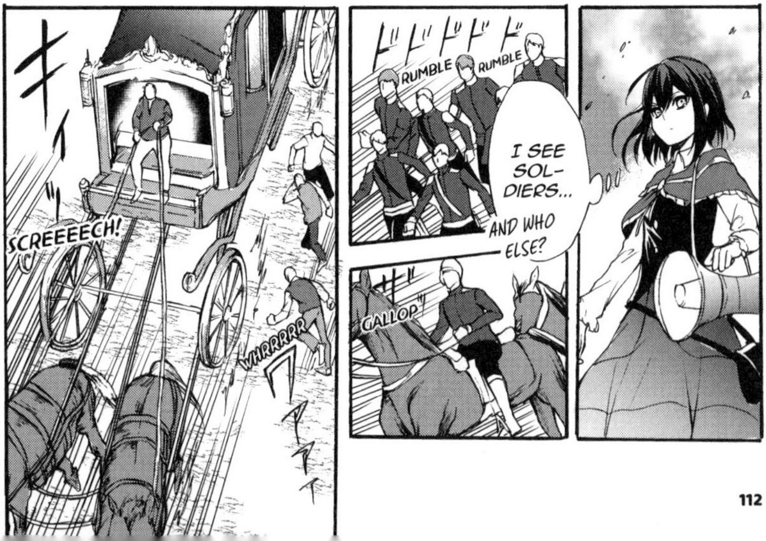
ドドドドド
RUMBLE
RUMBLE
I SEE SOL-DIERS...
AND WHO ELSE?
GALLOP
SCREEEECH!
WHRRRRR

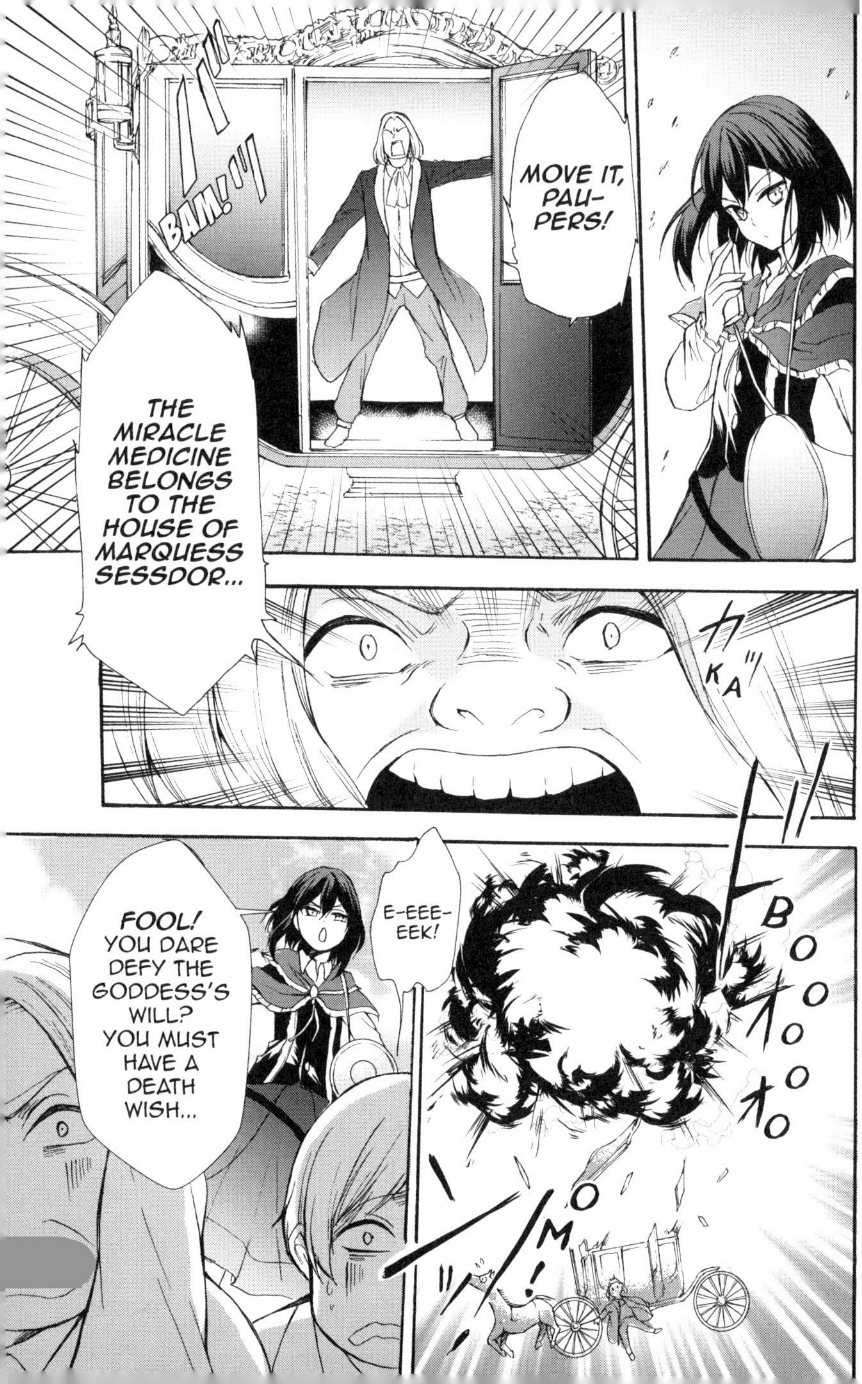
MOVE IT, PAUPERS!
BAM!
THE MIRACLE MEDICINE BELONGS TO THE HOUSE OF MARQUESS SESSDOR...
KA
BOOOOOOOM!
E-EEEE-EEK!
FOOL! YOU DARE DEFY THE GODDESS'S WILL? YOU MUST HAVE A DEATH WISH...

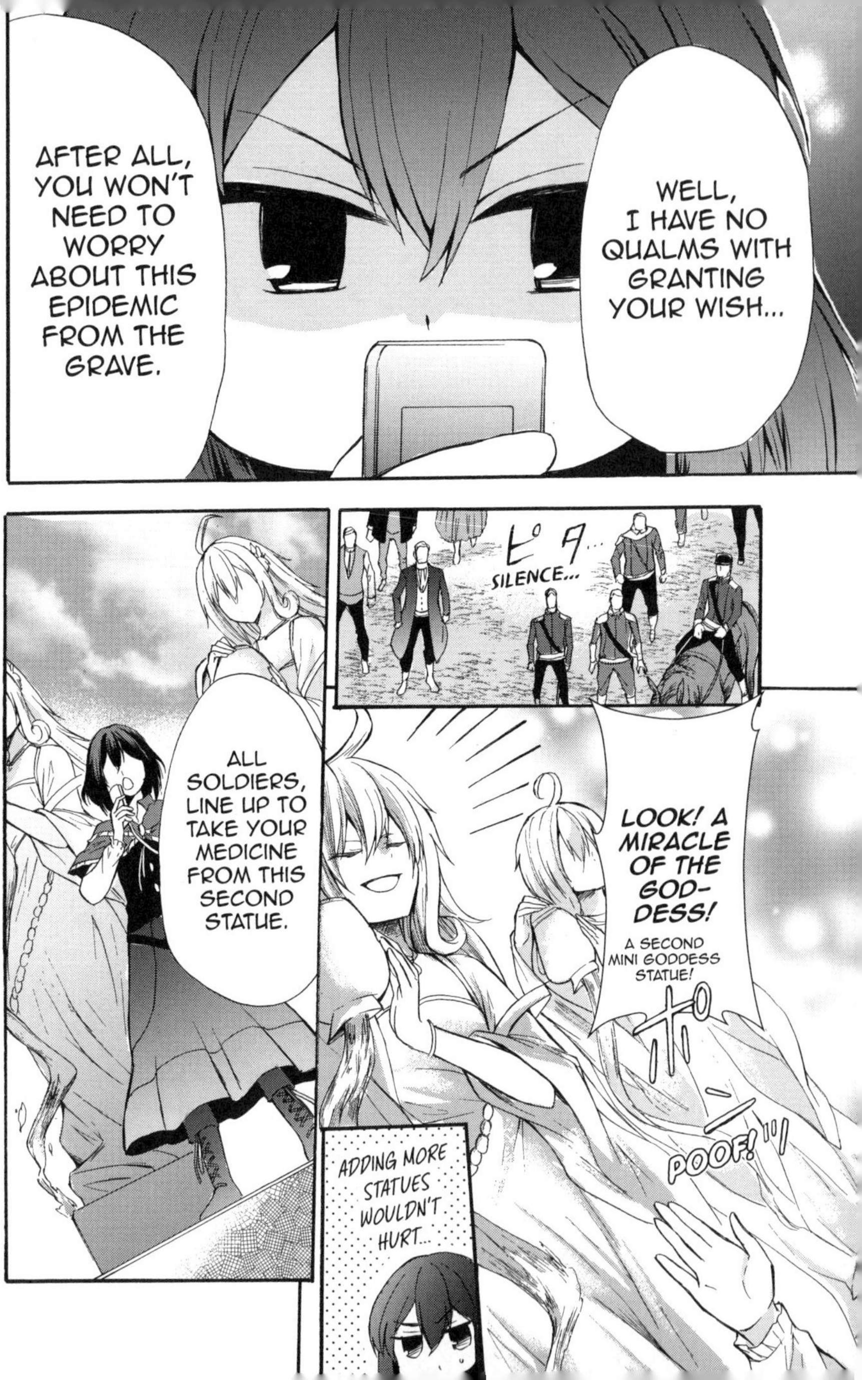
WELL, I HAVE NO QUALMS WITH GRANTING YOUR WISH...
AFTER ALL, YOU WON'T NEED TO WORRY ABOUT THIS EPIDEMIC FROM THE GRAVE.
ピタ...
SILENCE...
LOOK! A MIRACLE OF THE GOD-DESS!
A SECOND MINI GODDESS STATUE!
ポーー
POOF!
ADDING MORE STATUES WOULDN'T HURT...
ALL SOLDIERS, LINE UP TO TAKE YOUR MEDICINE FROM THIS SECOND STATUE.

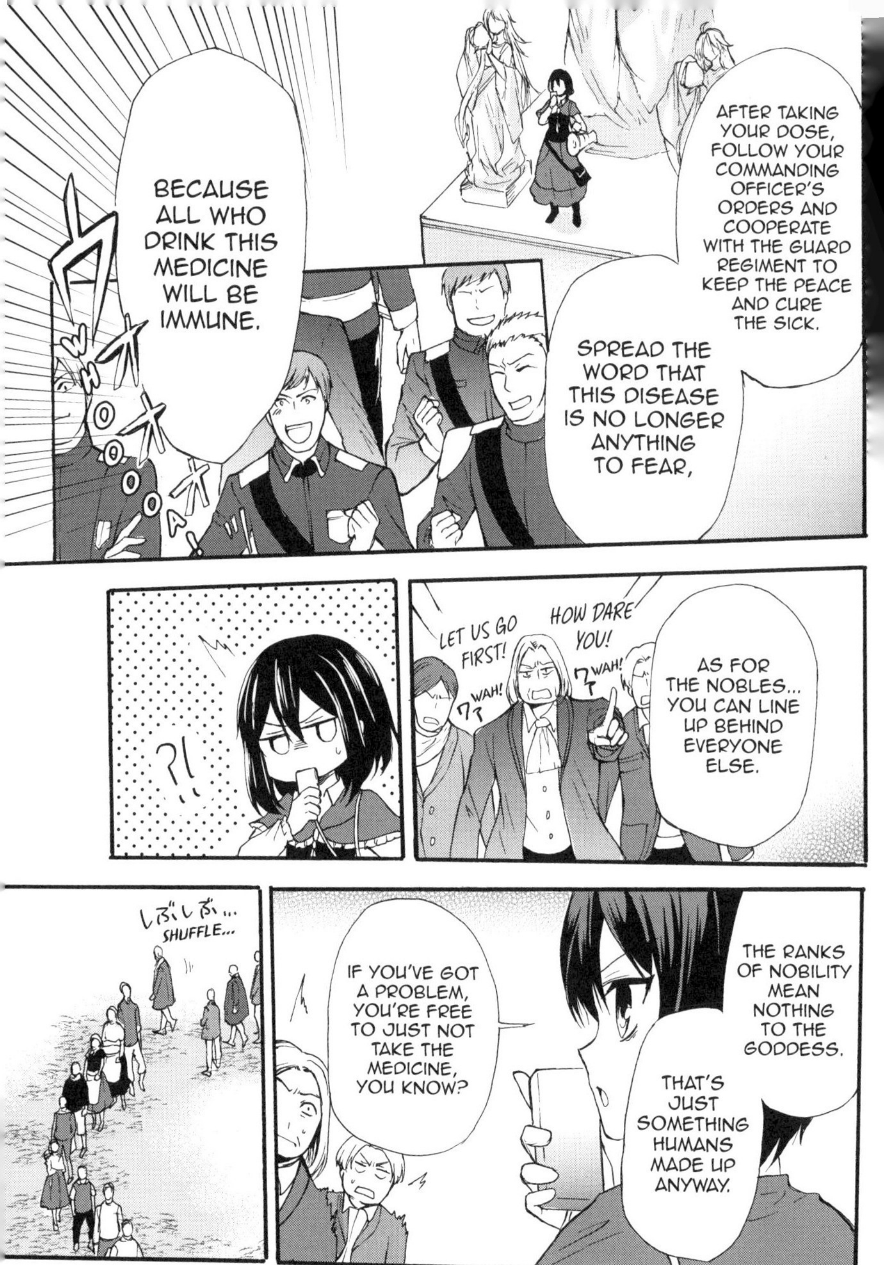
AFTER TAKING YOUR DOSE, FOLLOW YOUR COMMANDING OFFICER'S ORDERS AND COOPERATE WITH THE GUARD REGIMENT TO KEEP THE PEACE AND CURE THE SICK.
SPREAD THE WORD THAT THIS DISEASE IS NO LONGER ANYTHING TO FEAR,
BECAUSE ALL WHO DRINK THIS MEDICINE WILL BE IMMUNE.
WHOOOOOA!
AS FOR THE NOBLES... YOU CAN LINE UP BEHIND EVERYONE ELSE.
HOW DARE YOU!
WAH!
LET US GO FIRST!
WAH!
?!
THE RANKS OF NOBILITY MEAN NOTHING TO THE GODDESS.
THAT'S JUST SOMETHING HUMANS MADE UP ANYWAY.
IF YOU'VE GOT A PROBLEM, YOU'RE FREE TO JUST NOT TAKE THE MEDICINE, YOU KNOW?
しぶしぶ...
SHUFFLE...

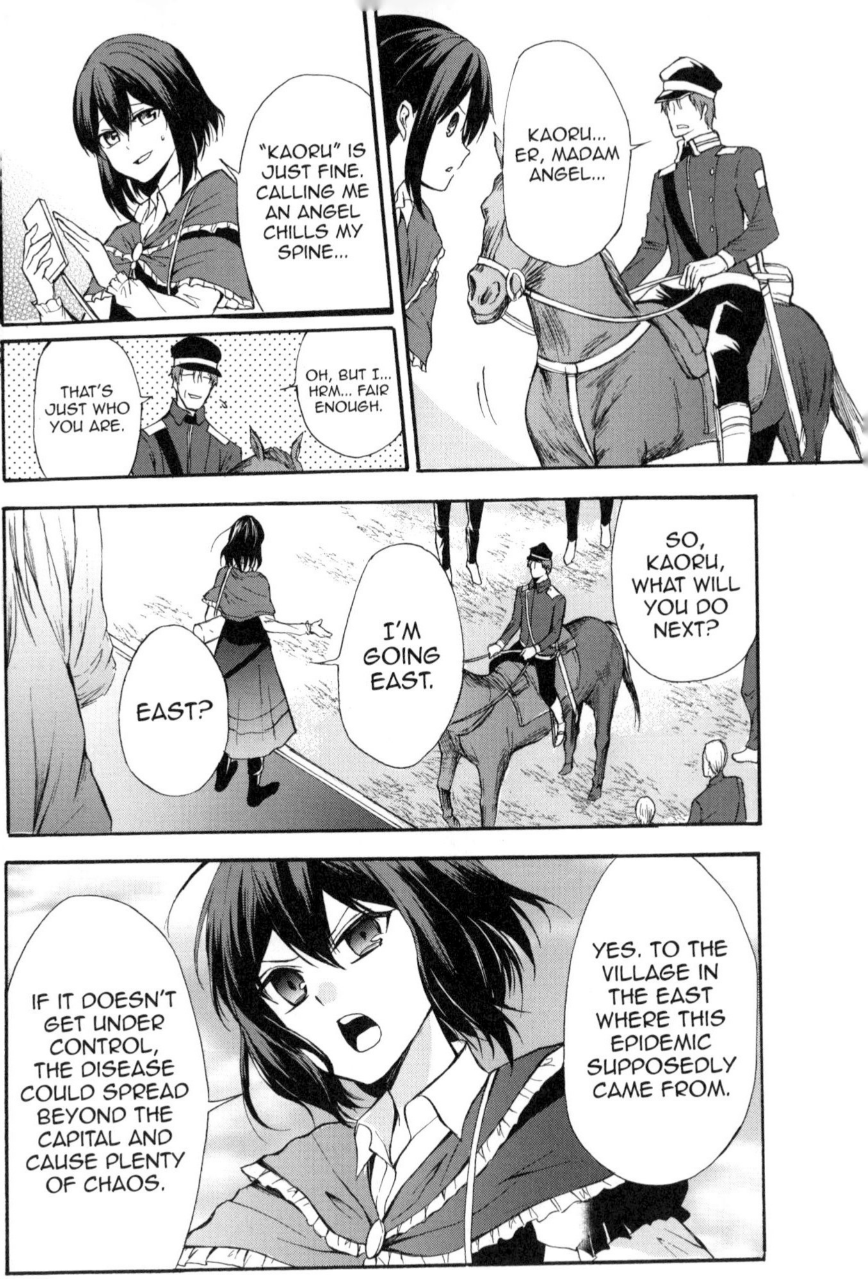
KAORU... ER, MADAM ANGEL...
"KAORU" IS JUST FINE. CALLING ME AN ANGEL CHILLS MY SPINE...
OH, BUT I... HRM... FAIR ENOUGH.
THAT'S JUST WHO YOU ARE.
SO, KAORU, WHAT WILL YOU DO NEXT?
I'M GOING EAST.
EAST?
YES. TO THE VILLAGE IN THE EAST WHERE THIS EPIDEMIC SUPPOSEDLY CAME FROM.
IF IT DOESN'T GET UNDER CONTROL, THE DISEASE COULD SPREAD BEYOND THE CAPITAL AND CAUSE PLENTY OF CHAOS.

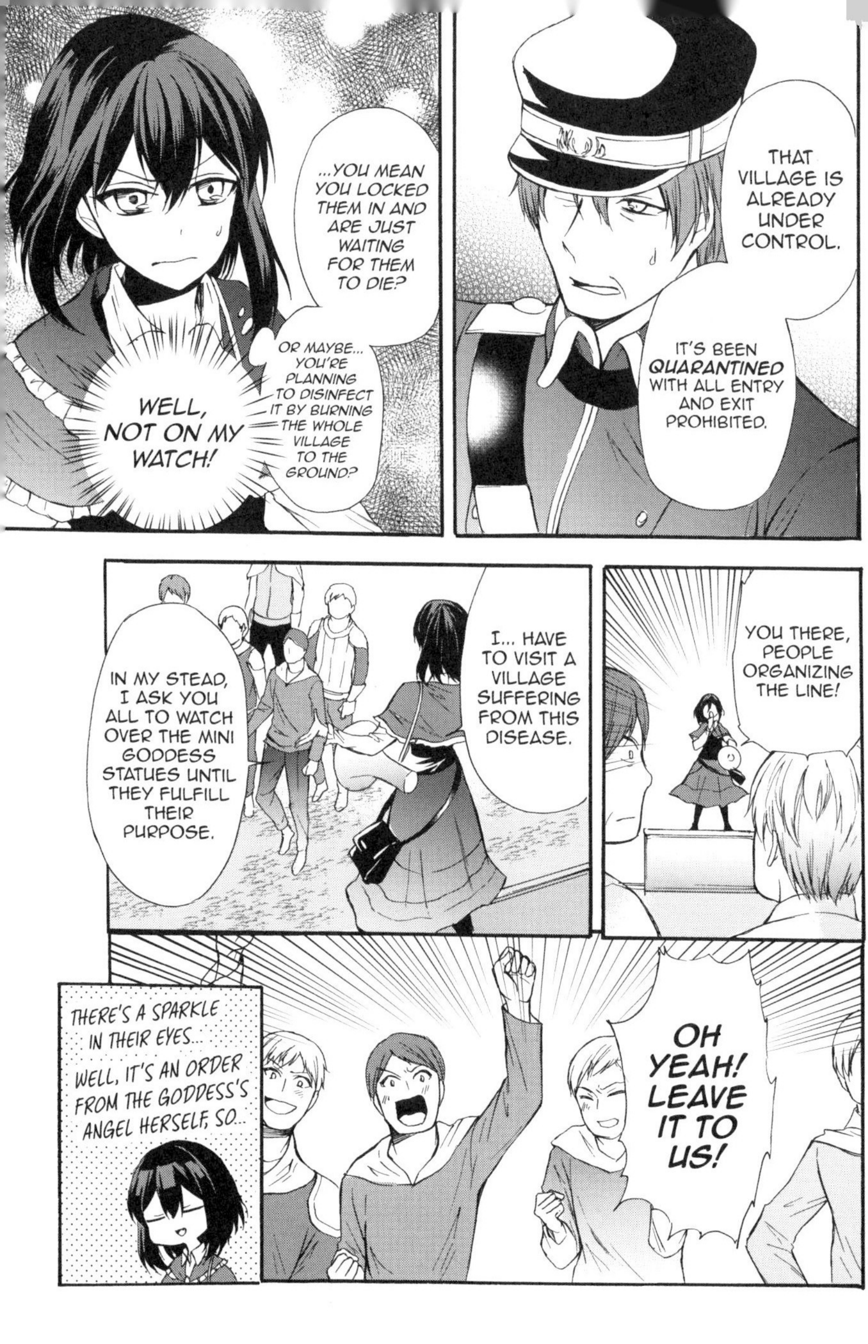
THAT VILLAGE IS ALREADY UNDER CONTROL.
IT'S BEEN QUARANTINED WITH ALL ENTRY AND EXIT PROHIBITED.
...YOU MEAN YOU LOCKED THEM IN AND ARE JUST WAITING FOR THEM TO DIE?
OR MAYBE... YOU'RE PLANNING TO DISINFECT IT BY BURNING THE WHOLE VILLAGE TO THE GROUND?
WELL, NOT ON MY WATCH!
YOU THERE, PEOPLE ORGANIZING THE LINE!
I... HAVE TO VISIT A VILLAGE SUFFERING FROM THIS DISEASE.
IN MY STEAD, I ASK YOU ALL TO WATCH OVER THE MINI GODDESS STATUES UNTIL THEY FULFILL THEIR PURPOSE.
OH YEAH! LEAVE IT TO US!
THERE'S A SPARKLE IN THEIR EYES... WELL, IT'S AN ORDER FROM THE GODDESS'S ANGEL HERSELF, SO...

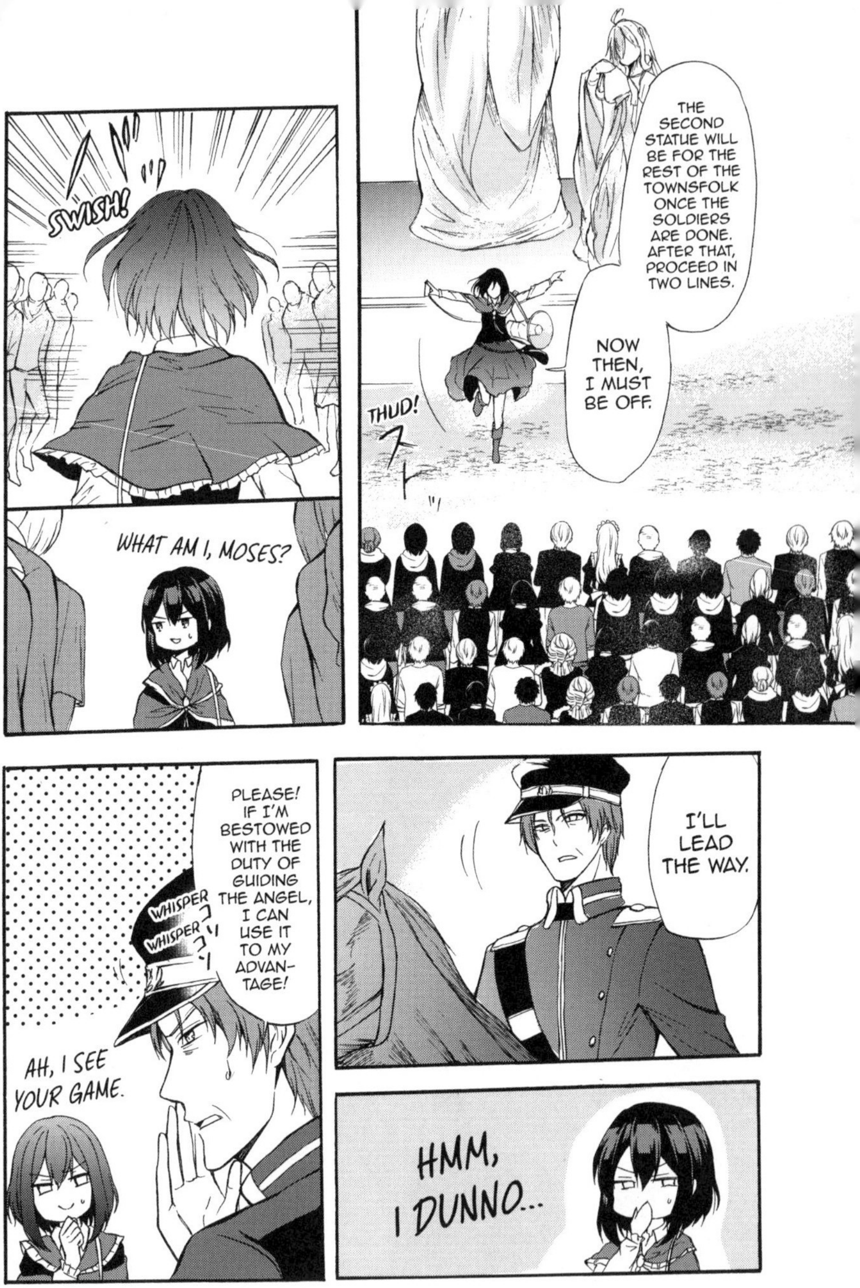
THE SECOND STATUE WILL BE FOR THE REST OF THE TOWNSFOLK ONCE THE SOLDIERS ARE DONE. AFTER THAT, PROCEED IN TWO LINES.
NOW THEN, I MUST BE OFF.
THUD!
SWISH!
WHAT AM I, MOSES?
I'LL LEAD THE WAY.
HMM, I DUNNO...
PLEASE! IF I'M BESTOWED WITH THE DUTY OF GUIDING THE ANGEL, I CAN USE IT TO MY ADVANTAGE!
WHISPER
WHISPER
AH, I SEE YOUR GAME.

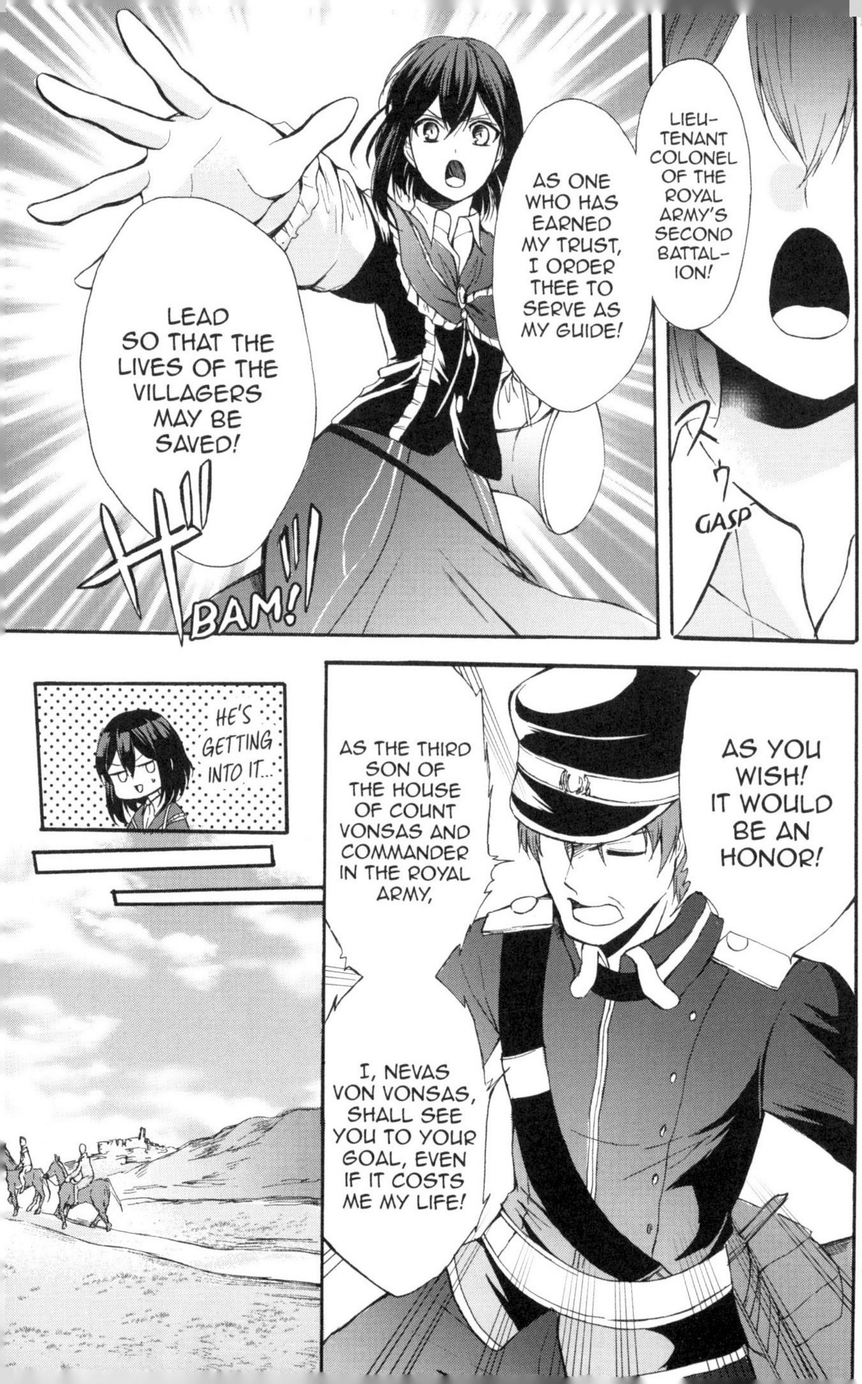
LIEU-TENANT COLONEL OF THE ROYAL ARMY'S SECOND BATTAL-ION!
GASP
AS ONE WHO HAS EARNED MY TRUST, I ORDER THEE TO SERVE AS MY GUIDE!
LEAD SO THAT THE LIVES OF THE VILLAGERS MAY BE SAVED!
BAM!
AS YOU WISH! IT WOULD BE AN HONOR!
AS THE THIRD SON OF THE HOUSE OF COUNT VONSAS AND COMMANDER IN THE ROYAL ARMY,
I, NEVAS VON VONSAS, SHALL SEE YOU TO YOUR GOAL, EVEN IF IT COSTS ME MY LIFE!
HE'S GETTING INTO IT...

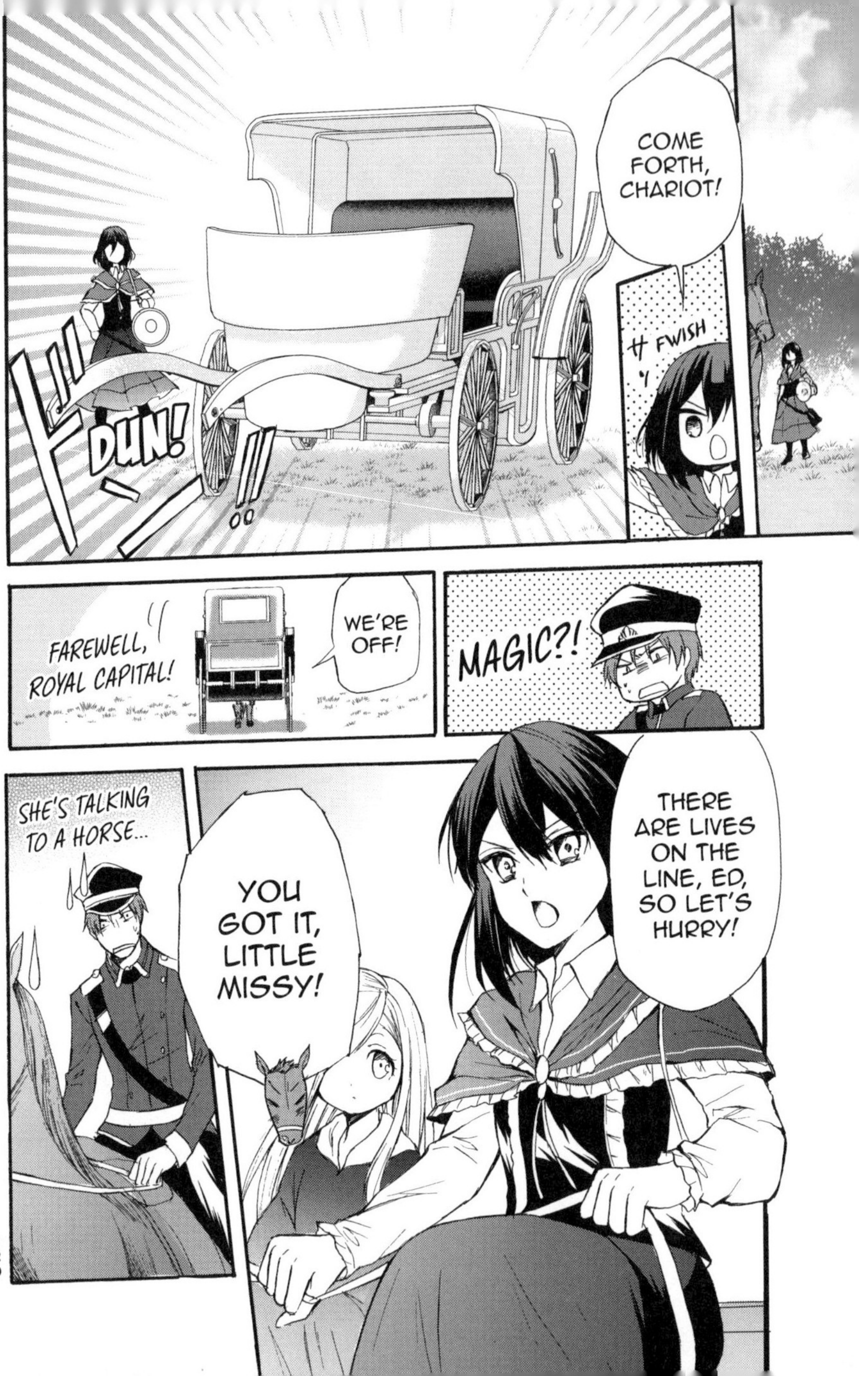

COME FORTH, CHARIOT!
FWISH
DUN!
MAGIC?!
WE'RE OFF!
FAREWELL, ROYAL CAPITAL!
THERE ARE LIVES ON THE LINE, ED, SO LET'S HURRY!
YOU GOT IT, LITTLE MISSY!
SHE'S TALKING TO A HORSE...

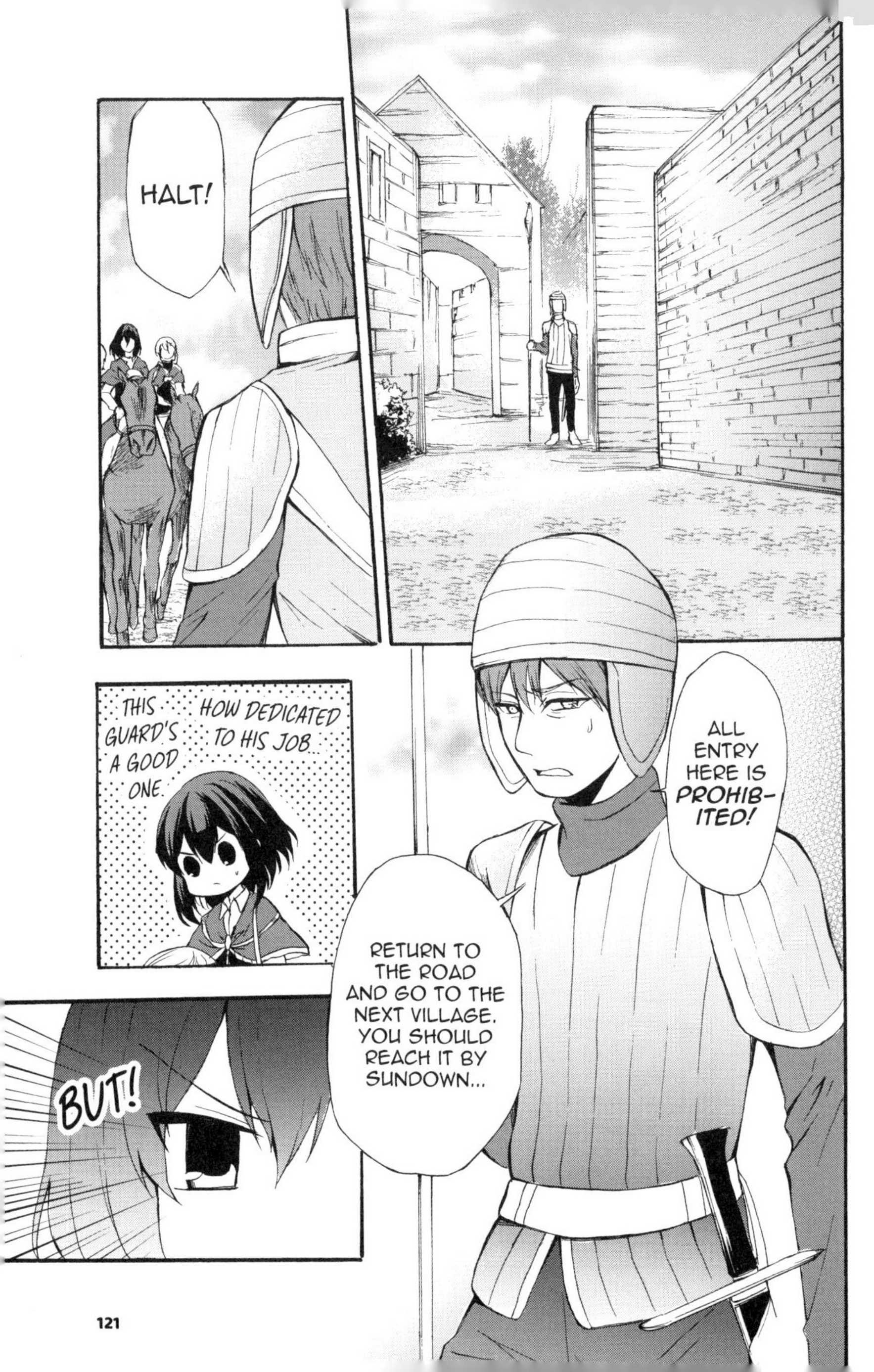
HALT!
ALL ENTRY HERE IS PROHIBITED!
RETURN TO THE ROAD AND GO TO THE NEXT VILLAGE. YOU SHOULD REACH IT BY SUNDOWN...
HOW DEDICATED TO HIS JOB...
THIS GUARD'S A GOOD ONE.
BUT!

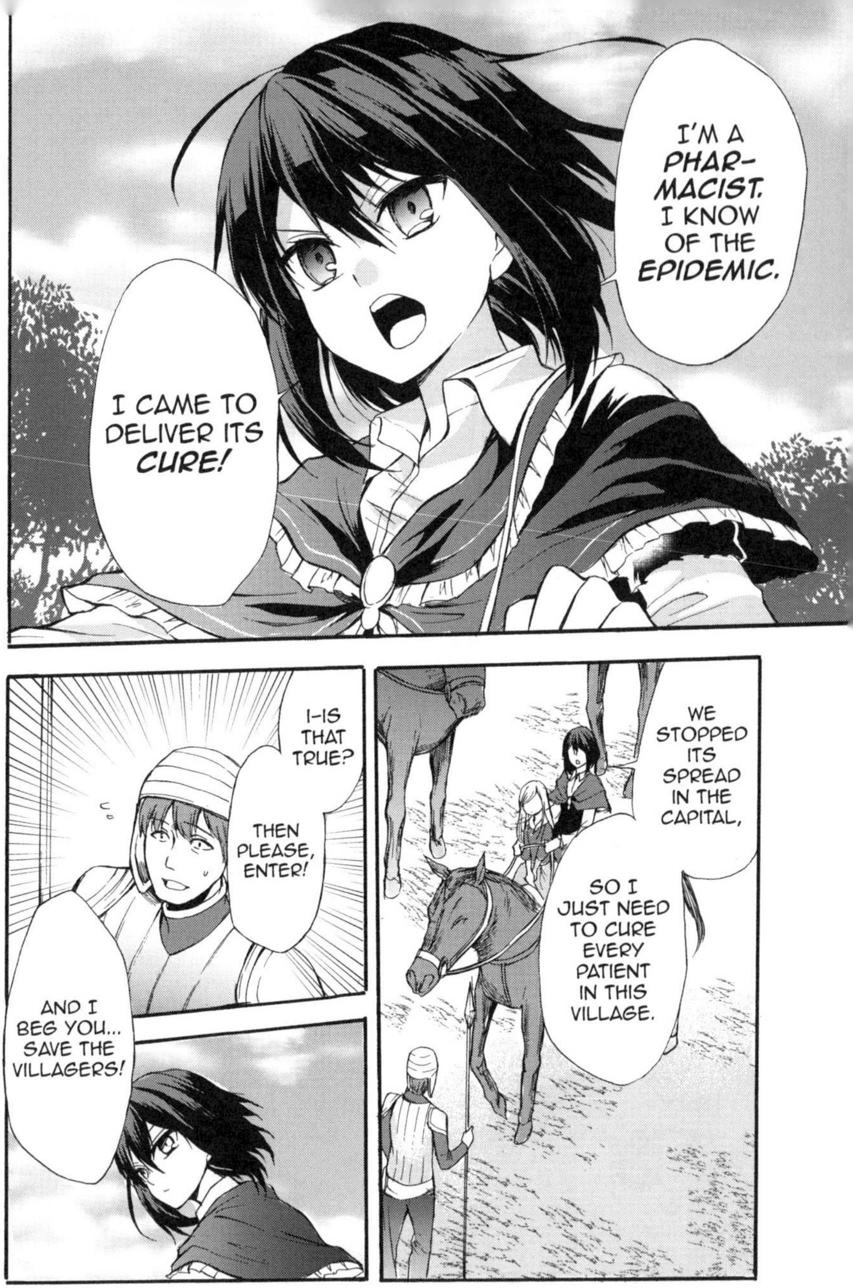
I'M A PHARMACIST. I KNOW OF THE EPIDEMIC.
I CAME TO DELIVER ITS CURE!
WE STOPPED ITS SPREAD IN THE CAPITAL,
SO I JUST NEED TO CURE EVERY PATIENT IN THIS VILLAGE.
I-IS THAT TRUE?
THEN PLEASE, ENTER!
AND I BEG YOU... SAVE THE VILLAGERS!

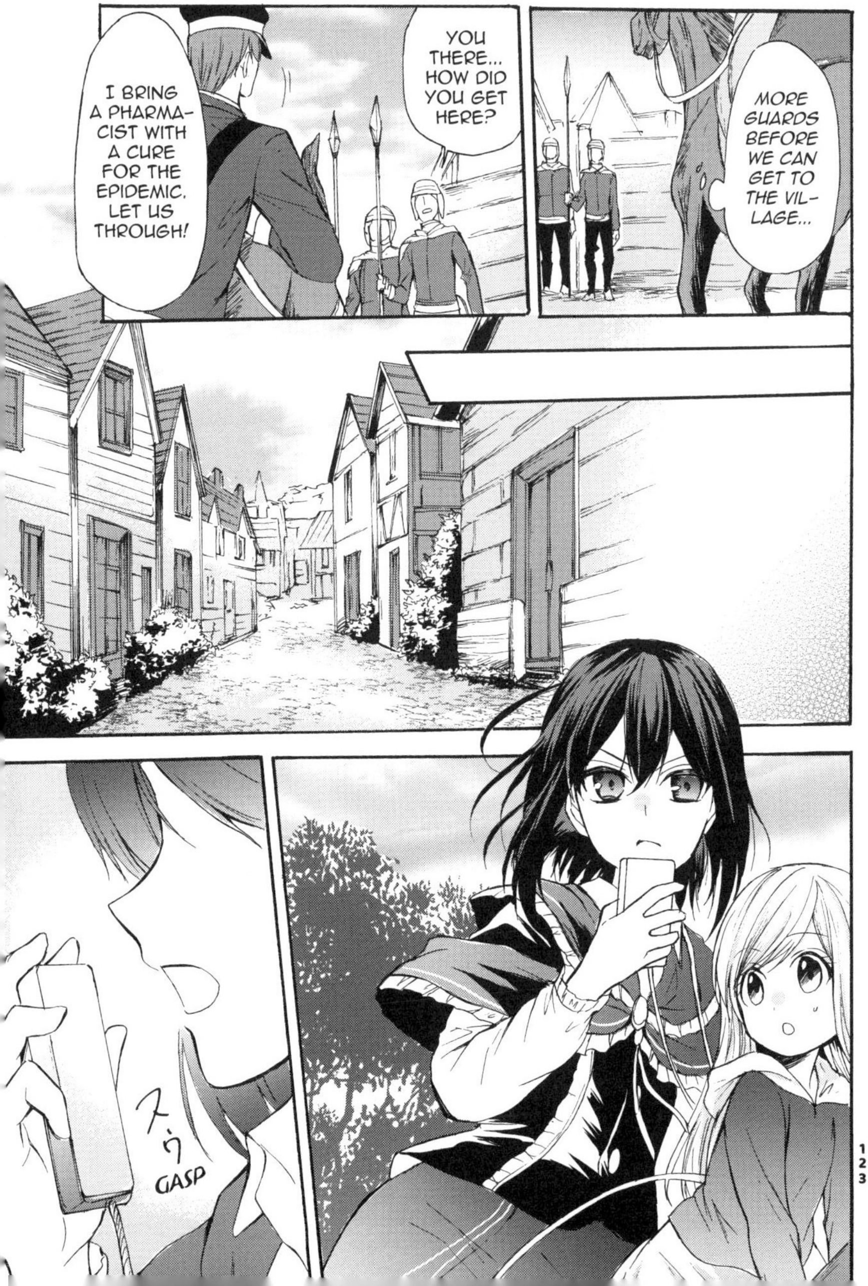
MORE GUARDS BEFORE WE CAN GET TO THE VIL-LAGE...
YOU THERE... HOW DID YOU GET HERE?
I BRING A PHARMA-CIST WITH A CURE FOR THE EPIDEMIC. LET US THROUGH!
スゥ
GASP

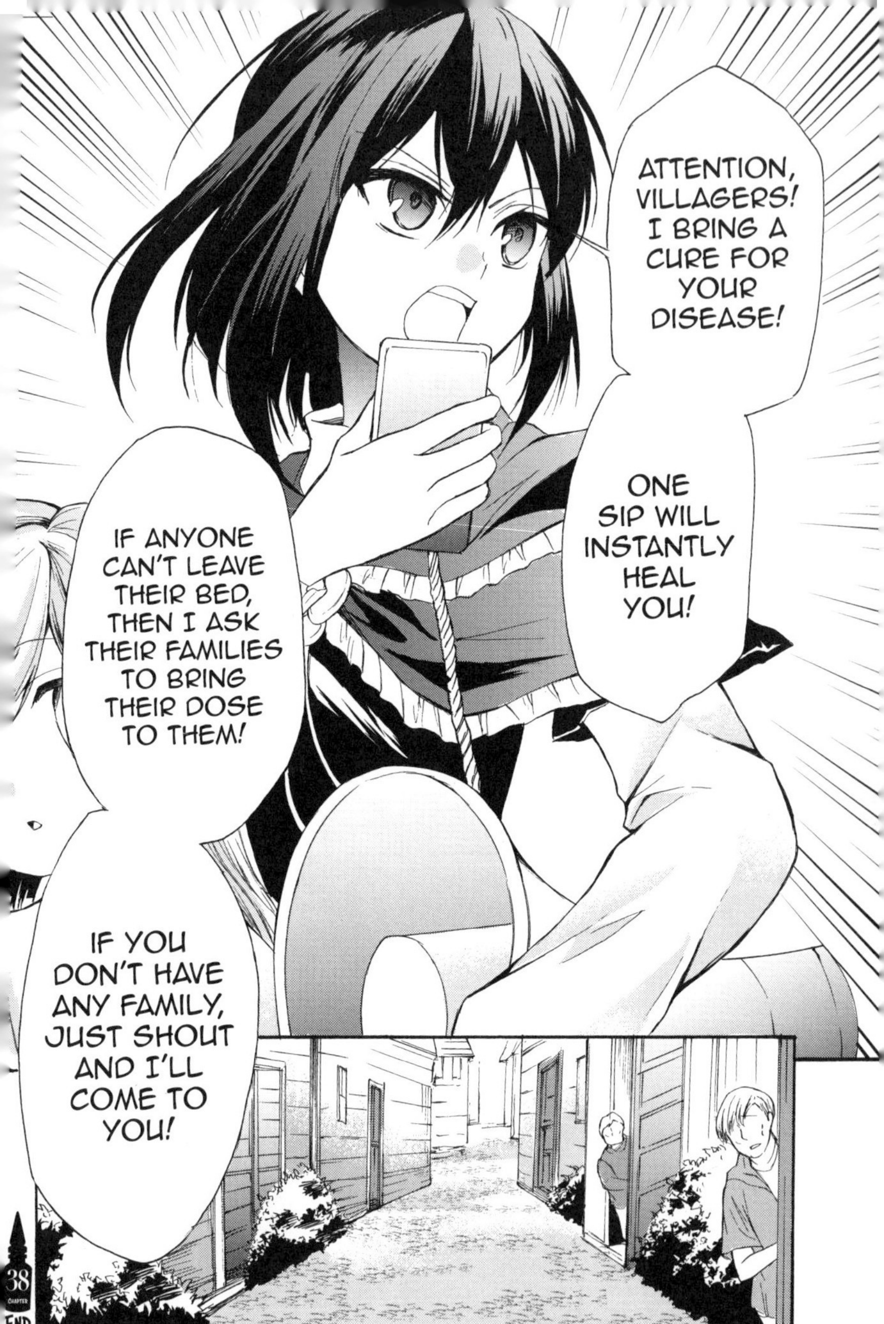
ATTENTION, VILLAGERS! I BRING A CURE FOR YOUR DISEASE!
ONE SIP WILL INSTANTLY HEAL YOU!
IF ANYONE CAN'T LEAVE THEIR BED, THEN I ASK THEIR FAMILIES TO BRING THEIR DOSE TO THEM!
IF YOU DON'T HAVE ANY FAMILY, JUST SHOUT AND I'LL COME TO YOU!
38 CHAPTER END

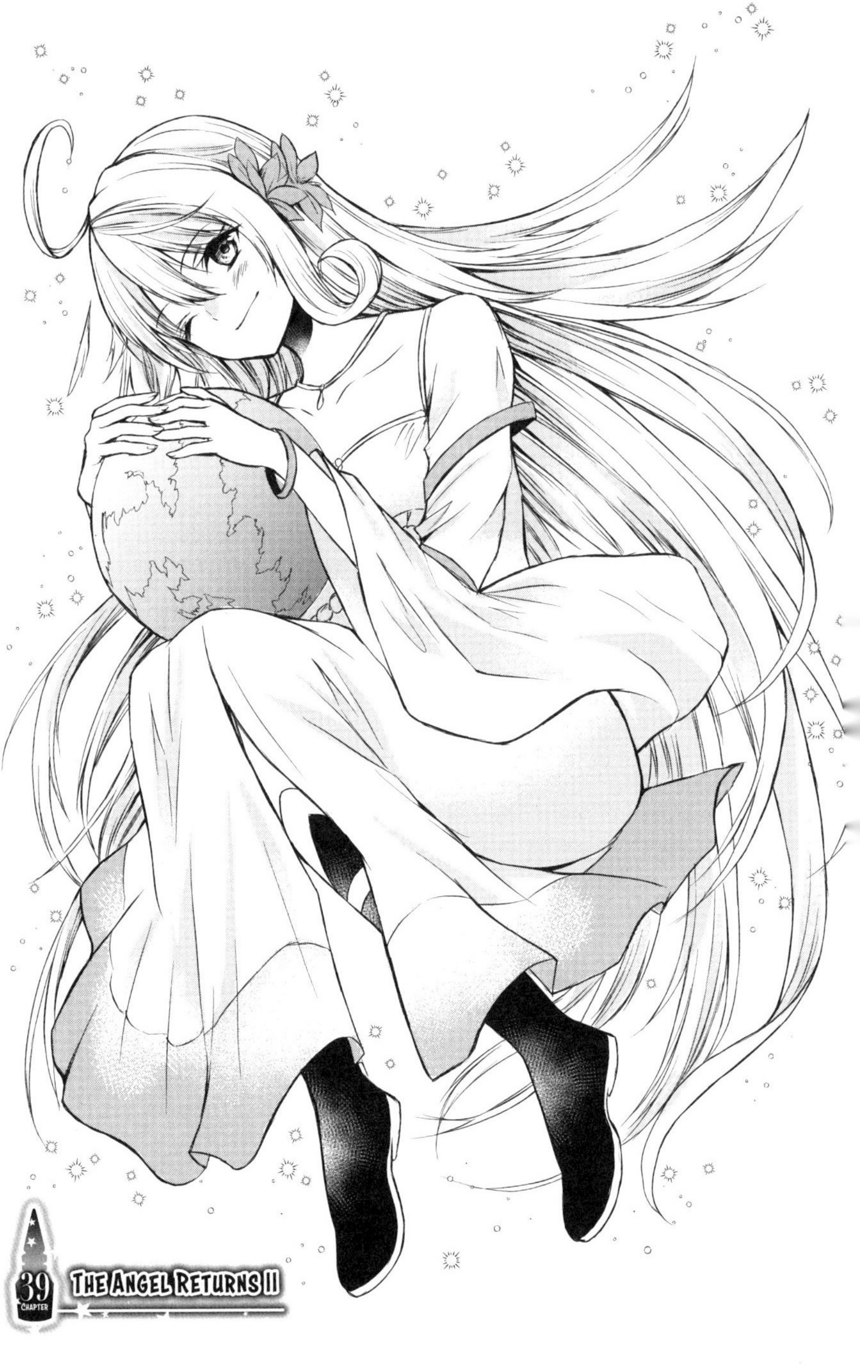

Chapter 39 The Angel Returns II

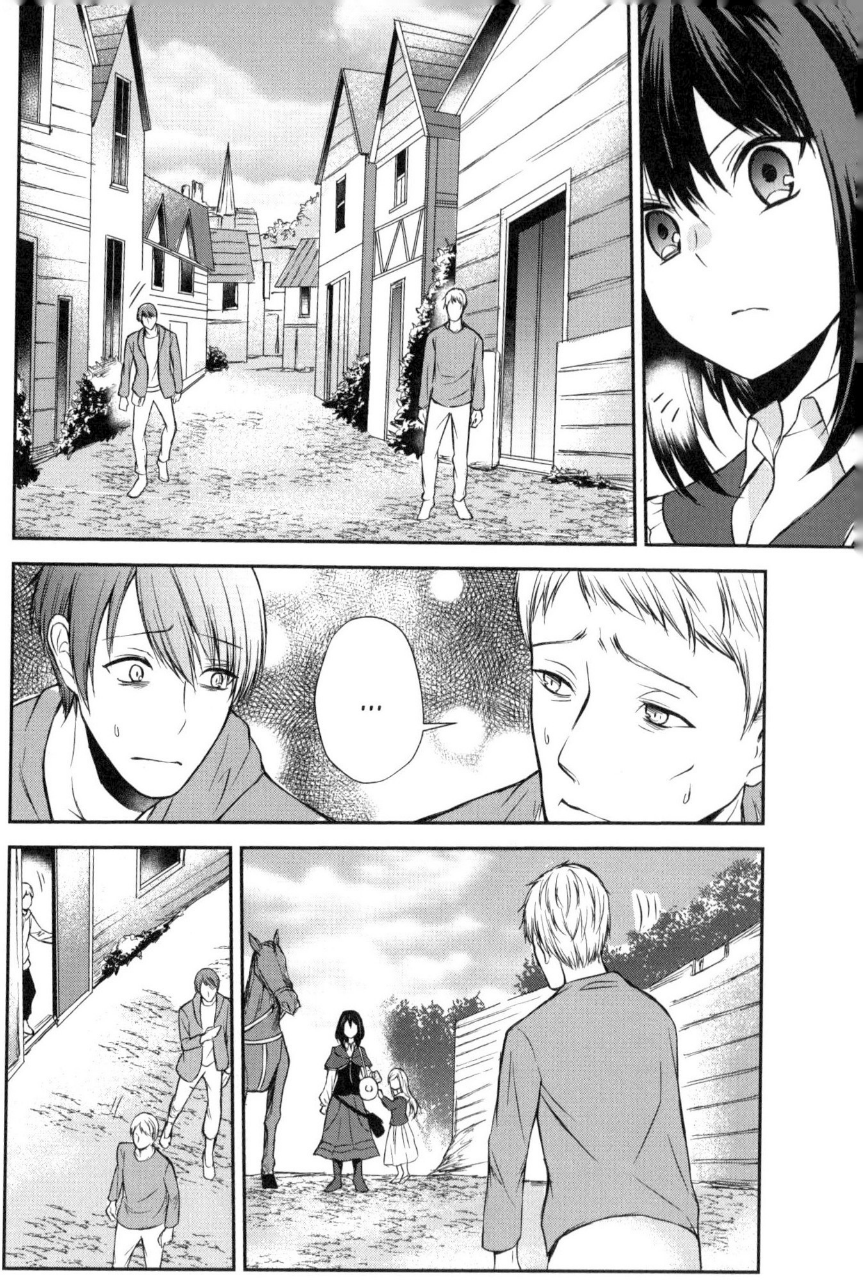
...

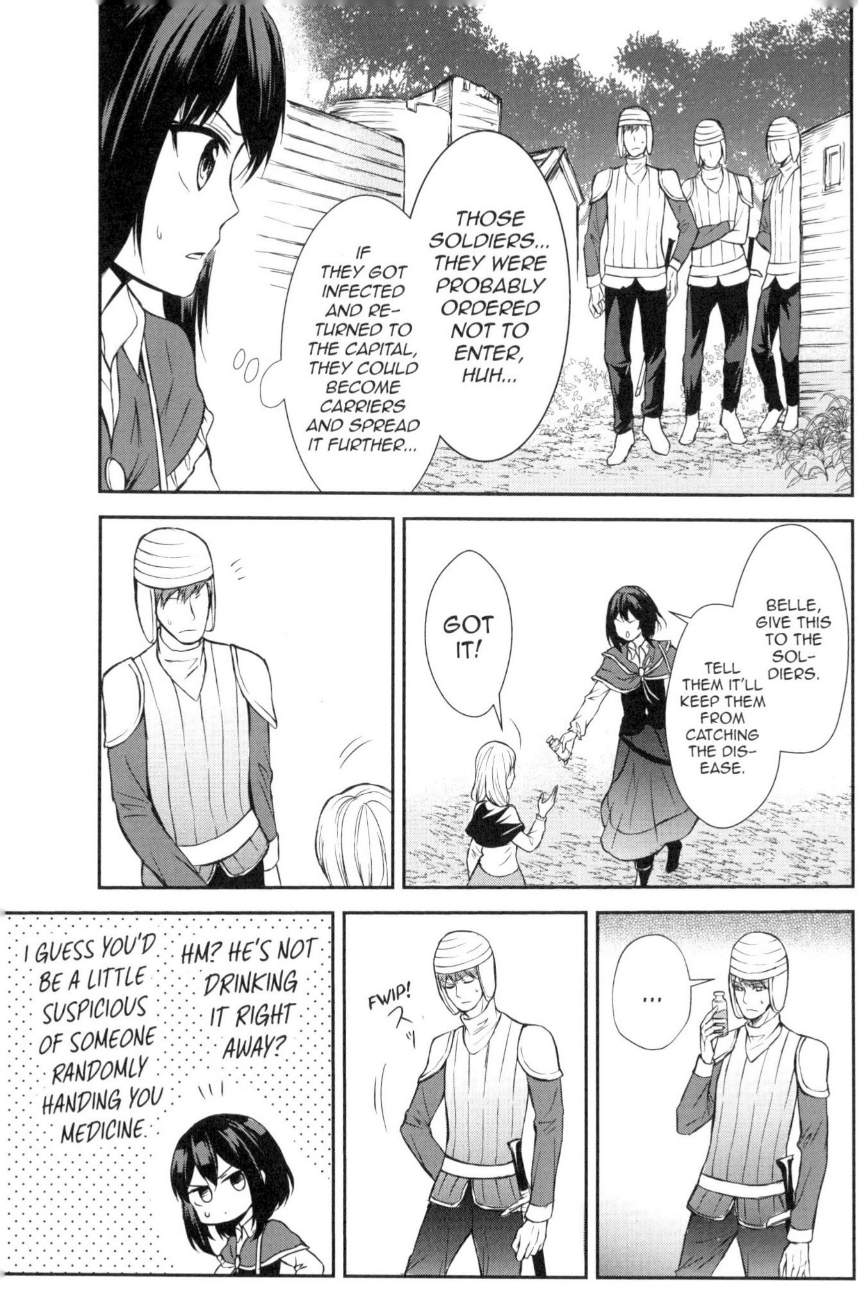
THOSE SOLDIERS... THEY WERE PROBABLY ORDERED NOT TO ENTER, HUH...
IF THEY GOT INFECTED AND RETURNED TO THE CAPITAL, THEY COULD BECOME CARRIERS AND SPREAD IT FURTHER...
BELLE, GIVE THIS TO THE SOLDIERS.
TELL THEM IT'LL KEEP THEM FROM CATCHING THE DISEASE.
GOT IT!
...
FWIP!
スッ
HM? HE'S NOT DRINKING IT RIGHT AWAY?
I GUESS YOU'D BE A LITTLE SUSPICIOUS OF SOMEONE RANDOMLY HANDING YOU MEDICINE.

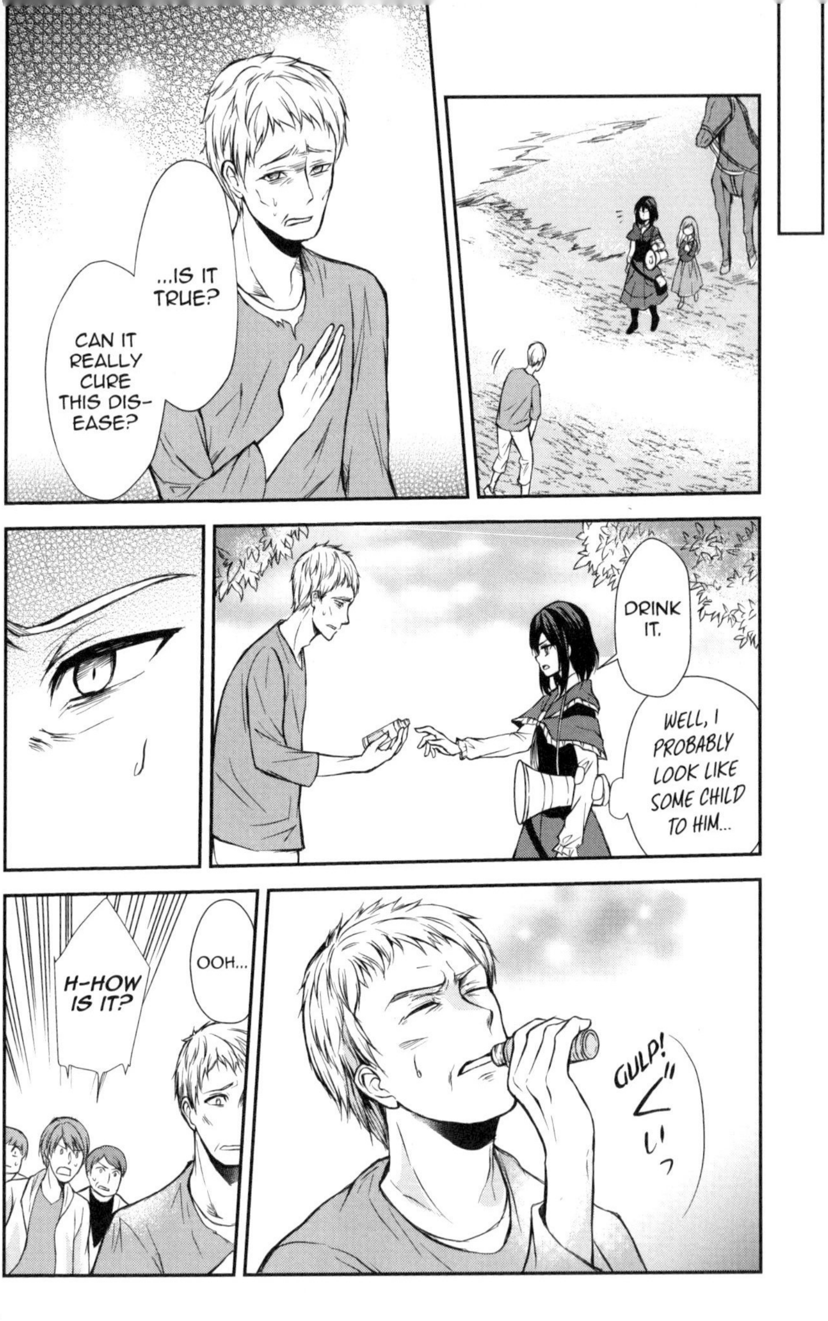
...IS IT TRUE?
CAN IT REALLY CURE THIS DIS-EASE?
DRINK IT.
WELL, I PROBABLY LOOK LIKE SOME CHILD TO HIM...
GULP!
ぐいっ
OOH...
H-HOW IS IT?

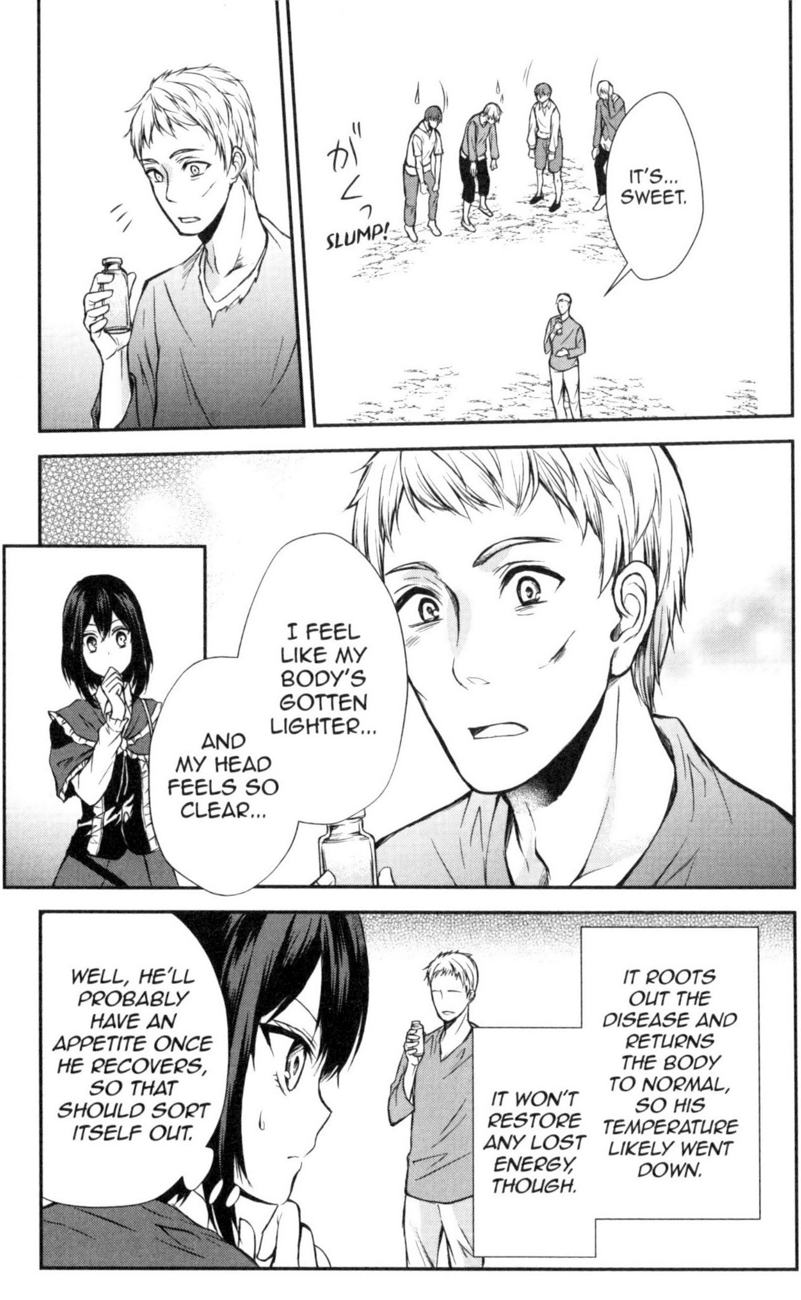
IT'S... SWEET.
がくっ
SLUMP!
I FEEL LIKE MY BODY'S GOTTEN LIGHTER...
AND MY HEAD FEELS SO CLEAR...
IT ROOTS OUT THE DISEASE AND RETURNS THE BODY TO NORMAL, SO HIS TEMPERATURE LIKELY WENT DOWN.
IT WON'T RESTORE ANY LOST ENERGY, THOUGH.
WELL, HE'LL PROBABLY HAVE AN APPETITE ONCE HE RECOVERS, SO THAT SHOULD SORT ITSELF OUT.

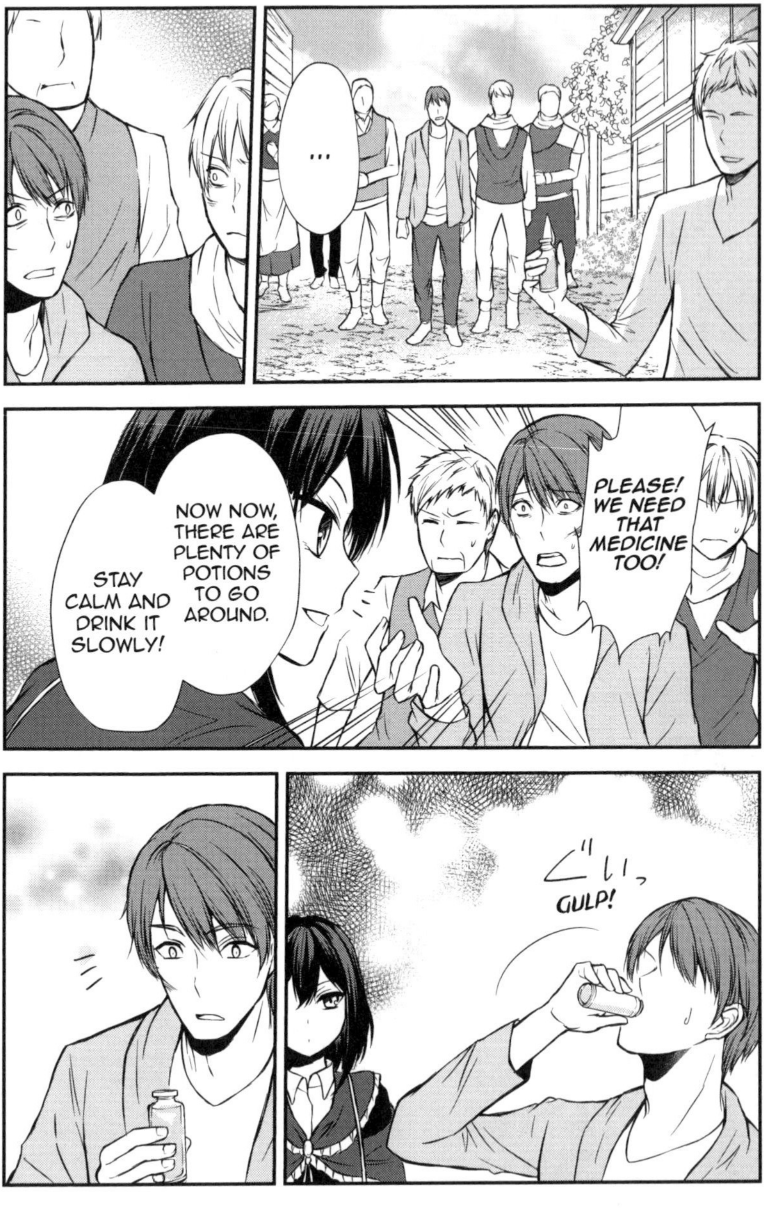
...
PLEASE! WE NEED THAT MEDICINE TOO!
NOW NOW, THERE ARE PLENTY OF POTIONS TO GO AROUND.
STAY CALM AND DRINK IT SLOWLY!
ぐいっ
GULP!

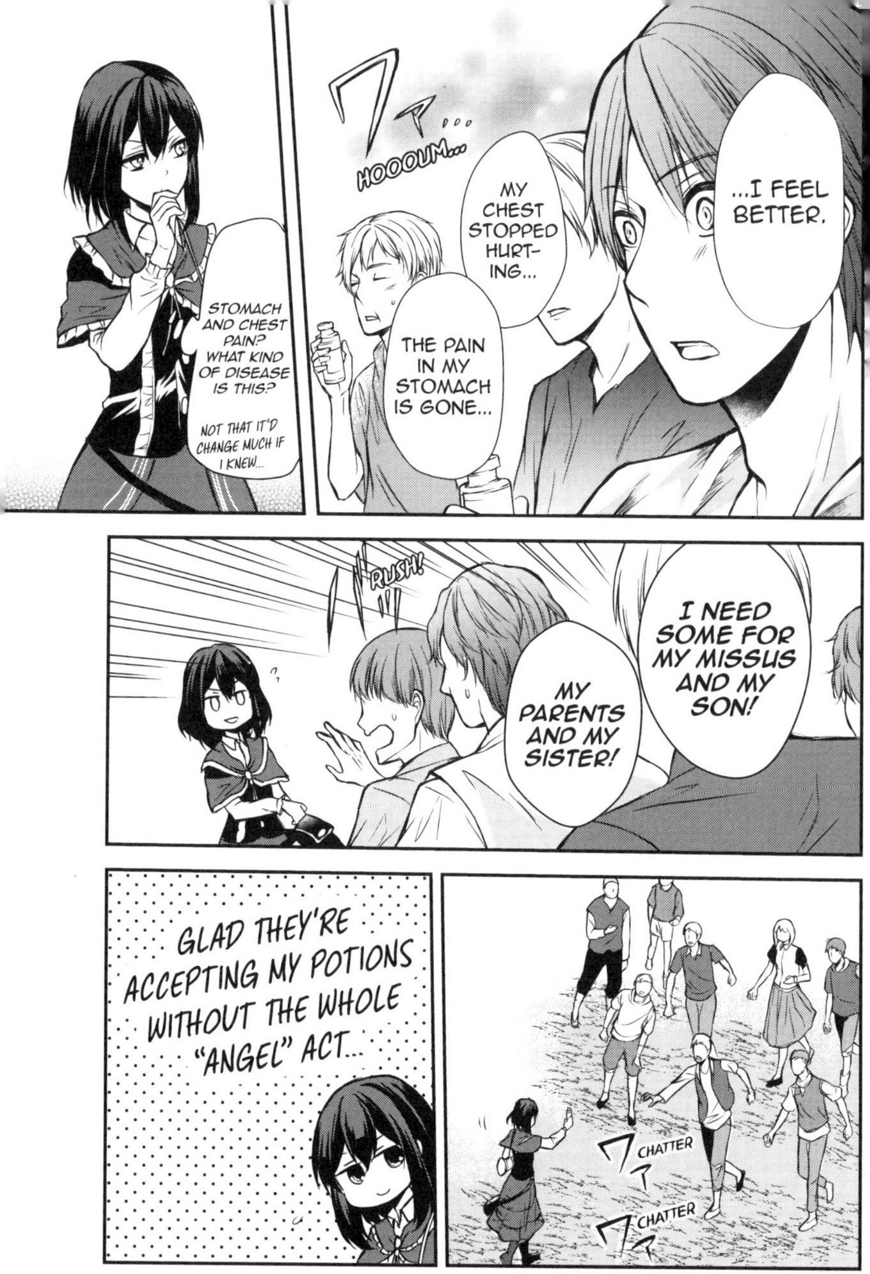
...I FEEL BETTER.
MY CHEST STOPPED HURT-ING...
THE PAIN IN MY STOMACH IS GONE...
HOOOUM...
STOMACH AND CHEST PAIN? WHAT KIND OF DISEASE IS THIS?
NOT THAT IT'D CHANGE MUCH IF I KNEW...
I NEED SOME FOR MY MISSUS AND MY SON!
MY PARENTS AND MY SISTER!
RUSH!
CHATTER
CHATTER
GLAD THEY'RE ACCEPTING MY POTIONS WITHOUT THE WHOLE "ANGEL" ACT...

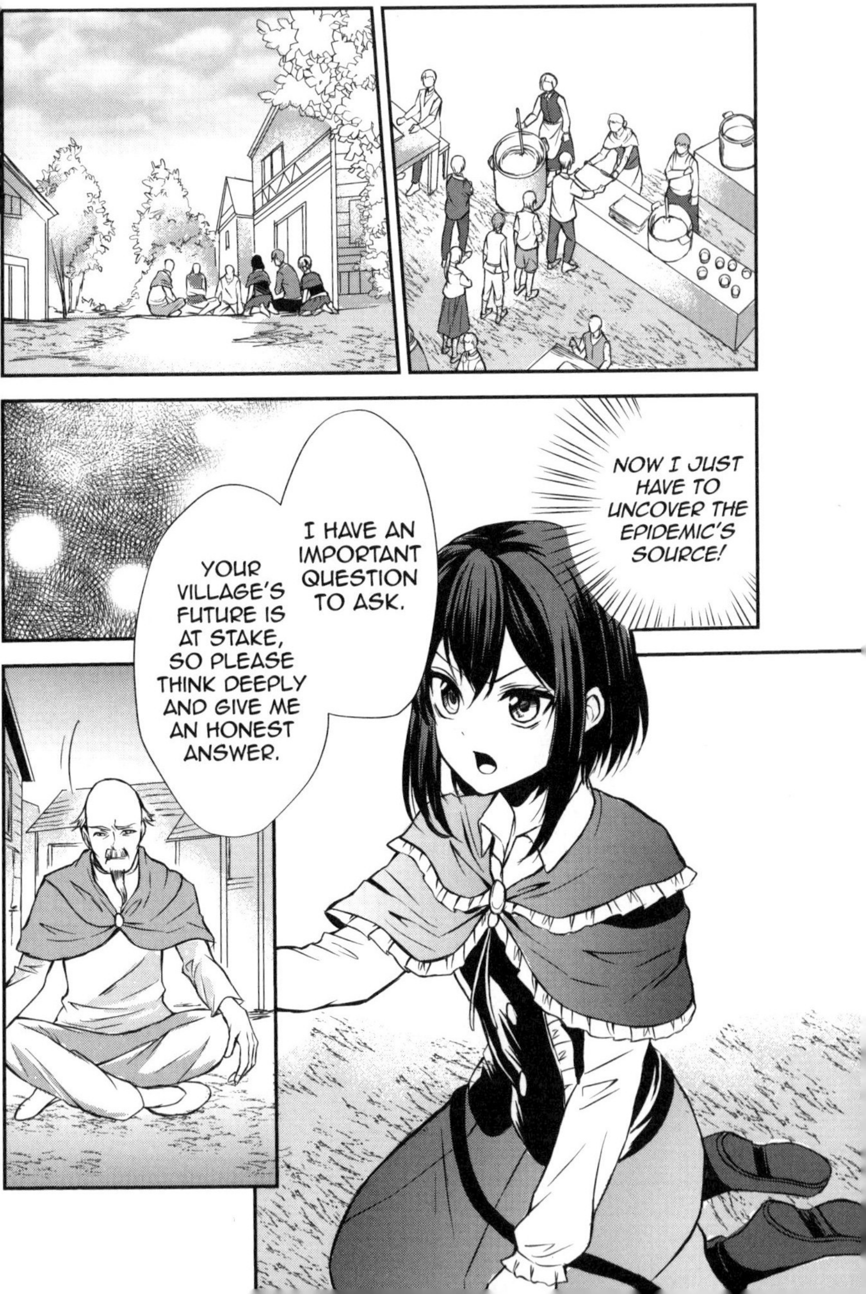
NOW I JUST HAVE TO UNCOVER THE EPIDEMIC'S SOURCE!
I HAVE AN IMPORTANT QUESTION TO ASK.
YOUR VILLAGE'S FUTURE IS AT STAKE, SO PLEASE THINK DEEPLY AND GIVE ME AN HONEST ANSWER.

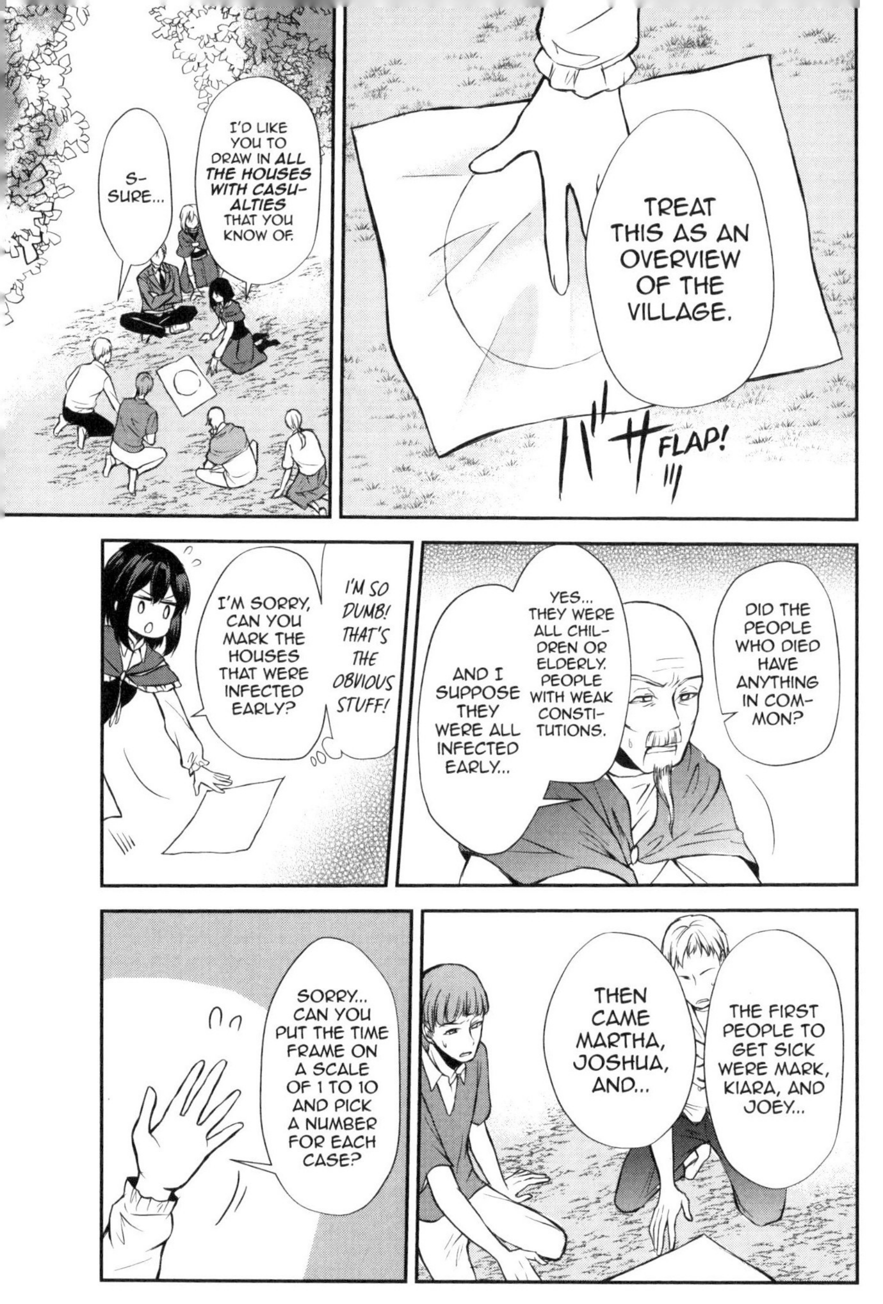
TREAT THIS AS AN OVERVIEW OF THE VILLAGE.
FLAP!
I'D LIKE YOU TO DRAW IN ALL THE HOUSES WITH CASUALTIES THAT YOU KNOW OF.
S-SURE...
DID THE PEOPLE WHO DIED HAVE ANYTHING IN COMMON?
YES... THEY WERE ALL CHILDREN OR ELDERLY. PEOPLE WITH WEAK CONSTITUTIONS.
AND I SUPPOSE THEY WERE ALL INFECTED EARLY...
I'M SO DUMB! THAT'S THE OBVIOUS STUFF!
I'M SORRY, CAN YOU MARK THE HOUSES THAT WERE INFECTED EARLY?
THE FIRST PEOPLE TO GET SICK WERE MARK, KIARA, AND JOEY...
THEN CAME MARTHA, JOSHUA, AND...
SORRY... CAN YOU PUT THE TIME FRAME ON A SCALE OF 1 TO 10 AND PICK A NUMBER FOR EACH CASE?

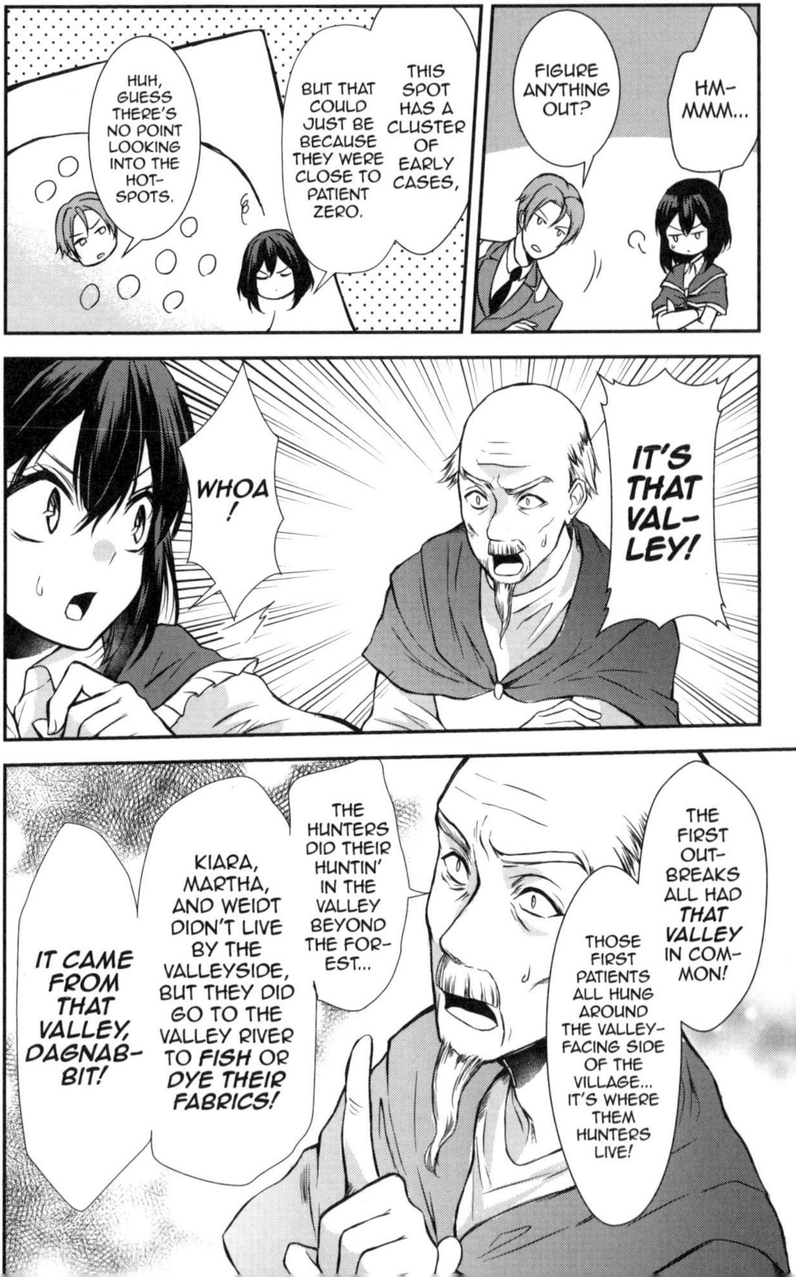
HMMMM...
FIGURE ANYTHING OUT?
THIS SPOT HAS A CLUSTER OF EARLY CASES,
BUT THAT COULD JUST BE BECAUSE THEY WERE CLOSE TO PATIENT ZERO.
HUH, GUESS THERE'S NO POINT LOOKING INTO THE HOT-SPOTS.
IT'S THAT VALLEY!
WHOA!
THE FIRST OUTBREAKS ALL HAD *THAT VALLEY* IN COMMON!
THOSE FIRST PATIENTS ALL HUNG AROUND THE VALLEY-FACING SIDE OF THE VILLAGE... IT'S WHERE THEM HUNTERS LIVE!
THE HUNTERS DID THEIR HUNTIN' IN THE VALLEY BEYOND THE FOREST...
KIARA, MARTHA, AND WEIDT DIDN'T LIVE BY THE VALLEYSIDE, BUT THEY DID GO TO THE VALLEY RIVER TO *FISH* OR *DYE THEIR FABRICS!*
IT CAME FROM THAT VALLEY, DAGNABBIT!

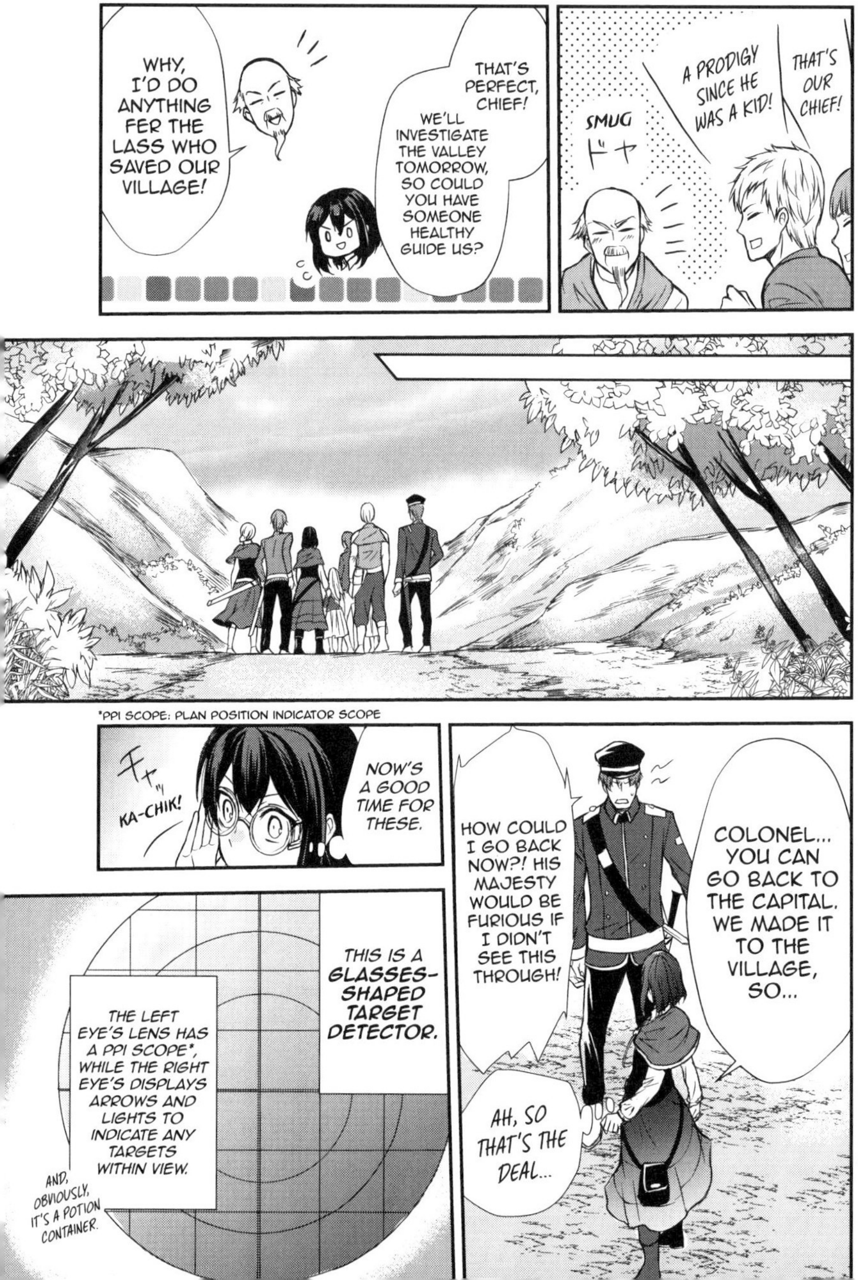
THAT'S OUR CHIEF!
A PRODIGY SINCE HE WAS A KID!
SMUG
ドヤ
THAT'S PERFECT, CHIEF!
WE'LL INVESTIGATE THE VALLEY TOMORROW, SO COULD YOU HAVE SOMEONE HEALTHY GUIDE US?
WHY, I'D DO ANYTHING FER THE LASS WHO SAVED OUR VILLAGE!
COLONEL... YOU CAN GO BACK TO THE CAPITAL. WE MADE IT TO THE VILLAGE, SO...
HOW COULD I GO BACK NOW?! HIS MAJESTY WOULD BE FURIOUS IF I DIDN'T SEE THIS THROUGH!
AH, SO THAT'S THE DEAL...
NOW'S A GOOD TIME FOR THESE.
チャ
KA-CHIK!
THIS IS A GLASSES-SHAPED TARGET DETECTOR.
THE LEFT EYE'S LENS HAS A PPI SCOPE*, WHILE THE RIGHT EYE'S DISPLAYS ARROWS AND LIGHTS TO INDICATE ANY TARGETS WITHIN VIEW.
AND, OBVIOUSLY, IT'S A POTION CONTAINER.

*PPI SCOPE: PLAN POSITION INDICATOR SCOPE

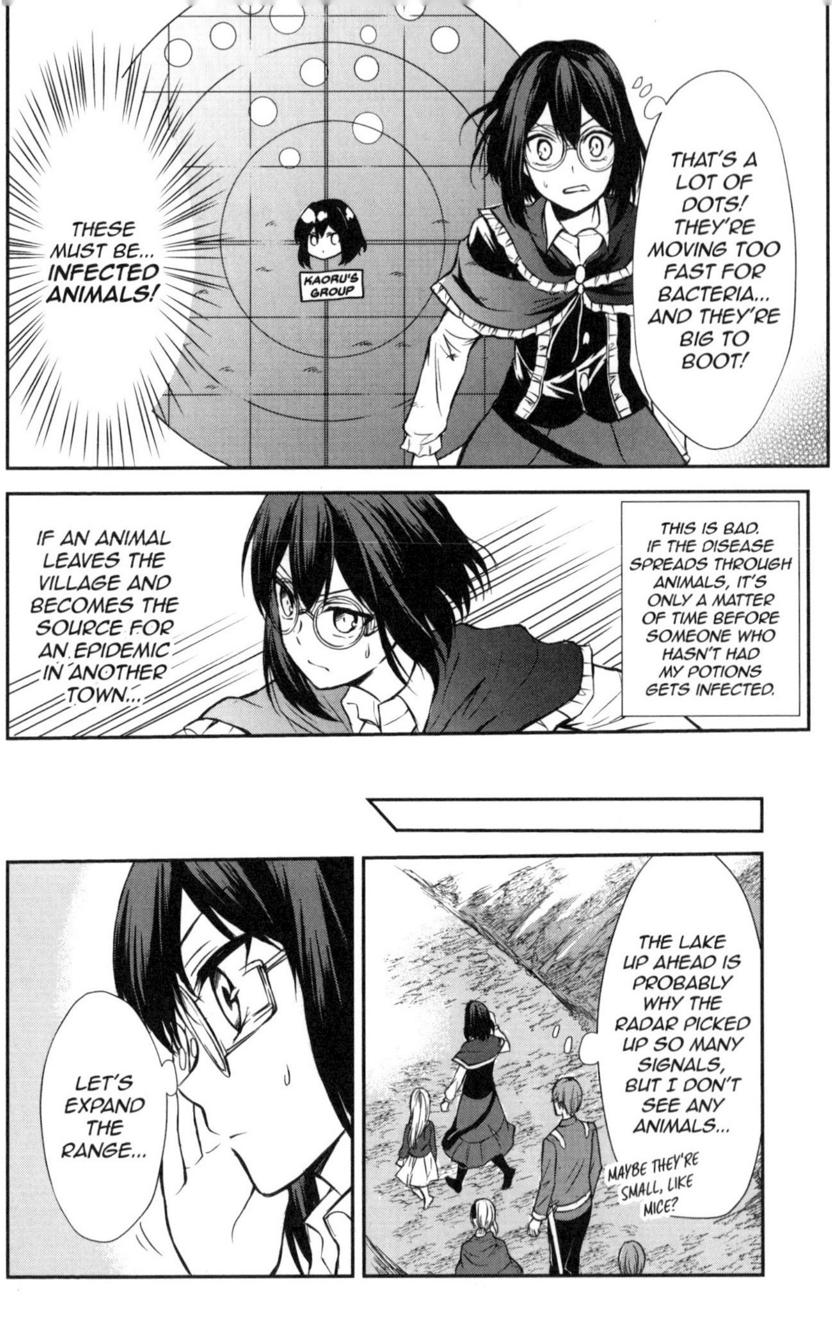

THAT'S A LOT OF DOTS! THEY'RE MOVING TOO FAST FOR BACTERIA... AND THEY'RE BIG TO BOOT!
THESE MUST BE... INFECTED ANIMALS!
KAORU'S GROUP
THIS IS BAD. IF THE DISEASE SPREADS THROUGH ANIMALS, IT'S ONLY A MATTER OF TIME BEFORE SOMEONE WHO HASN'T HAD MY POTIONS GETS INFECTED.
IF AN ANIMAL LEAVES THE VILLAGE AND BECOMES THE SOURCE FOR AN EPIDEMIC IN ANOTHER TOWN...
THE LAKE UP AHEAD IS PROBABLY WHY THE RADAR PICKED UP SO MANY SIGNALS, BUT I DON'T SEE ANY ANIMALS...
MAYBE THEY'RE SMALL, LIKE MICE?
LET'S EXPAND THE RANGE...

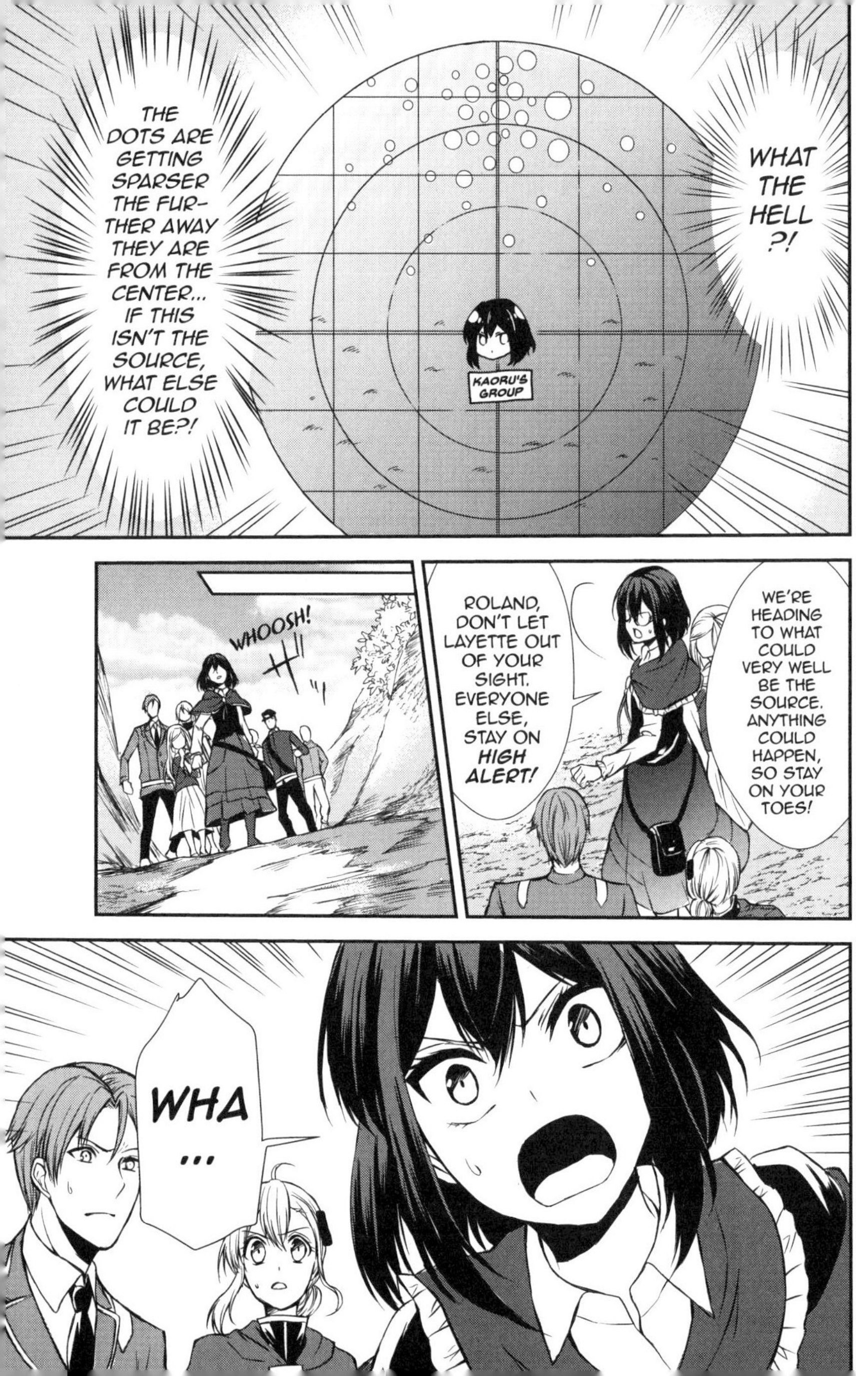
WHAT THE HELL ?!
THE DOTS ARE GETTING SPARSER THE FURTHER AWAY THEY ARE FROM THE CENTER... IF THIS ISN'T THE SOURCE, WHAT ELSE COULD IT BE?!
KAORU'S GROUP
WE'RE HEADING TO WHAT COULD VERY WELL BE THE SOURCE. ANYTHING COULD HAPPEN, SO STAY ON YOUR TOES!
ROLAND, DON'T LET LAYETTE OUT OF YOUR SIGHT. EVERYONE ELSE, STAY ON HIGH ALERT!
WHOOSH!
WHA ...

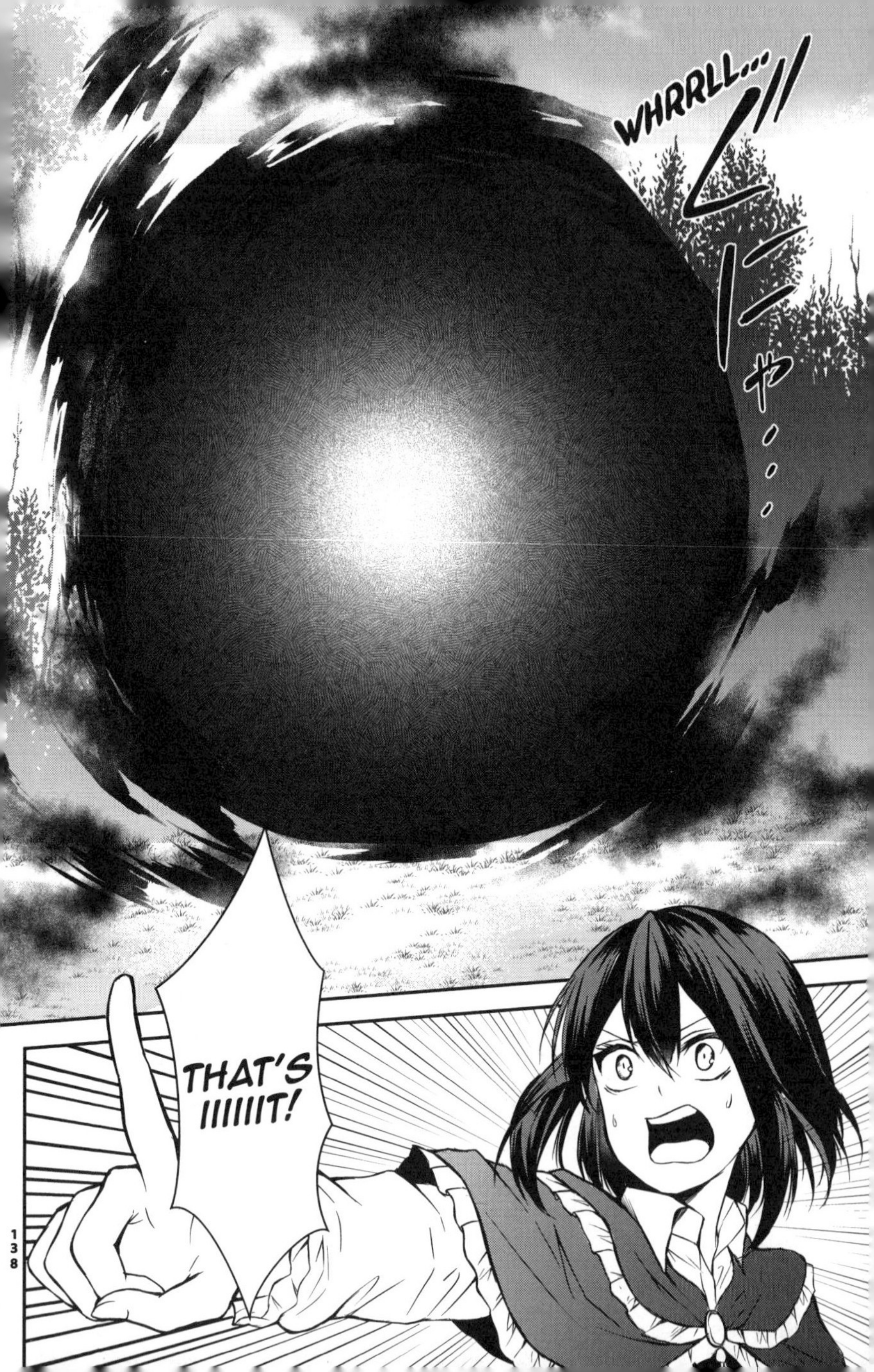
WHRRLL...
ぐにーゃ…
THAT'S IIIIIIT!

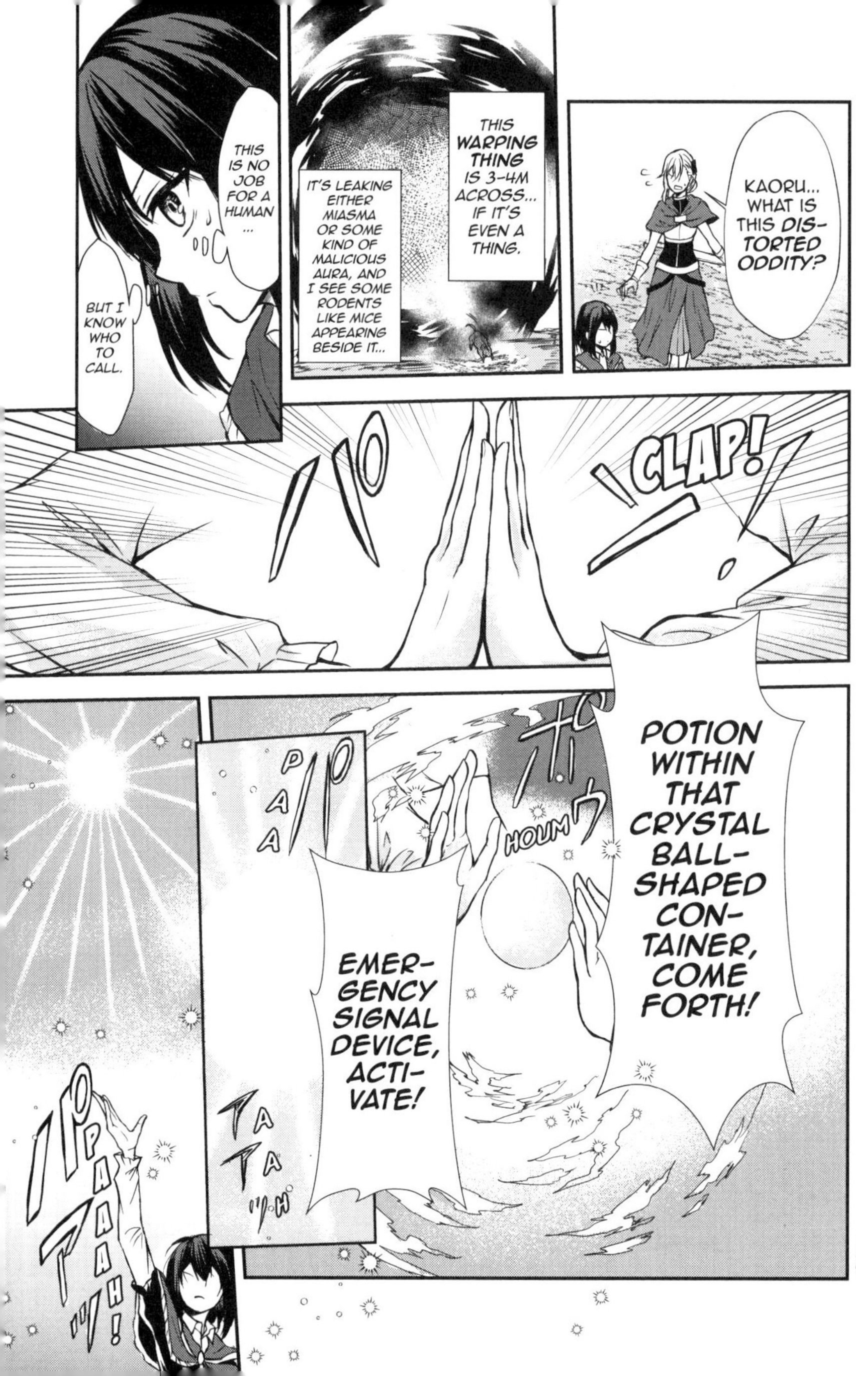
KAORU... WHAT IS THIS DIS-TORTED ODDITY?
THIS WARPING THING IS 3-4M ACROSS... IF IT'S EVEN A THING.
IT'S LEAKING EITHER MIASMA OR SOME KIND OF MALICIOUS AURA, AND I SEE SOME RODENTS LIKE MICE APPEARING BESIDE IT...
THIS IS NO JOB FOR A HUMAN ...
BUT I KNOW WHO TO CALL.
CLAP!
POTION WITHIN THAT CRYSTAL BALL-SHAPED CON-TAINER, COME FORTH!
HOUM
PAA
EMER-GENCY SIGNAL DEVICE, ACTI-VATE!
TA TA H
PAAAAH!

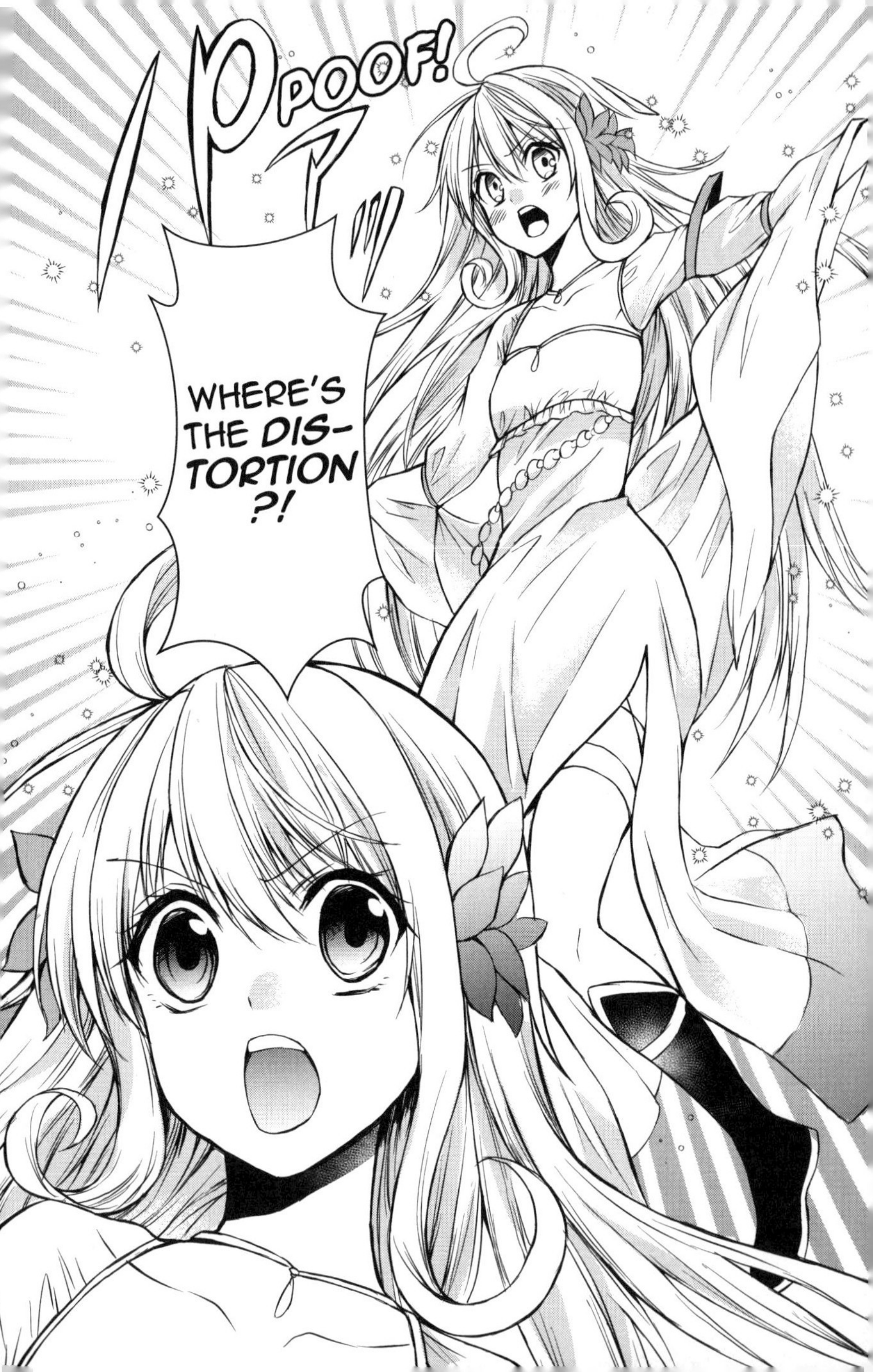
POOF!
WHERE'S THE DIS-TORTION ?!

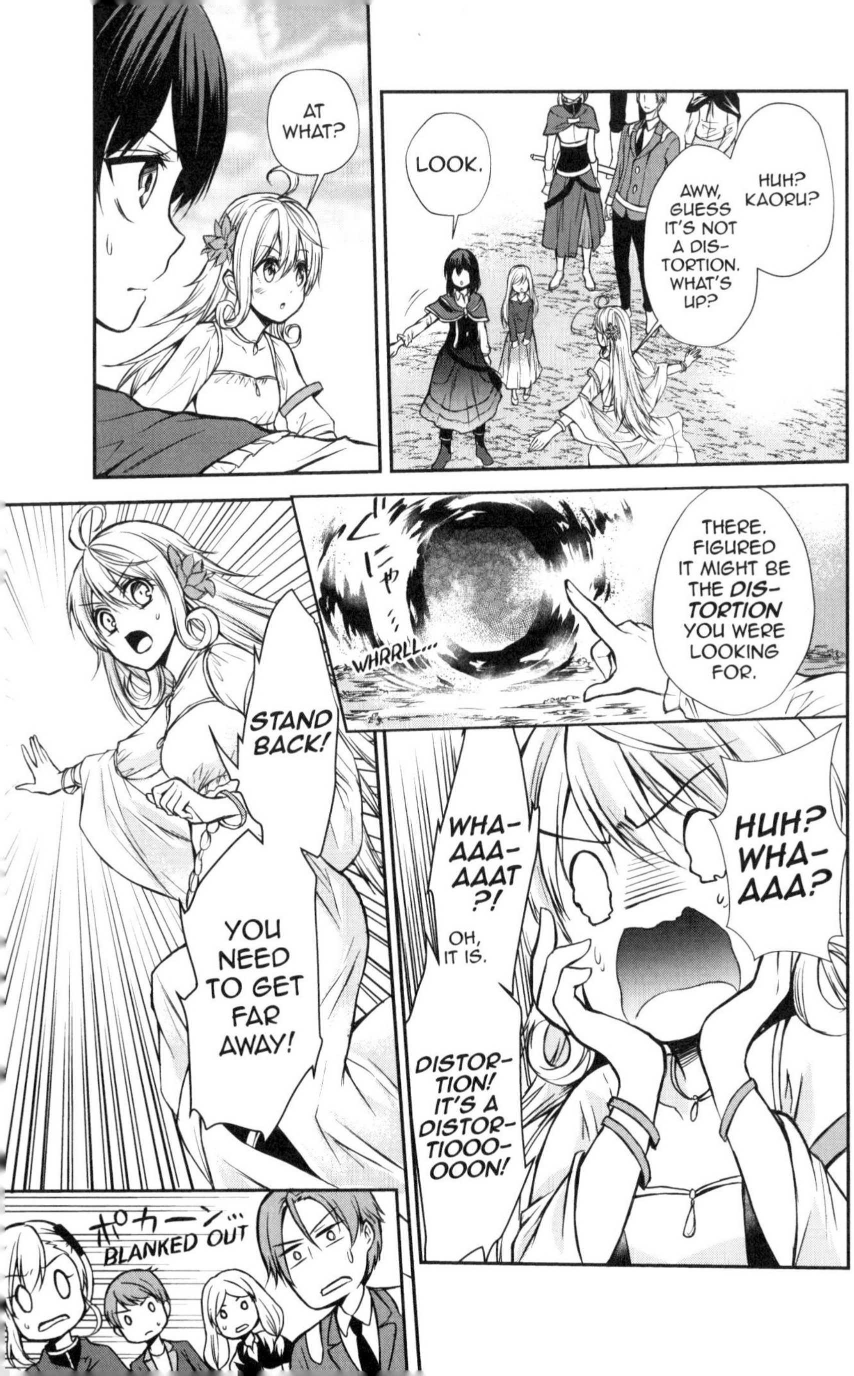
HUH? KAORU?
AWW, GUESS IT'S NOT A DISTORTION. WHAT'S UP?
LOOK.
AT WHAT?
THERE. FIGURED IT MIGHT BE THE *DISTORTION* YOU WERE LOOKING FOR.
ぐにゃ…
WHRRLL...
HUH? WHA-AAA?
WHA-AAA-AAAT?!
OH, IT IS.
DISTORTION! IT'S A DISTORTIOOO-OOON!
STAND BACK!
YOU NEED TO GET FAR AWAY!
ポカーン…
BLANKED OUT

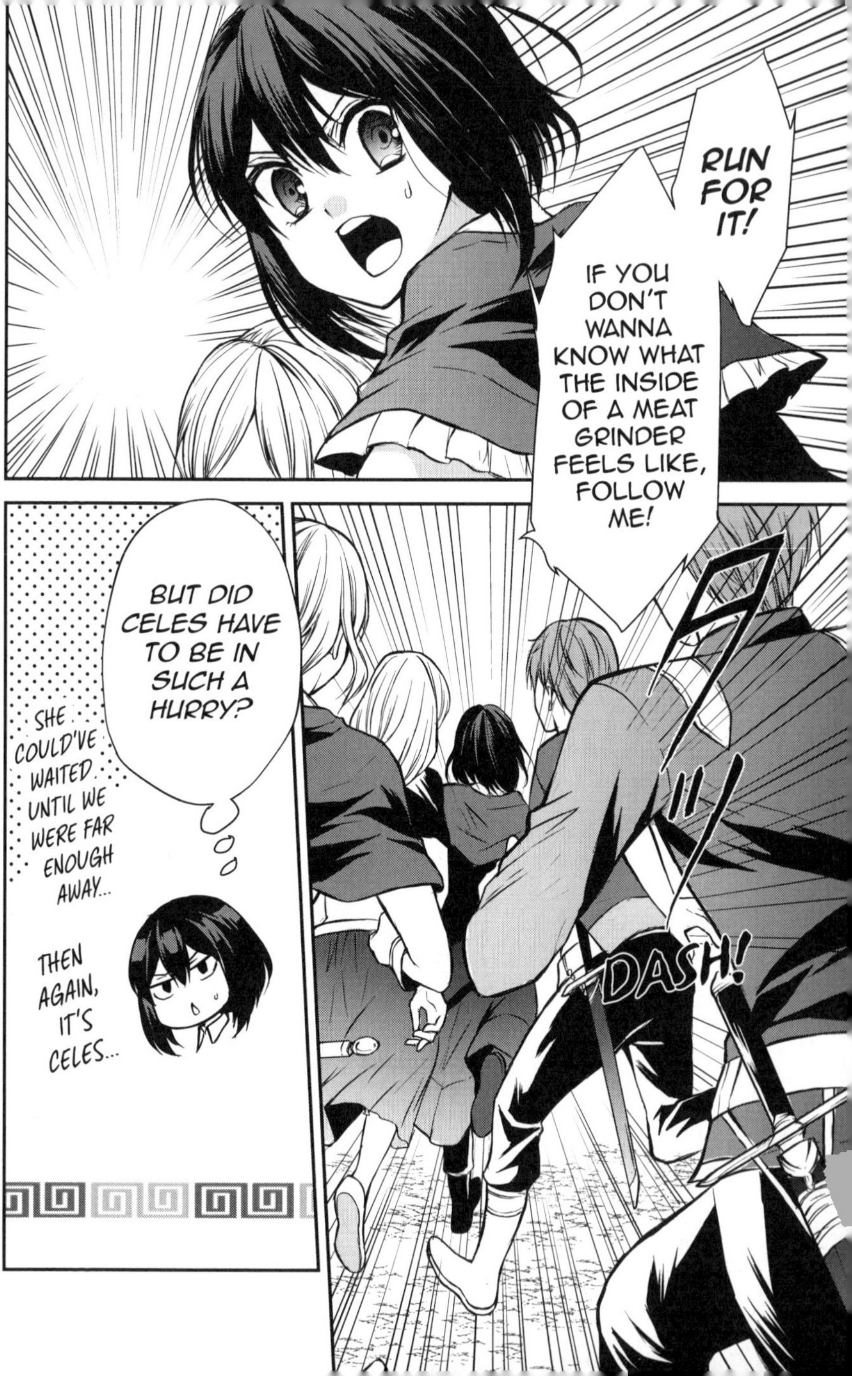
RUN FOR IT!
IF YOU DON'T WANNA KNOW WHAT THE INSIDE OF A MEAT GRINDER FEELS LIKE, FOLLOW ME!
DASH!
BUT DID CELES HAVE TO BE IN SUCH A HURRY?
SHE COULD'VE WAITED UNTIL WE WERE FAR ENOUGH AWAY...
THEN AGAIN, IT'S CELES...

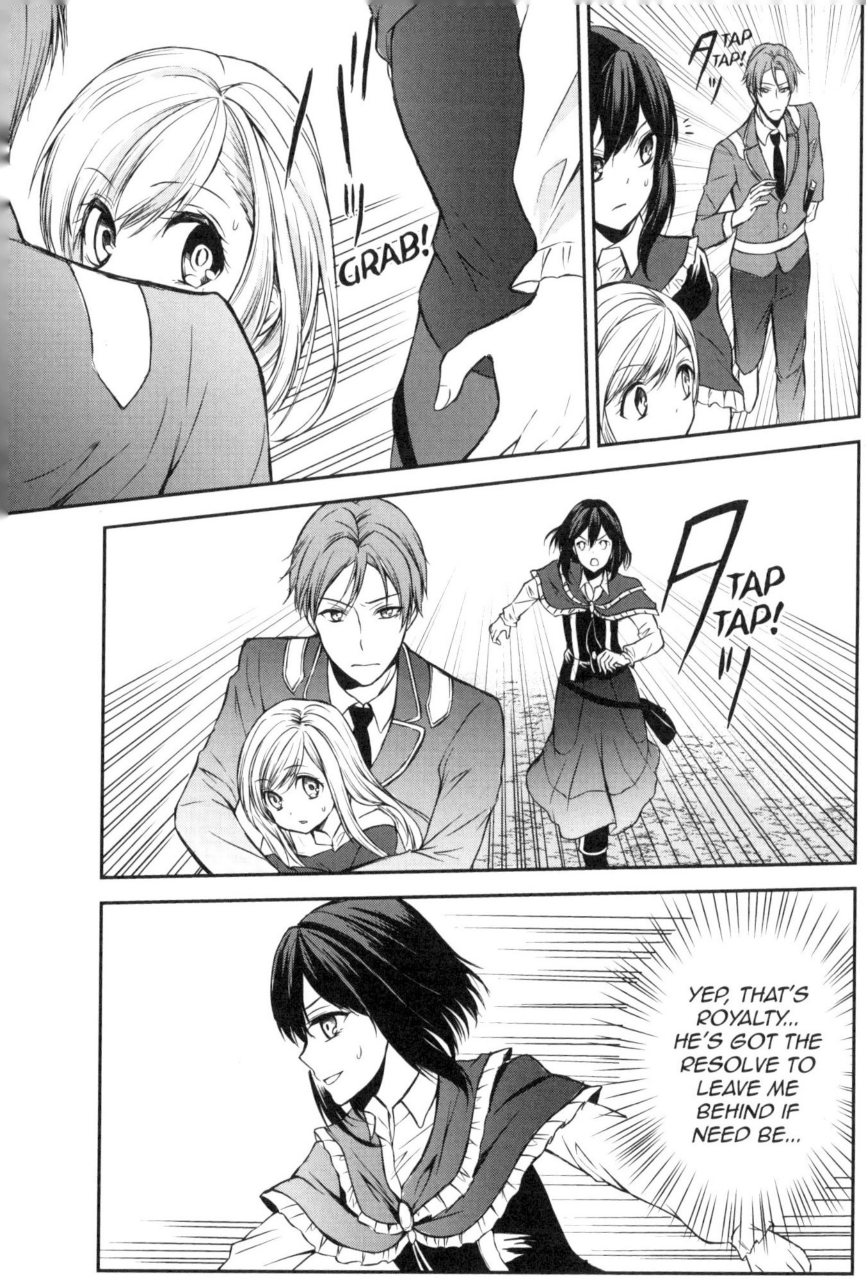

TAP TAP!
GRAB!
TAP TAP!
YEP, THAT'S ROYALTY... HE'S GOT THE RESOLVE TO LEAVE ME BEHIND IF NEED BE...

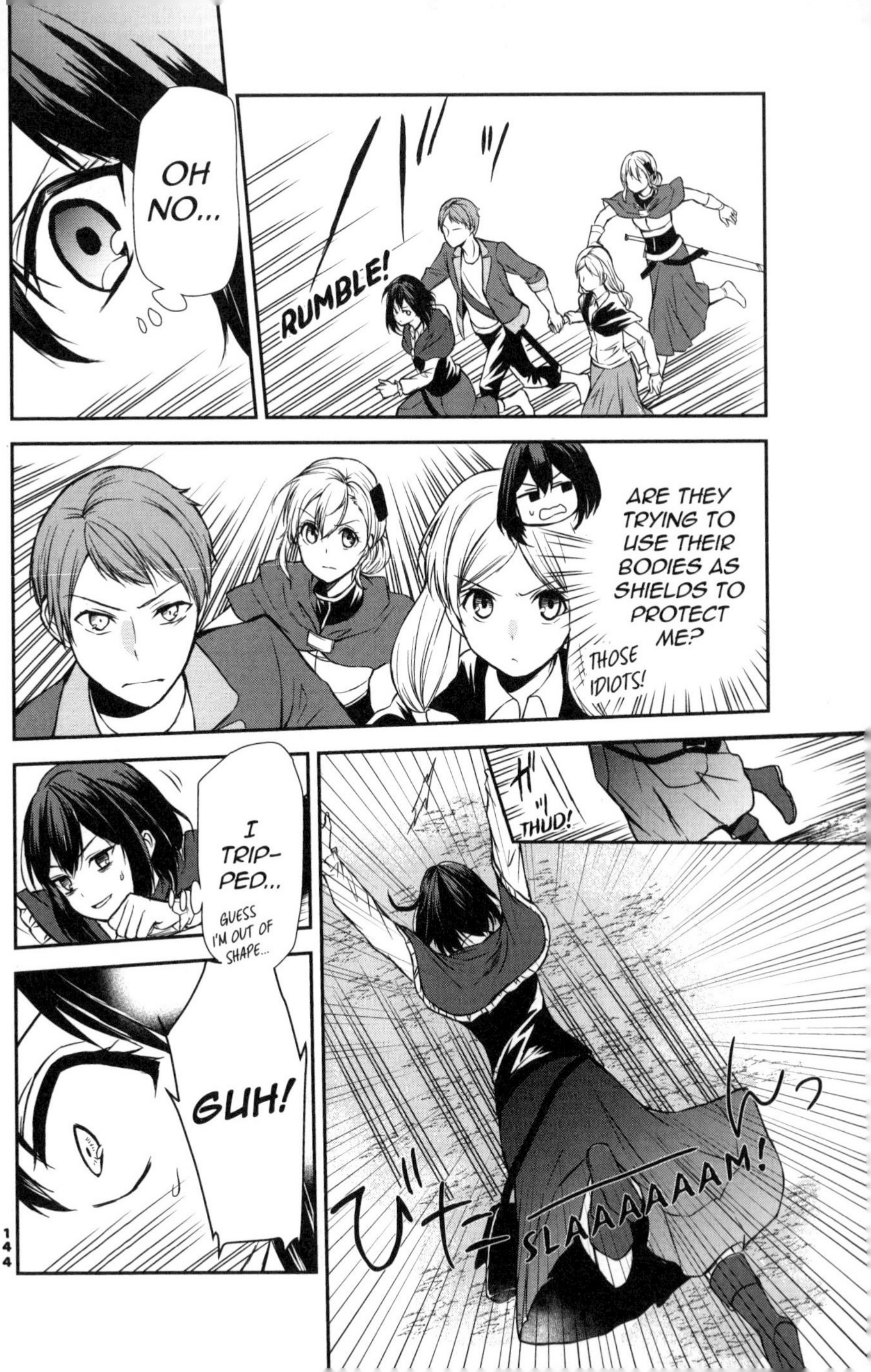
RUMBLE!
OH NO...
ARE THEY TRYING TO USE THEIR BODIES AS SHIELDS TO PROTECT ME?
THOSE IDIOTS!
THUD!
SLAAAAAAM!
I TRIP-PED...
GUESS I'M OUT OF SHAPE...
GUH!

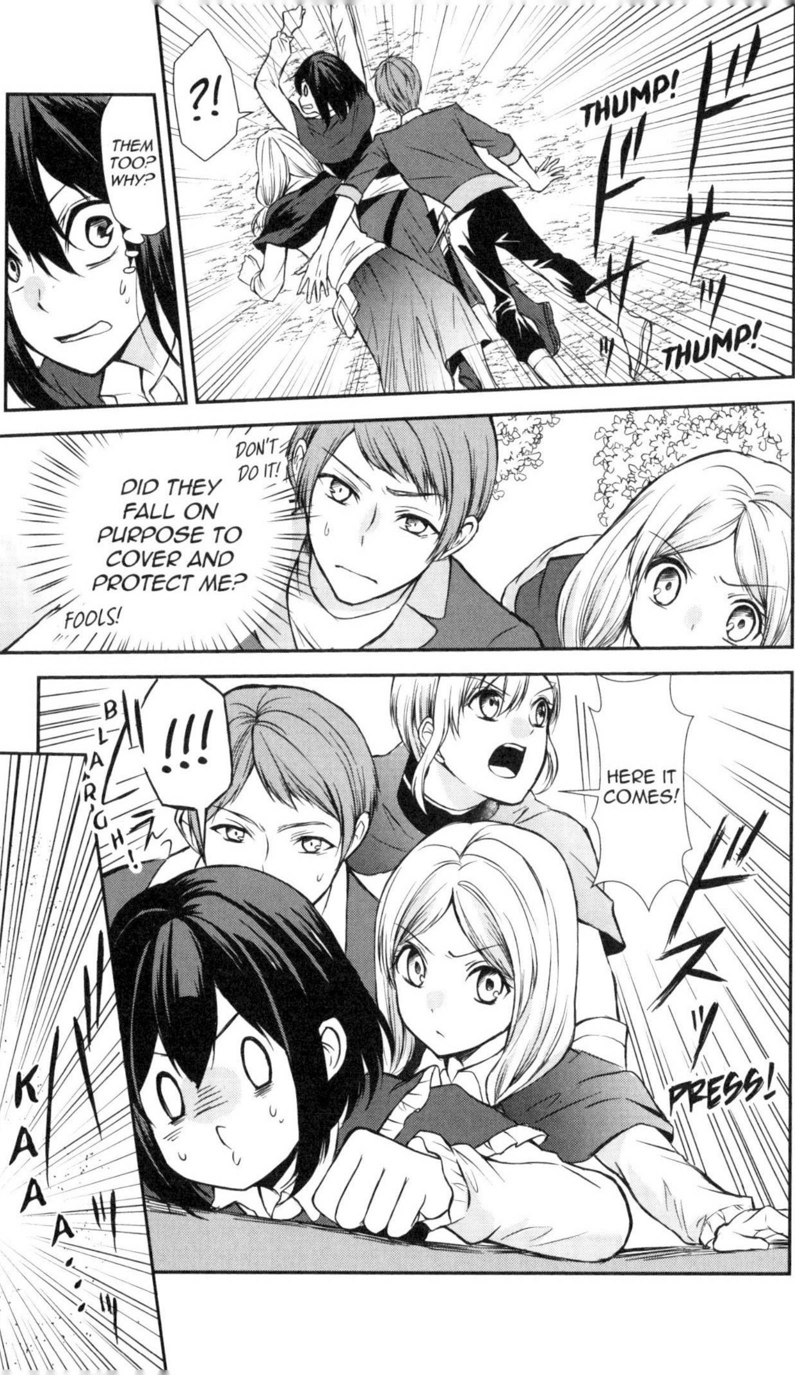

THUMP!
?!
THUMP!
THEM TOO? WHY?
DON'T DO IT!
DID THEY FALL ON PURPOSE TO COVER AND PROTECT ME?
FOOLS!
HERE IT COMES!
PRESS!
!!!
BLARGH!
KAAAA...!!!

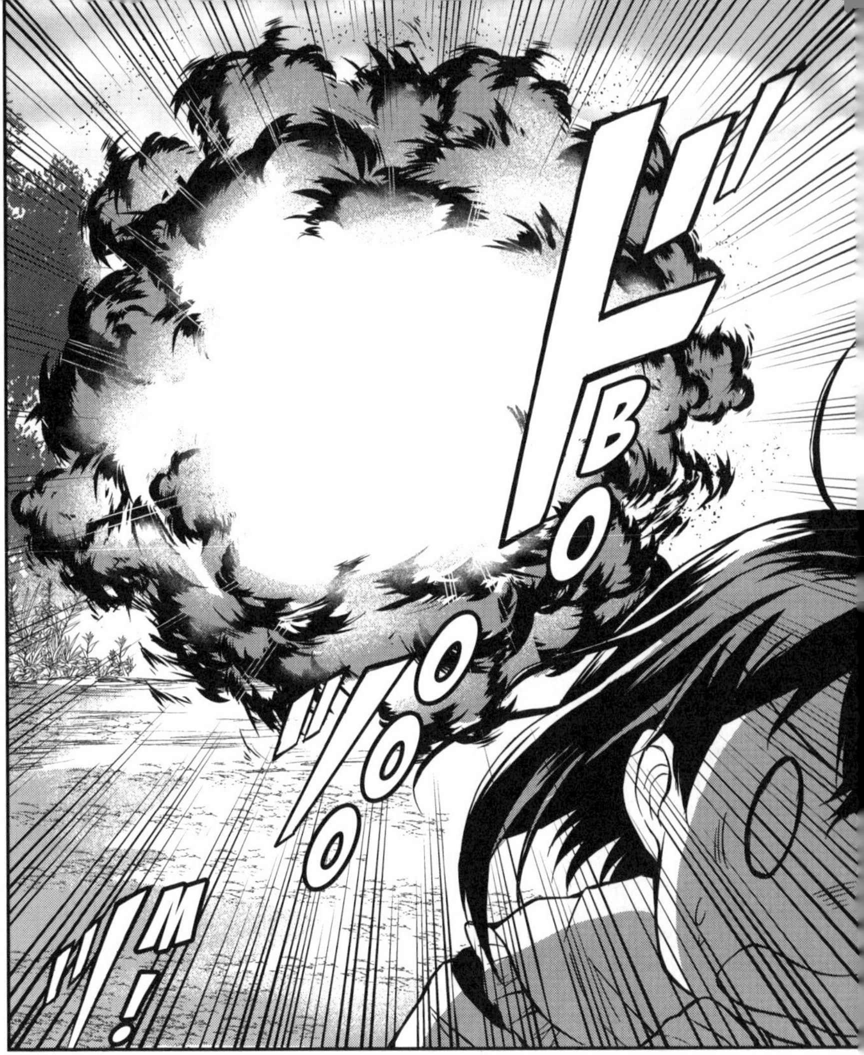
ド
BOOOOM!!

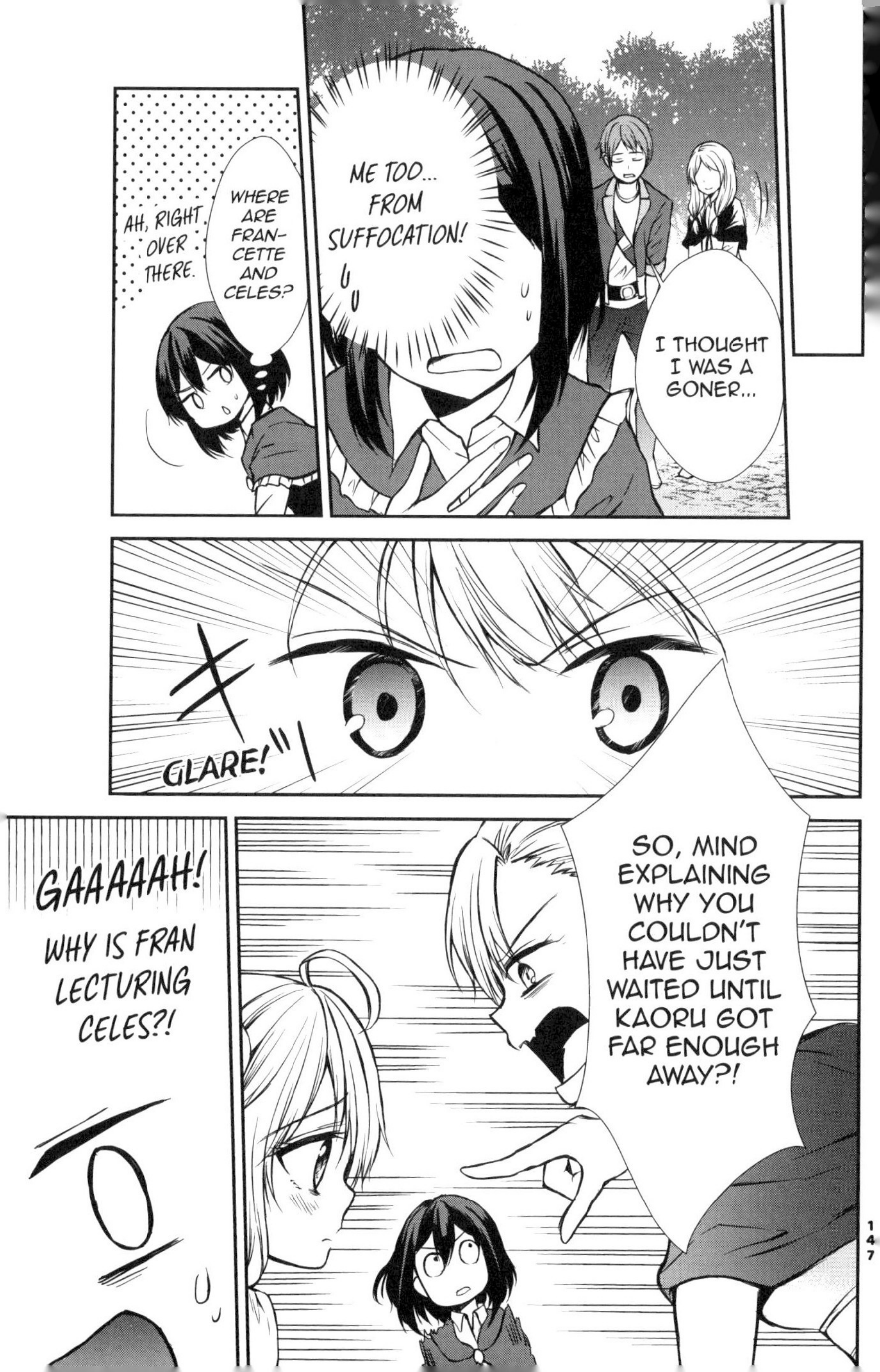

I THOUGHT I WAS A GONER...
ME TOO... FROM SUFFOCATION!
WHERE ARE FRAN-CETTE AND CELES?
AH, RIGHT OVER THERE.
GLARE!
SO, MIND EXPLAINING WHY YOU COULDN'T HAVE JUST WAITED UNTIL KAORU GOT FAR ENOUGH AWAY?!
GAAAAAH!
WHY IS FRAN LECTURING CELES?!

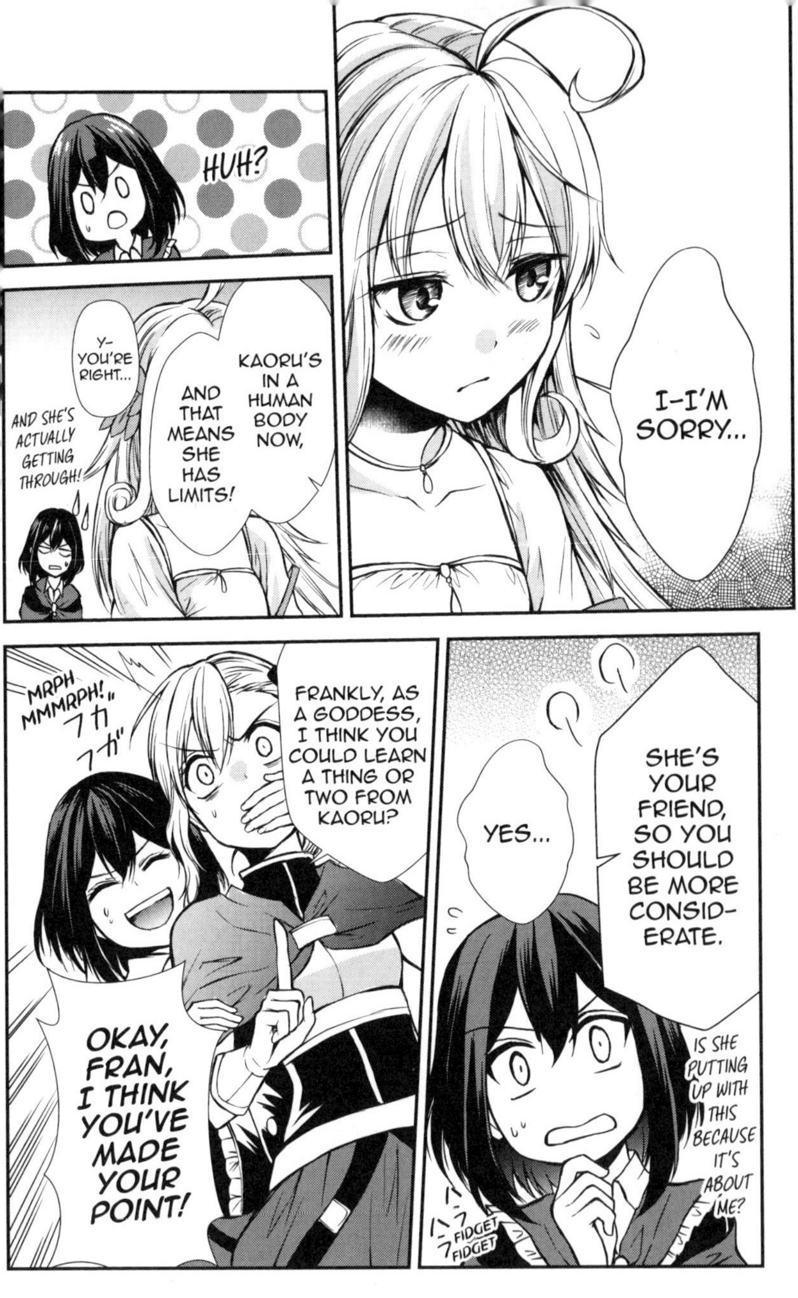
I-I'M SORRY...
HUH?
KAORU'S IN A HUMAN BODY NOW,
AND THAT MEANS SHE HAS LIMITS!
Y-YOU'RE RIGHT...
AND SHE'S ACTUALLY GETTING THROUGH!
SHE'S YOUR FRIEND, SO YOU SHOULD BE MORE CONSIDERATE.
YES...
IS SHE PUTTING UP WITH THIS BECAUSE IT'S ABOUT ME?
FIDGET FIDGET
FRANKLY, AS A GODDESS, I THINK YOU COULD LEARN A THING OR TWO FROM KAORU?
MRPH MMMRPH!
フガフガ
OKAY, FRAN, I THINK YOU'VE MADE YOUR POINT!

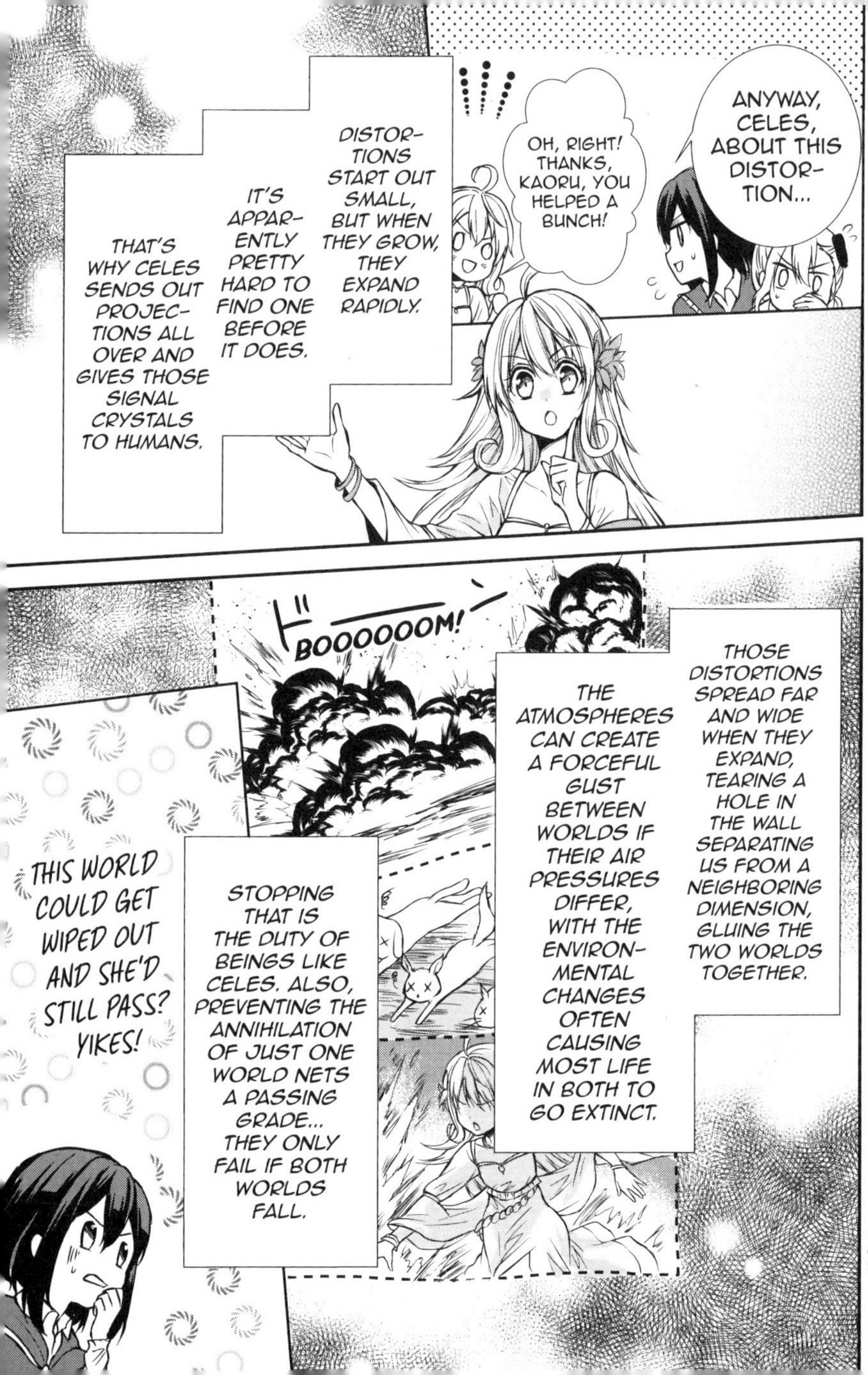
ANYWAY, CELES, ABOUT THIS DISTORTION...
OH, RIGHT! THANKS, KAORU, YOU HELPED A BUNCH!
DISTORTIONS START OUT SMALL, BUT WHEN THEY GROW, THEY EXPAND RAPIDLY.
IT'S APPARENTLY PRETTY HARD TO FIND ONE BEFORE IT DOES.
THAT'S WHY CELES SENDS OUT PROJECTIONS ALL OVER AND GIVES THOSE SIGNAL CRYSTALS TO HUMANS.
BOOOOOOM!
THOSE DISTORTIONS SPREAD FAR AND WIDE WHEN THEY EXPAND, TEARING A HOLE IN THE WALL SEPARATING US FROM A NEIGHBORING DIMENSION, GLUING THE TWO WORLDS TOGETHER.
THE ATMOSPHERES CAN CREATE A FORCEFUL GUST BETWEEN WORLDS IF THEIR AIR PRESSURES DIFFER, WITH THE ENVIRONMENTAL CHANGES OFTEN CAUSING MOST LIFE IN BOTH TO GO EXTINCT.
STOPPING THAT IS THE DUTY OF BEINGS LIKE CELES. ALSO, PREVENTING THE ANNIHILATION OF JUST ONE WORLD NETS A PASSING GRADE... THEY ONLY FAIL IF BOTH WORLDS FALL.
THIS WORLD COULD GET WIPED OUT AND SHE'D STILL PASS? YIKES!

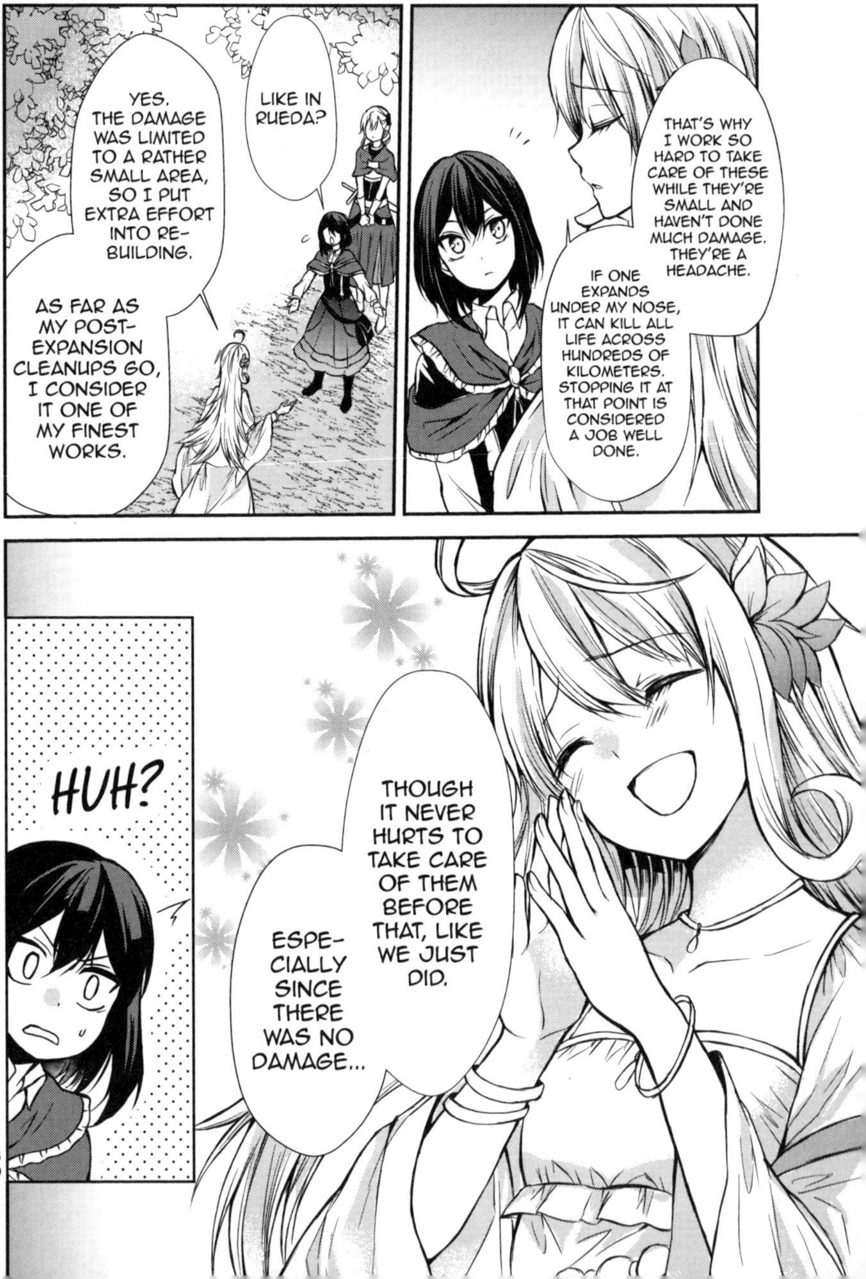

THAT'S WHY I WORK SO HARD TO TAKE CARE OF THESE WHILE THEY'RE SMALL AND HAVEN'T DONE MUCH DAMAGE. THEY'RE A HEADACHE.
IF ONE EXPANDS UNDER MY NOSE, IT CAN KILL ALL LIFE ACROSS HUNDREDS OF KILOMETERS. STOPPING IT AT THAT POINT IS CONSIDERED A JOB WELL DONE.
LIKE IN RUEDA?
YES. THE DAMAGE WAS LIMITED TO A RATHER SMALL AREA, SO I PUT EXTRA EFFORT INTO RE-BUILDING.
AS FAR AS MY POST-EXPANSION CLEANUPS GO, I CONSIDER IT ONE OF MY FINEST WORKS.
THOUGH IT NEVER HURTS TO TAKE CARE OF THEM BEFORE THAT, LIKE WE JUST DID.
ESPE-CIALLY SINCE THERE WAS NO DAMAGE...
HUH?

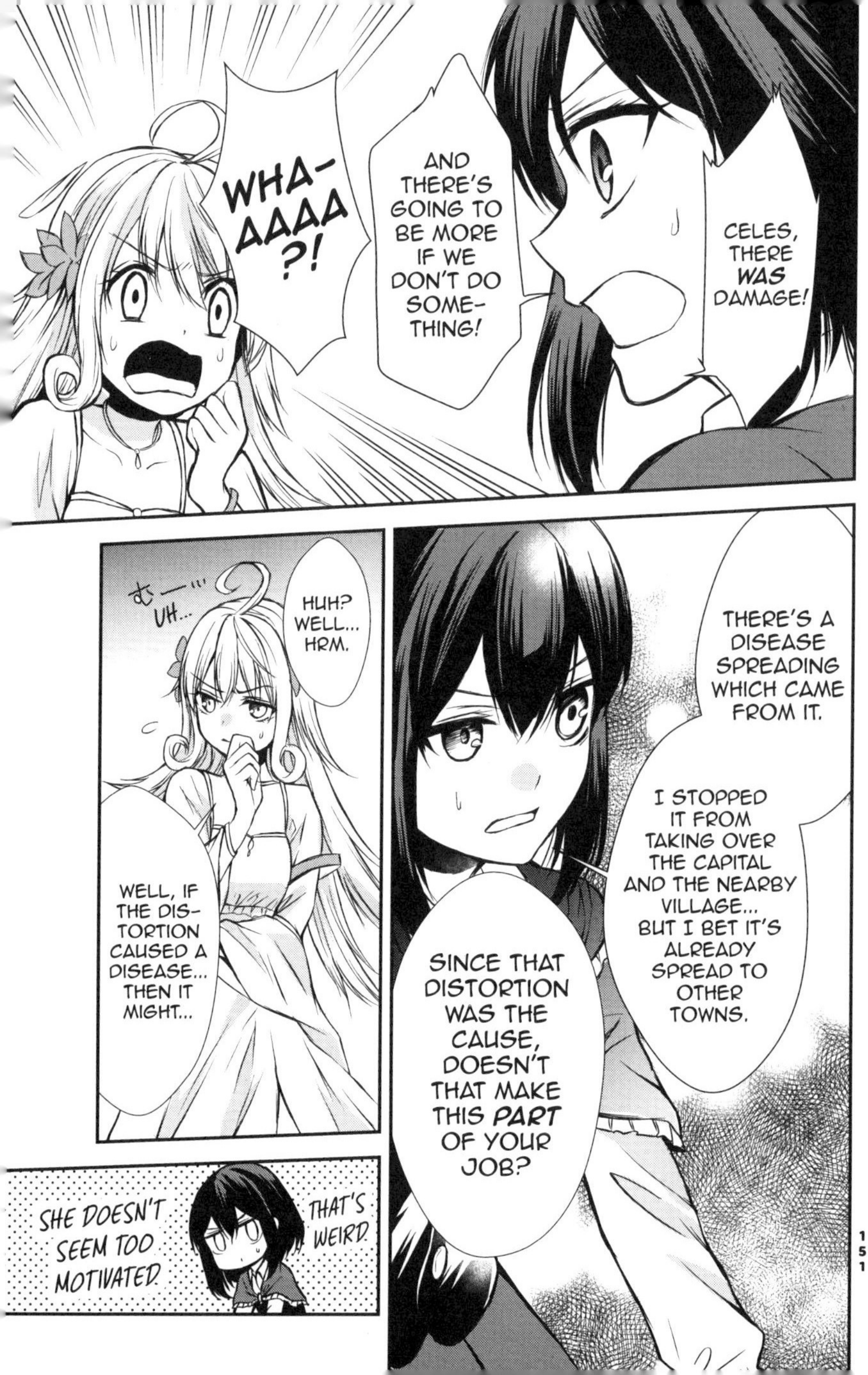
CELES, THERE *WAS* DAMAGE!
AND THERE'S GOING TO BE MORE IF WE DON'T DO SOME-THING!
WHA-AAAA?!
THERE'S A DISEASE SPREADING WHICH CAME FROM IT.
I STOPPED IT FROM TAKING OVER THE CAPITAL AND THE NEARBY VILLAGE... BUT I BET IT'S ALREADY SPREAD TO OTHER TOWNS.
SINCE THAT DISTORTION WAS THE CAUSE, DOESN'T THAT MAKE THIS *PART* OF YOUR JOB?
HUH? WELL... HRM.
むー" UH...
WELL, IF THE DIS-TORTION CAUSED A DISEASE... THEN IT MIGHT...
THAT'S WEIRD.
SHE DOESN'T SEEM TOO MOTIVATED.

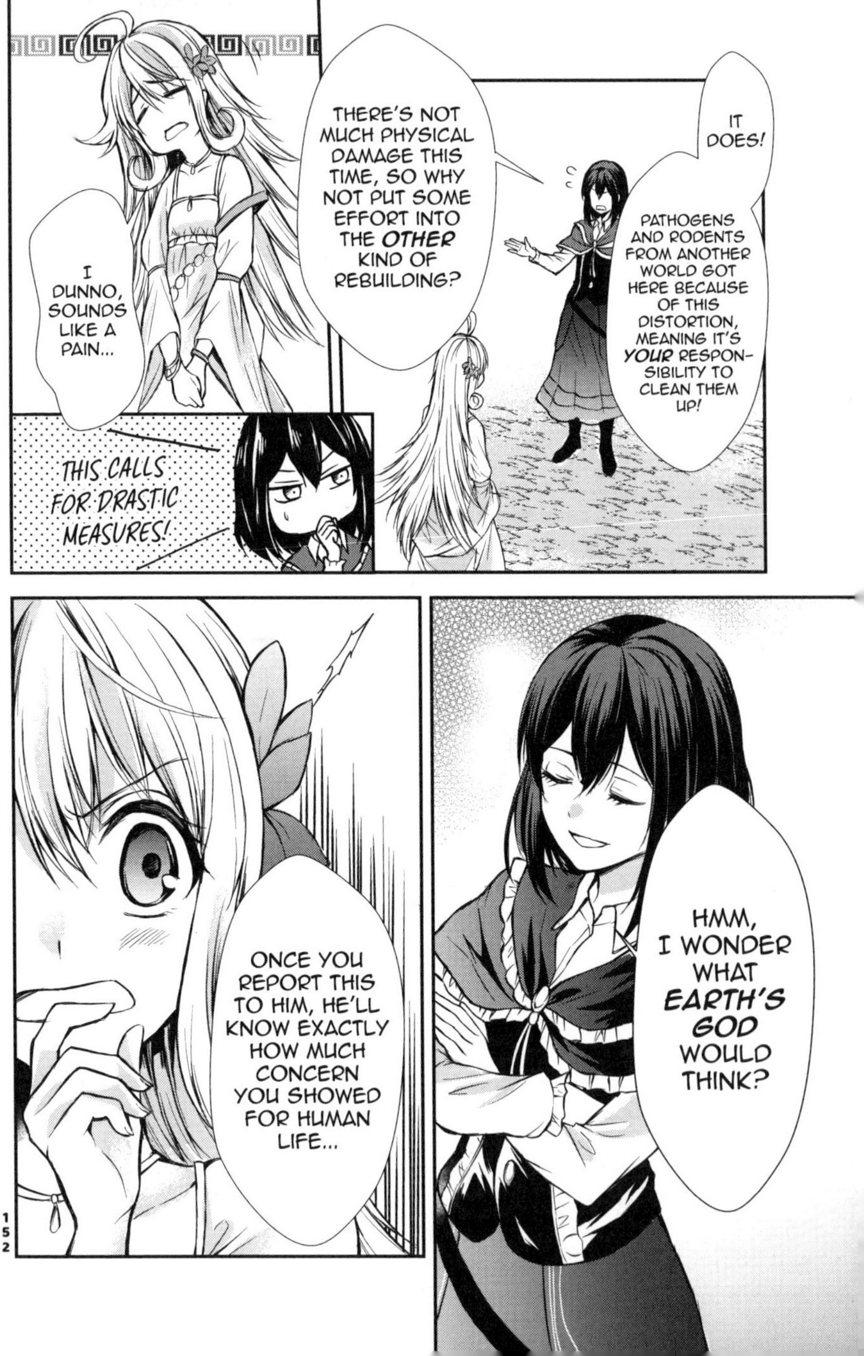
IT DOES!
PATHOGENS AND RODENTS FROM ANOTHER WORLD GOT HERE BECAUSE OF THIS DISTORTION, MEANING IT'S *YOUR* RESPONSIBILITY TO CLEAN THEM UP!
THERE'S NOT MUCH PHYSICAL DAMAGE THIS TIME, SO WHY NOT PUT SOME EFFORT INTO THE *OTHER* KIND OF REBUILDING?
I DUNNO, SOUNDS LIKE A PAIN...
THIS CALLS FOR DRASTIC MEASURES!
HMM, I WONDER WHAT *EARTH'S GOD* WOULD THINK?
ONCE YOU REPORT THIS TO HIM, HE'LL KNOW EXACTLY HOW MUCH CONCERN YOU SHOWED FOR HUMAN LIFE...

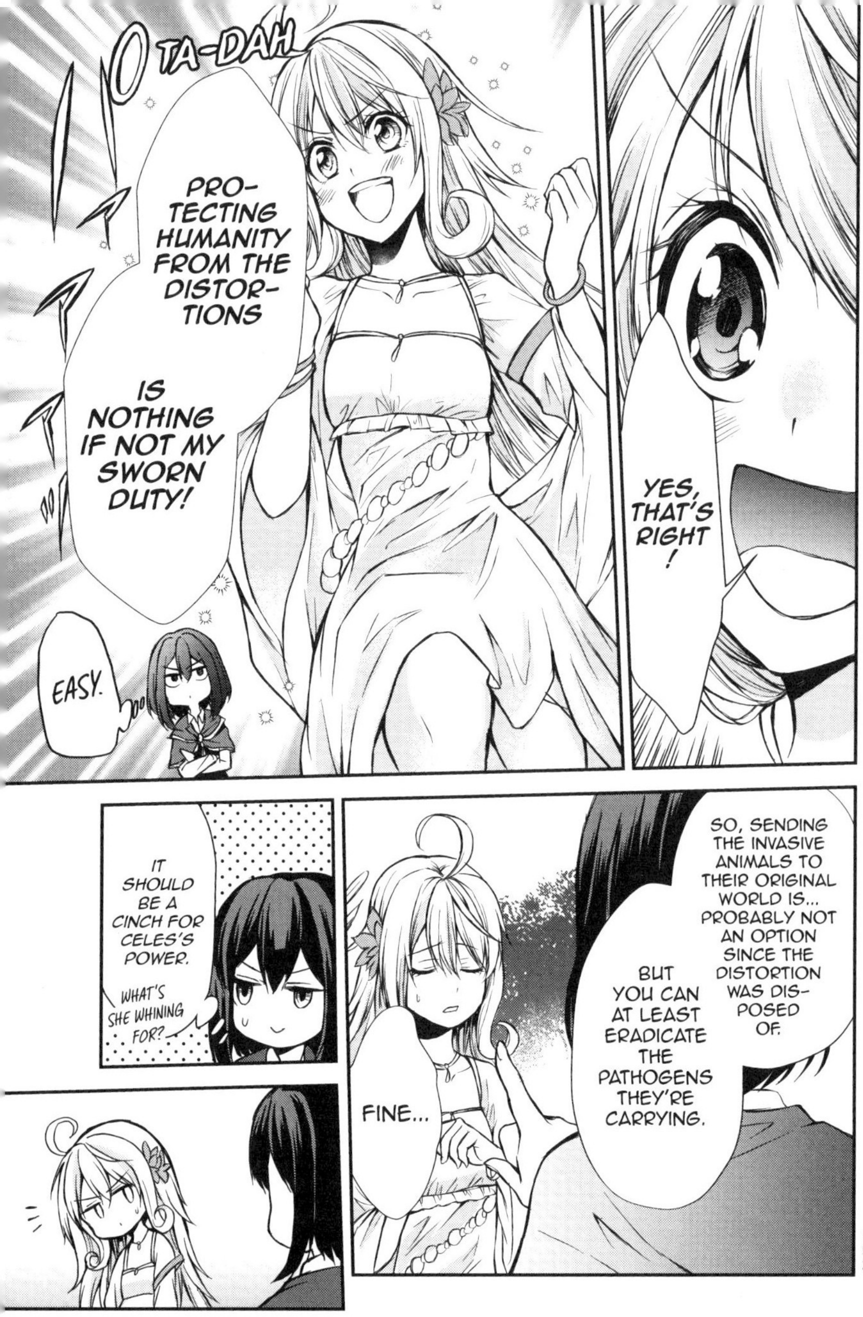
YES, THAT'S RIGHT!
TA-DAH
PRO-TECTING HUMANITY FROM THE DISTOR-TIONS
IS NOTHING IF NOT MY SWORN DUTY!
EASY.
SO, SENDING THE INVASIVE ANIMALS TO THEIR ORIGINAL WORLD IS... PROBABLY NOT AN OPTION SINCE THE DISTORTION WAS DIS-POSED OF.
BUT YOU CAN AT LEAST ERADICATE THE PATHOGENS THEY'RE CARRYING.
FINE...
IT SHOULD BE A CINCH FOR CELES'S POWER.
WHAT'S SHE WHINING FOR?

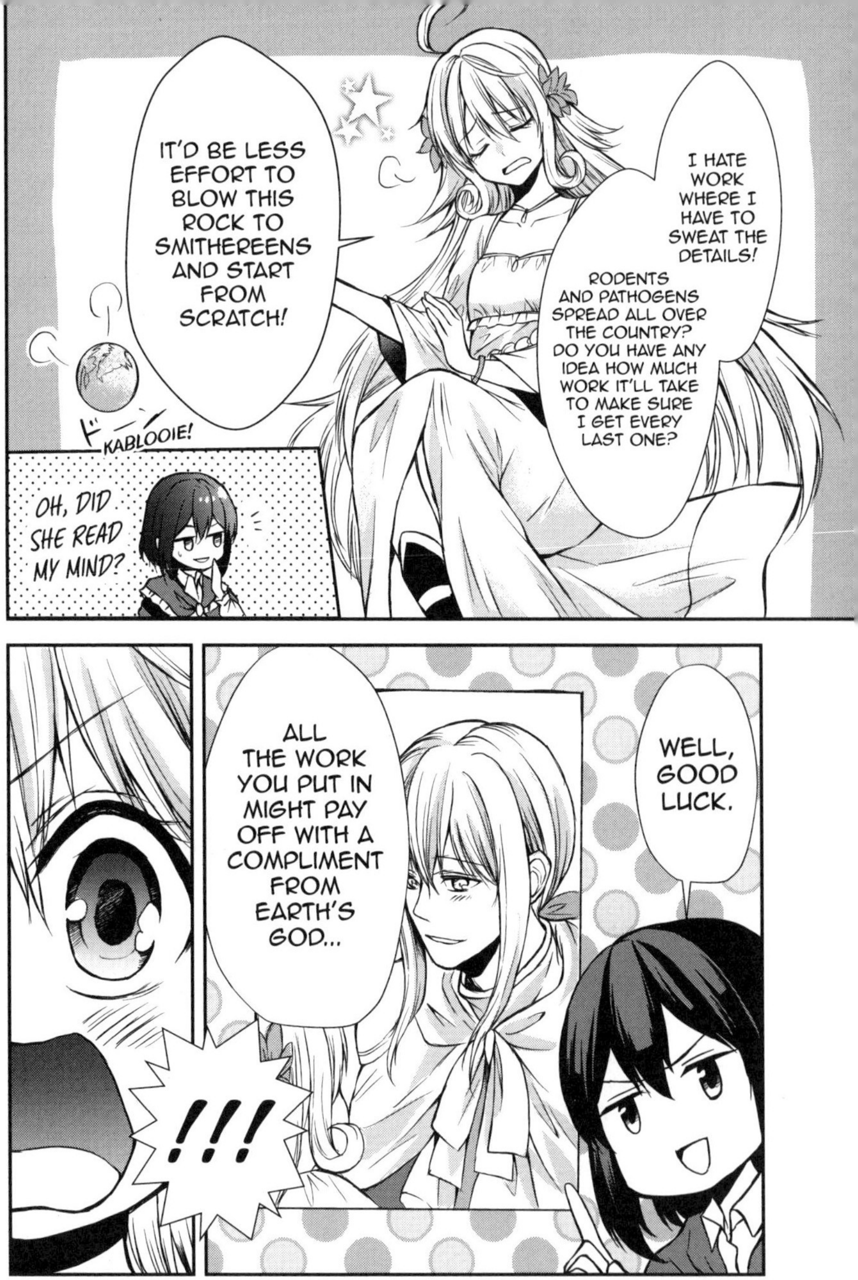
I HATE WORK WHERE I HAVE TO SWEAT THE DETAILS!
RODENTS AND PATHOGENS SPREAD ALL OVER THE COUNTRY? DO YOU HAVE ANY IDEA HOW MUCH WORK IT'LL TAKE TO MAKE SURE I GET EVERY LAST ONE?
IT'D BE LESS EFFORT TO BLOW THIS ROCK TO SMITHEREENS AND START FROM SCRATCH!
ドー
KABLOOIE!
OH, DID SHE READ MY MIND?
WELL, GOOD LUCK.
ALL THE WORK YOU PUT IN MIGHT PAY OFF WITH A COMPLIMENT FROM EARTH'S GOD...
!!!

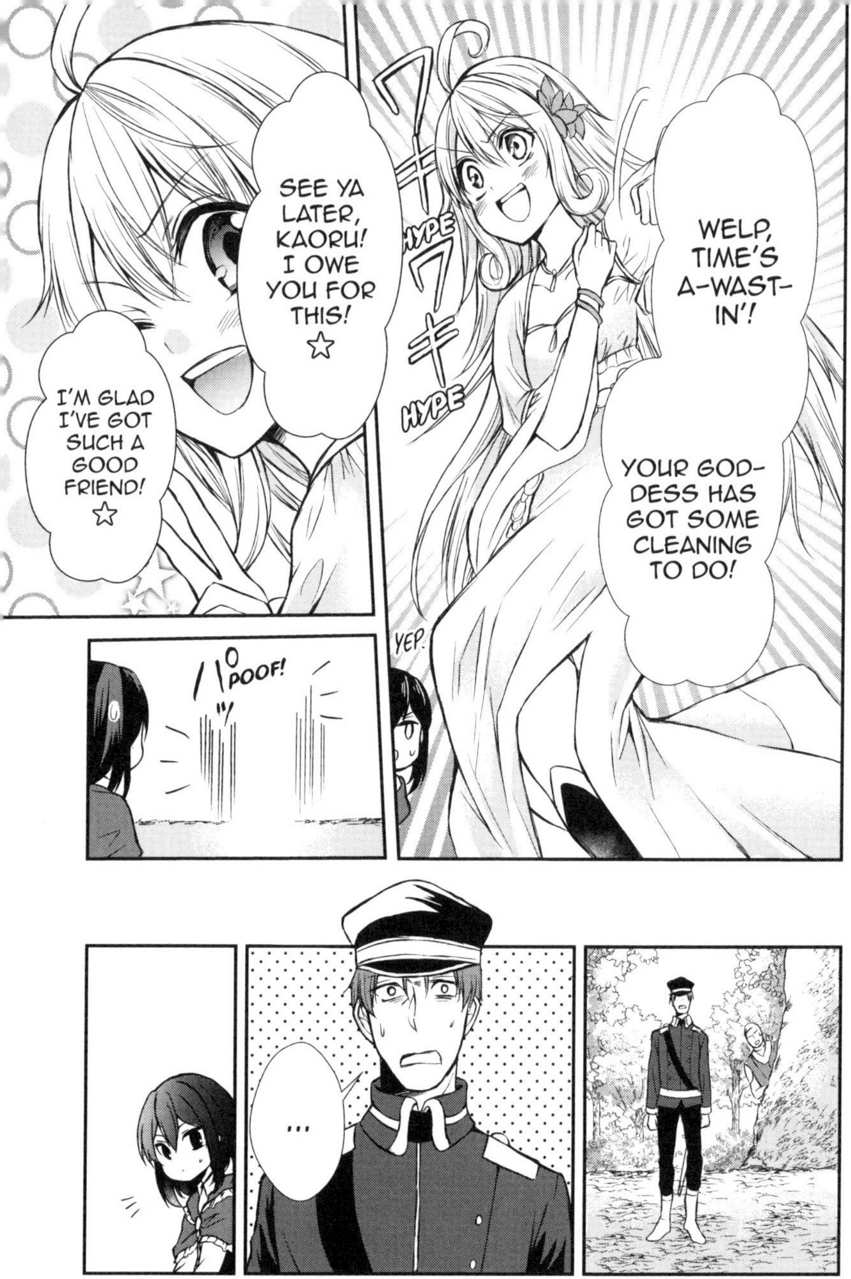
WELP, TIME'S A-WAST-IN'!
YOUR GOD-DESS HAS GOT SOME CLEANING TO DO!
HYPE
HYPE
YEP.
SEE YA LATER, KAORU! I OWE YOU FOR THIS! ☆
I'M GLAD I'VE GOT SUCH A GOOD FRIEND! ☆
POOF!
...

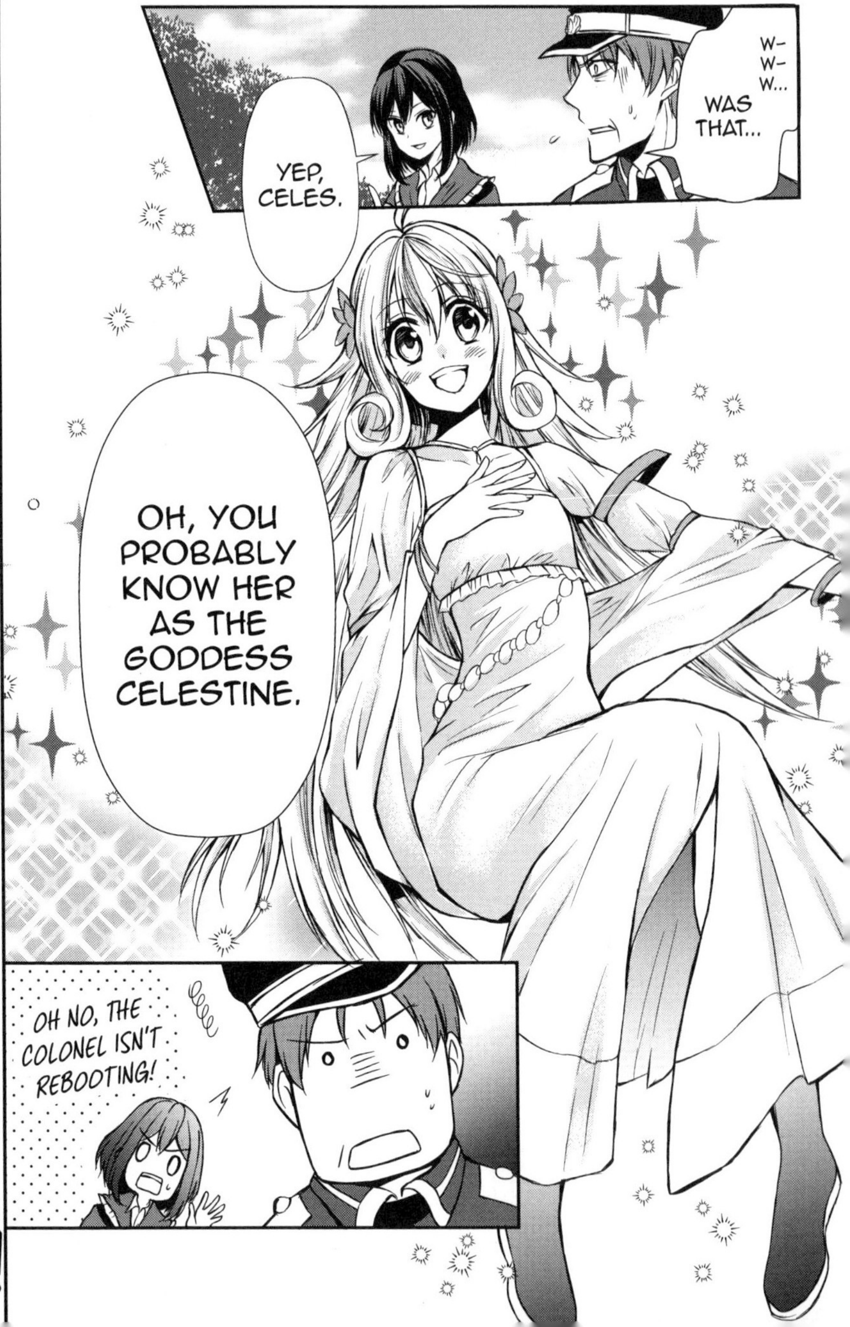
W- W- W... WAS THAT...
YEP, CELES.
OH, YOU PROBABLY KNOW HER AS THE GODDESS CELESTINE.
OH NO, THE COLONEL ISN'T REBOOTING!

39 CHAPTER END

END OF VOLUME 7

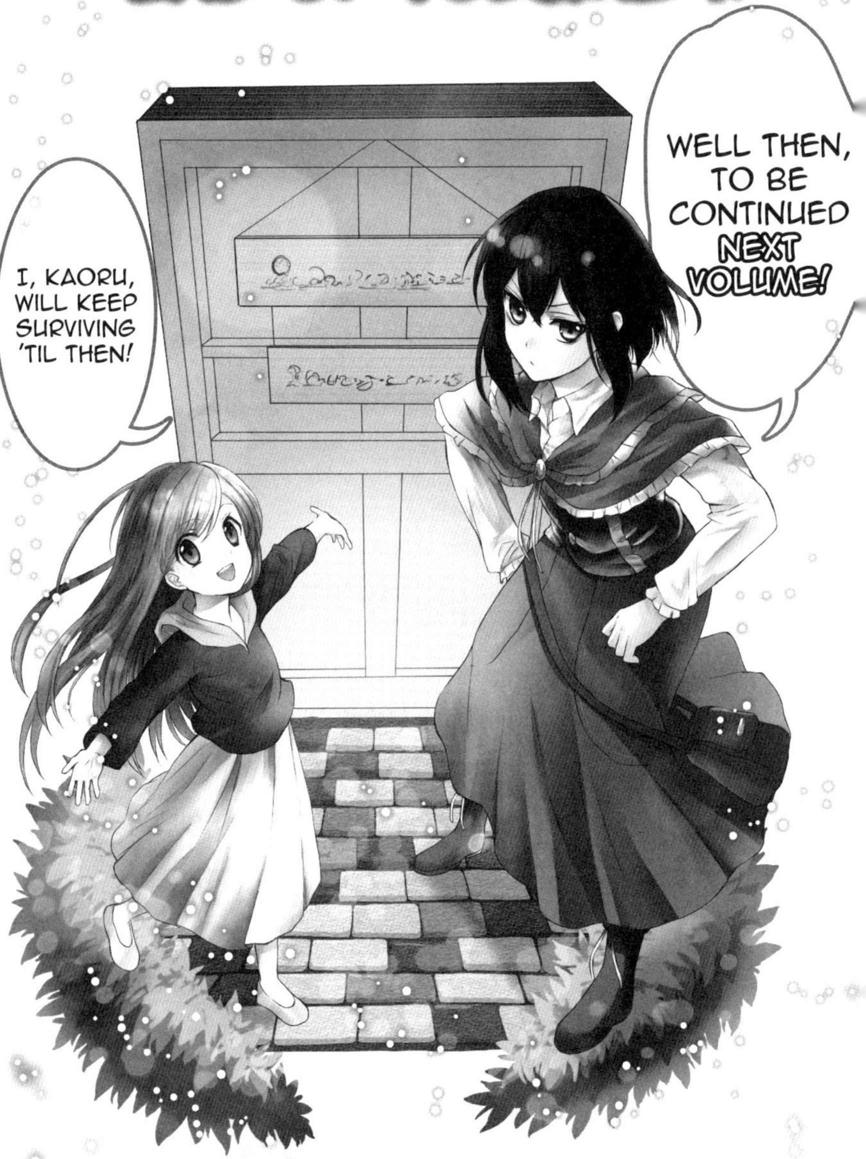
WELL THEN, TO BE CONTINUED NEXT VOLUME!
I, KAORU, WILL KEEP SURVIVING 'TIL THEN!

CONTINUED IN VOLUME 8

AFTERWORD

MANGA **HIBIKI KOKONOE** -SENSEI

LAYETTE'S ATELIER

How did you like volume 7?
I hope you all enjoyed it...
I switched to inking
digitally near the end.
How'd that turn out?
I just want to make
good art.

To my editor, FUNA, Sukima,
my assistant (who drew the
chariot), and all of my readers,
thank you very much!

 Hibiki Kokonoe

AUTHOR **FUNA** -SENSEI

CONGRATULATIONS ON

PUBLISHING VOLUME 7 OF THE MANGA!

A TREASURE HUNT, A WHIFF OF HER RARE SHOT AT MARRIAGE,

DEALING WITH BUSINESS RIVALS... AND SUDDENLY,

AN EPIDEMIC IN THE CAPITAL?! IS KAORU GOING BACK TO

THE ANGEL INDUSTRY? WELL, NOT AS A DAY JOB, JUST

AS A SIDE GIG. GOOD LUCK, KAORU! ONE DAY,

YOUR WEDDING DREAM WILL COME TRUE!

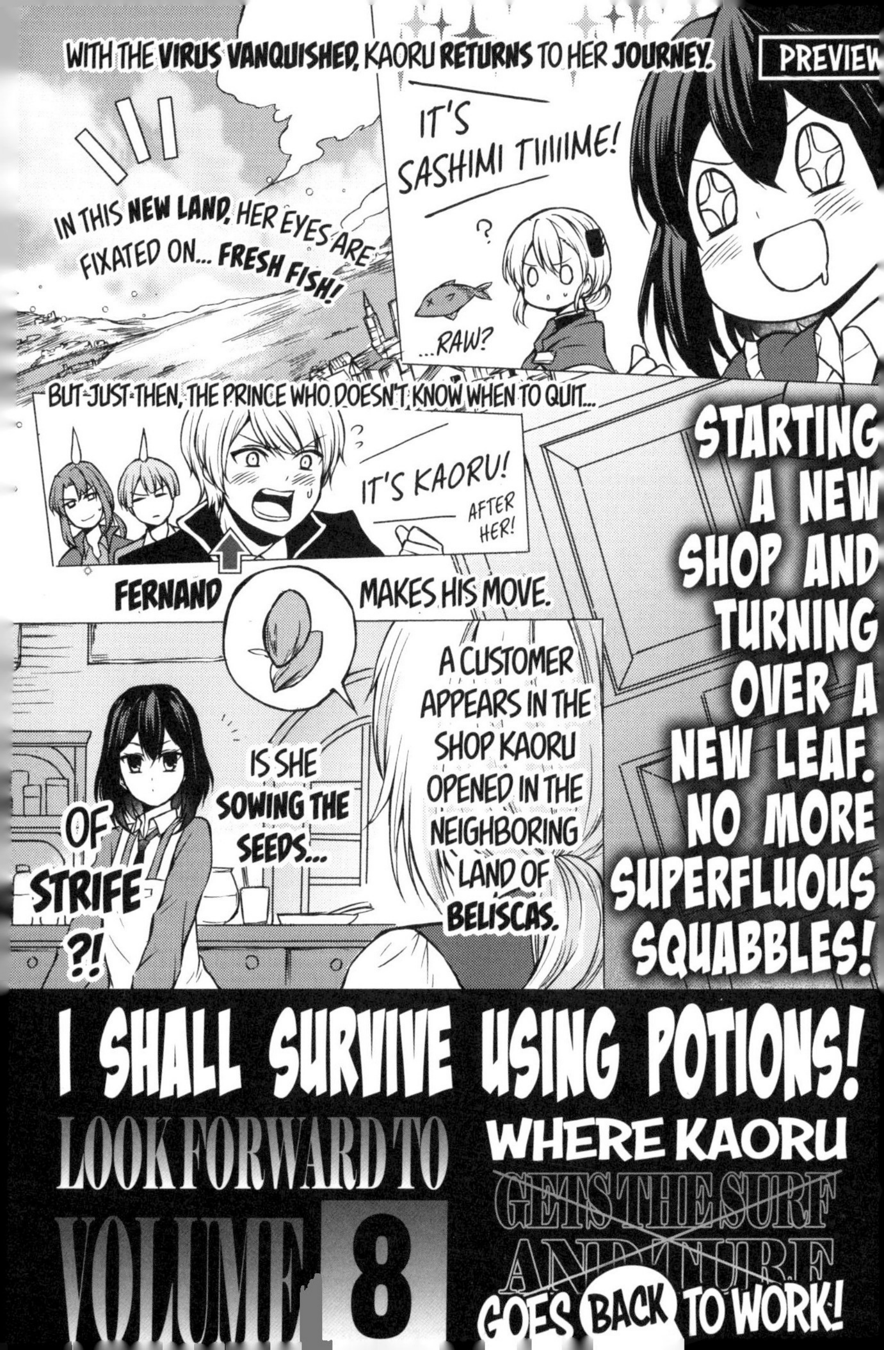
PREVIEW
WITH THE VIRUS VANQUISHED, KAORU RETURNS TO HER JOURNEY.
IN THIS NEW LAND, HER EYES ARE FIXATED ON... FRESH FISH!
IT'S SASHIMI TIIIIME!
?
...RAW?
BUT JUST THEN, THE PRINCE WHO DOESN'T KNOW WHEN TO QUIT...
STARTING A NEW SHOP AND TURNING OVER A NEW LEAF. NO MORE SUPERFLUOUS SQUABBLES!
IT'S KAORU!
AFTER HER!
FERNAND MAKES HIS MOVE.
A CUSTOMER APPEARS IN THE SHOP KAORU OPENED IN THE NEIGHBORING LAND OF BELISCAS.
IS SHE SOWING THE SEEDS...
OF STRIFE ?!

I SHALL SURVIVE USING POTIONS!

LOOK FORWARD TO VOLUME 8

WHERE KAORU ~~GETS THE SURF AND TURF~~ GOES BACK TO WORK!

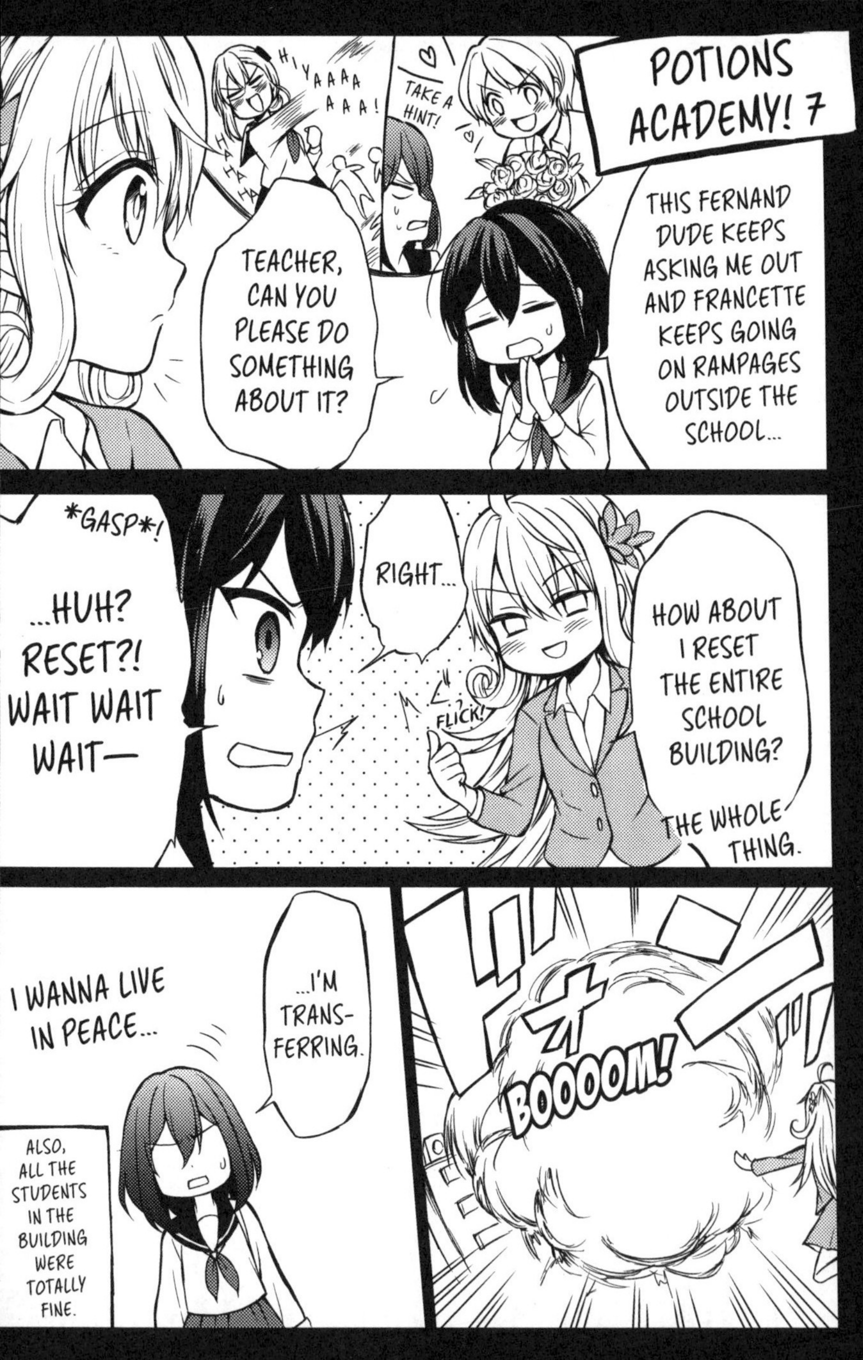
POTIONS ACADEMY! 7
THIS FERNAND DUDE KEEPS ASKING ME OUT AND FRANCETTE KEEPS GOING ON RAMPAGES OUTSIDE THE SCHOOL...
TAKE A HINT!
HIYAAAAAAA!
HAHAHA
TEACHER, CAN YOU PLEASE DO SOMETHING ABOUT IT?
HOW ABOUT I RESET THE ENTIRE SCHOOL BUILDING?
THE WHOLE THING.
FLICK!
RIGHT...
GASP!
...HUH? RESET?! WAIT WAIT WAIT—
BOOOOM!
...I'M TRANS-FERRING.
I WANNA LIVE IN PEACE...
ALSO, ALL THE STUDENTS IN THE BUILDING WERE TOTALLY FINE.

I SHALL SURVIVE USING POTIONS! (MANGA)VOLUME 7
by FUNA (story) and Hibiki Kokonoe (artwork)
Original character designs by Sukima

Translated by Airco
Edited by William Haggard
Lettered by Cedric Macias

First published in Japan in 2020 by Kodansha Ltd., Tokyo..
Publication rights for this English edition arranged through Kodansha Ltd., Tokyo.

Find more books like this one at www.j-novel.club!

Managing Director: Samuel Pinansky
Manga Line Manager: J. Collis
Managing Editor: Jan Mitsuko Cash
Managing Translator: Kristi Fernandez
QA Manager: Hannah N. Carter
Marketing Manager: Stephanie Hii

ISBN: 978-1-7183-4012-1
Printed in Korea
First Printing: May 2022
10 9 8 7 6 5 4 3 2 1

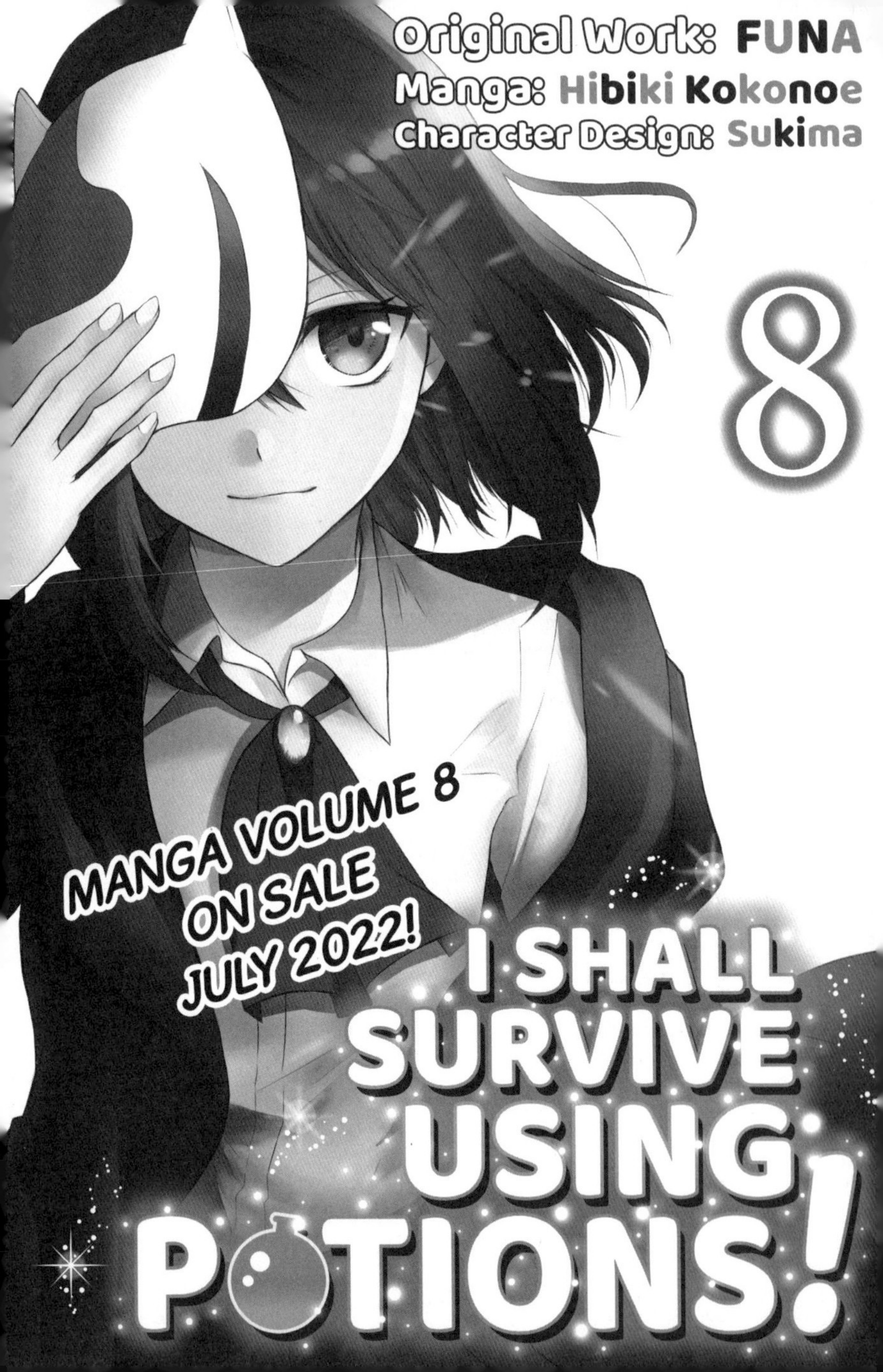
Original Work: FUNA
Manga: Hibiki Kokonoe
Character Design: Sukima
8
MANGA VOLUME 8
ON SALE
JULY 2022!
I SHALL SURVIVE USING POTIONS!

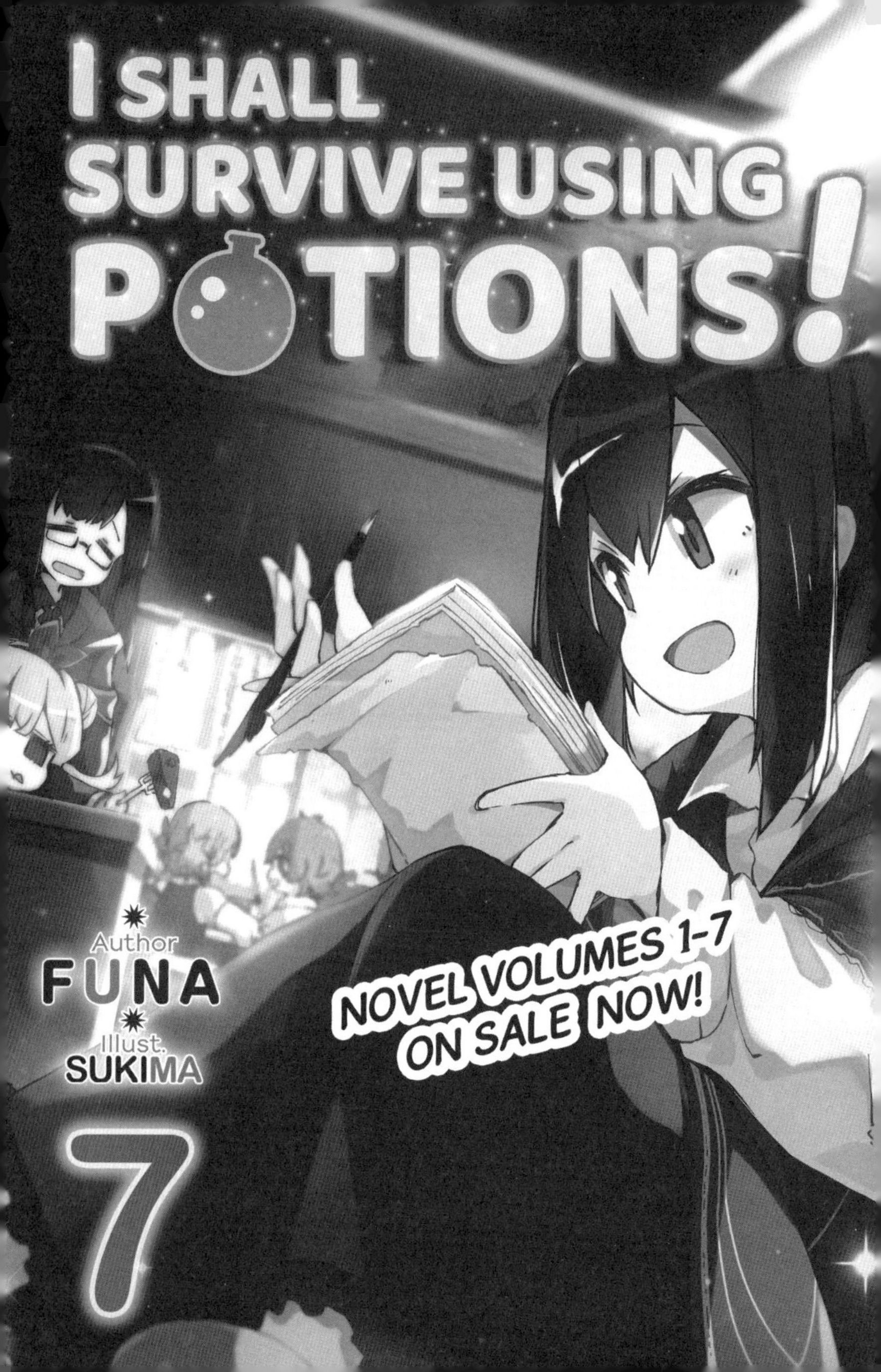

I SHALL SURVIVE USING POTIONS!
Author
FUNA
Illust.
SUKIMA
7
NOVEL VOLUMES 1–7
ON SALE NOW!

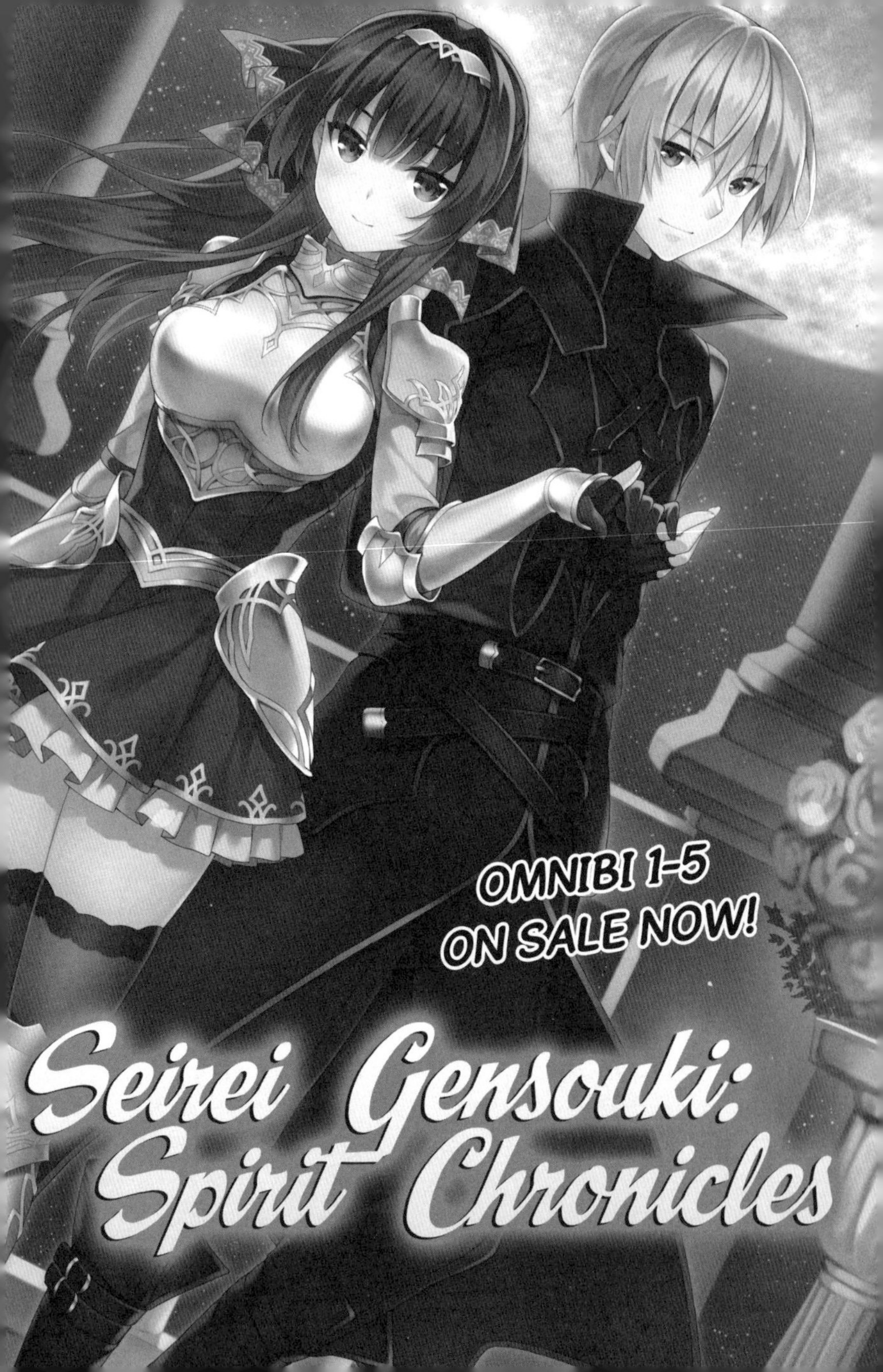
OMNIBI 1–5
ON SALE NOW!
Seirei Gensouki:
Spirit Chronicles

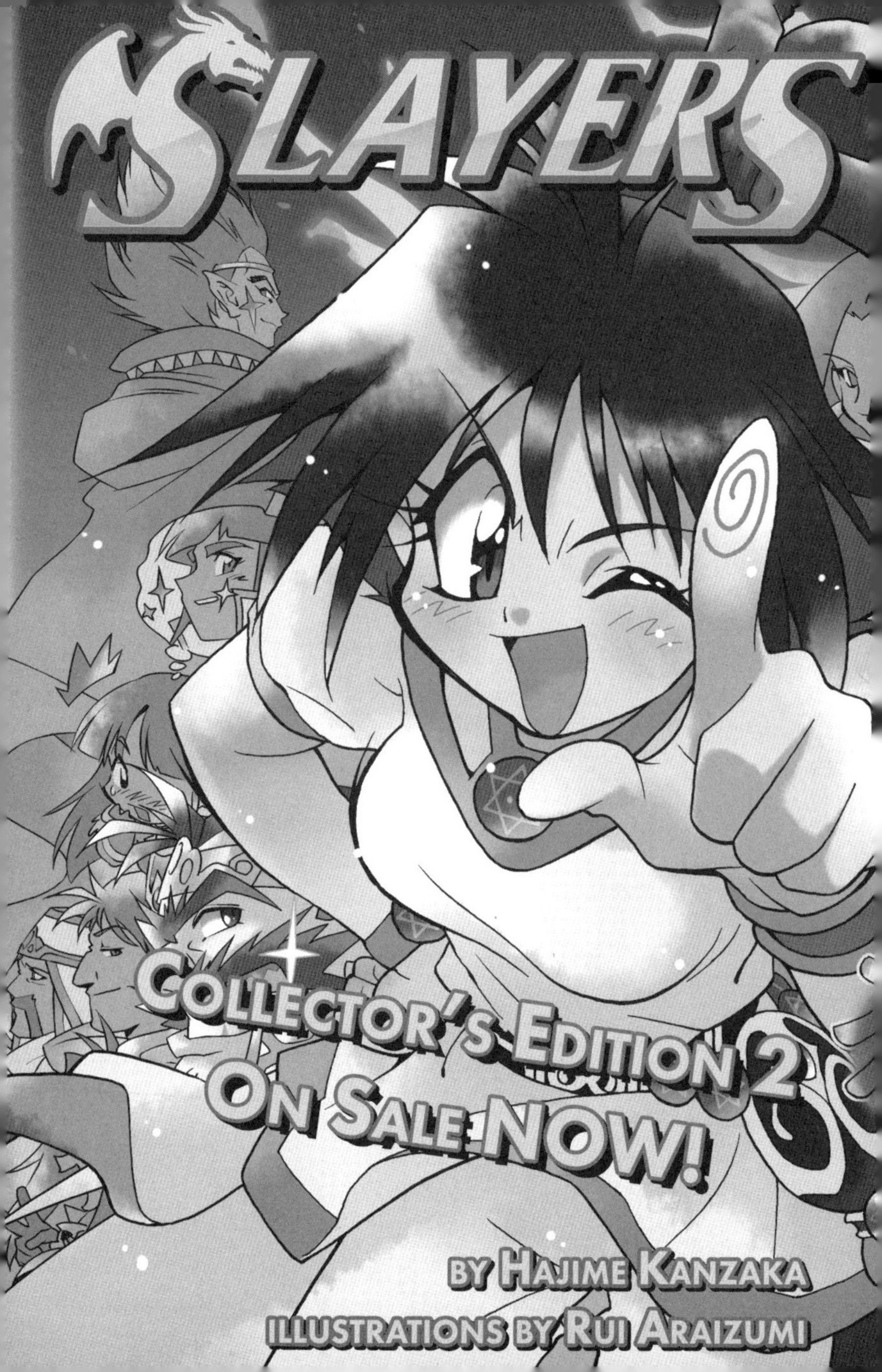
SLAYERS
COLLECTOR'S EDITION 2
ON SALE NOW!
BY HAJIME KANZAKA
ILLUSTRATIONS BY RUI ARAIZUMI

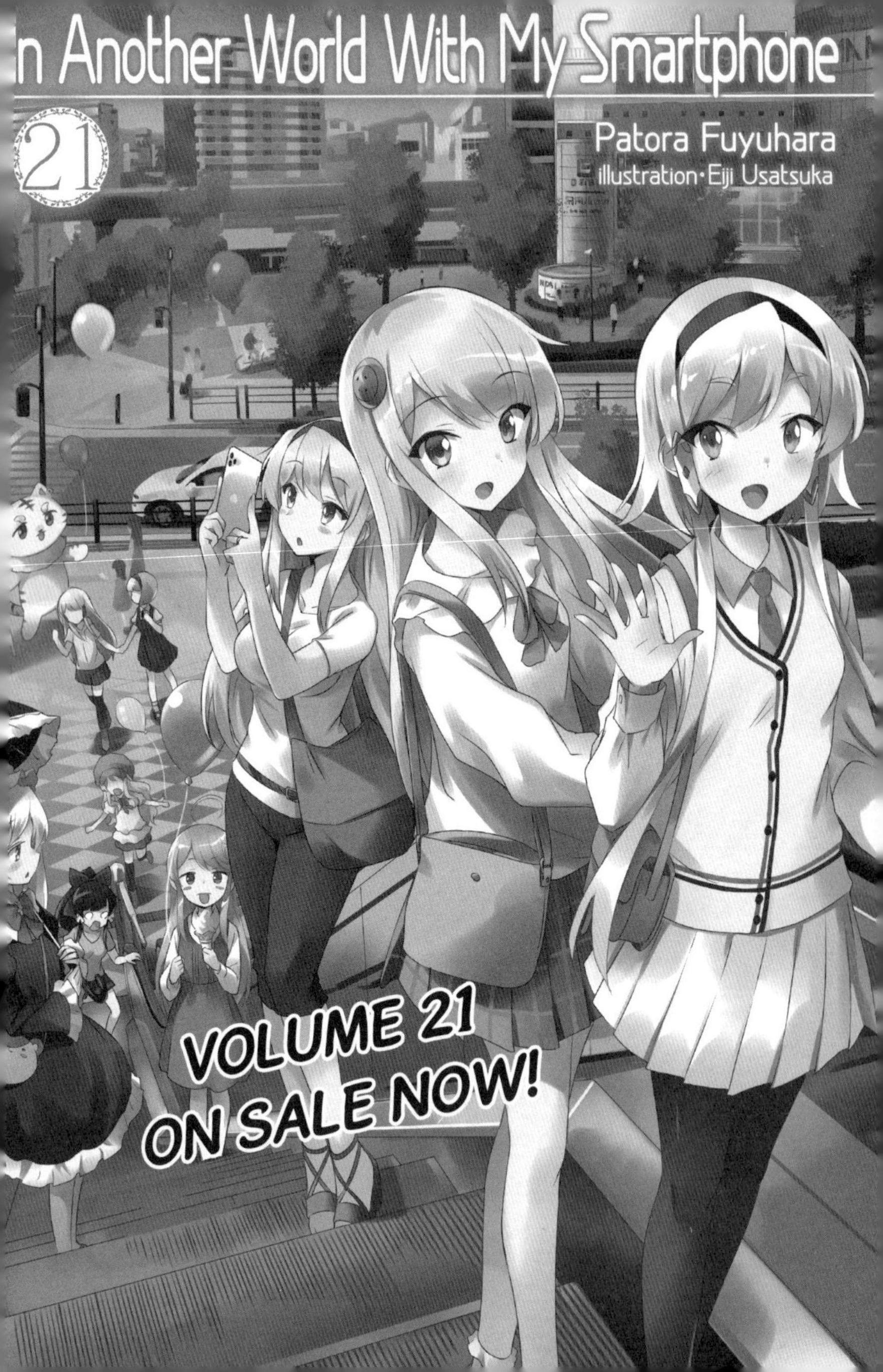
n Another World With My Smartphone
21
Patora Fuyuhara
illustration・Eiji Usatsuka
VOLUME 21
ON SALE NOW!